Curves and Surfaces for Computer Aided Geometric Design

Second Edition

This is a volume in
COMPUTER SCIENCE AND SCIENTIFIC COMPUTING

Werner Rheinboldt and Daniel Siewiorek, editors

Curves and Surfaces for Computer Aided Geometric Design

A Practical Guide

Second Edition

Gerald Farin
Department of Computer Science
Arizona State University
Tempe, Arizona

ACADEMIC PRESS, INC.
Harcourt Brace Jovanovich, Publishers
Boston   San Diego   New York
London   Sydney   Tokyo   Toronto

ACADEMIC PRESS, INC.
1250 Sixth Avenue, San Diego, CA 92101

United Kingdom Edition published by
ACADEMIC PRESS LIMITED
24–28 Oval Road, London NW1 7DX

Chapter 1 was written by P. Bézier.
Chapters 11 and 22 were written by W. Boehm.
Plates IX, X and XI reproduced courtesy of Silicon Graphics, Inc.

Library of Congress Cataloging-in-Publication Data
Farin, Gerald E.
    Curves and surfaces for computer aided geometric design: a
practical guide / Gerald Farin. — 2nd ed.
        p.   cm. — (Computer science and scientific computing)
    Includes bibliographical references.
    ISBN 0–12–249051–7 (alk. paper)
    1. Computer graphics.   I. Title.   II. Series.
T385.F37 1990
006.6—dc20   89–18389
                                                            CIP

Printed in the United States of America
    90 91 92 93   9 8 7 6 5 4 3 2 1

To My Parents

Contents

Preface

In the late 1950s, hardware became available that allowed the machining of 3D shapes out of blocks of wood or steel.[1] These shapes could then be used as stamps and dies for products such as the hood of a car. The bottleneck in this production method was soon found to be the lack of adequate software. In order to machine a shape using a computer, it became necessary to produce a computer-compatible description of that shape. The most promising description method was soon identified to be in terms of parametric surfaces. An example for this approach is provided by Plates I and III: Plate I shows the actual hood of a car; Plate III shows how it is represented internally as a collection of parametric surfaces.

The theory of parametric surfaces was well understood in differential geometry. Their potential for the representation of surfaces in a Computer Aided Design (CAD) environment were not known at all, however. The exploration of the use of parametric curves and surfaces can be viewed as the origin of Computer Aided Geometric Design (CAGD).

The major breakthroughs in CAGD were undoubtedly the theory of Bézier surfaces and Coons patches, later combined with B-spline methods. Bézier curves and surfaces were independently developed by P. de Casteljau at Citroën and by P. Bézier at Rénault. De Casteljau's development, slightly earlier than Bézier's, was never published, and so the whole theory of polynomial curves and surfaces in Bernstein form now bears Bézier's

---

[1] A process that is now called CAM for *Computer Aided Manufacturing*.

name. CAGD became a discipline in its own right after the 1974 conference at the University of Utah (see Barnhill and Riesenfeld [23]).

This book presents a unified treatment of the main ideas in CAGD. During the last years, there has been a trend towards more geometric insight into curve and surface schemes; I have followed this trend by basing most concepts on simple geometric algorithms. For instance, a student will be able to construct Bézier curves with hardly any knowledge of the concept of a parametric curve. Later, when parametric curves are discussed in the context of differential geometry, one can apply differential geometry ideas to the concrete curves that were developed before.

The theory of Bézier curves (and rational Bézier curves) plays a central role in this book. They are numerically the most stable among all polynomial bases currently used in CAD systems, as was recently shown by Farouki and Rajan [144]. Thus Bézier curves are the ideal geometric standard for the representation of piecewise polynomial curves. Also, Bézier curves lend themselves easily to a geometric understanding of many CAGD phenomena and may, for instance, be used to derive the theory of rational and nonrational B-spline curves.

While this book offers a comprehensive treatment of the basic methods in curve and surface design, it is not meant to provide solutions to application-oriented problems that arise in practice. In particular, no algorithms are included to handle intersection, rendering, or offset problems. At present, no unified approach exists for these "geometry processing" problems. However, the material presented here should enable the reader to read the advanced literature on these topics; on offsets: [124], [141], [139], [212], [214], [217], [228], [301], [338]; on intersections: [21], [115], [116], [165], [168], [183], [215], [199], [218], [235], [236], [239], [249], [327], [275], [289], [304], [329], [328]; on rendering: [1], [76], [158], [166], [240], [333].

Also, this is not a text on solid modeling. That branch of geometric modeling is concerned with the representation of objects that are enclosed by an assembly of surfaces, mostly very elementary ones such as planes, cylinders, or tori. When solid modeling systems become fully accepted, they will be able to incorporate the free-form curves and surfaces described in this book. The literature includes: [78], [142], [149], [207], [248], [257], [298], [342].

I have taught the material presented here in the form of both conference tutorials and university courses, typically at the intermediate level. The problems are mostly taken from graduate level courses. In general, the material in the text should enable readers to *use* the presented material. The problems are meant as a guide towards deeper understanding. They should be complemented with simpler exercises if this text is used at a lower level. In teaching this material, it is essential that students have access to computing and graphics facilities; practical experience greatly helps the understanding and appreciation of what might otherwise remain dry theory.

When I use this book as a text for a one semester CAGD class at the lower graduate / upper undergraduate level, I typically cover the following chapters: the first half of Chapter 2, Chapters 3, 4, 6, 8, 9, 16, and 17. Material from other chapters is sprinkled in as needed.

For the second edition, a sequence of C programs has been added to the text. These programs are my implementations of some (but not all) of the most important methods that are described here. The programs were tested for many examples, but they are not meant to be "industrial strength." In general, no checks are made for consistency or correctness of input data. Also, modularity was valued higher than efficiency. The programs are in C, but with non-C users in mind – in particular, all modules should be easily translatable into FORTRAN.

This book would not have been possible without the stimulating environment provided by the CAGD group at Arizona State University (and formerly at the University of Utah), led by Robert E. Barnhill. The book also greatly benefitted from numerous discussions I had with experts such as T. Foley, Q. Fu, H. Hagen, J. Hoschek, S. Kersey, G. Nielson, R. Patterson, and A. Worsey. I would also like to express my appreciation for the funding provided by the National Science Foundation and the Department of Energy.[2] Special thanks go to D. C. Hansford for the numerous helpful suggestions concerning the mathematical side of the material and also to W. Boehm, who was a critical and constructive consultant during all stages of this book.

For this revised edition, many improvements over the first versions were suggested by S. Abi-Ezzi, N. Beebe, W. Boehm, R. E. Barnhill, E. Clapp, P. J. Davis, D. Hansford, F. Kimura, S. Mann, G. Nielson, A. Swimmer, K. Voegele, W. Waggenspack, M. Wozny, and Y. Yamaguchi.

Tempe, Ariz.   Gerald Farin

---

[2]Grants DCR-8502858 and DE-FG02-87ER25041 respectively.

1

P. Bézier: How a Simple System Was Born

CAD/CAM mathematical problems have generated many solutions, each adapted to specific aspects of development. Most of the systems were invented by mathematicians, but UNISURF, at least at the start, was developed by mechanical engineers from the automotive industry. These engineers were familiar with parts described mainly by lines and circles; fillets and other blending auxiliary surfaces were scantly defined, their final shape being left to the skill and experience of patternmakers and die-setters.

Around 1960, designers of stamped parts such as car-body panels used French curves and sweeps. The final standard, however, was the "master model", whose shape, for many reasons, could not coincide with the curves traced on the drawing board. This inconsistency resulted in discussions, arguments, retouches, expenses and delay.

Obviously, no significant improvement could be expected as long as a method was not devised that provided an accurate, complete and indisputable definition of freeform shapes.

Computing and numerical control (NC) had made great progress at that time, and it was certain that only numbers, transmitted from drawing office to tool drawing office, manufacture, patternshop and inspection, could provide an answer; of course, drawings would remain necessary, but they

1

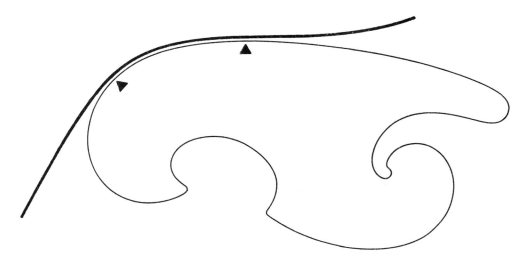

Figure 1.1. An arc of a handdrawn curve is approximated by a part of a template.

would only be explanatory, their accuracy having no importance. Numbers would be the only and final definition.

Certainly, no system could be devised without the help of mathematics—yet designers, in charge of operation, had good knowledge of geometry, especially descriptive geometry, but no basic training in algebra or analysis.

It should be noted that in France very little was known at that time about the work performed in the American aircraft industry. The papers by James Ferguson were not publicized before 1964, Citroen was secretive about the results obtained by Paul de Casteljau, and the famous technical report MAC-TR-41 (by S. A. Coons) did not appear until 1967. The works of W. Gordon and R. Riesenfield were printed in 1974.

The idea of UNISURF was initially oriented towards geometry rather than analysis, but kept in mind that every datum should be expressed exclusively by numbers.

For instance, an arc of a curve could be represented (Fig. 1.1) by the cartesian coordinates of its limit points, A and B, together with their curvilinear abscissae, related with a grid traced on the edge.

The shape of the middle line of a sweep is a cube, granted that its cross section is constant, its matter is homogeneous, and the effect of friction on the tracing cloth is not considered. It is difficult, however, to take into account the length between endpoints. Moreover, the curves employed for

Figure 1.2. A circular arc is obtained by connecting the points in this rectangular grid.

softwares for NC machine tools, i.e., 2D milling machines, were lines and circles and, sometimes, parabolas. Hence, a spline shape would be divided and subdivided into small arcs of circles put end to end.

In order to transform an arc of a circle into a portion of an ellipse, one could imagine (Fig. 1.2) a square frame containing two sets of strings, the intersections of which would be located on an arc of a circle; the frame sides being hinged, the square is transformed into a diamond (Fig. 1.3) and the circle becomes an arc of an ellipse, which would be defined entirely as soon as the coordinates of points A, B, and C were known. If the hinged sides of the frame were replaced by pantographs (Fig. 1.4), the diamond would become a parallelogram, and the definition of the arc of an ellipse would still result from the coordinates of the three points A, B, and C (Fig. 1.5).

This idea was not realistic, but it was easily replaced by the computation of coordinates of successive points on the curve; harmonic functions were available through the use of analog computers, which gave excellent results.

However, employing only arcs of ellipses limited by conjugate diameters was far too restrictive, and a more flexible definition was required.

Another idea came from the practice of a speaker projecting with a hand-held torch a small sign onto a screen displaying a figure printed on a slide. Replacing the sign with a curve and recording the exact location and orientation of the torch (Fig. 1.6) would define the image of the curve projected on the wall of the drawing office. One could even imagine having a variety of slides, each of which would bear a specific curve: circle, parabola, astroid, etc.

Figure 1.3. If the frame from the previous figure is sheared, an arc of an ellipse is obtained.

This was not a realistic idea, since the focal plane of the zoom would seldom be square to the axis; an optician's nightmare! but the principle could be translated, via projective geometry and matrix computation, into cartesian coordinates.

At that time, designers defined the shape of a car body by cross sections located one hundred millimeters apart, sometimes less. The advantage was that, from a drawing, one could derive templates for adjusting a clay model, a master or a stamping tool; the drawback was that a stylist does not define a shape by cross sections but with "character lines", which are seldom plane curves. Hence, a good system would be capable of manipulating and directly defining "space curves" or "free form curves". Of course, one could imagine working alternately (Fig. 1.7) on two projections of a space curve, but it is unlikely that a stylist would accept such a solution.

Theoretically, at least, a space curve could be expressed by a sweep having a circular section, constrained by springs or counterweights (Fig. 1.8), but this would prove quite impractical.

Would not the best solution be to revert to the basic idea of a frame? Instead of a curve inscribed in a square, it would be located in a cube (Fig. 1.9) that could become any parallelepiped (Fig. 1.10) by a linear transformation easy to compute. The first idea was to choose a basic curve that would be the intersection of two circular cylinders; the parallelepiped

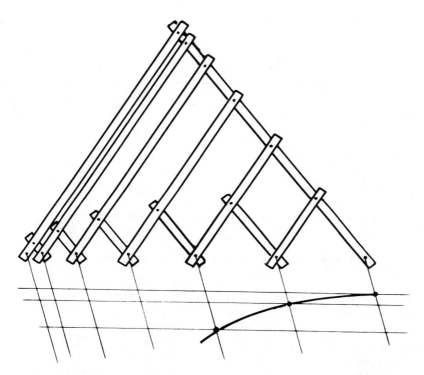

Figure 1.4. Pantograph construction of an arc of an ellipse.

would be defined (Fig. 1.10) by points O, X, Y, and Z. It is more practical, however, to put the basic vectors end to end to obtain a polygon OMNB (Fig. 1.10), which directly defines the end point B and its tangent NB; of course, points O, M, N, and B need not be coplanar and can define a space curve.

Polygons with three legs can define a large variety of curves (see Fig. 3.3 in section 3.3), but in order to increase it, we can make use of cubes and hypercubes of any order (Fig. 1.11) and the relevant polygons (Fig. 1.13).

At that point, it became necessary to do away with harmonic functions and revert to polynomials; this change was even more desirable since digital computers were gradually replacing analog computers. The polynomial functions were chosen according to the properties that were considered most important: tangency, curvature, etc.; later it was discovered that they could be considered as sums of Bernstein's functions.

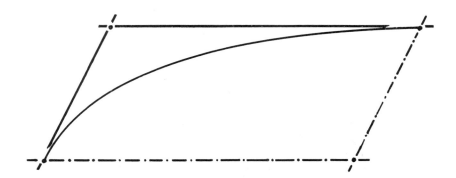

Figure 1.5. A "control polygon" for an arc of an ellipse.

When it was suggested that these curves replace sweeps and French curves, most stylists objected that they had invented their own templates and would not change their methods. It was therefore solemnly promised that their "secret" curves would be translated in secret listings and buried in the most secret part of the computer's memory, and that nobody but them would keep the key of the vaulted cellar. In fact, the standard curves were flexible enough and secret curves were soon forgotten; designers and draughtsmen easily understood the polygons and their relation with the shape of the corresponding curves.

In the traditional process of body engineering, a set of curves is carved in a 3D model and interpolation is left to the experience of highly skilled patternmakers; in order to obtain a satisfactory numerical definition, however, the surface had to be totally expressed with numbers.

At that time, circa 1960, very little if anything had been published about biparametric patches; the basic idea of UNISURF came from the study of a process often used in foundries to obtain a core: sand is compacted in a box (Fig. 1.12) and the shape of the upper surface of the core is obtained by scraping off the surplus with a timber plank cut as a template. Of course, a shape obtained by this method is relatively simple, since the shape of the plank is constant and that of the box edges is generally simple. To make the system more flexible, one could change the shape of the template at the same time as it is moved. This idea takes us back to a very old, and sometimes forgotten, definition of a surface: it is the locus of a curve which

Figure 1.6. A projector producing a "template curve" on the drawing of an object.

is at the same time moved and distorted. About 1970, a Dutch laboratory sculptured blocks of styrofoam with a flexible strip of steel, heated by electricity, whose shape was controlled by the flexion torque imposed on its extremities.

This process could not produce a large variety of shapes, but the principle could be translated into a mathematical solution: the guiding edges of the box are similar to the curves AB and CD of Fig. 1.13, which can be considered as directrices of a surface, defined by their characteristic polygon. A curve such as EF being generatrix, defined by its own polygon, the ends of which run along lines AB and CD, and the intermediate vertices of the polygon being on curves GH and JK, the surface ABDC is known as soon as the four polygons are defined. Connecting the corresponding vertices of the polygons defines the "characteristic net" of the patch, which plays, regarding the surface, the same part as a polygon a curve. Hence, the cartesian coordinates of the points of the patch are computed according to the values of two parameters.

After the expression of this basic idea, many problems remained to be solved: choosing adequate functions, blending curves and patches and dealing with degenerate patches, to name only a few. Resolving these was a matter of relatively simple mathematics, the basic principle remaining untouched.

A system has thus been progressively created. We observe that the first solution—parallelogram, pantograph—is the result of an education oriented towards kinematics, the conception of mechanisms. Then appeared geom-

Figure 1.7. Two imaginary projections of a car.

etry and optics, which very likely came from some training in the army, when geometry, cosmography and topography played an important part. Reflexion was oriented towards analysis, parametric spaces and, finally, data processing; a theory, as convenient as it may look, must not impose too heavy a task on the computer and must be easily understood, at least in its principle, by the operators.

We note that the various steps of this conception have a point in common: each idea must be related to the principle of a material system, simple and primitive though it may look, on which a variable solution could be based.

An engineer is a man who defines what is to be done and how it could be done; he not only describes the goal, but he leads the way toward it.

Before we look any deeper into this subject, it should be observed that elementary geometry played a major part in its development, and it should not gradually disappear from the courses of a mechanical engineer; each idea and each hypothesis was expressed by a figure or a sketch representing a mechanism. It would have been extremely difficult to build a mental image of a somewhat elaborate system without the help of pencil and paper. Let us consider, for instance, Figs. 1.9 and 1.11; they are equivalent to equations (4.7) and (16.6) in subsequent chapters. Evidently, these formulas conveniently are best suited to express data given to a computer, but

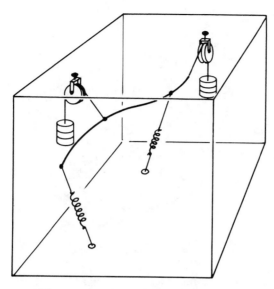

Figure 1.8. A curve held by springs.

most people would understand a simple figure better than the equivalent algebraic expression.

Napoleon said: "A short sketch is better than a long report."

Which are the parts played by experience, theory and imagination in the creation of a system? There is no definite answer to such a query. The importance of experience and of theoretical knowledge is not always clearly perceived; imagination seems a gift, a godsend or the result of a beneficial heredity; but is imagination not, in fact, the result of the maturation of knowledge gained during education and professional practice? Is it not born from facts apparently forgotten, stored in a distant part of the memory, and suddenly remembered when circumstances call them back? Is imagination not based partly on the ability to connect notions which, at first sight, look quite unrelated, such as mechanics, electronics, optics, foundry and data processing? Is it not the ability to catch barely seen analogies—as Alice in Wonderland did, to go "through the mirror"?

Will psychologists someday be able to detect in man such a gift that will be applicable to science and technology? Is it related to the sense of humor that can detect unexpected relationships between facts that look quite unconnected? Shall we learn how to develop it? Will it forever remain a gift, devoted by pure chance to some people while for others carefulness prevails?

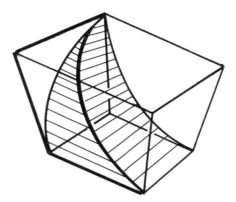

Figure 1.9. A curve defined inside a cube.

It is important that, sometimes, "sensible" men give free rein to imaginative people. "I succeeded," said Henry I. Ford, "because I let some fools try what wise people had advised me not to let them try."

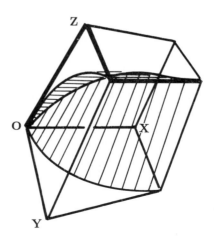

Figure 1.10. A curve defined inside a parallelepiped.

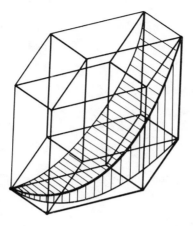

Figure 1.11. Higher order curves can be defined inside higher dimensional cubes.

Figure 1.12. A surface is being obtained by scraping off excess material with wooden templates.

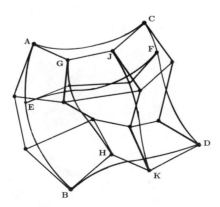

Figure 1.13. The characteristic net of a surface.

2

Introductory Material

2.1 Points and Vectors

When a designer or stylist works on an object, he or she does not think of
that object in very mathematical terms. A point on the object would not
be thought of as a triple of coordinates, but rather in functional terms: as a
corner, the midpoint between two other points, and so on. The objective of
this book, however, is to discuss objects that *are* defined in mathematical
terms, the language that lends itself best to computer implementations. As
a first step towards a mathematical description of an object, one therefore
defines a *coordinate system* in which it will be described analytically.

The space in which we describe our object does not possess a preferred
coordinate system – we have to define one ourselves. Many such systems
could be picked (and some will certainly be more practical than others).
But whichever one we choose, it should not affect any properties of the
object itself. Our interest is in the object and not in its relationship to
some arbitrary coordinate system; the methods that we will develop must
therefore be independent of a particular choice of a coordinate system. We
say that those methods must be *coordinate-free* or *coordinate-independent*.[1]

The concept of coordinate-free methods is stressed throughout in this

---

[1]More mathematically: the geometry of this book is affine geometry. The objects
that we will consider "live" in affine spaces, not in linear spaces.

book. It motivates the strict distinction between points and vectors as discussed next (for more details on this topic see R. Goldman [167]).

We shall denote *points*, elements of three-dimensional euclidean (or point) space $I\!\!E^3$, by lowercase boldface letters such as **a**, **b** etc. (The term "euclidean space" is used here because it is a relatively familiar term to most people. More correctly, we should have used the term "affine space.") A point identifies a location, often relative to other objects. Examples are the midpoint of a straight line segment or the center of gravity of a physical object.

The same notation (lowercase boldface) will be used for *vectors*, elements of three-dimensional linear (or vector) space $I\!\!R^3$. If we represent points or vectors by coordinates relative to some coordinate system, we shall adopt the convention of writing them as coordinate columns.

Although both points and vectors are described by triples of real numbers, we emphasize that there is a clear distinction between them: for any two points **a** and **b**, there is a unique vector **v** that points from **a** to **b**. It is computed by componentwise subtraction:

$$\mathbf{v} = \mathbf{b} - \mathbf{a}; \quad \mathbf{a}, \mathbf{b} \in I\!\!E^3, \ \ \mathbf{v} \in I\!\!R^3.$$

On the other hand, given a vector **v**, there are infinitely many pairs of points **a**, **b** such that $\mathbf{v} = \mathbf{b} - \mathbf{a}$. For if **a**, **b** is one such pair and if **w** is an arbitrary vector, then $\mathbf{a} + \mathbf{w}, \mathbf{b} + \mathbf{w}$ is another such pair since $\mathbf{v} = (\mathbf{b} + \mathbf{w}) - (\mathbf{a} + \mathbf{w})$ also. Figure 2.1 illustrates this fact.

Assigning the point $\mathbf{a} + \mathbf{w}$ to every point $\mathbf{a} \in I\!\!E^3$ is called a *translation*, and the above asserts that vectors are invariant under translations while points are not.

Elements of point space $I\!\!E^3$ can only be *subtracted* – this operation yields a vector. They cannot be *added* – this operation is not defined for points. (It is defined for vectors.) Figure 2.2 gives an example.

However, addition-like operations are defined for points: they are *barycentric combinations*.[2] These are weighted sums of points where the weights sum to one:

$$\mathbf{b} = \sum_{j=0}^{n} \alpha_j \mathbf{b}_j; \quad \begin{matrix} \mathbf{b}_j \in I\!\!E^3 \\ \alpha_0 + \cdots + \alpha_n = 1 \end{matrix} \cdot \tag{2.1}$$

At first glance, this looks like an undefined summation of points, but we can rewrite (2.1) as

$$\mathbf{b} = \mathbf{b}_0 + \sum_{j=1}^{n} \alpha_j (\mathbf{b}_j - \mathbf{b}_0),$$

which is clearly the sum of a point and a vector.

---

[2]They are also called *affine combinations*.

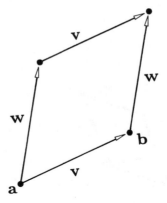

Figure 2.1. Points and vectors: vectors are not affected by translations.

An example of a barycentric combination is the centroid **g** of a triangle with vertices **a**, **b**, **c**, given by

$$\mathbf{g} = \frac{1}{3}\mathbf{a} + \frac{1}{3}\mathbf{b} + \frac{1}{3}\mathbf{c}.$$

The term "barycentric combination" is derived from "barycenter," meaning "center of gravity." The origin of this formulation is in physics: if the $\mathbf{b}_j$ are centers of gravity of objects with masses m_j, then their center of gravity **b** is located at $\mathbf{b} = \sum m_j \mathbf{b}_j / \sum m_j$ and has the combined mass $\sum m_j$. (If some of the m_j are negative, the notion of electric charges may provide a better analogy; see Coxeter [90], p.214.) Since a common factor in the m_j is immaterial for the determination of the center of gravity, we may normalize them by setting $\sum m_j = 1$.

An important special case of barycentric combinations are the *convex combinations*. These are barycentric combinations where the coefficients α_j, in addition to summing to one, are also nonnegative. A convex combination of points is always "inside" those points, which is an observation that leads to the definition of the *convex hull* of a point set: this is the set that is formed by all convex combinations of a point set. Figure 2.3 gives an example; see also Problems. More intuitively, the convex hull of a set is formed as follows: for a 2D set, imagine a string that is circumscribed around the set, where we imagine nails driven through the points in the set. Now pull the string tight – it will become the boundary of the convex hull.

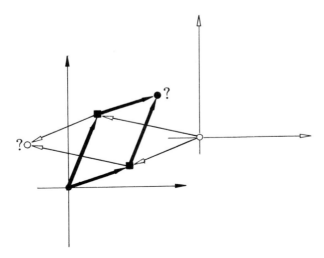

Figure 2.2. Addition of points: this is not a well-defined operation, since different coordinate systems would produce different "solutions." The two given points are marked by solid squares.

The convex hull of a point set is a *convex set*. Such a set is characterized by the following: for any two points in the the set, the straight line connecting them is also contained in the set. Examples are ellipses or parallelograms. It is an easy exercise to verify that affine maps preserve convexity.

Let us return to barycentric combinations, which generate points from points. If we want to generate a *vector* from a set of points, we may write

$$\mathbf{v} = \sum_{j=0}^{n} \sigma_j \mathbf{p}_j,$$

where we have a new restriction on the coefficients: now we must demand that the σ_j sum to zero.

The interplay between points and vectors is unusual at first. Later, it will turn out to be of invaluable theoretical and practical help. For example, we can perform quick *type checking* when we derive formulas. If the point coefficients fail to add up to one or zero – depending on the context – we know that something has gone wrong. In a more formal way, T. DeRose has developed the concept of "geometric programming," a graphics language that automatically performs type checks [109].

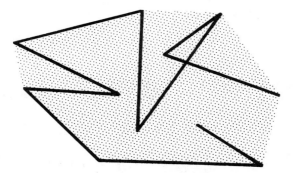

Figure 2.3. Convex hulls: a point set (a polygon) and its convex hull, shown shaded.

2.2 Affine Maps

Most of the transformations that are used to position or scale an object in a computer graphics or CAD environment are *affine* maps. (More complicated, so-called projective maps are discussed in Chapter 14.) The name 'affine map' is due to L. Euler; affine maps were first studied systematically by F. Moebius [258].

The fundamental operation for points is the barycentric combination. We will thus base the definition of an affine map on the notion of barycentric combinations. *A map* Φ *that maps* $I\!\!E^3$ *into itself is called an affine map if it leaves barycentric combinations invariant.* So if

$$\mathbf{x} = \sum \alpha_j \mathbf{a}_j; \quad \mathbf{x}, \mathbf{a}_j \in I\!\!E^3$$

and Φ is an affine map, then also

$$\Phi \mathbf{x} = \sum \alpha_j \Phi \mathbf{a}_j; \quad \Phi \mathbf{x}, \Phi \mathbf{a}_j \in I\!\!E^3. \tag{2.2}$$

This definition looks fairly abstract, yet has a simple interpretation. The expression $\mathbf{x} = \sum \alpha_j \mathbf{a}_j$ specifies how we have to weight the points $\mathbf{a}_j$ so that their weighted average is $\mathbf{x}$. This relation is still valid if we apply an affine map to all points $\mathbf{a}_j$ and to $\mathbf{x}$. As an example, the midpoint of a straight line segment will be mapped to the midpoint of the affine image of that straight line segment. Also, the centroid of a number of points will be mapped to the centroid of the image points.

Let us now be more specific. In a given coordinate system, a point $\mathbf{x}$ is represented by a coordinate triple, which we also denote by $\mathbf{x}$. An affine map now takes on the familiar form

$$\Phi\mathbf{x} = A\mathbf{x} + \mathbf{v}, \tag{2.3}$$

where A is a 3 x 3 matrix and $\mathbf{v}$ is a vector from $I\!\!R^3$.

A simple computation verifies that (2.3) does in fact describe an affine map, i.e., that barycentric combinations are preserved by maps of that form. For the following, recall that $\sum \alpha_j = 1$:

$$
\begin{aligned}
\Phi\left(\sum \alpha_j \mathbf{a}_j\right) &= A\left(\sum \alpha_j \mathbf{a}_j\right) + \mathbf{v} \\
&= \sum \alpha_j A\mathbf{a}_j + \sum \alpha_j \mathbf{v} \\
&= \sum \alpha_j \left(A\mathbf{a}_j + \mathbf{v}\right) \\
&= \sum \alpha_j \Phi\mathbf{a}_j,
\end{aligned}
$$

which concludes our proof.

Some examples of affine maps:

The identity. It is given by $\mathbf{v} = \mathbf{0}$, the zero vector, and by $A = I$, the identity matrix.

A translation. It is given by $A = I$, and a *translation vector* $\mathbf{v}$.

A scaling. It is given by $\mathbf{v} = \mathbf{0}$ and by a diagonal matrix A. The diagonal entries define by how much each component of the preimage $\mathbf{x}$ is to be scaled.

A rotation. If we rotate around the z-axis, then $\mathbf{v} = \mathbf{0}$ and

$$
A = \begin{bmatrix}
\cos \alpha & -\sin \alpha & 0 \\
\sin \alpha & \cos \alpha & 0 \\
0 & 0 & 1
\end{bmatrix}.
$$

A shear. An example is given by $\mathbf{v} = \mathbf{0}$ and

$$
A = \begin{bmatrix}
1 & a & b \\
0 & 1 & c \\
0 & 0 & 1
\end{bmatrix}.
$$

This family of shears maps the (x, y)-plane onto itself.

An important special case of affine maps are the *euclidean maps*, also called *rigid body motions*. They are characterized by orthonormal matrices A that are defined by the property $A^T A = I$. Euclidean maps leave lengths and angles unchanged; the most important examples are rotations and translations.

Affine maps can be combined, and a complicated map may be decomposed into a sequence of simpler maps. It can be shown that every affine map can be composed of translations, rotations, shears, and scalings.

The *rank* of A has an important geometric interpretation: if $\text{rank}(A) = 3$, then the affine map Φ maps three-dimensional objects to three-dimensional objects. If the rank is less than three, Φ is a parallel projection onto a plane (rank $= 2$) or even onto a straight line (rank $= 1$).

An affine map of $I\!\!E^2$ to $I\!\!E^2$ is uniquely determined by a (nondegenerate) triangle and its image. Thus any two triangles determine an affine map of the plane onto itself. In $I\!\!E^3$, an affine map is uniquely defined by a (nondegenerate) tetrahedron and its image.

More important facts about affine maps are discussed in the following section.

2.3 Linear Interpolation

Let $\mathbf{a}, \mathbf{b}$ be two distinct points in $I\!\!E^3$. The set of all points $\mathbf{x} \in I\!\!E^3$ of the form

$$\mathbf{x} = \mathbf{x}(t) = (1 - t)\mathbf{a} + t\mathbf{b}; \quad t \in I\!\!R \qquad (2.4)$$

is called the *straight line* through $\mathbf{a}$ and $\mathbf{b}$. Any three (or more) points on a straight line are said to be *collinear*.

For $t = 0$ the straight line passes through $\mathbf{a}$ and for $t = 1$ it passes through $\mathbf{b}$. For $0 \le t \le 1$, the point $\mathbf{x}$ is between $\mathbf{a}$ and $\mathbf{b}$, while for all other values of t it is outside; see Figure 2.4.

Equation (2.4) represents $\mathbf{x}$ as a barycentric combination of two points in $I\!\!E^3$. The same barycentric combination holds for the three points $0, t, 1$ in $I\!\!E^1$: $t = (1 - t) \cdot 0 + t \cdot 1$. So t is related to 0 and 1 by the same barycentric combination that relates $\mathbf{x}$ to $\mathbf{a}$ and $\mathbf{b}$. But then, by the definiton of affine maps, the three points $\mathbf{a}, \mathbf{x}, \mathbf{b}$ in three-space are an affine map of the three points $0, t, 1$ in one-space! *Thus linear interpolation is an affine map of the real line onto a straight line in $I\!\!E^3$.*[3]

It is now almost a tautology when we state: *linear interpolation is affinely invariant.* Written out as a formula: if Φ is an affine map of $I\!\!E^3$ onto itself,

---

[3]Strictly speaking, we should therefore use the term "affine interpolation" instead of "linear interpolation." We use "linear interpolation" because of its widespread use.

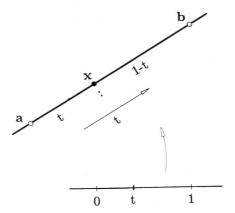

Figure 2.4. Linear interpolation: two points $\mathbf{a}, \mathbf{b}$ define a straight line through them. The point $\mathbf{x}$ on it divides the straight line segment between $\mathbf{a}$ and $\mathbf{b}$ in the ratio $t : 1 - t$.

and (2.4) holds, then also

$$\Phi \mathbf{x} = (1 - t)\Phi \mathbf{a} + t\Phi \mathbf{b}.$$

Closely related to linear interpolation is the concept of *barycentric coordinates*, due to Moebius [258]. Let $\mathbf{a}, \mathbf{x}, \mathbf{b}$ be three collinear points in $I\!E^3$:

$$\mathbf{x} = \alpha \mathbf{a} + \beta \mathbf{b}; \qquad \alpha + \beta = 1. \tag{2.5}$$

Then α and β are called *barycentric coordinates* of $\mathbf{x}$ with respect to $\mathbf{a}$ and $\mathbf{b}$. Note that by our previous definitions, $\mathbf{x}$ is a barycentric combination of $\mathbf{a}$ and $\mathbf{b}$.

The connection between barycentric coordinates and linear interpolation is obvious: we have $\alpha = 1 - t$ and $\beta = t$. This shows, by the way, that barycentric coordinates do not always have to be positive: for $t \notin [0, 1]$, either α or β is negative. For any three collinear points $\mathbf{a}, \mathbf{b}, \mathbf{c}$, the barycentric coordinates of $\mathbf{b}$ with respect to $\mathbf{a}$ and $\mathbf{c}$ are given by

$$\alpha = \frac{\mathrm{vol}_1(\mathbf{b}, \mathbf{c})}{\mathrm{vol}_1(\mathbf{a}, \mathbf{c})},$$

$$\beta = \frac{\mathrm{vol}_1(\mathbf{a}, \mathbf{b})}{\mathrm{vol}_1(\mathbf{a}, \mathbf{c})}.$$

where vol_1 denotes the one-dimensional volume, which is the signed distance between two points. Barycentric coordinates are not only defined on a straight line, but also on the plane. Section 18.1 has more details.

Another important concept in this context is that of *ratios*. The ratio of three collinear points $\mathbf{a}, \mathbf{b}, \mathbf{c}$ is defined by

$$\mathrm{ratio}(\mathbf{a}, \mathbf{b}, \mathbf{c}) = \frac{\mathrm{vol}_1(\mathbf{a}, \mathbf{b})}{\mathrm{vol}_1(\mathbf{b}, \mathbf{c})}. \tag{2.6}$$

If α and β are barycentric coordinates of $\mathbf{b}$ with respect to $\mathbf{a}$ and $\mathbf{c}$, it follows that

$$\mathrm{ratio}(\mathbf{a}, \mathbf{b}, \mathbf{c}) = \frac{\beta}{\alpha}. \tag{2.7}$$

The barycentric coordinates of a point do not change under affine maps, and neither does their quotient. Thus the ratio of three collinear points is not affected by affine transformations. So if (2.7) holds, then also

$$\mathrm{ratio}(\Phi\mathbf{a}, \Phi\mathbf{b}, \Phi\mathbf{c}) = \frac{\beta}{\alpha}, \tag{2.8}$$

where Φ is an affine map.

The last equation states that *affine maps are ratio preserving*. This property may be used to define affine maps: every map that takes straight lines to straight lines and is ratio preserving is an affine map.

The concept of ratio preservation may be used to derive another useful property of linear interpolation. We have defined the straight line segment $[\mathbf{a}, \mathbf{b}]$ to be the affine image of the *unit interval* $[0, 1]$, but we can also view that straight line segment as the affine image of any interval $[a, b]$. The interval $[a, b]$ may itself be obtained by an affine map from the interval $[0, 1]$ or vice versa. With $t \in [0, 1]$ and $u \in [a, b]$, that map is given by $t = (u - a)/(b - a)$. The interpolated point on the straight line is now given by both

$$\mathbf{x}(t) = (1 - t)\mathbf{a} + t\mathbf{b}$$

and

$$\mathbf{x}(u) = \frac{b - u}{b - a}\mathbf{a} + \frac{u - a}{b - a}\mathbf{b}. \tag{2.9}$$

Since a, u, b and $0, t, 1$ are in the same ratio as the triple $\mathbf{a}, \mathbf{x}, \mathbf{b}$, we have shown that *linear interpolation is invariant under affine domain transformations*. By affine domain transformation, we simply mean an affine map of the real line onto itself. The parameter t is sometimes called a *local parameter* of the interval $[a, b]$.

A concluding remark: we have demonstrated the interplay between the two concepts of linear interpolation and ratios. In this book, we will often describe methods by saying that points have to be collinear and must be in a given ratio. This is the geometric (descriptive) equivalent of the algebraic (algorithmic) statement that one of the three points may be obtained by linear interpolation from the other two.

2.4 Piecewise Linear Interpolation

Let $\mathbf{b}_0, \ldots, \mathbf{b}_n \in I\!\!E^3$ form a *polygon* $\mathbf{B}$. A polygon consists of a sequence of straight line segments, each interpolating to a pair of points $\mathbf{b}_i, \mathbf{b}_{i+1}$. It is therefore also called the *piecewise linear interpolant* $\mathcal{PL}$ to the points $\mathbf{b}_i$. If the points $\mathbf{b}_i$ lie on a curve $\mathbf{c}$, then $\mathbf{B}$ is said to be a piecewise linear interpolant to $\mathbf{c}$, and we write

$$\mathbf{B} = \mathcal{PL}\mathbf{c}. \tag{2.10}$$

One of the important properties of piecewise linear interpolation is *affine invariance*: if the curve $\mathbf{c}$ is mapped onto a curve $\Phi\mathbf{c}$ by an affine map Φ, then the piecewise linear interpolant to $\Phi\mathbf{c}$ is the affine map of the original piecewise linear interpolant:

$$\mathcal{PL}\ \Phi\mathbf{c} = \Phi\ \mathcal{PL}\ \mathbf{c}. \tag{2.11}$$

Another property is the *variation diminishing property*: consider a continuous curve $\mathbf{c}$ and a piecewise linear interpolant $\mathcal{PL}\mathbf{c}$, and also an arbitrary plane. Let cross $\mathbf{c}$ be the number of crossings that the curve $\mathbf{c}$ has with this plane, and let cross$\mathcal{PL}\mathbf{c}$ be the number of crossings that the piecewise linear interpolant has with this plane. (Special cases may arise; see Problems.) Then we always have

$$\text{cross}\mathcal{PL}\ \mathbf{c} \le \text{cross } \mathbf{c}. \tag{2.12}$$

This property follows from a simple observation: consider two points $\mathbf{b}_i$, $\mathbf{b}_{i+1}$. The straight line segment through them can cross a given plane at most at one point, while the curve segment from $\mathbf{c}$ that connects them may cross the same plane in arbitrarily many points. The variation diminishing property is illustrated in Figure 2.5.

2.5 Menelaos' Theorem

We use the concept of piecewise linear interpolation to prove one of the most important geometric theorems for the theory of CAGD: Menelaos' Theorem. This theorem can be used for the proof of many constructive algorithms, and its importance was already realized by de Casteljau [102].

Referring to Figure 2.6, let

$$\begin{aligned}
\mathbf{a}_t &= (1-t)\mathbf{p}_1 + t\mathbf{p}_2, \\
\mathbf{a}_s &= (1-s)\mathbf{p}_1 + s\mathbf{p}_2, \\
\mathbf{b}_t &= (1-t)\mathbf{p}_2 + t\mathbf{p}_3, \\
\mathbf{b}_s &= (1-s)\mathbf{p}_2 + s\mathbf{p}_3.
\end{aligned}$$

Figure 2.5. The variation diminishing property: a piecewise linear interpolant to a curve has no more intersections with any plane than the curve itself.

Let $\mathbf{c}$ be the intersection of the straight lines $\mathbf{a}_t\mathbf{b}_t$ and $\mathbf{a}_s\mathbf{b}_s$. Then

$$\text{ratio}(\mathbf{a}_t, \mathbf{c}, \mathbf{b}_t) = \frac{s}{1-s} \quad \text{and} \quad \text{ratio}(\mathbf{a}_s, \mathbf{c}, \mathbf{b}_s) = \frac{t}{1-t}. \qquad (2.13)$$

For a proof, we simply show that $\mathbf{c}$ satisfies the two equations

$$\mathbf{c} = (1-s)\mathbf{a}_t + s\mathbf{b}_t \quad \text{and} \quad \mathbf{c} = (1-t)\mathbf{a}_s + t\mathbf{b}_s,$$

which is straightforward. Notice also that the four collinear points $\mathbf{p}_1, \mathbf{a}_t, \mathbf{a}_s, \mathbf{p}_2$ as well as the four collinear points $\mathbf{p}_2, \mathbf{b}_t, \mathbf{b}_s, \mathbf{p}_3$ are affine maps the four points $0, t, s, 1$ on the real line.

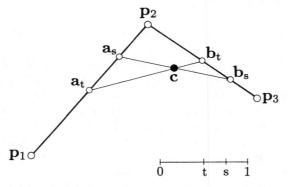

Figure 2.6. Menelaos' Theorem: the point $\mathbf{c}$ may be obtained from linear interpolation at t or at s.

Equation (2.13) is a "CAGD version" of the original Menelaos' Theorem, which may be stated as (see Coxeter [90]):

$$\text{ratio}(\mathbf{b}_s, \mathbf{b}_t, \mathbf{p}_2) \cdot \text{ratio}(\mathbf{p}_2, \mathbf{a}_t, \mathbf{a}_s) \cdot \text{ratio}(\mathbf{a}_s, \mathbf{c}, \mathbf{b}_s) = -1. \qquad (2.14)$$

The proof of (2.14) is a direct consequence of (2.13). Note the ordering of points in the second ratio! Menelaos' Theorem is closely related to Ceva's, which is given in Section 18.1.

2.6   Function Spaces

This section contains material that will later simplify our work by allowing very concise notation. Although we shall try to develop our material with an emphasis on geometric concepts, it will sometimes simplify our work considerably if we can resort to some elementary topics from functional analysis. Good references are the books by Davis [92] and de Boor [98].

Let $C[a, b]$ be the set of all real-valued continuous functions defined over the interval $[a, b]$ of the real axis. We can define addition and multiplication by a constant for elements $f, g \in C[a, b]$ by setting $(\alpha f + \beta g)(t) = \alpha f(t) + \beta g(t)$ for all $t \in [a, b]$. With these definitions, it is easy to show that $C[a, b]$ forms a *linear space* over the reals. The same is true for the sets $C^k[a, b]$, the sets of all real-valued functions defined over $[a, b]$ that are k-times continuously differentiable. Furthermore, for every k, C^{k+1} is a *subspace* of C^k.

We say that n functions $f_1, \ldots, f_n \in C[a, b]$ are *linearly independent* if $\sum c_i f_i = 0$ for all $t \in [a, b]$ implies $c_1 = \ldots = c_n = 0$.

We mention some subspaces of $C[a, b]$ that will be of interest later. The spaces $\mathcal{P}^n$ of all *polynomials* of degree n:

$$p^n(t) = a_0 + a_1 t + a_2 t^2 + \cdots + a_n t^n; \quad t \in [a, b].$$

For fixed n, the dimension of $\mathcal{P}^n$ is $n + 1$: each $p^n \in \mathcal{P}^n$ is determined uniquely by the $n + 1$ coefficients $a_0, \ldots, a_n$. These can be interpreted as a vector in $(n + 1)$-dimensional linear space $\mathbb{R}^{n+1}$, which has dimension $n + 1$. We can also name a *basis* for $\mathcal{P}^n$: the *monomials* $1, t, t^2, \ldots, t^n$ are $n + 1$ linearly independent functions and thus form a basis.

Another interesting class of subspaces of $C[a, b]$ is given by piecewise linear functions: let $a = t_0 < t_1 < \cdots < t_n = b$ be a *partition* of the interval $[a, b]$. A continuous function that is linear on each subinterval $[t_i, t_{i+1}]$ is called a piecewise linear function. Over a fixed partition of $[a, b]$, the piecewise linear functions form a linear function space. A basis for this

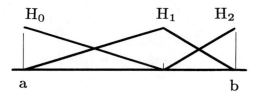

Figure 2.7. Hat functions: the piecewise linear function f can be written as $f = H_0 + 3H_1 + 2H_2$.

space is given by the *hat functions*: a hat function $H_i(t)$ is a piecewise linear function with $H_i(t_i) = 1$ and $H_i(t_j) = 0$ if $i \neq j$. A piecewise linear function f with $f(t_j) = f_j$ can always be written as

$$f(t) = \sum_{j=0}^{n} f_j H_j(t).$$

Figure 2.7 gives an example.

We will also consider *linear operators* that assign a function $\mathcal{A}f$ to a given function f. An operator $\mathcal{A} : C[a,b] \to C[a,b]$ is called *linear* if it leaves linear combinations invariant:

$$\mathcal{A}(\alpha f + \beta g) = \alpha \mathcal{A}f + \beta \mathcal{A}g; \quad \alpha, \beta \in \mathbb{R}.$$

An example is given by the derivative operator that assigns the derivative f' to a given function f: $\mathcal{A}f = f'$.

2.7 Problems

1. We have seen that affine maps leave the ratio of three collinear points constant, i.e., they are ratio-preserving. Show that the converse is also true: every ratio-preserving map is affine.

2. We defined the convex hull of a point set to be the set of all convex combinations formed by the elements of that set. Another definition is the following: the convex hull of a point set is the intersection of all convex sets that contain the given set. Show that both definitions are equivalent.

3. In the definition of the variation diminishing property we counted the crossings of a polygon with a plane. Discuss the case when the plane contains a whole polygon leg.

4. Show that the $n+1$ functions $f_i(t) = t^i$; $i = 0, \ldots, n$ are linearly independent.

5. Our definition of barycentric combinations gives the impression that it needs the involved points expressed in terms of some coordinate system. Show that this is not necessary: draw five points on a piece of paper, assign a weight to each one, and *construct* the barycenter of your points using a ruler (or compass and straightedge, if you are more classically inclined).

   Remark: For this construction, it is not necessary that the weights add to one. This is so since the geometric construction remains the same if we multiplied all weights by a common factor. In fact, one may replace the concept of points (having mass one and requiring barycentric combinations as the basic point operation) by that of *mass points*, having arbitrary weights and yielding their barycenter (with the combined mass of all points) as the basic operation. In such a setting, vectors would also be be mass points, but with mass zero.[4]

---

[4]I was introduced to this concept by A. Swimmer. It was developed by H. Grassmann in 1844.

3

The de Casteljau Algorithm

The algorithm described in this chapter is probably the most fundamental one in the field of curve and surface design, yet it is surprisingly simple. Its main attraction is the beautiful interplay between geometry and algebra: a very intuitive geometric construction leads to a powerful theory.

Historically, it is with this algorithm that the work of de Casteljau started in 1959. The only written evidence is in [103] and [102]; both technical reports that are not easily accessible. De Casteljau's work went unnoticed until W. Boehm obtained copies of the reports in 1975. From then on, de Casteljau's name gained more popularity.

3.1 Parabolas

We give a simple construction for the generation of a parabola; the straightforward generalization will then lead to Bézier curves. Let $\mathbf{b}_0, \mathbf{b}_1, \mathbf{b}_2$ be any three points in $I\!\!E^3$, and let $t \in I\!\!R$. Construct

$$\mathbf{b}_0^1(t) = (1-t)\mathbf{b}_0 + t\mathbf{b}_1$$
$$\mathbf{b}_1^1(t) = (1-t)\mathbf{b}_1 + t\mathbf{b}_2$$

$$\mathbf{b}_0^2(t) = (1-t)\mathbf{b}_0^1(t) + t\mathbf{b}_1^1(t).$$

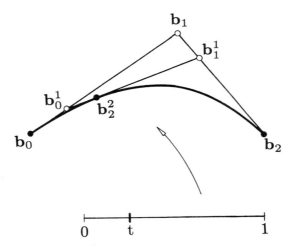

Figure 3.1. Parabolas: construction by repeated linear interpolation.

Inserting the first two equations into the third one, we obtain

$$\mathbf{b}_0^2(t) = (1 - t)^2 \mathbf{b}_0 + 2t(1 - t)\mathbf{b}_1 + t^2 \mathbf{b}_2. \tag{3.1}$$

This is a quadratic expression in t(the superscript denoting the degree), and so $\mathbf{b}_0^2(t)$ traces out a *parabola* as t varies from $-\infty$ to $+\infty$. We denote this parabola by $\mathbf{b}^2$. The above construction consists of *repeated linear interpolation*; its geometry is illustrated in Figure 3.1. For t between 0 and 1, $\mathbf{b}^2(t)$ is inside the triangle formed by $\mathbf{b}_0, \mathbf{b}_1, \mathbf{b}_2$, in particular $\mathbf{b}^2(0) = \mathbf{b}_0, \mathbf{b}^2(1) = \mathbf{b}_2$.

Inspecting the ratios of points in Figure 3.1, we see that

$$\text{ratio}(\mathbf{b}_0, \mathbf{b}_0^1, \mathbf{b}_1) = \text{ratio}(\mathbf{b}_1, \mathbf{b}_1^1, \mathbf{b}_2) = \text{ratio}(\mathbf{b}_0^1, \mathbf{b}_0^2, \mathbf{b}_1^1) = t/(1 - t).$$

Thus our construction of a parabola is *affinely invariant* because piecewise linear interpolation is affinely invariant; see Section 2.4.

We also note that a parabola is a plane curve, due to the fact that $\mathbf{b}^2(t)$ is always a barycentric combination of three points, as is clear from inspecting (3.1). A parabola is a special case of *conic sections*; these will be discussed in Chapter 14.

Finally we state a theorem from analytic geometry, closely related to our parabola construction. Let $\mathbf{a}, \mathbf{b}, \mathbf{c}$ be three distinct points on a parabola. Let the tangent at $\mathbf{b}$ intersect the tangents at $\mathbf{a}$ and $\mathbf{c}$ in $\mathbf{e}$ and $\mathbf{f}$, respectively. Let the tangents at $\mathbf{a}$ and $\mathbf{c}$ intersect in $\mathbf{d}$. Then ratio$(\mathbf{a}, \mathbf{e}, \mathbf{d}) =$

ratio$(\mathbf{e}, \mathbf{b}, \mathbf{f})$ = ratio$(\mathbf{d}, \mathbf{f}, \mathbf{c})$. This Three Tangent Theorem describes a property of parabolas; the de Casteljau algorithm can be viewed as the constructive counterpart.

3.2   The de Casteljau Algorithm

Parabolas are plane curves. Many applications require true space curves, however.[1] For those purposes, the above construction for a parabola can be generalized to generate a polynomial curve of arbitrary degree n:

de Casteljau algorithm:

Given: $\mathbf{b}_0, \mathbf{b}_1, \ldots, \mathbf{b}_n \in E^3$ and $t \in R$,

set

$$\mathbf{b}_i^r(t) = (1 - t)\mathbf{b}_i^{r-1}(t) + t\mathbf{b}_{i+1}^{r-1}(t) \qquad \left\{ \begin{array}{l} r = 1, \ldots, n \\ i = 0, \ldots, n - r \end{array} \right. \qquad (3.2)$$

and $\mathbf{b}_i^0(t) = \mathbf{b}_i$. Then $\mathbf{b}_0^n(t)$ is the point with parameter value t on the *Bézier curve* $\mathbf{b}^n$.

The polygon $\mathbf{P}$ formed by $\mathbf{b}_0, \ldots, \mathbf{b}_n$ is called the *Bézier polygon* or *control polygon* of the curve $\mathbf{b}^n$. Similarly, the polygon vertices $\mathbf{b}_i$ are called *control points* or *Bézier points*. Figure 3.2 illustrates the cubic case.

Sometimes we also write $\mathbf{b}^n(t) = \mathcal{B}[\mathbf{b}_0, \ldots, \mathbf{b}_n; t] = \mathcal{B}[\mathbf{P}; t]$ or, shorter, $\mathbf{b}^n = \mathcal{B}[\mathbf{b}_0, \ldots, \mathbf{b}_n] = \mathcal{B}\mathbf{P}$. This notation defines $\mathcal{B}$ to be the (linear) operator that associates the Bézier curve with its control polygon. We sometimes say that the curve $\mathcal{B}[\mathbf{b}_0, \ldots, \mathbf{b}_n]$ is the *Bernstein-Bézier approximation* to the control polygon, a terminology borrowed from approximation theory; see also Section 5.10.

The intermediate coefficients $\mathbf{b}_i^r(t)$ are conveniently written into a triangular array of points, the *de Casteljau scheme* – we give the example of the cubic case:

$$\begin{array}{llll} \mathbf{b}_0 & & & \\ \mathbf{b}_1 & \mathbf{b}_0^1 & & \\ \mathbf{b}_2 & \mathbf{b}_1^1 & \mathbf{b}_0^2 & \\ \mathbf{b}_3 & \mathbf{b}_2^1 & \mathbf{b}_1^2 & \mathbf{b}_0^3. \end{array} \qquad (3.3)$$

This triangular array of points seems to suggest the use of a two-dimensional array in writing code for the de Casteljau algorithm. That would be a waste of storage, however: it is sufficient to use the left column only and to overwrite it appropriately.

---

[1] Compare the comments by P. Bézier in Chapter 1!

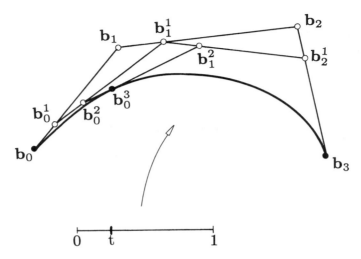

Figure 3.2. The de Casteljau algorithm: the point $\mathbf{b}_0^3(t)$ is obtained from repeated linear interpolation. The cubic case $n = 3$ is shown for $t = 1/4$.

3.3   Some Properties of Bézier Curves

The de Casteljau algorithm allows us to infer several important properties of Bézier curves. We will infer these properties from the geometry underlying the algorithm. In the next chapter, we will show also how they can be derived analytically.

Affine invariance. Affine maps were discussed in Section 2.2. They are in the toolkit of every CAD system: objects must be repositioned, scaled, and so on. An important property of Bézier curves is that they are invariant under affine maps, which means that the following two procedures yield the same result: a) first, compute the point $\mathbf{b}^n(t)$ and then apply an affine map to it; b) first, apply an affine map to the control polygon and then evaluate the mapped polygon at parameter value t.

Affine invariance is, of course, a direct consequence of the de Casteljau algorithm: the algorithm is composed of a sequence of linear interpolations (or, equivalently, of a sequence of affine maps). These are themselves affinely invariant, and so is a finite sequence of them.

Let us discuss a practical aspect of affine invariance. Suppose we plot a cubic curve $\mathbf{b}^3$ by evaluating at 100 points and then plotting the resulting point array. Suppose now that we would like to plot the curve after a rotation has been applied to it. We can take the hundred computed points, apply the rotation to each of them and plot. Or, we can apply the rotation to the four control points, then evaluate one hundred times and plot. The first method needs one hundred applications of the rotation, while the second needs only four!

Affine invariance may not seem to be a very exceptional property for a useful curve scheme; in fact, it is not straightforward to think of a curve scheme that does not have it (exercise!). It is perhaps worth noting that Bézier curves do *not* enjoy another, also very important, property: they are not *projectively invariant*. Projective maps are used in computer graphics when an object is to be rendered realistically. So if we try to make life easy and simplify a perspective map of a Bézier curve by mapping the control polygon and then computing the curve, we have actually cheated: that curve is not the perspective image of the original curve! More details on perspective maps can be found in Chapter 14.

Invariance under affine parameter transformations. Very often, one thinks of a Bézier curve as being defined over the interval $[0, 1]$. This is done because it is convenient, not because it is necessary: the de Casteljau algorithm is "blind" to the actual interval that the curve is defined over because it uses ratios only. One may therefore think of the curve as being defined over any arbitrary interval $a \leq u \leq b$ of the real line – after the introduction of local coordinates $t = (u-a)/(b-a)$, the algorithm proceeds as usual. This property is inherited from linear interpolation, as described in Section 2.3.

The transition from the interval $[0, 1]$ to the interval $[a, b]$ is an *affine map*. Therefore, we can say that Bézier curves are invariant under affine parameter transformations. Sometimes, one sees the term *linear parameter transformation* in this context, but this terminology is not quite correct: the transformation of the interval $[0, 1]$ to $[a, b]$ typically includes a translation, which is not a linear map.

Convex hull property. For $t \in [0, 1]$, $\mathbf{b}^n(t)$ lies in the convex hull (see Section 2.3) of the control polygon. This follows since every intermediate $\mathbf{b}_i^r$ is obtained as a convex barycentric combination of previous $\mathbf{b}_j^{r-1}$ – at no step of the de Casteljau algorithm do we produce points outside the convex hull of the $\mathbf{b}_i$.

A simple consequence of the convex hull property is that a planar control polygon always generates a planar curve.

The importance of the convex hull property lies in what is known as *interference checking.* Suppose we want to know if two Bézier curves intersect each other – for example, each might represent the path of a robot arm, and our aim is to make sure that the two paths do not intersect, thus avoiding expensive collisions of the robots. Instead of actually computing a possible intersection, we can perform a much cheaper test: circumscribe the smallest possible box around the control polygon of each curve such that it has its edges parallel to some coordinate system. Such boxes are called *minmax boxes*, since their faces are created by the minimal and maximal coordinates of the control polygons. Clearly each box contains its control polygon, and, by the convex hull property, also the corresponding Bézier curve. If we can verify that the two boxes do not overlap (a trivial test!), we are assured that the two curves do not intersect. If the boxes do overlap, we would have to perform more checks on the curves. The possibility for a quick decision of no interference is extremely important, since in practice one often has to check one object against thousands of others, most of which can be labeled as "no interference" by the minmax box test.[2]

Endpoint interpolation. The Bézier curve passes through $\mathbf{b}_0$ and $\mathbf{b}_n$: we have $\mathbf{b}^n(0) = \mathbf{b}_0, \mathbf{b}^n(1) = \mathbf{b}_n$. This is easily verified by writing down the scheme (3.3) for the cases $t = 0$ and $t = 1$. In a design situation, the endpoints of a curve are certainly two very important points. It is therefore essential to have direct control over them, which is assured by endpoint interpolation.

Designing with Bézier curves. Figure 3.3 shows several Bézier curves. From the inspection of these examples, one gets the impression that in some sense the Bézier curve "mimicks" the Bézier polygon – this statement will be made more precise later. This is the reason why Bézier curves provide such a handy tool for the *design* of curves: In order to reproduce the shape of a handdrawn curve, it is sufficient to specify a control polygon that somehow 'exaggerates' the shape of the curve. One lets the computer draw the Bézier curve defined by the polygon, and, if necessary, adjusts the location (possibly also the number) of the polygon vertices. Typically, an experienced person will reproduce a given curve after two to three iterations of this *interactive* procedure.

We will subsequently derive more properties of Bézier curves; in order to do so, we shall develop the so-called Bernstein representation in the next chapter.

---

[2] It is possible to create volumes (or areas, in the 2D case) that hug the given curve closer than the minmax box does. See Sederberg *et al.* [331].

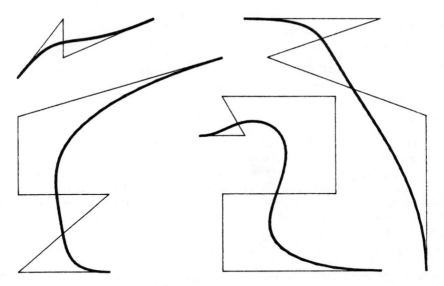

Figure 3.3. Bézier curves: some examples.

3.4   Implementation

Here is a C implementation of the de Casteljau algorithm:

```
float decas(degree,coeff,t)
/*    uses  de Casteljau to compute one coordinate
      value of a  Bezier curve. Has to be called
      for each coordinate  (x,y, and/or z) of a control polygon.
Input:    degree: degree of curve.
          coeff:  array with coefficients of curve.
          t:      parameter value.
Output: coordinate value.
*/
      float coeff[];
      float t;
      int degree;
      {
      int r,i;
      float t1;
      float coeffa[10];             /* an auxiliary array*/

      t1 = 1.0 - t;
      for(i=0; i<=degree; i++)
          coeffa[i]=coeff[i];       /* save input array */
```

```
for (r=1; r<= degree; r++)
for (i=0; i<= degree - r; i++)
{
    coeffa[i]= t1* coeffa[i]  +   t * coeffa[i+1] ;
}
return (coeffa[0]);
}
```

This procedure invites several comments. First, we see that it requires the use of an auxiliary array coeffa. Moreover, this auxiliary array has to be filled for each function call! So on top of the already high computational cost of the de Casteljau algorithm we add another burden to the routine, keeping it from being very efficient. A faster evaluation method is given at the end of the next chapter.

To plot a Bézier curve, we would then call the routine several times:

```
void bez_to_points(degree,npoints,coeff,points)
/*      Converts Bezier curve into point sequence. Works on
        one coordinate only.
   Input:   degree:  degree of curve.
            npoints: # of coordinates to be generated. (counting
                     from 0!)
            coeff:   coordinates of control polygon.
   Output:  points:  coordinates of points on curve.

        Remark: For a 2D curve, this routine needs to be called twice,
                once for the x-coordinates and once for y.
*/
        int degree, npoints;
        float coeff[],points[];


{
        float t,delt;
        int i;
        float decas();

        delt=1.0/(float)npoints; /* step length */
        t=0.0;
        for(ri=0; i<=npoints; i++)
        {
            points[i]=decas(degree,coeff,t);
            t = t+delt;
        }
}
```

The last subroutine has to be called once for each coordinate, i.e., two or three times. Once arrays `points_x`, `points_y`, `points_z` have been generated, they may be plotted by calls to a polygon-draw routine, typically named `polyline_abs_3` (or, in the 2D case, `polyline_abs_2`).

3.5 Problems

1. Use the notation $\mathbf{b}^n(t) = \mathcal{B}[\mathbf{b}_0, \ldots, \mathbf{b}_n; t]$ to formulate the de Casteljau algorithm. Comment on the computation count if you implement such a recursive algorithm in a language like C.

2. Suppose a planar Bézier curve has a control polygon that is symmetric with respect to the y-axis. Is the curve also symmetric with respect to the y-axis? Be sure to consider the control polygon $(-1, 0), (0, 1), (1, 1), (0, 2), (0, 1), (-1, 1), (0, 2), (0, 1), (1, 0)$. Generalize to other symmetry properties.

3. Show that every nonplanar cubic in $I\!E^3$ can be obtained as an affine map of the *standard cubic* (see Boehm [55])

$$\mathbf{x}(t) = \begin{bmatrix} t \\ t^2 \\ t^3 \end{bmatrix}.$$

4

The Bernstein Form of a Bézier Curve

Bézier curves can be defined by a recursive algorithm, and this is how de Casteljau first developed them. It is also necessary, however, to have an *explicit* representation for them, i.e., to express a Bézier curve in terms of a nonrecursive formula rather than in terms of an algorithm. This will facilitate further theoretical development considerably.

4.1 Bernstein Polynomials

We will express Bézier curves in terms of *Bernstein polynomials*, defined explicitly by

$$B_i^n(t) = \binom{n}{i} t^i (1-t)^{n-i}, \qquad (4.1)$$

where the binomial coefficients are given by

$$\binom{n}{i} = \begin{cases} \frac{n!}{i!(n-i)!} & \text{if } 0 \le i \le n \\ 0 & \text{else.} \end{cases}$$

There is a fair amount of literature on these polynomials. We cite just a few: Bernstein [40], Lorentz [245], Davis [92], Korovkin [229]. An extensive bibliography is in Gonska and Meier [172].

Before we explore the importance of Bernstein polynomials to Bézier curves, let us first examine them more closely. One of their important properties is that they satisfy the following recursion:

$$B_i^n(t) = (1 - t)B_i^{n-1}(t) + tB_{i-1}^{n-1}(t) \tag{4.2}$$

with

$$B_0^0(t) \equiv 1 \tag{4.3}$$

and

$$B_j^n(t) \equiv 0 \quad \text{for } j \notin \{0, \dots, n\}. \tag{4.4}$$

The proof is simple:

$$
\begin{aligned}
B_i^n(t) &= \binom{n}{i} t^i (1-t)^{n-i} \\
&= \binom{n-1}{i} t^i (1-t)^{n-i} + \binom{n-1}{i-1} t^i (1-t)^{n-i} \\
&= (1-t)B_i^{n-1}(t) + tB_{i-1}^{n-1}(t).
\end{aligned}
$$

Another important property is that Bernstein polynomials form a *partition of unity*:

$$\sum_{j=0}^{n} B_j^n(t) \equiv 1. \tag{4.5}$$

This fact is proved with the help of the binomial theorem:

$$1 = (t + (1 - t))^n = \sum_{j=0}^{n} \binom{n}{j} t^j (1-t)^{n-j} = \sum_{j=0}^{n} B_j^n(t).$$

Figure 4.1 shows the family of the five quartic Bernstein polynomials. Note that the B_i^n are nonnegative over the interval $[0, 1]$.

We are now ready to see why Bernstein polynomials are important for the development of Bézier curves. The intermediate de Casteljau points $\mathbf{b}_i^r$ can be expressed in terms of Bernstein polynomials of degree r:

$$\mathbf{b}_i^r(t) = \sum_{j=0}^{r} \mathbf{b}_{i+j} B_j^r(t) \quad \begin{aligned} &\in \{0, \dots, n\} \\ i &\in \{0, \dots, n - r\}. \end{aligned} \tag{4.6}$$

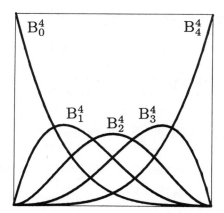

Figure 4.1. Bernstein polynomials: the quartic case.

This equation shows exactly how the intermediate point $\mathbf{b}_i^r$ depends on the given Bézier points $\mathbf{b}_i$. The main importance of (4.6), however, is for the case $r = n$. The corresponding de Casteljau point is the point on the curve and is given by

$$\mathbf{b}^n(t) = \mathbf{b}_0^n(t) = \sum_{j=0}^{n} \mathbf{b}_j B_j^n(t). \tag{4.7}$$

We still have to prove (4.6). To that end, we use the recursive definition of the $\mathbf{b}_i^r$ (Equation 3.2) and the recursion for the Bernstein polynomials (4.2) and (4.4) in an inductive proof:

$$\begin{aligned}
\mathbf{b}_i^r(t) &= (1-t)\mathbf{b}_i^{r-1}(t) + t\mathbf{b}_{i+1}^{r-1}(t) \\
&= (1-t)\sum_{j=i}^{i+r-1} \mathbf{b}_j B_{j-i}^{r-1}(t) + t\sum_{j=i+1}^{i+r} \mathbf{b}_j B_{j-i-1}^{r-1}(t).
\end{aligned}$$

Reindexing and invoking (4.4), we can rewrite this as

$$\begin{aligned}
\mathbf{b}_i^r(t) &= (1-t)\sum_{j=i}^{i+r} \mathbf{b}_j B_{j-i}^{r-1}(t) + t\sum_{j=i}^{i+r} \mathbf{b}_j B_{j-i-1}^{r-1}(t) \\
&= \sum_{j=i}^{i+r} \mathbf{b}_j[(1-t)B_{j-i}^{r-1}(t) + tB_{j-i-1}^{r-1}(t)].
\end{aligned}$$

Application of (4.2) then completes the proof. Note that (4.2) also defines B_0^n and B_n^n, since $B_{-1}^{n-1} = B_n^{n-1} = 0$ by (4.4).

4.2   Properties of Bézier Curves

Many of the properties in this section have already appeared in the previous
chapter. They were derived using geometric arguments. We shall now
rederive several of them, using algebraic arguments. If the same heading
is used as in the last chapter, the reader should look there for a complete
description of the property in question.

Affine invariance. Barycentric combinations are invariant under affine
maps, and so (4.5) gives the algebraic verification of this property.

Invariance under affine parameter transformations. Algebraically, this
property reads

$$\sum_{i=0}^{n} \mathbf{b}_i B_i^n(t) = \sum_{i=0}^{n} \mathbf{b}_i B_i^n \left(\frac{u-a}{b-a}\right). \tag{4.8}$$

Convex hull property. This follows, since for $t \in [0,1]$, the Bernstein
polynomials are nonnegative. They sum to one as shown in (4.5).

Endpoint interpolation. This is a consequence of the identities

$$\begin{aligned}
B_i^n(0) = 1 \quad &\text{iff} \quad i = 0, \\
B_i^n(1) = 1 \quad &\text{iff} \quad i = n
\end{aligned} \tag{4.9}$$

and (4.5).

Symmetry. Looking at the examples in Figure 3.3, it is clear that it
does not matter if the Bézier points are labeled $\mathbf{b}_0, \mathbf{b}_1, \ldots, \mathbf{b}_n$ or
$\mathbf{b}_n, \mathbf{b}_{n-1}, \ldots, \mathbf{b}_0$. The curves that correspond to the two different
orderings look the same; they only differ in the direction in which
they are traversed. Written out as a formula:

$$\sum_{j=0}^{n} \mathbf{b}_j B_j^n(t) = \sum_{j=0}^{n} \mathbf{b}_{n-j} B_j^n(1-t). \tag{4.10}$$

This follows from the identity

$$B_j^n(t) = B_{n-j}^n(1-t), \tag{4.11}$$

which follows from inspection of (4.1). We say that Bernstein polynomials are *symmetric* with respect to t and $1-t$.

Invariance under barycentric combinations. The process of forming the Bézier curve from the Bézier polygon leaves barycentric combinations invariant: for $\alpha + \beta = 1$, we get

$$\sum_{j=0}^{n}(\alpha\mathbf{b}_j + \beta\mathbf{c}_j)B_j^n(t) = \alpha\sum_{j=0}^{n}\mathbf{b}_j B_j^n(t) + \beta\sum_{j=0}^{n}\mathbf{c}_j B_j^n(t). \qquad (4.12)$$

In words: we can construct the weighted average of two Bézier curves either by taking the weighted average of corresponding points on the curves, or by taking the weighted average of corresponding control vertices and then computing the curve.

This linearity property is essential for many theoretical purposes, the most important one being the definition of tensor product surfaces in Chapter 16.

Linear precision. A useful identity is the following:

$$\sum_{j=0}^{n}\frac{j}{n}B_j^n(t) = t, \qquad (4.13)$$

which has the following application: suppose the polygon vertices $\mathbf{b}_j$ are uniformly distributed on a straight line joining two points $\mathbf{p}$ and $\mathbf{q}$:

$$\mathbf{b}_j = (1 - \frac{j}{n})\mathbf{p} + \frac{j}{n}\mathbf{q}; \quad j = 0,\ldots,n.$$

The curve that is generated by this polygon is the straight line between $\mathbf{p}$ and $\mathbf{q}$, i.e., the initial straight line is reproduced. This property is called *linear precision*.[1]

Pseudo-local control. The Bernstein polynomial B_i^n has only one maximum and attains it at $t = i/n$. This has a design application: if we move only one of the control polygon vertices, say, $\mathbf{b}_i$, then the curve is mostly affected by this change in the region of the curve around the parameter value i/n. This makes the effect of the change reasonably predictable, although the change does affect the whole curve.

---

[1] If the points are not uniformly spaced, we will also recapture the straight line segment. However, it will not be linearly parametrized.

4.3   The Derivative of a Bézier Curve

The derivative of a Bernstein polynomial B_i^n is obtained as

$$
\begin{aligned}
\frac{\mathrm{d}}{\mathrm{d}t} B_i^n(t) &= \frac{\mathrm{d}}{\mathrm{d}t} \binom{n}{i} t^i (1-t)^{n-i} \\
&= \frac{i\, n!}{i!(n-i)!} t^{i-1}(1-t)^{n-i} - \frac{(n-i)n!}{i!(n-i)!} t^i (1-t)^{n-i-1} \\
&= \frac{n(n-1)!}{(i-1)!(n-i)!} t^{i-1}(1-t)^{n-i} - \frac{n(n-1)!}{i!(n-i-1)!} t^i (1-t)^{n-i-1} \\
&= n(B_{i-1}^{n-1}(t) - B_i^{n-1}(t)).
\end{aligned}
$$

Thus

$$
\frac{\mathrm{d}}{\mathrm{d}t} B_i^n(t) = n\left(B_{i-1}^{n-1}(t) - B_i^{n-1}(t) \right). \tag{4.14}
$$

We can now determine the derivative of a Bézier curve $\mathbf{b}^n$:

$$
\frac{\mathrm{d}}{\mathrm{d}t} \mathbf{b}^n(t) = n \sum_{j=0}^{n} \left(B_{j-1}^{n-1}(t) - B_j^{n-1}(t) \right) \mathbf{b}_j.
$$

Because of (4.4), this can be simplified to

$$
\frac{\mathrm{d}}{\mathrm{d}t} \mathbf{b}^n(t) = n \sum_{j=1}^{n} B_{j-1}^{n-1}(t)\mathbf{b}_j - n \sum_{j=0}^{n-1} B_j^{n-1}(t)\mathbf{b}_j,
$$

and now an index transformation of the first sum yields

$$
\frac{\mathrm{d}}{\mathrm{d}t} \mathbf{b}^n(t) = n \sum_{j=0}^{n-1} B_j^{n-1}(t)\mathbf{b}_{j+1} - n \sum_{j=0}^{n-1} B_j^{n-1}(t)\mathbf{b}_j,
$$

and finally

$$
\frac{\mathrm{d}}{\mathrm{d}t} \mathbf{b}^n(t) = n \sum_{j=0}^{n-1} (\mathbf{b}_{j+1} - \mathbf{b}_j) B_j^{n-1}(t).
$$

The last formula can be simplified somewhat by the introduction of the *forward difference operator* Δ:

$$
\Delta \mathbf{b}_j = \mathbf{b}_{j+1} - \mathbf{b}_j. \tag{4.15}
$$

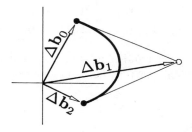

Figure 4.2. Derivatives: a Bézier curve and its first derivative curve (scaled down by a factor of three). Note that this derivative curve does not change if a translation is applied to the original curve.

We now have for the derivative of a Bézier curve:

$$\frac{\mathrm{d}}{\mathrm{d}t}\mathbf{b}^n(t) = n \sum_{j=0}^{n-1} \Delta\mathbf{b}_j B_j^{n-1}(t); \quad \Delta\mathbf{b}_j \in I\!\!R^3. \qquad (4.16)$$

The derivative of a Bézier curve is thus another Bézier curve, obtained by differencing the original control polygon. However, this derivative Bézier curve does not "live" in $I\!\!E^3$ any more! Its coefficients are differences of points, i.e., *vectors*, which are elements of $I\!\!R^3$. In order to visualize the derivative curve and polygon in $I\!\!E^3$, we can construct a polygon in $I\!\!E^3$ that consists of the points $\mathbf{a} + \Delta\mathbf{b}_0, \dots, \mathbf{a} + \Delta\mathbf{b}_{n-1}$. Here $\mathbf{a}$ is arbitrary; one reasonable choice is $\mathbf{a} = \mathbf{0}$. Figure 4.2 illustrates a Bézier curve and its derivative curve (with the choice $\mathbf{a} = \mathbf{0}$). This derivative curve is sometimes called a *hodograph*. For more information on hodographs, see Forrest [156].

4.4 Higher Order Derivatives

In order to compute higher derivatives, we first generalize the forward difference operator (4.15): the *iterated forward difference operator* Δ^r is defined
by

$$\Delta^r \mathbf{b}_j = \Delta^{r-1}\mathbf{b}_{j+1} - \Delta^{r-1}\mathbf{b}_j. \tag{4.17}$$

We list a few examples:

$$
\begin{aligned}
\Delta^0 \mathbf{b}_i &= \mathbf{b}_i \\
\Delta^1 \mathbf{b}_i &= \mathbf{b}_{i+1} - \mathbf{b}_i \\
\Delta^2 \mathbf{b}_i &= \mathbf{b}_{i+2} - 2\mathbf{b}_{i+1} + \mathbf{b}_i \\
\Delta^3 \mathbf{b}_i &= \mathbf{b}_{i+3} - 3\mathbf{b}_{i+2} + 3\mathbf{b}_{i+1} - \mathbf{b}_i.
\end{aligned}
$$

The factors on the right-hand sides are binomial coefficients, forming a
Pascal-like triangle. This pattern holds in general:

$$\Delta^r \mathbf{b}_i = \sum_{j=0}^{r} \binom{r}{j} (-1)^{r-j}\mathbf{b}_{i+j}. \tag{4.18}$$

We are now in a position to give the formula for the r-th derivative of a
Bézier curve:

$$\frac{d^r}{dt^r}\mathbf{b}^n(t) = \frac{n!}{(n-r)!}\sum_{j=0}^{n-r}\Delta^r\mathbf{b}_j B_j^{n-r}(t). \tag{4.19}$$

The proof of (4.19) is by repeated application of (4.16).

Two important special cases of (4.19) are given by $t = 0$ and $t = 1$.
Because of (4.9) we get

$$\frac{d^r}{dt^r}\mathbf{b}^n(0) = \frac{n!}{(n-r)!}\Delta^r\mathbf{b}_0, \tag{4.20}$$

$$\frac{d^r}{dt^r}\mathbf{b}^n(1) = \frac{n!}{(n-r)!}\Delta^r\mathbf{b}_{n-r}. \tag{4.21}$$

Thus the r-th derivative of a Bézier curve at an endpoint depends only
on the $r + 1$ Bézier points near (and including) that endpoint. For $r = 0$,
we get the already established property of endpoint interpolation. The case
$r = 1$ states that $\mathbf{b}_0$ and $\mathbf{b}_1$ define the tangent at $t = 0$, provided they are
distinct.[2] Similarly, $\mathbf{b}_{n-1}$ and $\mathbf{b}_n$ determine the tangent at $t = 1$. The
cases $r = 1$, $r = 2$ are illustrated in Figure 4.3.

---

[2]In general, the tangent at $\mathbf{b}_0$ is determined by $\mathbf{b}_0$ and the first $\mathbf{b}_i$ that is distinct
from $\mathbf{b}_0$. Thus the tangent may be defined even if the tangent vector is the zero vector.

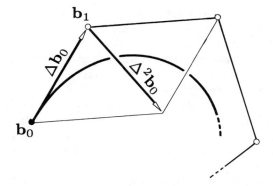

Figure 4.3. Endpoint derivatives: the first and second derivative vectors at $t = 0$ are multiples of the first and second difference vectors at $\mathbf{b}_0$.

4.5 Derivatives and the de Casteljau Algorithm

Derivatives of a Bézier curve can be expressed in terms of the intermediate points generated by the de Casteljau algorithm:

$$\frac{\mathrm{d}^r}{\mathrm{d}t^r}\mathbf{b}^n(t) = \frac{n!}{(n-r)!}\Delta^r\mathbf{b}_0^{n-r}(t). \tag{4.22}$$

This follows since summation and taking differences commute:

$$\sum_{j=0}^{n-1}\Delta\mathbf{b}_j = \sum_{j=1}^{n}\mathbf{b}_j - \sum_{j=0}^{n-1}\mathbf{b}_j = \Delta\sum_{j=0}^{n-1}\mathbf{b}_j. \tag{4.23}$$

Using this, we have

$$\frac{\mathrm{d}^r}{\mathrm{d}t^r}\mathbf{b}^n(t) = \frac{n!}{(n-r)!}\sum_{j=0}^{n-r}\Delta^r\mathbf{b}_j B_j^{n-r}(t) \tag{4.24}$$

$$= \frac{n!}{(n-r)!}\Delta^r\sum_{j=0}^{n-r}\mathbf{b}_j B_j^{n-r}(t) \tag{4.25}$$

$$= \frac{n!}{(n-r)!}\Delta^r\mathbf{b}_0^{n-r}(t). \tag{4.26}$$

The first and the last of these three equations suggest two different ways of computing the rth derivative of a Bézier curve: for the first method (4.24), compute all r^{th} forward differences of the control points, then interpret them as a new Bézier polygon of degree $n - r$ and evaluate it at t.

The second method, using (4.26), computes the rth derivative as a "byproduct" of the de Casteljau algorithm. If we compute a point on a Bézier curve using a triangular arrangement as in (3.3), then for any $n - r$, the corresponding $\mathbf{b}_i^{n-r}$ form a column (with r entries) in that scheme. To obtain the rth derivative at t, we simply take the rth difference of these points and then multiply by the constant $n!/(n-r)!$. In some applications (curve/plane intersection, for example), one needs not only a point on the curve, but its first and/or second derivative at the same time. The de Casteljau algorithm offers a quick solution to this problem.

A summary of both methods: in order to compute the rth derivative of a Bézier curve, perform r difference steps and $n - r$ evaluation steps. It does not matter in which order we perform these two steps.

The case $r = 1$ is important enough to warrant special attention:

$$\frac{\mathrm{d}}{\mathrm{d}t}\mathbf{b}^n(t) = n(\mathbf{b}_1^{n-1}(t) - \mathbf{b}_0^{n-1}(t)). \tag{4.27}$$

The intermediate points $\mathbf{b}_0^{n-1}$ and $\mathbf{b}_1^{n-1}$ thus determine the *tangent vector* at $\mathbf{b}^n(t)$, which is illustrated in Figures 3.1 and 3.2.

4.6   The Matrix Form of a Bézier Curve

Some authors (Faux and Pratt [145], Mortenson [259], Chang [73]) prefer to write Bézier curves and other polynomial curves in matrix form. A curve of the form

$$\mathbf{x}(t) = \sum_{j=0}^{n} \mathbf{c}_i C_i(t)$$

can be interpreted as a dot product:

$$\mathbf{x}(t) = \begin{bmatrix} \mathbf{c}_0 & \cdots & \mathbf{c}_n \end{bmatrix} \begin{bmatrix} C_0(t) \\ \vdots \\ C_n(t) \end{bmatrix}.$$

One can take this one step further and write

$$\begin{bmatrix} C_0(t) \\ \vdots \\ C_n(t) \end{bmatrix} = \begin{bmatrix} m_{00} & \cdots & m_{0n} \\ \vdots & & \vdots \\ m_{n0} & \cdots & m_{nn} \end{bmatrix} \begin{bmatrix} t^0 \\ \vdots \\ t^n \end{bmatrix}. \tag{4.28}$$

The matrix $M = \{m_{ij}\}$ describes the basis transformation between the basis polynomials $C_i(t)$ and the *monomial basis* t^i.

If the C_i are Bernstein polynomials, $C_i = B_i^n$, the matrix M has elements

$$m_{ij} = (-1)^{j-i} \binom{n}{j} \binom{j}{i}. \tag{4.29}$$

We list the cubic case explicitly:

$$M = \begin{bmatrix} 1 & -3 & 3 & -1 \\ 0 & 3 & -6 & 3 \\ 0 & 0 & 3 & -3 \\ 0 & 0 & 0 & 1 \end{bmatrix}.$$

Why the matrix form? Mathematically, it is equivalent to other curve formulations. When it comes to computer implementations, however, the matrix form may be advantageous if matrix multiplication is hard-wired.

A warning is in place: the monomial form is *numerically unstable* and should be avoided where accuracy in computation is of any importance. See the discussion in Section 24.3 for more details.

4.7 Implementation

First, we give a routine that evaluates a Bézier curve more efficiently than decas from the last chapter. It will have the flavor of Horner's scheme for the evaluation of a polynomial in monomial form. To give an example of Horner's scheme, also called nested multiplication, we list the cubic case:

$$\mathbf{c}_0 + t\mathbf{c}_1 + t^2\mathbf{c}_2 + t^3\mathbf{c}_3 = \mathbf{c}_0 + t(\mathbf{c}_1 + t(\mathbf{c}_2 + t\mathbf{c}_3)).$$

A similar nested form can be devised for Bézier curves; again, the cubic case:

$$\mathbf{b}^3(t) = \left(\left(\binom{3}{0}s\mathbf{b}_0 + \binom{3}{1}t\mathbf{b}_1\right)s + \binom{3}{2}t^2\mathbf{b}_2\right)s + \binom{3}{3}t^3\mathbf{b}_3,$$

where $s = 1 - t$. Recalling the identity

$$\binom{n}{i} = \frac{n-i+1}{i}\binom{n}{i-1}; \quad i > 0,$$

we arrive at the following program (for the general case):

```
float hornbez(degree,coeff,t)
/*   uses   a Horner-like  scheme to compute one coordinate
       value of a  Bezier curve. Has to be called
       for each coordinate  (x,y, and/or z) of a control polygon.
Input:    degree: degree of curve.
          coeff:  array with coefficients of curve.
          t:      parameter value.
Output:           coordinate value.
*/
       int degree;
       float coeff[];
       float t;
{
       int i,n_choose_i;   /* Warning: on 16 bit machines, this will
                              blow up if degree > 16 ! */
       float fact,t1,aux;

       t1=1.0 - t;  fact=1.0;
       n_choose_i=1;

       aux=coeff[0]*t1;          /* starting the evaluation
                                    loop */
       for(i=1; i<degree; i++)
       {
            fact=fact*t;
            n_choose_i=n_choose_i*(degree-i+1)/i; /* always int! */
            aux=(aux + fact*n_choose_i*coeff[i])*t1;
       }
       aux = aux + fact*t*coeff[degree];

       return aux;
}
```

To use this routine for plotting a Bézier curve, we would replace the call to decas in bez_to_points by an identical call to hornbez. Replacing decas by hornbez results in a significant savings of time: we do not have to save the control polygon in an auxiliary array; also, hornbez is of order n, whereas decas is of order n^2.

This is not to say, however, that we have produced super efficient code for plotting points on a Bézier curve. For instance, we have to call hornbez once for each coordinate, and thus have to generate the binomial coefficents n_choose_i twice. This could be improved by writing a routine that combines the two calls. A further improvement could be to compute the sequence of binomial coefficents only once, and not over and over for each new value of t. All these (and possibly more) improvements would speed up the program, but would be less modular and thus less understandable. For the code in this book, modularity is placed above efficiency (in most cases).

4.8   Problems

1. Show that the Bernstein polynomials B_i^n form a basis for the linear space of all polynomials of degree n.

2. Show that the Bernstein polynomial B_i^n attains its maximum at $t = i/n$. Find the maximum value. What happens for large n?

3. A cusp is a point on a curve where the first derivative vector vanishes. Can a nonplanar cubic Bézier curve have a cusp?

5

Bézier Curve Topics

5.1   Degree Elevation

Suppose we were designing with Bézier curves as described in Section 3.3, trying to use a Bézier curve of degree n. After modifying the polygon a few times, it may turn out that a degree n curve does not possess sufficient flexibility to model the desired shape. One way to proceed in such a situation is to increase the flexibility of the polygon by adding another vertex to it. As a first step, one might want to add another vertex yet leave the shape of the curve unchanged – this corresponds to raising the degree of the Bézier curve by one. The new vertices $\mathbf{b}_j^{(1)}$ must satisfy

$$\sum_{j=0}^{n} \mathbf{b}_j \binom{n}{j} t^j (1-t)^{n-j} = \sum_{j=0}^{n+1} \mathbf{b}_j^{(1)} \binom{n+1}{j} t^j (1-t)^{n+1-j}. \tag{5.1}$$

We multiply the left hand side by $(t + (1 - t))$ and get

$$\sum_{j=0}^{n} \mathbf{b}_j \binom{n}{j} \left(t^j (1-t)^{n+1-j} + t^{j+1} (1-t)^{n-j} \right)$$

$$= \sum_{j=0}^{n+1} \mathbf{b}_j^{(1)} \binom{n+1}{j} t^j (1-t)^{n+1-j}.$$

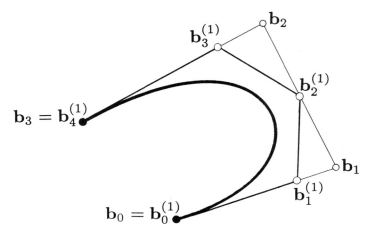

Figure 5.1. Degree elevation: both polygons define the same (degree three) curve.

We now compare coefficients of $t^j(1-t)^{n+1-j}$ on both sides and obtain

$$\mathbf{b}_j^{(1)}\binom{n+1}{j} = \mathbf{b}_j\binom{n}{j} + \mathbf{b}_{j-1}\binom{n}{j-1},$$

which is equivalent to

$$\mathbf{b}_j^{(1)} = \frac{j}{n+1}\mathbf{b}_{j-1} + (1 - \frac{j}{n+1})\mathbf{b}_j; \quad j = 0,\ldots,n+1. \qquad (5.2)$$

Thus the new vertices $\mathbf{b}_j^{(1)}$ are obtained from the old polygon by piecewise linear interpolation at the parameter values $j/(n+1)$. It follows that the new polygon $\mathcal{E}\mathbf{P}$ lies in the convex hull of the old one. Figure 5.1 gives an example. Note how $\mathcal{E}\mathbf{P}$ is "closer" to the curve $\mathcal{B}\mathbf{P}$ than the original polygon $\mathbf{P}$.

Degree elevation has important application in surface design: for several algorithms that produce surfaces from curve input, it is necessary that these curves be of the same degree. Using degree elevation, we may achieve this by raising the degree of all input curves to the one of the highest degree. Another application lies in the area of *data transfer* between different CAD/CAM or graphics systems: Suppose you have generated a parabola (i.e., a degree two Bézier curve), and you want to feed it into a system that only knows about cubics. All you have to do is to degree elevate your parabola.

5.2 Repeated Degree Elevation

The process of degree elevation assigns a polygon $\mathcal{E}\mathbf{P}$ to an original polygon $\mathbf{P}$. We may repeat this process and obtain a sequence of polygons $\mathbf{P}, \mathcal{E}\mathbf{P}, \mathcal{E}^2\mathbf{P}$, etc. After r degree elevations, the polygon $\mathcal{E}^r\mathbf{P}$ has the vertices $\mathbf{b}_0^{(r)}, \ldots, \mathbf{b}_{n+r}^{(r)}$, and each $\mathbf{b}_i^{(r)}$ is explicitly given by

$$\mathbf{b}_i^{(r)} = \sum_{j=0}^{n} \mathbf{b}_j \binom{n}{j} \frac{\binom{r}{i-j}}{\binom{n+r}{i}}. \tag{5.3}$$

This formula is easily proved by induction (see Problems).

Let us now investigate what happens if we repeat the process of degree elevation again and again. As we shall see, the polygons $\mathcal{E}^r\mathbf{P}$ converge to the curve that all of them define:

$$\lim_{r \to \infty} \mathcal{E}^r\mathbf{P} = \mathcal{B}\mathbf{P}. \tag{5.4}$$

In order to prove this result, fix some parameter value t. For each r, find the index i such that $i/(n+r)$ is closest to t. We can think of $i/(n+r)$ as a parameter on the polygon $\mathcal{E}^r\mathbf{P}$, and as $r \to \infty$, this ratio tends to t. One can now show (using Stirling's formula) that

$$\lim_{i/(n+r) \to t} \frac{\binom{r}{i-j}}{\binom{r+n}{i}} = t^j(1-t)^{n-j},$$

and therefore

$$\lim_{i/(n+r) \to t} \mathbf{b}_i^{(r)} = \sum_{j=0}^{n} \mathbf{b}_j B_j^n(t) = [\mathcal{B}\mathbf{P}](t).$$

Figure 5.2 shows an example of the limit behavior of the polygons $\mathcal{E}^r\mathbf{P}$.

The polygons $\mathcal{E}^r\mathbf{P}$ approach the curve very slowly; this convergence result has no practical consequences. However, it helps in the investigations of some theoretical properties, as in the next section.

The convergence of the polygons $\mathcal{E}^r\mathbf{P}$ to the curve was conjectured by R. Forrest [156] and proved in Farin [126]. The above proof follows an approach taken by J. Zhou [355]. Degree elevation may be generalized to "corner-cutting;" for a brief description, see Section 10.7.

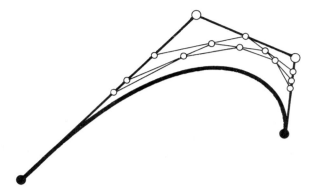

Figure 5.2. Degree elevation: a sequence of polygons approaching the curve that is defined by each of them.

5.3   The Variation Diminishing Property

We can now show that Bézier curves enjoy the *variation diminishing property:*[1] the curve $\mathcal{B}\mathbf{P}$ has no more intersections with any plane than the polygon $\mathbf{P}$. Degree elevation is an instance of piecewise linear interpolation, and we know that operation is variation diminishing (see Section 2.4). Thus each $\mathcal{E}^r\mathbf{P}$ has fewer intersections with a given plane than its predecessor $\mathcal{E}^{(r-1)}\mathbf{P}$ has. Since the curve is the limit of these polygons, we have proved our statement. For high degree Bézier curves, variation diminution may become so strong that the control polygon has no resemblance to the curve any more.

A special case is obtained for *convex* polygons: a planar polygon (or curve) is said to be convex if it has no more than two intersections with any plane. The variation diminishing property thus asserts that a convex polygon generates a convex curve. Note that the inverse statement is not true: there exist convex curves that have a nonconvex control polygon!

5.4   Degree Reduction

Degree elevation can be viewed as a process that introduces redundancy: a curve is described by more information than is actually necessary. The inverse process might seem more interesting: can we *reduce* possible redundancy in a curve representation? More specifically, can we write a given

---

[1]The variation diminishing property was first investigated by I. Schoenberg [320] in the context of B-spline approximation.

curve of degree n as one of degree $n - 1$? We shall call this process *degree reduction*.

In general, exact degree reduction is not possible. For example, a cubic with a point of inflection cannot possibly be written as a quadratic. Degree reduction, therefore, can be viewed only as a method to *approximate* a given curve by one of lower degree. Our problem can now be stated as follows: given a Bézier curve with control vertices $\mathbf{b}_i; i = 0, \ldots, n$ can we find a Bézier curve with control vertices $\hat{\mathbf{b}}_i; i = 0, \ldots, n - 1$ that approximates the first curve?

Let us now pretend that the $\mathbf{b}_i$ were obtained from the $\hat{\mathbf{b}}_i$ by the process of degree elevation (this is not true, in general, but makes a good working assumption). Then they would be related by

$$\mathbf{b}_i = \frac{i}{n}\hat{\mathbf{b}}_{i-1} + \frac{n-i}{n}\hat{\mathbf{b}}_i; \quad i = 0, 1, \ldots, n. \tag{5.5}$$

This equation can be used to derive two recursive formulas for the generation of the $\hat{\mathbf{b}}_i$ from the $\mathbf{b}_i$:

$$\hat{\mathbf{b}}_i = \frac{n\mathbf{b}_i - i\hat{\mathbf{b}}_{i-1}}{n-i}; \quad i = 0, 1, \ldots, n - 1 \tag{5.6}$$

and

$$\hat{\mathbf{b}}_{i-1} = \frac{n\mathbf{b}_i - (n-i)\hat{\mathbf{b}}_i}{i}; \quad i = n, n - 1, \ldots, 1. \tag{5.7}$$

Figure 5.3 illustrates the first of the two recursive formulas: the polygon of the $\mathbf{b}_i$ is given, and the degree $n - 1$ approximation to it is constructed by "unraveling" the degree elevation process from left to right. If the given n^{th} degree curve had actually been of degree $n - 1$, formula (5.6) would have produced the lower degree polygon. Since this is in general not true, we only obtain an approximation – quite a bad one in most cases. The reason is that both (5.6) and (5.7) are *extrapolation* formulas, which tend to be numerically unstable.

One observes that (5.6) tends to produce reasonable approximations near $\mathbf{b}_0$ and that (5.7) behaves decently near $\mathbf{b}_n$. We may take advantage of this and combine both approximations; for example, we could take the left half of the polygon from (5.6) and the right half of the polygon from (5.7) and merge them to obtain the final polygon of degree $n - 1$ (caution: there is a case distinction depending on n being even or odd!). An example is shown in Figure 5.4.

The first appearance of degree reduction is in Forrest [156]. It has been used for curve rendering by F. Little. A detailed treatment is in Watkins and Worsey [349].

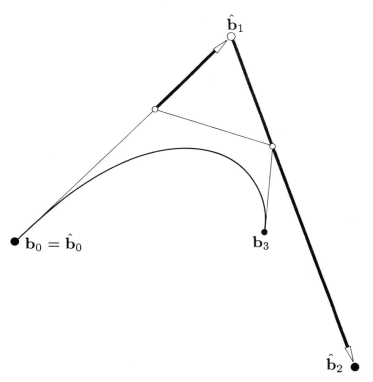

Figure 5.3. Degree reduction I: a cubic is approximated by a quadratic. The approximation is very poor.

5.5 Nonparametric Curves

We have so far considered three-dimensional parametric curves $\mathbf{b}(t)$. Now we shall restrict ourselves to *functional curves* of the form $y = f(x)$, where f denotes a polynomial. These (planar) curves can be written in parametric form:

$$\mathbf{b}(t) = \left[\begin{array}{c} x(t) \\ y(t) \end{array} \right] = \left[\begin{array}{c} t \\ f(t) \end{array} \right].$$

We are interested in functions f that are expressed in terms of the Bernstein basis:

$$f(t) = b_0 B_0^n(t) + \cdots + b_n B_n^n(t);$$

note that now the coefficients b_j are real numbers, not points. The b_j therefore do not form a polygon, yet functional curves are a subset of parametric

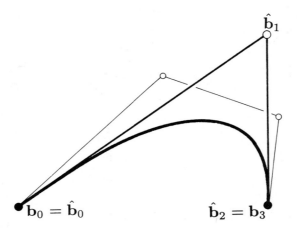

Figure 5.4. Degree reduction II: combining the two degree reduction methods (solving from left to right and from right to left), a reasonable approximation is obtained. Here, $\hat{\mathbf{b}}_1$ is the midpoint of the two corresponding points from the two methods.

curves and therefore must possess a control polygon. In order to find it, we recall the linear precision property of Bézier curves, as defined by (4.13). We can now write our functional curve as

$$\mathbf{b}(t) = \sum_{j=0}^{n} \begin{bmatrix} j/n \\ b_j \end{bmatrix} B_j^n(t). \tag{5.8}$$

Thus the control polygon of the function $f(t) = \sum b_j B_j^n$ is given by the points $(j/n, b_j); j = 0, \ldots, n$. If we want to distinguish clearly between the parametric and the nonparametric cases, we call $f(t)$ a *Bézier function.* Figure 5.5 illustrates the cubic case. We also emphasize that the b_i are real numbers, not points; we call the b_i *Bézier ordinates.*

Because Bézier curves are invariant under affine reparametrizations, we may consider any interval $[a, b]$ instead of the special interval $[0, 1]$. Then the abscissae values are $a + i(b - a)/n; \quad i = 0, \ldots, n$.

5.6 Cross Plots

Parametric Bézier curves are composed of coordinate functions: each component is a Bézier function. For two dimensional curves, this can be used to construct the *cross plot* of a curve. Figure 5.6 shows the decomposition of a Bézier curve into its two coordinate functions. A cross plot can be a very helpful tool for the investigationnot only of Bézier curves, but of

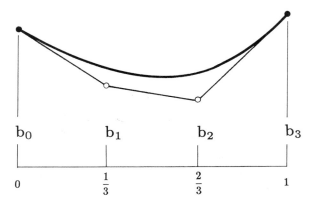

Figure 5.5. Functional curves: the control polygon of a cubic polynomial has abscissae values 0,1/3,2/3,1.

general two dimensional curves. We will use it for the analysis of Bézier and B-spline curves. It can be generalized to more than two dimensions, but is not as useful then.

5.7   Integrals

As we have seen, the Bézier polygon $\mathbf{P}$ of a Bézier function is formed by points $(j/n, b_j)$. Let us assign an area $\mathcal{A}\mathbf{P}$ to $\mathbf{P}$ by

$$\mathcal{A}\mathbf{P} = \frac{1}{n+1} \sum_{j=0}^{n} b_j. \tag{5.9}$$

An example for this area is shown in Figure 5.7; it corresponds to approximating the area under the polygon by a particular Riemann sum (of the polygon).

It is now easy to show that this "approximation area" is the same for the polygon $\mathcal{E}\mathbf{P}$, obtained from degree elevation (Section 5.1):

$$
\begin{aligned}
\mathcal{A}\mathcal{E}\mathbf{P} &= \frac{1}{n+2} \sum_{j=0}^{n+1} \frac{j}{n+1} b_{j-1} + \left(1 - \frac{j}{n+1}\right) b_j \\
&= \frac{1}{n+2} \sum_{j=0}^{n} \frac{n+2}{n+1} b_j \\
&= \mathcal{A}\mathbf{P}.
\end{aligned}
$$

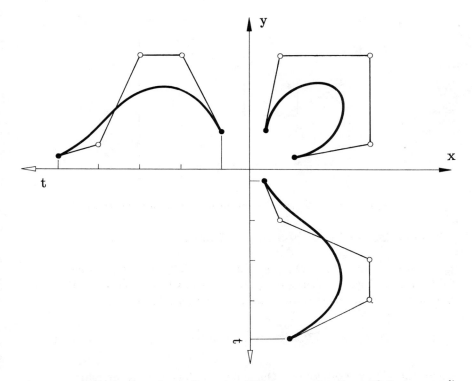

Figure 5.6. Cross plots: A two dimensional Bézier curve together with its two coordinate functions.

If we repeat the process of degree elevation, we know that the polygons $\mathcal{E}^r\mathbf{P}$ converge to the function $\mathcal{B}\mathbf{P}$. Their area $\mathcal{A}\mathcal{E}^r\mathbf{P}$ stays the same, and so in the limit is equal to the Riemann sum of the function, which converges to the integral:

$$\int_0^1 \sum_{j=0}^n b_j B_j^n(x)\mathrm{d}x = \frac{1}{n+1}\sum_{j=0}^n b_j. \qquad (5.10)$$

The special case $b_i = \delta_{i,j}$ gives

$$\int_0^1 B_i^n(x)\mathrm{d}x = \frac{1}{n+1}, \qquad (5.11)$$

i.e., all basis functions B_i^n (for a fixed n) have the same integral.

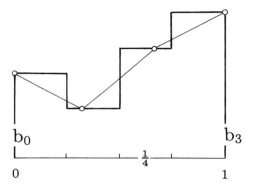

Figure 5.7. Integrals: an approximation to the area under **P**.

5.8 The Bézier Form of a Bézier Curve

In his work ([42], [43], [49], [48], [46], [44], [47], see also Vernet [343]), Bézier did not use the Bernstein polynomials as basis functions. He wrote the curve $\mathbf{b}^n$ as a linear combination of functions F_i^n:

$$\mathbf{b}^n(t) = \sum_{j=0}^{n} \mathbf{c}_j F_j^n(t), \tag{5.12}$$

where the F_j^n are polynomials that obey the following recursion:

$$F_i^n(t) = (1-t)F_i^{n-1}(t) + tF_{i-1}^{n-1}(t) \tag{5.13}$$

with

$$F_0^0(t) = 1, \quad F_{r+1}^r(t) = 0, \quad F_{-1}^r(t) = 1. \tag{5.14}$$

Note that the third condition in the last equation is the only instance where the definition of the F_i^n differs from that of the B_i^n! An explicit expression for the F_i^n is given by

$$F_i^n = \sum_{j=i}^{n} B_j^n. \tag{5.15}$$

A consequence of (5.14) is that $F_0^n \equiv 1$ for all n. Since $F_j^n(t) \geq 0$ for $t \in [0,1]$, it follows that (5.12) is not a barycentric combination of the $\mathbf{c}_j$. In fact, $\mathbf{c}_0$ is a point while the other $\mathbf{c}_j$ are vectors. The following relations hold:

$$\mathbf{c}_0 = \mathbf{b}_0 \tag{5.16}$$

$$\mathbf{c}_j = \Delta\mathbf{b}_{j-1}; \quad j > 0. \tag{5.17}$$

This undesirable distinction between points and vectors was abandoned soon after R. Forrest's discovery that the Bézier form (5.12) of a Bézier curve could be written in terms of Bernstein polynomials (see the appendix in [48]).

5.9   The Barycentric Form of a Bézier Curve

In this section, we present a different notation for Bézier curves that will be useful later. Let $\mathbf{p}_1$ and $\mathbf{p}_2$ be two distinct points on a straight line. Then, as described in Section 2.3, we can write any point $\mathbf{p}$ on the straight line in terms of barycentric coordinates of $\mathbf{p}_1$ and $\mathbf{p}_2$: $\mathbf{p} = u\mathbf{p}_1 + v\mathbf{p}_2$, thus identifying $\mathbf{p}$ with $\mathbf{u} = (u, v)$ and $u + v = 1$. The straight line can be mapped into $I\!\!E^3$, where it defines a polynomial curve $\mathbf{x}$

$$
\mathbf{x}(\mathbf{u}) = \sum_{\substack{i + j = n \\ i, j \geq 0}} \binom{n}{i, j} u^i v^j \mathbf{b}_{i,j},
\tag{5.18}
$$

where

$$
\binom{n}{i, j} = \frac{n!}{i!j!}.
$$

It is important to note that, although (5.18) *looks* bivariate, it really isn't: the condition $u + v = 1$ ensures that we still define a curve, not a surface. The connection with the standard Bézier form is established by setting $t = v, \mathbf{b}_i = \mathbf{b}_{i,j}$.

We can also define Bernstein polynomials in barycentric form:

$$
B^n_{i,j}(\mathbf{u}) = \binom{n}{i, j} u^i v^j; \quad i + j = n.
$$

The barycentric form brings out nicely two important properties of Bézier curves: invariance under affine parameter transformations and, as a consequence, symmetry, as discussed in Section 3.3. The location of the two points $\mathbf{p}_1$ and $\mathbf{p}_2$ becomes completely irrelevant – all that matters is the relative location of $\mathbf{p}$ with respect to them, described by u and v.

Here is what the de Casteljau algorithm becomes in barycentric notation:

$$
\mathbf{b}^r_{i,j}(\mathbf{u}) = u\mathbf{b}^{r-1}_{i+1,j}(\mathbf{u}) + v\mathbf{b}^{r-1}_{i,j+1}(\mathbf{u}) \quad \begin{cases} r = 1, \ldots, n \\ i + j = n - r \end{cases}.
\tag{5.19}
$$

The point on the curve is then given by $\mathbf{b}^n_{0,0}(\mathbf{u})$.

The barycentric form allows an intriguing way of writing derivatives: instead of evaluating at a *point* $\mathbf{u}$ with $u+v=1$, let us evaluate at a *vector* $\mathbf{d} = (d,e)$ with $d+e=0$. If we pick $\mathbf{d} = (1,-1)$, the de Casteljau algorithm (5.19) becomes

$$\mathbf{b}_{i,j}^r(\mathbf{d}) = \mathbf{b}_{i+1,j}^{r-1}(\mathbf{d}) - \mathbf{b}_{i,j+1}^{r-1}(\mathbf{d}).$$

Thus a *vector* argument for the de Casteljau algorithm produces forward differences! In other words,

$$\mathbf{b}_{i,j}^r(\mathbf{d}) = \Delta^r \mathbf{b}_i,$$

where the term on the right-hand side is in standard, nonbarycentric, notation.

We can combine the point and vector evaluations into one scheme: define

$$\mathbf{b}_{i,j}^{r,s}(\mathbf{u},\mathbf{d}) = \sum_{\rho=0}^{r}\sum_{\sigma=0}^{s} \mathbf{b}_{i+\rho,j+\sigma} B_\rho^r(\mathbf{u}) B_\sigma^s(\mathbf{d}); \quad i+j+r+s = n. \tag{5.20}$$

A term $\mathbf{b}_{0,0}^{r,s}(\mathbf{u},\mathbf{d})$ is obtained by r applications of the point-valued de Casteljau algorithm and by s applications of the vector-valued de Casteljau algorithm. Using (5.20), it is not hard to show that each $\mathbf{b}_{i,j}^{r,s}(\mathbf{u},\mathbf{d})$ may be obtained through either one of the following two recursions (Farin [130]):

$$\mathbf{b}_{i,j}^{r,s}(\mathbf{u},\mathbf{d}) = u\mathbf{b}_{i+1,j}^{r-1,s} + v\mathbf{b}_{i,j+1}^{r-1,s} \tag{5.21}$$

and

$$\mathbf{b}_{i,j}^{r,s}(\mathbf{u},\mathbf{d}) = d\mathbf{b}_{i+1,j}^{r,s-1} + e\mathbf{b}_{i,j+1}^{r,s-1}. \tag{5.22}$$

Figure 5.8 shows an example; each set $\{\mathbf{b}_{ij}^{rs}\}$ has $n-r-s$ elements. The term $\mathbf{b}_{0,0}^{n,0}(\mathbf{u},\mathbf{d})$ denotes the point on the curve (no dependence on $\mathbf{d}$), and $\mathbf{b}_{0,0}^{0,n}(\mathbf{u},\mathbf{d})$ denotes the nth derivative (no dependence on $\mathbf{u}$).

In general, the terms $\mathbf{b}_{0,0}^{r,s}(\mathbf{u},\mathbf{d})$ (after multiplication by $\frac{n!}{(n-s)!}$) give the sth derivative of the curve at the point with barycentric coordinates $\mathbf{u}$. Any path leading to $\mathbf{b}_{0,0}^{r,s}(\mathbf{u},\mathbf{d})$ from the original $\mathbf{b}_{i,j}$, indicated by arrows in Figure 5.8, is a valid way to compute the sth derivative. This approach of applying the de Casteljau algorithm for several arguments simultaneously is also known as *blossoming*.

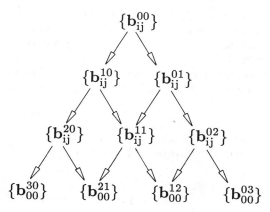

Figure 5.8. Generalizing the de Casteljau algorithm: evaluating at a point $\mathbf{u}$ and a vector $\mathbf{d}$ simultaneously, one gets all derivatives. In particular, for $n = 3$, $\mathbf{b}_{00}^{30}$ corresponds to the point on the curve, $3 \cdot \mathbf{b}_{00}^{21}$ corresponds to the first derivative etc.

5.10 The Weierstrass Approximation Theorem

One of the most important results in approximation theory is the Weierstrass approximation Theorem. S. Bernstein invented the polynomials that now bear his name in order to formulate a constructive proof of this theorem. The interested reader is referred to Davis [92].

We will give a "customized" version of the theorem, namely, we state it in the context of parametric curves. So let $\mathbf{c}$ be a continuous curve that is defined over $[0, 1]$. For some fixed n, we can sample $\mathbf{c}$ at parameter values i/n. The points $\mathbf{c}(i/n)$ can now be interpreted as the Bézier polygon of a polynomial curve $\mathbf{x}_n$:

$$\mathbf{x}_n(t) = \sum_{i=0}^{n} \mathbf{c}(\frac{i}{n}) B_i^n(t).$$

We say that $\mathbf{x}_n$ is the nth degree Bernstein-Bézier approximation to $\mathbf{c}$.

We are next going to increase the density of our samples, i.e., we increase n. This generates a sequence of approximations $\mathbf{x}_n, \mathbf{x}_{n+1}, \ldots$. The Weierstrass approximation Theorem states that this sequence of polynomials converges to the curve $\mathbf{c}$:

$$\lim_{n \to \infty} \mathbf{x}_n(t) = \mathbf{c}(t).$$

At first sight, this looks like a handy way to approximate a given curve by polynomials: we just have to pick a degree n that is sufficiently large, and we are as close to the curve as we like. This is only theoretically true, however. In practice, one would have to choose values of n in the thousands or even millions in order to obtain a reasonable closeness of fit (see Korovkin [229] for more details).

The value of the theorem is therefore more of a theoretical nature. It shows that every curve may be approximated arbitrarily closely by a polynomial curve.

5.11   Formulas for Bernstein Polynomials

This section is a collection of formulas; some appeared in the text, some did not. Credit for some of these goes to R. Goldman, R. Farouki, and V. Rajan [143].

A Bernstein polynomial is defined by

$$B_i^n(t) = \left\{ \begin{array}{ll} \binom{n}{i} t^i (1-t)^{n-i} & \text{if } i \in [0,n], \\ 0 & \text{else.} \end{array} \right.$$

The power basis $\{t^i\}$ and the Bernstein basis $\{B_i^n\}$ are related by

$$t^i = \sum_{j=i}^{n} \frac{\binom{j}{i}}{\binom{n}{i}} B_j^n(t) \tag{5.23}$$

and

$$B_i^n(t) = \sum_{j=i}^{n} (-1)^{j-i} \binom{n}{j} \binom{j}{i} t^j. \tag{5.24}$$

Recursion:

$$B_i^n(t) = (1-t)B_i^{n-1}(t) + tB_{i-1}^{n-1}(t).$$

Subdivision:

$$B_i^n(ct) = \sum_{j=0}^{n} B_i^j(c)B_j^n(t). \tag{5.25}$$

Derivative:

$$\frac{d}{dt}B_i^n(t) = n\big(B_{i-1}^{n-1}(t) - B_i^{n-1}(t)\big).$$

Integral:

$$\int_0^t B_i^n(x)\mathrm{d}x = \frac{1}{n+1} \sum_{j=i+1}^{n+1} B_j^{n+1}(t),\tag{5.26}$$

$$\int_0^1 B_i^n(x)\mathrm{d}x = \frac{1}{n+1}.$$

Three degree elevation formulas:

$$(1-t)B_i^n(t) = \frac{n+1-i}{n+1} B_i^{n+1}(t),\tag{5.27}$$

$$tB_i^n(t) = \frac{i+1}{n+1} B_{i+1}^{n+1}(t),\tag{5.28}$$

$$B_i^n(t) = \frac{n+1-i}{n+1} B_i^{n+1}(t) + \frac{i+1}{n+1} B_{i+1}^{n+1}(t).\tag{5.29}$$

Product:

$$B_i^m(u)B_j^n(u) = \frac{\binom{m}{i}\binom{n}{j}}{\binom{m+n}{i+j}} B_{i+j}^{m+n}(u).\tag{5.30}$$

5.12 Implementation

A C routine for degree elevation follows. Note that we have to treat the cases $i = 0$ and $i = n + 1$ separately: the program would not like the corresponding nonexisting array elements.

```
float degree_elevate(degree,coeff,cx)
/*   Degree elevates one coordinate of a Bezier control polygon.
     Has to be called for each coordinate
     (x,y, and/or z) of a 'real' control polygon.
Input:    degree: degree of curve.
          coeff:  array with coefficients of control polygon.
Output:   cx:     array with degree elevated coefficients.
*/

        float coeff[],cx[];
        int   degree;
{
        int i,degree1;

        degree1 = degree+1;
        cx[0] = coeff[0];
```

```
for(i=1; i<= degree; i++)
    {
    cx[i]=i*coeff[i-1] + (degree1 - i)*coeff[i];
    }

cx[degree1]= coeff[degree];
}
```

5.13 Problems

1. Prove formula (5.15).

2. Prove the relationship between the "Bézier" and the Bernstein form for a Bézier curve (5.17).

3. For this problem, you should be familiar with the subdivision formula (7.7) from Chapter 7. Prove that

$$\int_0^t b^n(x)\mathrm{d}x = \frac{t}{n+1}\sum_{j=0}^n b_0^j(t).$$

4. With the result from the previous problem, prove

$$F_i^n(t) = n\int_0^t B_i^{n-1}(x)\mathrm{d}x.$$

5. Degree reduction: let $\hat{\mathbf{b}}_{n-1}$ be the polygon endpoint obtained from (5.6). Show that

$$\hat{\mathbf{b}}_{n-1} - \mathbf{b}_n = \Delta^n \mathbf{b}_0.$$

Hint: find an explicit form for the $\hat{\mathbf{b}}_i$ first.

6. Prove formula (5.3).

6

Polynomial Interpolation

Polynomial interpolation is the most fundamental of all interpolation concepts; the earliest method is probably due to I. Newton. Nowadays, polynomial interpolation is mostly of theoretical value; faster and more accurate methods have been developed. Those methods are *piecewise polynomial*; thus they intrinsically rely on the polynomial methods that are presented in this chapter.

6.1 Aitken's Algorithm

A common problem in curve design is *point data interpolation*: from data points $\mathbf{p}_i$ with corresponding parameter values t_i, find a curve that passes through the $\mathbf{p}_i$.[1] One of the oldest techniques to solve this problem is to find an *interpolating polynomial* through the given points. That polynomial must satisfy the interpolatory constraints

$$\mathbf{p}(t_i) = \mathbf{p}_i; \quad i = 0, \ldots, n.$$

Several algorithms exist for this problem – any textbook on numerical

---

[1]The shape of the curve depends heavily on the parameter values t_i. Methods for their determination will be discussed later in the context of spline interpolation, see Section 9.4.

analysis will discuss several of them. In this section we shall present a recursive technique that is due to A. Aitken.

We have already solved the linear case, $n = 1$, in Section 2.3. The Aitken recursion computes a point on the interpolating polynomial through a sequence of repeated linear interpolations, starting with

$$\mathbf{p}_i^1(t) = \frac{t_{i+1} - t}{t_{i+1} - t_i}\mathbf{p}_i + \frac{t - t_i}{t_{i+1} - t_i}\mathbf{p}_{i+1}; \quad i = 0, \ldots, n - 1.$$

Let us now suppose (as one does in recursive techniques) that we have already solved the problem for the case $n - 1$. To be more precise, assume that we have found a polynomial $\mathbf{p}_0^{n-1}$ that interpolates to the n first data points $\mathbf{p}_0, \ldots, \mathbf{p}_{n-1}$, and also a polynomial $\mathbf{p}_1^{n-1}$ that interpolates to the n last data points $\mathbf{p}_1, \ldots, \mathbf{p}_n$. Under these assumptions, it is easy to write down the form of the final interpolant, now called $\mathbf{p}_0^n$:

$$\mathbf{p}_0^n(t) = \frac{t_n - t}{t_n - t_0}\mathbf{p}_0^{n-1}(t) + \frac{t - t_0}{t_n - t_0}\mathbf{p}_1^{n-1}(t). \tag{6.1}$$

Figure 6.1 illustrates this form for the cubic case.

Let us verify that (6.1) does in fact interpolate to all given data points $\mathbf{p}_i$: for $t = t_0$,

$$\mathbf{p}_0^n(t_0) = 1 * \mathbf{p}_0^{n-1}(t_0) + 0 * \mathbf{p}_1^{n-1}(t_0) = \mathbf{p}_0.$$

A similar result is derived for $t = t_n$. Under our assumption, we have $\mathbf{p}_0^{n-1}(t_i) = \mathbf{p}_1^{n-1}(t_i) = \mathbf{p}_i$ for all other values of i.

Since the weights in (6.1) sum to one identically, we get the desired $\mathbf{p}_0^n(t_i) = \mathbf{p}_i$.

We can now generalize (6.1) to solve the polynomial interpolation problem: starting with the given parameter values t_i and the data points $\mathbf{p}_i = \mathbf{p}_i^0$, we set

$$\mathbf{p}_i^r(t) = \frac{t_{i+r} - t}{t_{i+r} - t_i}\mathbf{p}_i^{r-1}(t) + \frac{t - t_i}{t_{i+r} - t_i}\mathbf{p}_{i+1}^{r-1}(t); \begin{cases} r = 1, \ldots, n; \\ i = 0, \ldots, n - r \end{cases}. \tag{6.2}$$

It is clear from the above consideration that $\mathbf{p}_0^n(t)$ is indeed a point on the interpolating polynomial. The recursive evaluation (6.2) is called *Aitken's algorithm*.[2]

It has the following geometric interpretation: to find $\mathbf{p}_i^r$, map the interval $[t_i, t_{i+r}]$ onto the straight line segment through $\mathbf{p}_i^{r-1}, \mathbf{p}_{i+1}^{r-1}$. That affine map

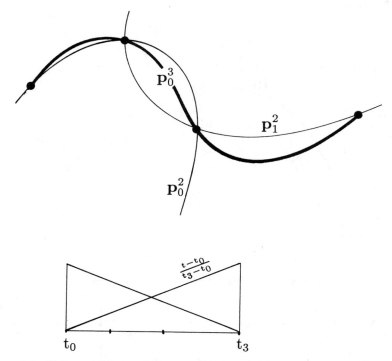

Figure 6.1. Polynomial interpolation: a cubic interpolating polynomial may be obtained as a "blend" of two quadratic interpolants.

takes t to $\mathbf{p}_i^r$. The geometry of Aitken's algorithm is illustrated in Figure 6.2 for the cubic case.

It is convenient to write the intermediate $\mathbf{p}_i^r$ in a triangular array; the cubic case would look like

$$
\begin{array}{llll}
\mathbf{p}_0 & & & \\
\mathbf{p}_1 & \mathbf{p}_0^1 & & \\
\mathbf{p}_2 & \mathbf{p}_1^1 & \mathbf{p}_0^2 & \\
\mathbf{p}_3 & \mathbf{p}_2^1 & \mathbf{p}_1^2 & \mathbf{p}_0^3.
\end{array}
\tag{6.3}
$$

We can infer several properties of the interpolating polynomial from Aitken's algorithm:

- *Affine invariance:* This follows since the Aitken algorithm uses only barycentric combinations.

---

[2]The particular organization of the algorithm as presented here is due to Neville.

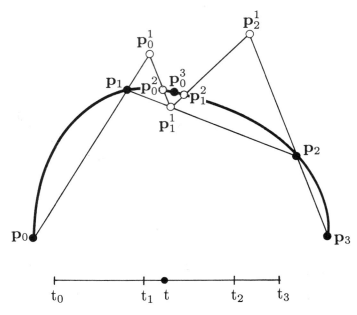

Figure 6.2. Aitken's algorithm: a point on an interpolating polynomial may be found from repeated linear interpolation.

- *Linear precision*: If all $\mathbf{p}_i$ are uniformly distributed[3] on a straight line segment, all intermediate $\mathbf{p}_i^r(t)$ are identical for $r > 0$. Thus the straight line segment is reproduced.

- *No convex hull property:* The parameter t in (6.2) by no means has to lie between t_i and t_{i+r}. Therefore, Aitken's algorithm does not use convex combinations only : $\mathbf{p}_0^n(t)$ is not guaranteed to lie within the convex hull of the $\mathbf{p}_i$. We should note, however, that no smooth curve interpolation scheme exists that has the convex hull property.

- *No variation diminishing property:* By the same reasoning, we do not get the variation diminishing property. Again, no "decent" interpolation scheme has this property. However, interpolating polynomials can be variation augmenting to an extent that renders them useless for practical problems.

---

[3]If the points are on a straight line, but distributed unevenly, we will still recapture the graph of the straight line, but it will not be parametrized linearly.

6.2 Lagrange Polynomials

Aitken's algorithm allows us to compute a point $\mathbf{p}^n(t)$ on the interpolating polynomial through $n+1$ data points. It does not provide an answer to the following questions: a) is the interpolating polynomial unique? b) what is a closed form for it? Both questions are resolved by the use of the *Lagrange polynomials* L_i^n.

The explicit form of the interpolating polynomial $\mathbf{p}$ is given by

$$\mathbf{p}(t) = \sum_{i=0}^{n} \mathbf{p}_i L_i^n(t), \tag{6.4}$$

where the L_i^n are *Lagrange polynomials*

$$L_i^n(t) = \frac{\prod_{\substack{j=0 \\ j \neq i}}^{n} (t - t_j)}{\prod_{\substack{j=0 \\ j \neq i}}^{n} (t_i - t_j)}. \tag{6.5}$$

Before we proceed further, we should note that the L_i^n must sum to one in order for (6.4) to be a barycentric combination and thus be geometrically meaningful; we will return to this topic below.

We verify (6.4) by observing that the Lagrange polynomials are *cardinal*: they satisfy

$$L_i^n(t_j) = \delta_{i,j}, \tag{6.6}$$

$\delta_{i,j}$ being the Kronecker delta. In other words, the ith Lagrange polynomial vanishes at all knots except at the ith one, where it assumes the value 1. Because of this property of Lagrange polynomials, (6.4) is called the *cardinal* form of the interpolating polynomial $\mathbf{p}$. The polynomial $\mathbf{p}$ has many other representations, of course (we can rewrite it in monomial form, for example), but (6.4) is the only form in which the data points appear explicitly.

We have thus justified our use of the term *the* interpolating polynomial. In fact, the polynomial interpolation problem always has a solution, and it always has a *unique* solution. The reason is that, because of (6.6), the L_i^n form a basis of all polynomials of degree n. Thus, (6.4) is the unique representation of the polynomial $\mathbf{p}$ in this basis. This is why one sometimes refers to all polynomial interpolation schemes as *Lagrange interpolation*.[4]

We can now be sure that Aitken's algorithm yields the same point as does (6.4). Based on that knowlegde, we can conclude a property of Lagrange

---

[4]More precisely: to all those schemes that interpolate to given set of data points. Other forms of polynomial interpolation exist, and are discussed later.

polynomials that was already mentioned right after (6.5), namely, that they sum to one:

$$\sum_{i=0}^{n} L_i^n(t) \equiv 1.$$

This is a simple consequence of the affine invariance of polynomial interpolation, as shown for Aitken's algorithm.

6.3   The Vandermonde Approach

Suppose we want the interpolating polynomial $\mathbf{p}^n$ in the monomial basis:

$$\mathbf{p}^n(t) = \sum_{j=0}^{n} \mathbf{a}_j t^j. \tag{6.7}$$

The standard approach to finding the unknown coefficients from the known data is simply to write down everything one knows about the problem:

$$
\begin{aligned}
\mathbf{p}^n(t_0) = \mathbf{p}_0 &= \mathbf{a}_0 + \mathbf{a}_1 t_0 + \ldots + \mathbf{a}_n t_0^n, \\
\mathbf{p}^n(t_1) = \mathbf{p}_1 &= \mathbf{a}_0 + \mathbf{a}_1 t_1 + \ldots + \mathbf{a}_n t_1^n, \\
&\vdots \\
\mathbf{p}^n(t_n) = \mathbf{p}_n &= \mathbf{a}_0 + \mathbf{a}_1 t_n + \ldots + \mathbf{a}_n t_n^n.
\end{aligned}
$$

In matrix form:

$$
\begin{bmatrix} \mathbf{p}_0 \\ \mathbf{p}_1 \\ \vdots \\ \mathbf{p}_n \end{bmatrix} = \begin{bmatrix} 1 & t_0 & t_0^2 & \cdots & t_0^n \\ 1 & t_1 & t_1^2 & \cdots & t_1^n \\ \vdots & \vdots & \vdots & & \vdots \\ 1 & t_n & t_n^2 & \cdots & t_n^n \end{bmatrix} \begin{bmatrix} \mathbf{a}_0 \\ \mathbf{a}_1 \\ \vdots \\ \mathbf{a}_n \end{bmatrix}. \tag{6.8}
$$

We can shorten this to

$$\mathbf{p} = T\mathbf{a}. \tag{6.9}$$

We already know that a solution $\mathbf{a}$ to this linear system exists, but one can show independently that the determinant $\det T$ is nonzero (for distinct parameter values t_i). This determinant is known as the *Vandermonde* of the interpolation problem. The solution, i.e., the vector $\mathbf{a}$ containing the coefficients $\mathbf{a}_i$, can be found from

$$\mathbf{a} = T^{-1}\mathbf{p}. \tag{6.10}$$

This should be taken only as a shorthand notation for the solution – not as an algorithm! Note that the linear system (6.9) really consists of *three* linear systems with the same coefficient matrix, one system for each coordinate. It is known from numerical analysis that in such cases the LU decomposition of T is a more economical way to obtain the solution $\mathbf{a}$. This will be even more important when we discuss tensor product surface interpolation in Section 17.4.

The interpolation problem can also be solved if we use basis functions other than the monomials. Let $\{F_i^n\}_{i=0}^n$ be such a basis. We then seek an interpolating polynomial of the form

$$\mathbf{p}^n(t) = \sum_{j=0}^n \mathbf{c}_j F_i^n(t). \tag{6.11}$$

The above reasoning again leads to a linear system (three linear systems, to be more precise) for the coefficients $\mathbf{c}_j$, this time with the *generalized Vandermonde F*

$$F = \begin{bmatrix} F_0^n(t_0) & F_1^n(t_0) & \cdots & F_n^n(t_0) \\ F_0^n(t_1) & F_1^n(t_1) & \cdots & F_n^n(t_1) \\ \vdots & \vdots & & \vdots \\ F_0^n(t_n) & F_1^n(t_n) & \cdots & F_n^n(t_n) \end{bmatrix}. \tag{6.12}$$

Since the F_i^n form a basis for all polynomials of degree n, it follows that the generalized Vandermonde $\det F$ is nonzero.

Thus, for instance, we are able to find the Bézier curve that passes through a given set of data points: the F_i^n would then be the Bernstein polynomials B_i^n.

6.4   Limits of Lagrange Interpolation

We have seen that polynomial interpolation is simple, unique, and has a nice geometric interpretation. One might therefore expect this interpolation scheme to be used frequently; however, nobody uses it in a design situation. The main reason is illustrated in Figure 6.3: polynomial interpolants *oscillate*. For quite reasonable data points and parameter values, the polynomial interpolant exhibits wild wiggles that are not inherent in the data. One may say thatpolynomial interpolation is not *shape preserving*.

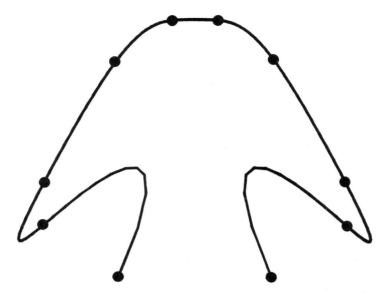

Figure 6.3. Lagrange interpolation: while the data points suggest a convex interpolant, the Lagrange interpolant exhibits extraneous wiggles.

This phenomenon is not due to numerical effects; it is actually inherent in the polynomial interpolation process. Suppose we are given a finite arc of a smooth curve **c**. We can then sample the curve at parameter values t_i and pass the interpolating polynomial through those points. If we increase the number of points on the curve, thus producing interpolants of higher and higher degree, one would expect the corresponding interpolants to converge to the sampled curve **c**. This, however, is not generally true: there exist smooth curves for which this sequence of interpolants diverges. This fact is dealt with in numerical analysis, where it is known by the name of its discoverer: it is called the "Runge phenomenon" [303].

As a second consideration, let us examine the cost of polynomial interpolation, i.e., the number of operations necessary to construct and then evaluate the interpolant. Solving the Vandermonde system (6.8) requires roughly n^3 operations; subsequent computation of a point on the curve requires n operations. The operation count for the construction of the interpolant is much smaller for other schemes, as is the cost of evaluations (here piecewise schemes are far superior). This latter cost is the more important one, of course: construction of the interpolant happens once, but it may be evaluated thousands of times!

6.5 Cubic Hermite Interpolation

Polynomial interpolation is not restricted to interpolation to point data; one can also interpolate to other information, such as derivative data. This leads to an interpolation scheme that is more useful than Lagrange interpolation: it is called *Hermite interpolation*. We treat the cubic case first: there, one is given two points $\mathbf{p}_0, \mathbf{p}_1$ and two tangent vectors $\mathbf{m}_0, \mathbf{m}_1$. The objective is to find a cubic polynomial curve $\mathbf{p}$ that interpolates to these data:

$$
\begin{aligned}
\mathbf{p}(0) &= \mathbf{p}_0, \\
\dot{\mathbf{p}}(0) &= \mathbf{m}_0, \\
\dot{\mathbf{p}}(1) &= \mathbf{m}_1, \\
\mathbf{p}(1) &= \mathbf{p}_1,
\end{aligned}
$$

where the dot denotes differentiation.

We will write $\mathbf{p}$ in cubic Bézier form, and therefore must determine four Bézier points $\mathbf{b}_0, \ldots, \mathbf{b}_3$. Two of them are quickly determined:

$$
\mathbf{b}_0 = \mathbf{p}_0, \quad \mathbf{b}_3 = \mathbf{p}_1.
$$

For the remaining two, we recall (from Section 4.3) the endpoint derivative for Bézier curves:

$$
\dot{\mathbf{p}}(0) = 3\Delta\mathbf{b}_0, \quad \dot{\mathbf{p}}(1) = 3\Delta\mathbf{b}_2.
$$

We can easily solve for $\mathbf{b}_1$ and $\mathbf{b}_2$:

$$
\mathbf{b}_1 = \mathbf{p}_0 + \frac{1}{3}\mathbf{m}_0, \quad \mathbf{b}_2 = \mathbf{p}_1 - \frac{1}{3}\mathbf{m}_1.
$$

This situation is shown in Figure 6.4.

Having solved the interpolation problem, we now attempt to write it in *cardinal form*; we would like to have the given data appear *explicitly* in the equation for the interpolant. So far, our interpolant is in Bézier form:

$$
\mathbf{p}(t) = \mathbf{p}_0 B_0^3(t) + (\mathbf{p}_0 + \frac{1}{3}\mathbf{m}_0)B_1^3(t) + (\mathbf{p}_1 - \frac{1}{3}\mathbf{m}_1)B_2^3(t) + \mathbf{p}_1 B_3^3(t).
$$

In order to get the cardinal form, we simply rearrange:

$$
\mathbf{p}(t) = \mathbf{p}_0 H_0^3(t) + \mathbf{m}_0 H_1^3(t) + \mathbf{m}_1 H_2^3(t) + \mathbf{p}_1 H_3^3(t), \tag{6.13}
$$

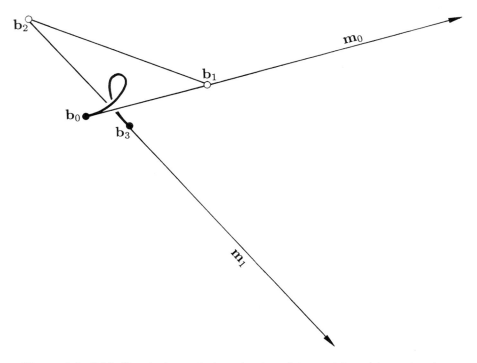

Figure 6.4. Cubic Hermite interpolation: the given data – points and tangent vectors
– together with the interpolating cubic in Bézier form.

where we have set[5]

$$
\begin{aligned}
H_0^3(t) &= B_0^3(t) + B_1^3(t) \\
H_1^3(t) &= \tfrac{1}{3} B_1^3(t) \\
H_2^3(t) &= -\tfrac{1}{3} B_2^3(t) \\
H_3^3(t) &= B_2^3(t) + B_3^3(t).
\end{aligned}
\tag{6.14}
$$

The H_i^3 are called "cubic Hermite polynomials;" they are graphed in Figure
6.5.

What are the properties necessary to make the H_i^3 cardinal functions
for the cubic Hermite interpolation problem? They must be cardinal with

---

[5]This is a deviation from standard notation. Standard notation groups by orders of
derivatives, i.e, first the two positions, then the two derivatives. The form (6.13) was
chosen since it groups coefficients according to their geometry.

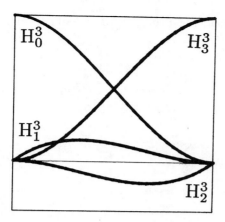

Figure 6.5. Cubic Hermite polynomials: the four H_i^3 are shown over the interval $[0, 1]$.

respect to evaluation and differentiation at $t = 0$ and $t = 1$, i.e., each of the H_i^3 equals 1 for one of these four operations and is zero for the remaining three:

$$
\begin{array}{llll}
H_0^3(0) = 1, & \frac{d}{dt}H_0^3(0) = 0, & \frac{d}{dt}H_0^3(1) = 0, & H_0^3(1) = 0, \\
H_1^3(0) = 0, & \frac{d}{dt}H_1^3(0) = 1, & \frac{d}{dt}H_1^3(1) = 0, & H_1^3(1) = 0, \\
H_2^3(0) = 0, & \frac{d}{dt}H_2^3(0) = 0, & \frac{d}{dt}H_2^3(1) = 1, & H_2^3(1) = 0, \\
H_3^3(0) = 0, & \frac{d}{dt}H_3^3(0) = 0, & \frac{d}{dt}H_3^3(1) = 0, & H_3^3(1) = 1.
\end{array}
$$

Another important property of the H_i^3 follows from the geometry of the interpolation problem; (6.13) contains combinations of points and vectors. We know that the point coefficients must sum to one in order for (6.13) to be geometrically meaningful:

$$
H_0^3(t) + H_3^3(t) \equiv 1.
$$

This is of course also verified by inspection of (6.14).

Cubic Hermite interpolation has one annoying peculiarity: it is not invariant under affine domain transformations. Let a cubic Hermite interpolant be given as in (6.13), i.e., having the interval $[0, 1]$ as its domain. Now apply an affine domain transformation to it by changing t to $\hat{t} = (1 - t)a + tb$, thereby changing $[0, 1]$ to some $[a, b]$. The interpolant (6.13) becomes

$$
\hat{\mathbf{p}}(\hat{t}) = \mathbf{p}_0 \hat{H}_0^3(\hat{t}) + \mathbf{m}_0 \hat{H}_1^3(\hat{t}) + \mathbf{m}_1 \hat{H}_2^3(\hat{t}) + \mathbf{p}_1 \hat{H}_3^3(\hat{t}), \tag{6.15}
$$

where the $\hat{H}_i^3(\hat{t})$ are defined through their cardinal properties:

$$
\begin{array}{llll}
\hat{H}_0^3(a) = 1, & \frac{\mathrm{d}}{\mathrm{d}t}\hat{H}_0^3(a) = 0, & \frac{\mathrm{d}}{\mathrm{d}t}\hat{H}_0^3(b) = 0, & \hat{H}_0^3(b) = 0, \\
\hat{H}_1^3(a) = 0, & \frac{\mathrm{d}}{\mathrm{d}t}\hat{H}_1^3(a) = 1, & \frac{\mathrm{d}}{\mathrm{d}t}\hat{H}_1^3(b) = 0, & \hat{H}_1^3(b) = 0, \\
\hat{H}_2^3(a) = 0, & \frac{\mathrm{d}}{\mathrm{d}t}\hat{H}_2^3(a) = 0, & \frac{\mathrm{d}}{\mathrm{d}t}\hat{H}_2^3(b) = 1, & \hat{H}_2^3(b) = 0, \\
\hat{H}_3^3(a) = 0, & \frac{\mathrm{d}}{\mathrm{d}t}\hat{H}_3^3(a) = 0, & \frac{\mathrm{d}}{\mathrm{d}t}\hat{H}_3^3(b) = 0, & \hat{H}_3^3(b) = 1.
\end{array}
$$

In order to satisfy these requirements, the new $\hat{H}_i^3$ must differ from the original H_i^3: we obtain

$$
\begin{aligned}
\hat{H}_0^3(\hat{t}) &= H_0^3(t), \\
\hat{H}_1^3(\hat{t}) &= (b-a)H_1^3(t), \\
\hat{H}_2^3(\hat{t}) &= (b-a)H_2^3(t), \\
\hat{H}_3^3(\hat{t}) &= H_3^3(t),
\end{aligned}
\tag{6.16}
$$

where $t \in [0,1]$ is the local parameter of the interval $[a,b]$.

Evaluation of (6.15) at $\hat{t} = a$ and $\hat{t} = b$ yields $\hat{\mathbf{p}}(a) = \mathbf{p}_0, \hat{\mathbf{p}}(b) = \mathbf{p}_1$. The derivatives have changed, however: invoking the chain rule, we find that $\mathrm{d}\hat{\mathbf{p}}(a)/\mathrm{d}t = (b-a)\mathbf{m}_0$ and, similarly, $\mathrm{d}\hat{\mathbf{p}}(b)/\mathrm{d}t = (b-a)\mathbf{m}_1$.

Thus an affine domain transformation changes the curve unless the defining tangent vectors are changed accordingly – a result quite unlike the Bézier curve case.

In order to maintain the same curve after a domain transformation, we must change the length of the tangent vectors: if the length of the domain interval is changed by a factor α, we must replace $\mathbf{m}_0$ and $\mathbf{m}_1$ by $\mathbf{m}_0/\alpha$ and $\mathbf{m}_1/\alpha$, respectively. There is an intuitive argument for this: interpreting the parameter as time, assume we had one time unit to traverse the curve. After changing the interval length by a factor of ten, for example, we have ten time units to traverse the same curve, resulting in a much smaller speed of traversal. Since the magnitude of the derivative equals that speed, it must also shrink by a factor of ten.

An illustration is given in Figure 6.6. It shows — using a parametric cubic and the x-portion of its cross plot — how a stretching of the domain interval "flattens" the x-component function. This results in a shorter tangent vector of the parametric curve. In this figure, we have made use of the fact that the slope of a function may be expressed as the height of a right triangle with base length one.

We also note that the Hermite form is not symmetric: if we replace t by $1 - t$ (assuming again the interval $[0,1]$ as the domain), the curve coefficientscannot simply be renumbered (as in the case of Bézier curves).

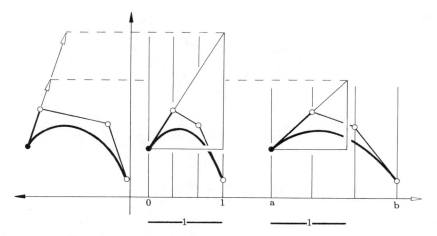

Figure 6.6. Lengths of tangent vectors and domain intervals: the longer the domain interval (right cubic function), the shorter the tangent vector of the parametric curve.

Rather, the tangent vectors must be *reversed*. This follows from the above by applying the affine map to $[0,1]$ that maps that interval to $[1,0]$, thus reversing its direction.

The dependence of the cubic Hermite form on the domain interval is rather unpleasant — it is often not accounted for and can be blamed for countless programming errors by both students and professionals. We will use the Bézier form whenever possible.

6.6   Quintic Hermite Interpolation

Instead of prescribing only position and first derivative information at two points, one might add that for second order derivatives. Then our data are $\mathbf{p}_0, \mathbf{m}_0, \mathbf{s}_0$ and $\mathbf{p}_1, \mathbf{m}_1, \mathbf{s}_1$, "$\mathbf{s}'''$" denoting second derivative. The lowest order polynomial to interpolate to these data is of degree five. Its Bézier points are easily obtained following the approach above. If we rearrange the Bézier form to obtain a cardinal form of the interpolant $\mathbf{p}$, we find

$$\mathbf{p}(t) = \mathbf{p}_0 H_0^5(t) + \mathbf{m}_0 H_1^5(t) + \mathbf{s}_0 H_2^5(t) + \mathbf{s}_1 H_3^5(t) + \mathbf{m}_1 H_4^5(t) + \mathbf{p}_1 H_5^5(t),$$

$$(6.17)$$

where

$$
\begin{aligned}
H_0^5 &= B_0^5 + B_1^5 + B_2^5 \\
H_1^5 &= \frac{1}{5}[B_1^5 + 2B_2^5] \\
H_2^5 &= \frac{1}{20}B_2^5 \\
H_3^5 &= \frac{1}{20}B_3^5 \\
H_4^5 &= -\frac{1}{5}[2B_3^5 + B_4^5] \\
H_5^5 &= B_3^5 + B_4^5 + B_5^5.
\end{aligned}
$$

It is easy to verify the cardinal properties of the H_i^5: they are the straight-forward generalization of the cardinal properties for cubic Hermite polynomials.

6.7   The Newton Form and Forward Differencing

We finish this chapter with a Lagrange-type polynomial interpolant of which a spinoff, called forward differencing, has established itself in the Computer Graphics community. We will assume that the underlying parametrization is uniform, i.e., $t_{j+1} = t_j + h$ for some interval length h. It can be shown that a form of the nth degree interpolating polynomial $\mathbf{p}^n(t)$ is given by

$$
\mathbf{p}^n(t) = \mathbf{p}_0 + \frac{1}{h}\Delta\mathbf{p}_0(t - t_0) + \ldots + \frac{1}{h^n}\Delta^n\mathbf{p}_0(t - t_0)\cdots(t - t_{n-1}). \quad (6.18)
$$

The derivation of this *Newton form* is in any standard text on numerical analysis.

The differences $\Delta^i\mathbf{p}_j$ are defined as

$$
\Delta^i\mathbf{p}_j = \Delta^{i-1}\mathbf{p}_{j+1} - \Delta^{i-1}\mathbf{p}_j. \quad (6.19)
$$

The coefficients in (6.18) are conveniently written in a table like this (setting $g = 1/h$):

$$
\begin{array}{llll}
\mathbf{p}_0 & & & \\
\mathbf{p}_1 & g\Delta\mathbf{p}_0 & & \\
\mathbf{p}_2 & g\Delta\mathbf{p}_1 & g^2\Delta^2\mathbf{p}_0 & \\
\mathbf{p}_3 & g\Delta\mathbf{p}_2 & g^2\Delta^2\mathbf{p}_1 & g^3\Delta^3\mathbf{p}_0.
\end{array}
$$

The last row contains the coefficients of the Newton form. We have only considered the cubic case here, and shall continue to do so: the general case is a very straightforward generalization.

We could now evaluate $\mathbf{p}^3$ at any parameter value t by simply evaluating (6.18) there. For the case of our evaluation points t_j being equally spaced, again with $t_{j+1} = t_j + h$, there is a much faster way. Suppose we had computed $\mathbf{p}_j = \mathbf{p}^3(t_j)$ etc. from (6.18). Then we could compute all entries in the following table:

$$
\begin{array}{lllll}
\mathbf{p}_0 & & & & \\
\mathbf{p}_1 & g\Delta\mathbf{p}_0 & & & \\
\mathbf{p}_2 & g\Delta\mathbf{p}_1 & g^2\Delta^2\mathbf{p}_0 & & \\
\mathbf{p}_3 & g\Delta\mathbf{p}_2 & g^2\Delta^2\mathbf{p}_1 & g^3\Delta^3\mathbf{p}_0 & \\
\mathbf{p}_4 & g\Delta\mathbf{p}_3 & g^2\Delta^2\mathbf{p}_2 & g^3\Delta^3\mathbf{p}_1 & \\
\mathbf{p}_5 & g\Delta\mathbf{p}_4 & g^2\Delta^2\mathbf{p}_3 & g^3\Delta^3\mathbf{p}_2 & \\
\;\vdots & \;\;\vdots & \;\;\;\vdots & \;\;\;\vdots &
\end{array}
\tag{6.20}
$$

Now consider the last column of this table, containing terms of the form $g^3\Delta^3\mathbf{p}_j$. All these terms are equal! This is so since the nth derivative of an nth degree polynomial is constant, and since the nth derivative of (6.18) is given by $n!g^n\Delta^n\mathbf{p}_0 = n!g^n\Delta^n\mathbf{p}_1 = \ldots$.

We thus have a new way of constructing the table (6.20) from *right to left*: instead of computing the entry $\mathbf{p}_4$ from (6.18), first compute $g^2\Delta^2\mathbf{p}_2$ from equation (6.19):

$$g^2\Delta^2\mathbf{p}_2 = g^3\Delta^3\mathbf{p}_1 + g^2\Delta^2\mathbf{p}_1,$$

then compute $g\Delta\mathbf{p}_3$ from

$$g\Delta\mathbf{p}_3 = g^2\Delta\mathbf{p}_2 + g\Delta\mathbf{p}_2,$$

and finally

$$\mathbf{p}_4 = g\Delta\mathbf{p}_3 + \mathbf{p}_3.$$

Then compute $\mathbf{p}_5$ in the same manner, and so on. The general formula is, with $\mathbf{q}_j^i = g^i\Delta^i\mathbf{p}_j$:

$$\mathbf{q}_j^i = \mathbf{q}_{j-1}^{i+1} + \mathbf{q}_{j-1}^i; \quad i = 2, 1, 0. \tag{6.21}$$

It yields the points $\mathbf{p}_j = \mathbf{q}_j^0$.[6]

---

[6]It also holds for any degree n if we replace $i = 2, 1, 0$ by $i = n-1, n-2, \ldots, 0$.

This way of computing the $\mathbf{p}_j$ does not involve a single multiplication after the startup phase! It is therefore extremely fast and has been implemented in many graphics systems, known under the name *forward differencing*. Given four initial points $\mathbf{p}_0, \mathbf{p}_1, \mathbf{p}_2, \mathbf{p}_3$ and a stepsize h, it generates a sequence of points on the cubic polynomial through the initial four points. Typically the polynomial will be given in Bézier form, so those four points have to be computed as a start-up operation.

In a graphics environment, it is desirable to adjust the step size h such that each pixel along the curve is hit. One way of doing this is to adjust the step size while marching along the curve. This is called *adaptive forward differencing* and is described by Lien, Shantz, and Pratt [242] and by Chang, Shantz, and Rochetti [76].

Although fast, forward differencing is not foolproof: As we compute more and more points on the curve, they begin to be affected by roundoff. So while we intend to march along our curve, we may instead leave its path, deviating from it more and more as we continue on. For more literature on this method, see Abi-Ezzi [1], Bartels et al. [34], or Shantz and Chang [333].

6.8   Implementation

The code for Aitken's algorithm is very similar to that for the de Casteljau algorithm:

```
float aitken(degree,coeff,t)
/*   uses  Aitken to compute one coordinate
     value of a  Lagrange interpolating polynomial. Has to be called
     for each coordinate  (x,y, and/or z) of data points.
Input:   degree: degree of curve.
         coeff:  array with coordinates to be interpolated.
         t:      parameter value.
Output:  coordinate value.

         Note: we  assume a uniform knot sequence!
*/
     float coeff[];
     float t;
     int degree;
{
     int r,i;
     float t1;
     float coeffa[20];  /* an auxiliary array */
```

```
for (i=0; i<=degree; i++) coeffa[i]=coeff[i]; /* save input */

for (r=1; r<= degree; r++)
for (i=0; i<= degree - r; i++)
{
     t1=(degree*t-i)/((float) r);
     coeffa[i]= (1.0-t1)* coeffa[i]   +   t1 * coeffa[i+1] ;
}
return (coeffa[0]);
}
```

6.9 Problems

1. The de Casteljau algorithm for Bézier curves has as its "counterpart" the recursion formula (4.2) for Bernstein polynomials. Deduce a recursion formula for Lagrange polynomials from Aitken's algorithm.

2. Aitken's algorithm looks very similar to the de Casteljau algorithm. Use both to define a whole class of algorithms, of which each would be a special case. (See [133].)

3. The Hermite form is not invariant under affine domain transformations, while the Bézier form is. What about the Lagrange and monomial forms? What are the general conditions for a curve scheme to be invariant under affine domain transformations?

4. In Lagrange interpolation, each $\mathbf{p}_i$ is assigned a corresponding parameter value t_i. Experiment (graphically) by interchanging two parameter values t_i and t_j without interchanging $\mathbf{p}_i$ and $\mathbf{p}_j$. Explain your results.

5. Show that the cubic and quintic Hermite polynomials are linearly independent.

7

Spline Curves in Bézier Form

Bézier curves provide a powerful tool in curve design, but they have some limitations: if the curve to be modeled has a complex shape, then its Bézier representation will have a prohibitively high degree (for practical purposes, degrees exceeding 10 are prohibitive). Such complex curves can, however, be modeled using *composite Bézier curves*. We shall also use the name *spline curves* for such *piecewise polynomial curves*. This chapter describes the main properties of cubic and quadratic spline curves. More general spline curves will be presented in Chapter 10.

7.1   Global and Local Parameters

Before we start to develop a theory for piecewise curves, let us establish the main definitions that we will use later. When we considered single Bézier curves, we assumed that they were the map of the interval $0 \leq t \leq 1$. We could make this assumption because of the invariance of Bézier curves under affine parameter transformations; see Section 3.3. Life is not quite that easy with piecewise curves: while we can assume that each individual segment of a spline curve s is the map of the interval $[0, 1]$, the curve as a whole is the map of a collection of intervals, and their relative lengths play an important role.

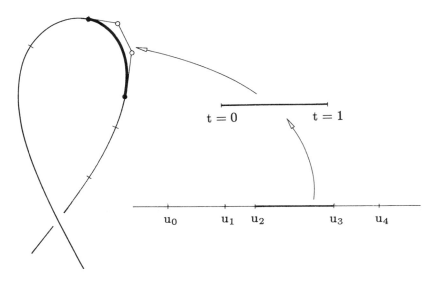

Figure 7.1. Local coordinates: the interval $[u_2, u_3]$ has been endowed with a local coordinate t. The third segment of the spline curve is shown with its Bézier polygon.

A *spline curve* **s** is the continuous map of a collection of intervals $u_0 < \ldots < u_L$ into $I\!\!E^3$, where each interval $[u_i, u_{i+1}]$ is mapped onto a polynomial curve segment. Each real number u_i is called a *breakpoint* or a *knot*. The collection of all u_i is called the *knot sequence*. For every parameter value u we thus have a corresponding point **s**(u) on the curve **s**. Let this value u be from an interval $[u_i, u_{i+1}]$. We can introduce a *local coordinate* (or local parameter) t for the interval $[u_i, u_{i+1}]$ by setting

$$t = \frac{u - u_i}{u_{i+1} - u_i} = \frac{u - u_i}{\Delta_i}. \tag{7.1}$$

One checks that t varies from 0 to 1 as u varies from u_i to u_{i+1}.

When we talk about the whole curve **s**, it will be more convenient to do so in terms of the global parameter u. (An example of such a property is the concept of differentiablity.) The individual segments of **s** may be written as Bézier curves, and it is often easier to describe each one of them in terms of local coordinates. We adopt the definition **s**$_i$ for the i-th segment of **s**, and we write **s**$(u) = $ **s**$_i(t)$ to denote a point on it. Figure 7.1 illustrates the interplay between local and global coordinates.

The introduction of local coordinates has some ramifications concerning

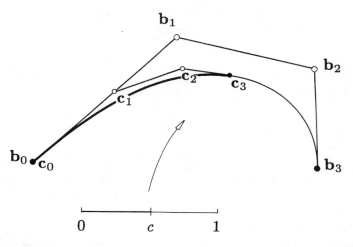

Figure 7.2. Subdivision: two Bézier polygons describe the same cubic polynomial; one is associated with the interval $[0, 1]$, the other with $[0, 1/2]$.

the use of derivatives. For $u \in [u_i, u_{i+1}]$, the chain rule gives

$$\frac{\mathrm{d}s(u)}{\mathrm{d}u} = \frac{\mathrm{d}s_i(t)}{\mathrm{d}t}\frac{\mathrm{d}t}{\mathrm{d}u} \qquad (7.2)$$

$$= \frac{1}{\Delta_i}\frac{\mathrm{d}s_i(t)}{\mathrm{d}t}. \qquad (7.3)$$

Two more definitions: the points $s(u_i) = s_i(0) = s_{i-1}(1)$ are called *junction points* or *joints*. The collection of the Bézier polygons for all curve segments itself forms a polygon; it is called the *piecewise Bézier polygon* of **s**.

7.2   Subdivision I

A Bézier curve $\mathbf{b}^n$ is usually defined over the interval (the domain) $[0, 1]$, but it can also be defined over any interval $[0, c]$. The part of the curve that corresponds to $[0, c]$ can also be defined by a Bézier polygon, as illustrated in Figure 7.2. Finding this Bézier polygon is referred to as *subdivision* of the Bézier curve. The following short development shows how the geometry underlying the de Casteljau algorithm can be utilized for this task.

Let us introduce a *local parameter* s for the interval $[0, c]$: it is defined by $s = t/c$. We check that for $s = 0$, we get $t = 0$ and that for $s = 1$, we get $t = c$. Let us denote the Bézier polygon corresponding to the interval $[0, c]$ by $c_0, \ldots, c_n$ – it defines a Bézier curve c^n (which is part of the same polynomial curve as b^n is, of course).

In order to find the unknown c_j from the known b_j, let us consider derivatives at $s = t = 0$. Since b^n and c^n are parts of the same polynomial curve, all their derivatives at $s = t = 0$ must coincide:

$$\frac{d^r}{dt^r} b^n(0) = \frac{d^r}{ds^r} c^n(0); \quad r = 0, \ldots, n. \tag{7.4}$$

We recall that a derivative of a Bézier curve, when taken at an endpoint, depends only on the Bézier points nearby; see (4.21). Thus the r-th derivative of b^n only depends on $b_0, \ldots, b_r$ and the r-th derivative of c^n depends only on $c_0, \ldots, c_r$.

Now let us interpret the first $r + 1$ control points of each curve as control polygons of two degree r Bézier curves, which we called b_0^r and c_0^r in Section 3.2. These two Bézier curves are identical since they agree in all derivatives at $t = 0$ and $s = 0$:

$$c_0^r(s) = b_0^r(t) \quad \text{for all } s, t, \tag{7.5}$$

since they agree in all derivatives up to order r at $t = s = 0$, as follows from inspection of (4.21). The last equation must also hold for the particular value $s = 1$, corresponding to $t = c$:

$$c_0^r(1) = b_0^r(c). \tag{7.6}$$

Now, since $c_0^r(1) = c_r$ by equation (4.6), we have found the unknown c_j:

$$c_j = b_0^j(c). \tag{7.7}$$

This formula is called the *subdivision formula* for Bézier curves.

Thus it turns out that the de Casteljau algorithm not only computes the point $b^n(c)$, but also provides the control vertices of the Bézier curve corresponding to the interval $[0, c]$. Because of the symmetry property (4.10), it follows that the control vertices of the part corresponding to $[c, 1]$ are given by the b_{n-j}^j. Thus, in Figures 3.1 and 3.2, we see the two subpolygons defining the arcs $b^n(0), b^n(c)$ and $b^n(c), b^n(1)$.

We may use the above subdivision arguments to *extrapolate* a Bézier curve. Suppose we are given the Bézier points c_j of the curve segment corresponding to $t \in [0, c]$ and want the Bézier points d_j of the curve segment corresponding to $t \in [c, 1]$. By the above reasoning, the polygons $c_0, \ldots, c_n$ and $d_0, \ldots, d_n$ must be the product of a subdivision process of a polygon $\mathbf{b}_0, \ldots, \mathbf{b}_n$. The $\mathbf{d}_j$ correspond to the $\mathbf{b}_{n-j}^j$ and are given by

$$\mathbf{d}_j = \mathbf{c}_{n-j}^j(d), \tag{7.8}$$

where $d = 1/c$ is the local coordinate of 1 with respect to the interval $[0, c]$.

A final remark: the subdivision formula (7.7) makes use of only *local* interval coordinates. In other words, we can use (7.7) to subdivide a Bézier curve that is defined over an arbitrary interval $[a, b]$ after we introduce local coordinates for it. This, of course, is a consequence of the invariance of Bézier curves under affine parameter transformations, as described in Section 3.3.

Subdivision for Bézier curves, although mentioned by de Casteljau [102], was rigorously proved by E. Staerk [335].

7.3   Subdivision II

Because of the subject's importance, we give a second proof for the subdivision procedure; this one will not require the use of derivatives. Instead of subdividing at just one parameter value, let us subdivide at *two* parameter values simultaneously. Let our two parameter values be u and t. We may evaluate the curve at u or at t using a de Casteljau algorithm:

$$\mathbf{b}_i^r(u) = (1-u)\mathbf{b}_i^{r-1}(u) + u\mathbf{b}_{i+1}^{r-1}(u) \quad \left\{ \begin{array}{l} r = 1, \ldots, n \\ i = 0, \ldots, n-r \end{array} \right. \tag{7.9}$$

to get the point $\mathbf{b}_0^n(u)$ and

$$\mathbf{b}_j^r(t) = (1-t)\mathbf{b}_j^{r-1}(t) + t\mathbf{b}_{j+1}^{r-1}(t) \quad \left\{ \begin{array}{l} r = 1, \ldots, n \\ j = 0, \ldots, n-r \end{array} \right. \tag{7.10}$$

to get the point $\mathbf{b}_0^n(t)$.

Both algorithms may be combined into one "generalized de Casteljau algorithm" by defining a set of intermediate points $\mathbf{b}_{i,j}^{r,s}(u, t)$ according to

$$\mathbf{b}_{i,j}^{r,s}(u, t) = (1-u)\mathbf{b}_{i+1,j}^{r-1,s} + u\mathbf{b}_{i,j+1}^{r-1,s} \tag{7.11}$$

and

$$\mathbf{b}_{i,j}^{r,s}(u, t) = (1-t)\mathbf{b}_{i+1,j}^{r,s-1} + t\mathbf{b}_{i,j+1}^{r,s-1}. \tag{7.12}$$

We compute all $\mathbf{b}_{i,j}^{r,s}(u, t)$ for which $i + j + r + s = n$. We then have that, for example, $\mathbf{b}_{0,0}^{n,0}(u, t)$ is the point on the curve corresponding to u and that $\mathbf{b}_{0,0}^{0,n}(u, t)$ is the point on the curve corresponding to t.

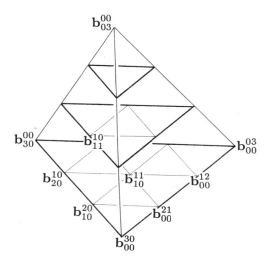

Figure 7.3. The generalized de Casteljau algorithm: all intermediate $\mathbf{b}_{i,j}^{r,s}$ form a tetrahedral scheme, shown for the case $n = 3$.

In general, the points $\mathbf{b}_{i,j}^{r,s}$ are obtained by performing r de Casteljau steps with respect to u and s de Casteljau steps with respect to t. It does not matter in which order these steps are carried out; thus each $\mathbf{b}_{i,j}^{r,s}$ is uniquely defined. A geometric justification of this fact is given by the "CAGD version" of Menelaos' Theorem, as outlined in Section 2.5.

We may write all $\mathbf{b}_{i,j}^{r,s}$ in a tetrahedral scheme, shown in Figure 7.3. Let us now think of u as being fixed while t is allowed to vary. We know that the point $\mathbf{b}_{0,0}^{0,n}$ may be obtained by a de Casteljau algorithm which utilizes all points of the "back face" of the tetrahedron in Figure 7.3. What is somewhat surprising is the fact that it may also be obtained by a second de Casteljau algorithm, namely one that utilizes the elements of the "bottom face," with points $\mathbf{b}_{n-i,0}^{i,0}$ as input and $\mathbf{b}_{0,0}^{0,n}$ as the result. It may be written as

$$\mathbf{b}_{i,0}^{r,s} = \frac{u-t}{u}\mathbf{b}_{i+1,0}^{r,s-1} + \frac{t}{u}\mathbf{b}_{i,0}^{r+1,s-1}, \qquad (7.13)$$

a relationship that is readily deduced from (7.11) and (7.12).[1] This is a de Casteljau algorithm since $\frac{t}{u}$ is the local coordinate of t with respect to the interval $[0, u]$.

---

[1] Referring to Figure 7.3, we have for example that $\mathbf{b}_{10}^{20} = (1-u)\mathbf{b}_{20}^{10} + u\mathbf{b}_{11}^{10}$ and $\mathbf{b}_{10}^{11} = (1-t)\mathbf{b}_{20}^{10} + t\mathbf{b}_{20}^{10}$. Using these two expressions to express $\mathbf{b}_{10}^{11}$ in terms of $\mathbf{b}_{10}^{10}$ and $\mathbf{b}_{10}^{20}$ yields (7.13).

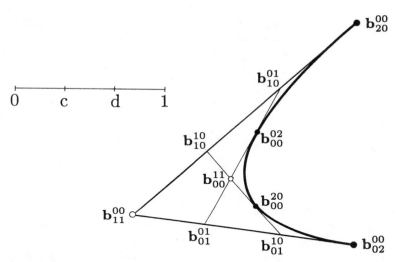

Figure 7.4. Generalized subdivision: The two de Casteljau algorithms for the parameter values u and t can be merged to yield the vertices of all subdivision control polygons.

We can thus obtain the point $\mathbf{b}_{0,0}^{0,n}$ both from the original control polygon $\mathbf{b}_{i,j}^{0,0}$ and from the "subdivision polygon" $\mathbf{b}_{n-i,0}^{i,0}$, and we can do this for any value of t – hence both polygons define the same curve! In terms of the standard de Casteljau algorithm, one easily identifies that the $\mathbf{b}_{n-i,0}^{i,0}$ correspond to the $\mathbf{b}_0^i$, i.e., the "left" subpolygon, corresponding to the interval $[0, u]$.

Similar arguments may be used to show that *every edge* of the tetrahedron in Figure 7.3 represents a control polygon corresponding to one of the six intervals formed by $0, u, t, 1$, in particular, the $\mathbf{b}_{0,0}^{r,s}$ correspond to the interval $[u, t]$. A more geometric example is given by Figure 7.4 for the case $n = 2$.

An extensive treatment of the generalized subdivision process is in Goldman [169]. The process of combining several de Casteljau steps for different parameter values is called *blossoming* after L. Ramshaw [292]. It was independently developed by de Casteljau [104].

7.4   Smoothness Conditions

Suppose we are given two Bézier curves $\mathbf{s}_0$ and $\mathbf{s}_1$, with polygons $\mathbf{b}_0, \ldots, \mathbf{b}_n$ and $\mathbf{b}_n, \ldots, \mathbf{b}_{2n}$, respectively. We maythink of each curve as existing by itself, defined over the interval $t \in [0,1]$ or some other interval. We may also think of the two curves as two segments of one *composite* curve, defined as the map of the interval $[u_0, u_2]$ into $I\!E^3$. The "left" segment $\mathbf{s}_0$ is defined over an interval $[u_0, u_1]$, while the "right" segment $\mathbf{s}_1$ is defined over $[u_1, u_2]$ (see Section 7.1).

Let us pretend for a moment that both curves are arcs of one global polynomial curve $\mathbf{b}^n(u)$, defined over the interval $[u_0, u_2]$. Section 7.2 tells us that the two polygons $\mathbf{b}_0, \ldots, \mathbf{b}_n$ and $\mathbf{b}_n, \ldots, \mathbf{b}_{2n}$ must be the result of a subdivision process. Then their control vertices must be related by

$$\mathbf{b}_{n+i} = \mathbf{b}_{n-i}^i(t); \quad i = 0, \ldots, n, \tag{7.14}$$

where $t = (u_2 - u_0)/(u_1 - u_0)$ is the local coordinate of u_2 with respect to the interval $[u_0, u_1]$; see (7.8).

Now suppose we arbitrarily change $\mathbf{b}_{2n}$: the two curves then no longer describe the same global polynomial. However, they still agree in all derivatives of order $0, \ldots, n-1$ at $u = u_1$! This is simply because $\mathbf{b}_{2n}$ has no influence on derivatives of order less than n at $u = u_1$. Similarly, we may change $\mathbf{b}_{2n-r}$ and still maintain continuity of all derivatives of order $0, \ldots, n-r-1$.

We therefore have the C^r condition for Bézier curves: the two Bézier curves defined over $u_0 \le u \le u_1$ and $u_1 \le u \le u_2$, by the polygons $\mathbf{b}_0, \ldots, \mathbf{b}_n$ and $\mathbf{b}_n, \ldots, \mathbf{b}_{2n}$ respectively, are r times continuously differentiable at $u = u_1$ if and only if

$$\mathbf{b}_{n+i} = \mathbf{b}_{n-i}^i(t); \quad i = 0, \ldots, r, \tag{7.15}$$

where $t = (u_2 - u_0)/(u_1 - u_0)$ is the local coordinate of u_2 with respect to the interval $[u_0, u_1]$.

Thus the de Casteljau algorithm also governs the continuity conditions between adjacent Bézier curves. Note that (7.15) is a theoretical tool; it should not be used to *construct* C^r curves – this would lead to numerical problems because of the extrapolations that are used in (7.15).

Another condition for C^r continuity should also be mentioned here. By equating derivatives using (4.19) and applying the chain rule,[2] we obtain

$$(\frac{1}{\Delta_0})^i \Delta^i \mathbf{b}_{n-i} = (\frac{1}{\Delta_1})^i \Delta^i \mathbf{b}_n \quad i = 0, \ldots, r. \tag{7.16}$$

Conditions for continuity of higher derivatives of Bézier curves were first derived by E. Staerk [335] in 1976. The cases $r = 1$ and $r = 2$ are probably the ones of most practical relevance, and we shall discuss them in more detail next.

---

[2]Equation (4.19) is with respect to the local parameter of an interval. We are interested in differentiability with respect to the global parameter.

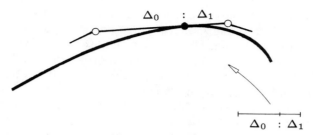

Figure 7.5. C^1 condition: the three shown Bézier points must be collinear with ratio $\Delta_0 : \Delta_1$.

7.5 C^1 **Continuity**

We know that only the three Bézier points $\mathbf{b}_{n-1}, \mathbf{b}_n, \mathbf{b}_{n+1}$ influence the first derivatives at the junction point $\mathbf{b}_n$. According to (7.15), $\mathbf{b}_{n+1}$ is obtained by linear interpolation of the two points $\mathbf{b}_{n-1}, \mathbf{b}_n$. These three points must therefore be collinear and must also be in the ratio $(u_1 - u_0) : (u_2 - u_1) = \Delta_0 : \Delta_1$. This is illustrated in Figure 7.5.

We can also obtain this result in a different way: let s and t be local parameters of the intervals $[u_0, u_1]$ and $[u_1, u_2]$, respectively. Let the C^1 curve consisting of the two polynomial segments be called $\mathbf{s}$, having the global parameter u. Then (cf. Section 7.1)

$$\frac{\mathrm{d}}{\mathrm{d}u}\mathbf{s}(u) = \frac{1}{\Delta_0}\frac{\mathrm{d}}{\mathrm{d}s}\mathbf{s}_0(s) = \frac{1}{\Delta_1}\frac{\mathrm{d}}{\mathrm{d}t}\mathbf{s}_1(t).$$

Since

$$\frac{\mathrm{d}}{\mathrm{d}s}\mathbf{s}_0(1) = n\Delta\mathbf{b}_{n-1}$$
$$\frac{\mathrm{d}}{\mathrm{d}t}\mathbf{s}_1(0) = n\Delta\mathbf{b}_n,$$

we get

$$\Delta_1\Delta\mathbf{b}_{n-1} = \Delta_0\Delta\mathbf{b}_n, \tag{7.17}$$

which confirms the above result.

It is important to note that collinearity of three distinct control points $\mathbf{b}_{n-1}, \mathbf{b}_n, \mathbf{b}_{n+1}$ is not sufficient to guarantee C^1 continuity! This is because the notion of C^1 continuity is based on the interplay between domain and range configurations. Collinearity of three points is purely a range phenomenon. Without additional information on the domain of the curve under consideration, we cannot make any statements concerning differentiability. However, collinearity of three distinct control points $\mathbf{b}_{n-1}, \mathbf{b}_n, \mathbf{b}_{n+1}$ does guarantee a continuously varying tangent.

A special situation arises if $\Delta\mathbf{b}_{n-1} = \Delta\mathbf{b}_n = \mathbf{0}$, i.e., if all three points $\mathbf{b}_{n-1}, \mathbf{b}_n, \mathbf{b}_{n+1}$ coincide. In this case, the composite curve $\mathbf{s}$ has a zero tangent vector at the junction point $\mathbf{b}_n$, and is differentiable no matter what the interval lengths Δ_0, Δ_1 are. Zero tangent vectors may give rise to corners or cusps in curves, a fact that intuitively contradicts the concept of differentiability.

Smoothness and differentiability only agree for functional curves – the connection between them is lost in the parametric case. Differentiable curves may not be smooth (see cusps above) and smooth curves may not be differentiable (see Figures 7.9 and 7.10).

7.6 C^2 Continuity

As above, let $\mathbf{s}$ be a spline curve that consists of two segments $\mathbf{s}_0$ and $\mathbf{s}_1$, defined over $[u_0, u_1]$ and $[u_1, u_2]$, respectively. Let us assume that $\mathbf{s}$ is C^1, so that (7.17) is met. The additional C^2 condition, with $r = 2$ in (7.15), states that the two quadratic polynomials with control polygons $\mathbf{b}_{n-2}, \mathbf{b}_{n-1}, \mathbf{b}_n$ and $\mathbf{b}_n, \mathbf{b}_{n+1}, \mathbf{b}_{n+2}$, defined over $[u_0, u_1]$ and $[u_1, u_2]$, describe the same global quadratic polynomial. Therefore, a polygon $\mathbf{b}_{n-2}, \mathbf{d}, \mathbf{b}_{n+2}$ must exist that describes that polynomial over the interval $[u_0, u_2]$. The two above subpolygons are then obtained from it by subdivision at the parameter value u_1.

The C^2 condition for a C^1 curve $\mathbf{s}$ at u_1 is thus the existence of a point $\mathbf{d}$ such that

$$\mathbf{b}_{n-1} = (1 - t_1)\mathbf{b}_{n-2} + t_1\mathbf{d}, \tag{7.18}$$
$$\mathbf{b}_{n+1} = (1 - t_1)\mathbf{d} + t_1\mathbf{b}_{n+2}, \tag{7.19}$$

where $t_1 = \Delta_0/(u_2 - u_0)$ is the local parameter of u_1 with respect to the interval $[u_0, u_2]$. Figure 7.6 gives an example.

This condition provides us with an easy test to see if a curve is C^2 at a given breakpoint u_i: we simply construct the auxiliary point $\mathbf{d}$ from both the right and the left and check for equality. Figure 7.7 shows two curve segments that fail the C^2 test.

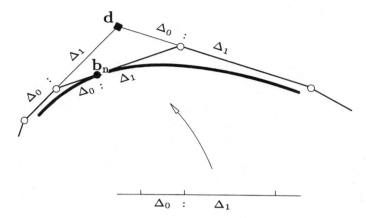

Figure 7.6. C^2 condition: two Bézier curves are twice differentiable at the junction point $\mathbf{b}_n$ if the auxiliary point $\mathbf{d}$ exists uniquely.

Another derivation of the C^2 condition would be to compute the left and right second derivatives at the junction point $\mathbf{b}_n$ and to equate them. The second derivatives at a junction point are essentially second differences of nearby Bézier points. For the simpler case of uniform parameter spacing, $\Delta_0 = \Delta_1$, Figure 7.8 shows how this approach leads to the same C^2 condition as above.

7.7 Finding a C^1 Parametrization

Let $\mathbf{s}$ be a C^r spline curve over the domain $u_0 < \ldots < u_L$. An affine parameter transformation $v = \alpha + \beta u$ leaves the curve invariant: we know that each curve segment $\mathbf{s}_i$ remains unchanged since Bézier curves are invariant under affine parameter transformations; cf. Section 3.3. The smoothness conditions (7.15) between segments are formulated in terms of the de Casteljau algorithm, which operates with constant ratios $\Delta_i : \Delta_{i+1}$ only. These ratios are left invariant under an affine parameter transformation.

This invariance property can be expressed in a different way: a C^r spline curve is determined not by *one* knot sequence, but in fact by a whole family of knot sequences that can be obtained from one another by scalings and translations (i.e., by affine maps of the real line onto itself).

We can determine these knot sequences from inspection of the piecewise Bézier polygon: if it has "corners" at the junction points, it cannot define a C^1 spline curve, and the notion of a knot sequence is meaningless. (A

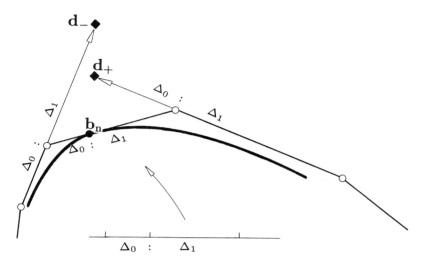

Figure 7.7. C^2 condition: the two shown segments generate different auxiliary points $\mathbf{d}_{\pm}$, hence they are only C^1.

C^0 spline curve is C^0 over *any* knot sequence.) Suppose then that we have a piecewise Bézier polygon with $\mathbf{b}_{in-1}, \mathbf{b}_{in}, \mathbf{b}_{in+1}$ collinear for all i. We can now construct a knot sequence as follows: set $u_0 = 0$, $u_1 = 1$ and for $i = 2, \ldots, L$ determine u_i from

$$\frac{\Delta_{i-1}}{\Delta_i} = \frac{||\Delta \mathbf{b}_{in-1}||}{||\Delta \mathbf{b}_{in}||}. \tag{7.20}$$

Of course, this is only one member of the family of C^1 parametrizations of the given curve. We may for instance normalize the u_i by dividing through by u_L. This forces all u_i to be in the unit interval $[0,1]$.

Any other choice of parameter intervals will not change the shape of the piecewise curve – that shape is uniquely determined by the Bézier polygons. However, different knot spacing *will* change the continuity class of the curve defined by its Bézier polygons: the cross plots that are shown in Figures 7.9 and 7.10 demonstrate this. We see that the continuity class of a curve is not a geometric property that is intrinsically linked to the shape of the curve – it is a result of the parametrization.

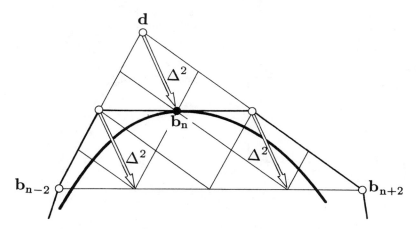

Figure 7.8. C^2 condition for uniform parameter spacing: if $\Delta^2\mathbf{b}_{n-2} = \Delta^2\mathbf{b}_n = \Delta^2$, a unique auxiliary point **d** exists. (Proof by the use of similar triangles.)

7.8 C^1 **Quadratic B-spline Curves**

Let us consider a C^1 piecewise quadratic spline curve **s** that is defined over L intervals $u_0 < \ldots < u_L$, as in Figure 7.11. We call the Bézier points $\mathbf{b}_{2i+1}$ *inner Bézier points*, and the $\mathbf{b}_{2i}$ *junction points*.

We can completely determine a quadratic spline curve by prescribing the knot sequence and the Bézier points

$$\mathbf{b}_0, \mathbf{b}_1, \mathbf{b}_3, \ldots, \mathbf{b}_{2i+1}, \ldots, \mathbf{b}_{2L-1}, \mathbf{b}_{2L}.$$

The remaining junction points are computed from the C^1 conditions

$$\mathbf{b}_{2i} = \frac{\Delta_i}{\Delta_{i-1} + \Delta_i}\mathbf{b}_{2i-1} + \frac{\Delta_{i-1}}{\Delta_{i-1} + \Delta_i}\mathbf{b}_{2i+1}. \qquad (7.21)$$

We can thus define a C^1 quadratic Bézier curve with fewer data than are necessary to define the complete piecewise Bézier polygon. The minimum amount of information that is needed is a) the polygon $\mathbf{b}_0, \mathbf{b}_1, \mathbf{b}_3, \ldots$, $\mathbf{b}_{2i+1} \ldots, \mathbf{b}_{2L-1}, \mathbf{b}_{2L}$, called the *B-spline polygon* or *de Boor polygon* of **s**, and b) the knot sequence $u_0, \ldots, u_L$. If the curve is described in terms of this B-spline polygon, it is sometimes called a *B-spline curve*. We also denote the quadratic B-spline polygon by $\mathbf{d}_{-1}, \mathbf{d}_0, \ldots, \mathbf{d}_{L-1}, \mathbf{d}_L$; see Figure 7.11. Each B-spline polygon, together with a knot sequence, determines a C^1 quadratic spline curve, and, conversely, each quadratic C^1 spline curve possesses a unique B-spline polygon.

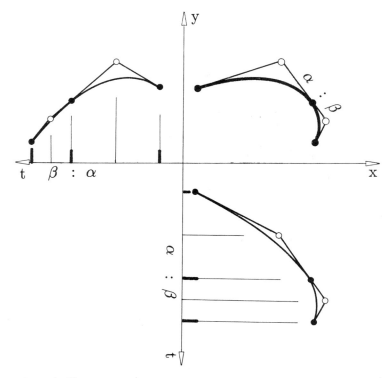

Figure 7.9. A C^1 parametrization: the piecewise quadratic Bézier curve is C^1 when the parameter intervals are chosen to be in the same ratio $\alpha : \beta$ as the Bézier points $\mathbf{b}_1, \mathbf{b}_2, \mathbf{b}_3$.

From the definition of a quadratic B-spline polygon, we can deduce several properties, which we shall simply list since their derivation is a direct consequence of the above definitions:

- convex hull property
- linear precision
- affine invariance
- symmetry
- endpoint interpolation
- variation diminishing property

The last property follows since the piecewise Bézier polygon of **s** is obtained by piecewise linear interpolation of the B-spline polygon, a process which is variation diminishing, as seen in Section 2.3.

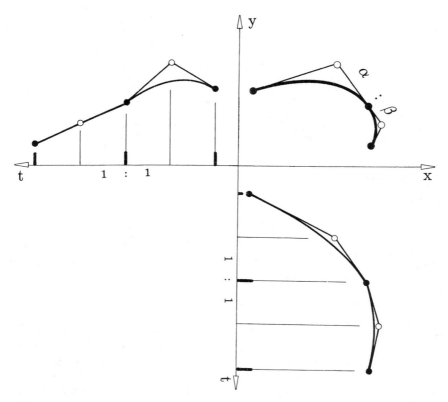

Figure 7.10. A C^0 parametrization: the piecewise Bézier curve is the same as in the previous figure. It is *not* a C^1 curve with the choice of uniform parameter intervals as indicated in the cross plot.

All of the above properties are shared with Bézier curves, although the convex hull property may be sharpened considerably for quadratic B-spline curves: the curve **s** lies in the union of the convex hulls of the triangles $\mathbf{b}_{2i-1}, \mathbf{b}_{2i+1}, \mathbf{b}_{2i+3}$; $i = 1 \ldots, L - 2$ and the triangles $\mathbf{b}_0, \mathbf{b}_1, \mathbf{b}_3$ and $\mathbf{b}_{2L-3}, \mathbf{b}_{2L-1}, \mathbf{b}_{2L}$, as shown in Figure 7.12. A Bézier curve of degree $2L$ could only be guaranteed to lie within the convex hull of the whole polygon $\mathbf{b}_0, \ldots, \mathbf{b}_{2L}$.

By definition, quadratic B-spline curves consist of parabolic segments, i.e., planar curves. However, the B-spline control polygon may be truly three-dimensional – we thus have a method to generate C^1 space curves that are piecewise planar.

There is one important property that single Bézier curves do not share

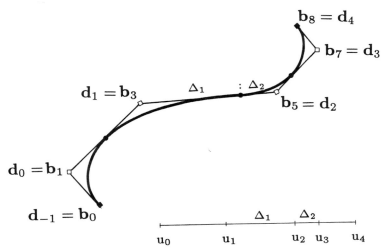

Figure 7.11. C^1 quadratic splines: the junction points $\mathbf{b}_{2i}$ are determined by the inner Bézier points and the knot sequence.

with B-spline curves : *local control.* If we are dealing with a single Bézier curve,[3] we know that a change of one of the control vertices affects the whole curve – it is a *global* change. Changing a control vertex of a quadratic B-spline curve, on the other hand, affects at most three curve segments. It is this local control property that made B-spline curves as popular as they are. If a part of a curve is completely designed, it is highly undesirable to jeopardize this result by changing the curve in other regions. With single Bézier curves, this is unavoidable.

As a consequence of the local control property, we may include straight line segments in a quadratic B-spline curve: if three subsequent control vertices are collinear, the quadratic segment that is determined by them must be linear. A single (higher degree) Bézier curve cannot contain linear segments unless it is itself linear; this is yet another reason why B-spline curves are much more flexible than single Bézier curves. Figure 7.13 shows a quadratic B-spline curve that includes straight line segments. Such curves occur frequently in technical design applications, as well as in font design.

From inspection of Figure 7.11, we see that the endpoints of a B-spline curve are treated in a special way.This is not the case with *closed curves.*

---

[3]In this context, we do not consider Bézier curves as parts of composite curves!

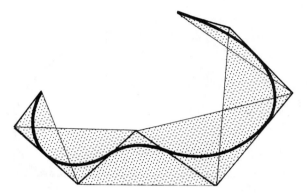

Figure 7.12. The convex hull property: a C^1 quadratic B-spline curve lies in the union of a set of triangles. The triangles are formed by triples of consecutive control vertices.

These are curves that are defined by $\mathbf{s}(u_0) = \mathbf{s}(u_L)$. Figure 7.14 shows two closed quadratic B-spline curves. For such curves, C^1 continuity is defined by the additional constraint $(\mathrm{d}/\mathrm{d}u)\mathbf{s}(u_0) = (\mathrm{d}/\mathrm{d}u)\mathbf{s}(u_L)$.

The figure also shows that a B-spline curve depends not only on the B-spline polygon, but also on the knot sequence.

7.9 C^2 Cubic B-spline Curves

We are now interested in C^2 piecewise cubic spline curves, again defined over L intervals $u_0 < \ldots < u_L$. Consider any two adjacent curve segments $\mathbf{s}_{i-1}$ and $\mathbf{s}_i$. In order to be C^1 at u_i, the relevant Bézier points must be in the ratio $\Delta_{i-1} : \Delta_i$, or

$$\mathbf{b}_{3i} = \frac{\Delta_i}{\Delta_{i-1} + \Delta_i}\mathbf{b}_{3i-1} + \frac{\Delta_{i-1}}{\Delta_{i-1} + \Delta_i}\mathbf{b}_{3i+1}. \tag{7.22}$$

In order to be C^2 as well, an auxiliary point $\mathbf{d}_i$ must exist such that the points $\mathbf{b}_{3i-2}, \mathbf{b}_{3i-1}, \mathbf{d}_i$ and $\mathbf{d}_i, \mathbf{b}_{3i+1}, \mathbf{b}_{3i+2}$ are in the same ratio $\Delta_{i-1} : \Delta_i$, as follows from the C^2 conditions (7.19); Figure 7.15 illustrates this point.

A C^2 cubic spline curve defines the auxiliary points $\mathbf{d}_i$, which form a polygon $\mathbf{P}$. Conversely, a polygon $\mathbf{P}$ and a knot sequence $\{u_i\}$ also define a C^2 cubic spline curve: set

$$\mathbf{b}_{3i-2} = \frac{\Delta_{i-1} + \Delta_i}{\Delta}\mathbf{d}_{i-1} + \frac{\Delta_{i-2}}{\Delta}\mathbf{d}_i \tag{7.23}$$

$$\mathbf{b}_{3i-1} = \frac{\Delta_i}{\Delta}\mathbf{d}_{i-1} + \frac{\Delta_{i-2} + \Delta_{i-1}}{\Delta}\mathbf{d}_i, \tag{7.24}$$

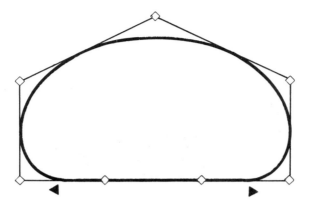

Figure 7.13. Quadratic B-spline curves: curves can be designed that include straight line segments.

where

$$\Delta = \Delta_{i-2} + \Delta_{i-1} + \Delta_i. \tag{7.25}$$

With the junction points $\mathbf{b}_{3i}$ defined in (7.22), the piecewise Bézier curve defined by the $\mathbf{d}_i$ meets the C^2 conditions at every knot u_i; $i = 2, \ldots, L-2$.

Near the ends, things are a little more complicated. We define the cubic B-spline polygon to have vertices $\mathbf{d}_{-1}, \mathbf{d}_0, \ldots, \mathbf{d}_L, \mathbf{d}_{L+1}$ and then set

$$\begin{aligned}
\mathbf{b}_0 &= \mathbf{d}_{-1} \\
\mathbf{b}_1 &= \mathbf{d}_0 \\
\mathbf{b}_2 &= \frac{\Delta_1}{\Delta_0+\Delta_1}\mathbf{d}_0 + \frac{\Delta_0}{\Delta_0+\Delta_1}\mathbf{d}_1
\end{aligned} \tag{7.26}$$

$$\begin{aligned}
\mathbf{b}_{3L-2} &= \frac{\Delta_{L-1}}{\Delta_{L-2}+\Delta_{L-1}}\mathbf{d}_{L-1} + \frac{\Delta_{L-2}}{\Delta_{L-2}+\Delta_{L-1}}\mathbf{d}_L \\
\mathbf{b}_{3L-1} &= \mathbf{d}_L \\
\mathbf{b}_{3L} &= \mathbf{d}_{L+1}.
\end{aligned} \tag{7.27}$$

Now the spline curve is C^2 at every interior knot. This construction is due to W. Boehm [51]. An illustration is given in Figure 7.16.

If a cubic spline curve is expressed in terms of the *B-spline polygon* (the polygon consisting of the $\mathbf{d}_i$), it is usually called a C^2 cubic B-spline curve.

Cubic B-spline curves enjoy the same properties as do quadratic ones:

- convex hull property
- linear precision
- affine invariance
- symmetry

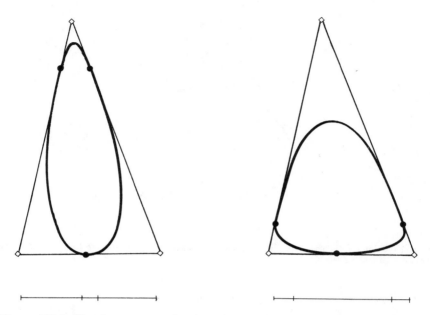

Figure 7.14. Closed curves: two closed quadratic B-spline curves are shown that have the same control polygon but different knot sequences.

- endpoint interpolation
- variation diminishing property
- local control

Local control for cubic B-spline curves is not quite as local as it it for quadratic ones. If a control vertex $\mathbf{d}_i$ of a cubic B-spline curve is moved, *four* segments of the curve will be changed, as shown in Figure 7.17.

7.10   Parametrizations

"Given the de Boor polygon and the knot sequence, construct the corresponding piecewise Bézier polygon:" that was the topic of the last two sections. In free-form design, one creates the de Boor polygon interactively, but how does one create the knot sequence? An easy answer is to set $u_i = i$, or some other (equivalent) uniform spacing, but this method is too rigid in many cases. The jury is still out on what constitutes an "optimal" parametrization. As a rule of thumb, better curves are obtained from a given polygon if the geometry of the polygon is incorporated into the knot sequence.

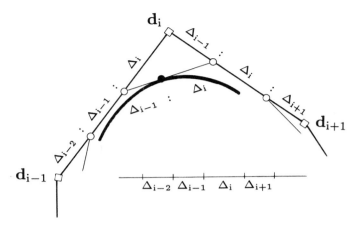

Figure 7.15. C^2 cubic B-spline curves: the auxiliary points $\mathbf{d}_i$ define the B-spline polygon of the curve.

For example, one may set (in the cubic case)

$$
\begin{aligned}
u_0 &= 0, \\
u_1 &= \|\mathbf{d}_1 - \mathbf{d}_{-1}\|, \\
u_i &= u_{i-1} + \|\mathbf{d}_i - \mathbf{d}_{i-1}\|; \quad i = 2, \ldots, L-1, \\
u_L &= u_{L-1} + \|\mathbf{d}_{L+1} - \mathbf{d}_{L-1}\|.
\end{aligned}
\tag{7.28}
$$

This is a *chord length parametrization* for cubic B-spline curves when the polygon is given.[4] This parametrization often produces "smoother" curves than the uniform one described above (see Sapidis [315]).

7.11   Design and Inverse Design

Quadratic B-spline curves seemed to do a pretty good job at producing complex shapes, so why increase the degree to cubic? Cubic polynomials are *true space curves*, i.e., they are not planar. For 2D shapes, piecewise quadratics might suffice, but when it comes to 3D, they can only produce piecewise 2D segments. Two examples why this is not desirable: 3D curves that are used to describe robot paths will exhibit jumps in their torsion – this is bad for the joints of the robot arm. Secondly, 3D curves that

---

[4]Another chord length parametrization exists if data points are given for an interpolatory spline. It is described in Chapter 9.

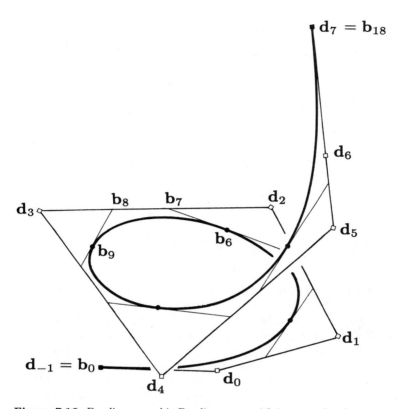

Figure 7.16. B-splines: a cubic B-spline curve with its control polygon.

have to satisfy aesthetic requirements would simply *look* bad if described by piecewise planar shapes.[5]

Another advantage of piecewise cubics is the fact that they may have inflection points *inside* a segment. With piecewise quadratics, one would have to make sure that there is a junction point at every inflection point.

How do we design curves using cubic B-splines? The typical free-form design takes place in a 2D environment, using a mouse, light pen, or some other interactive input device. A control polygon is sketched out on the terminal, the resulting curve is drawn, the control polygon is adjusted, and so on. The parametrization that is being used should be kept away from the designer, and would most likely be one of the two methods described

---

[5]Of course, this could be overcome by using a large number of quadratic pieces. But then, why not go a step further and do everything piecewise linear, with even more pieces?

Figure 7.17. Local control: as one control vertex is moved, only the four "nearby" curve segments change.

in the previous section. To obtain a 3D curve, one would then change to another view (by rotating the curve), and continue adjusting control points. The final result might look reasonable on the terminal, but should probably undergo a final smoothing process as discussed in Chapter 23.

Sometimes designers just don't like to deal with control polygons, and prefer to manipulate the curve directly. In that case, the curve should be obtained from an interpolation process as described in Chapter 8 or 9. It may be represented internally in B-spline or piecewise Bézier form. If the designer wants to change a certain junction point x_i to a new location, this may easily be done *locally* using B-spline technology as follows.

If we were to displace $\mathbf{x}(u_i)$ by a vector $\Delta\mathbf{x}_i$, then we would have to change $\mathbf{d}_i$ by a vector

$$\mathbf{e}_i = \frac{1}{c_i}\Delta\mathbf{x}_i. \tag{7.29}$$

The value of c_i may be computed to

$$c_i = \frac{1}{u_{i+1} - u_{i-1}}(\Delta_i \frac{u_i - u_{i-2}}{u_{i+1} - u_{i-2}} + \Delta_{i-1}\frac{u_{i+2} - u_i}{u_{i+2} - u_{i-1}}). \tag{7.30}$$

Thus we have solved our problem, called *inverse design*. In this mode, we would directly move the junction point $\mathbf{x}_i$ and simply hide the equivalent change in the control polygon from the designer. We need to keep in mind that this procedure (since it changes $\mathbf{d}_i$) will also change $\mathbf{x}_{i-1}$ and $\mathbf{x}_{i+1}$, although by smaller amounts.

7.12   Implementation

Here is the C subdivision routine for Bézier curves:

```
void subdiv(degree,coeff,t,bleft,bright)
/*
      subdivides Bezier curve at parameter value t.
      Only one coordinate is treated.
Input:    degree:            degree of curve.
          coeff:             array with coefficients of curve.
Output:   bleft,bright:      arrays with left and right coefficients.

      Note:     Ordering of right polygon is reversed.
*/
      float coeff[],bleft[],bright[];
      float t;
      int degree;
{
      int r,i;
      float t1;
      t1 = 1.0 - t;

/*
      first, obtain right subpolygon from  de Casteljau
*/
      for (i=0;i <= degree; i++) bright[i] = coeff[i];

      for (r=1; r<= degree; r++)
      for (i=0; i<= degree - r; i++)
      {
            bright[i]=  t1 * bright[i]  +   t  * bright[i+1] ;
      }

/*    use same as above in order to get left half. Idea:
      reverse ordering; then the above yields left half. */

      t = 1.0 - t; t1 = 1.0 - t;

      for (i=0;i <= degree; i++) bleft[degree-i] = coeff[i];

      for (r=1; r<= degree; r++)
      for (i=0; i<= degree - r; i++)
      {
            bleft[i]=  t1 * bleft[i]  +  t * bleft[i+1] ;
      }

}
```

A program for the conversion of a cubic B-spline curve to piecewise Bézier form:

```
void bspline_to_bezier(bspl,knot,l,bez)
/*    converts  cubic B-spline polygon into piecewise Bezier polygon.
Input:    bspl: B-spline control polygon
          knot: knot sequence
          l:    no. of intervals
Output:   bez:  piecewise Bezier polygon. Each junction point b_3i is
                only stored once.
Remark:   bspl starts from 0 and not -1 as in the text. All
          subscripts are therefore shifted by one. For those familiar
          with Chapter 10: don't try to use multiple knots here --
          in terms of that chapter, the end knots u_0 and u_l
          have multiplicity 3, but  all other
          knots are simple, and the curve is C2.
*/

      float bspl[],  knot[], bez[];
      int l;
{
      int i, i3, l3;
/* The first points need special attention:  */

      bez[0]=bspl[0];
      bez[1]=bspl[1];
      if(l>1)
      {
          bez[2]=((knot[2]-knot[1])*bspl[1]
                  +(knot[1]-knot[0])*bspl[2]     )/(knot[2]-knot[0]);
      }
      if(l>2)
      {
          bez[4]=(  (knot[3]-knot[1])*bspl[2]
                  +(  knot[1]-knot[0])*bspl[3]  )/(knot[3]-knot[0]);
          bez[3]=(  (knot[2]-knot[1])*bez[2]
                  + (knot[1]-knot[0])*bez[4]     )/(knot[2]-knot[0]);
      }
/* Now the main part:   */

      for(i=2; i<l-1; i++)
      {
      i3=3*i;
      bez[i3-1]=(  (knot[i+1]-knot[i])*bspl[i]
              +   (knot[i]-knot[i-2])*bspl[i+1] )/(knot[i+1]-knot[i-2]);
```

```
     bez[i3+1]=( (knot[i+2]-knot[i])*bspl[i+1]
            +( knot[i]-knot[i-1])*bspl[i+2]  )/(knot[i+2]-knot[i-1]);
     bez[i3]  =( (knot[i+1]-knot[i])*bez[i3-1]
            + (knot[i]-knot[i-1])*bez[i3+1]   )/(knot[i+1]-knot[i-1]);
     }
/* The last points need special attention:  */

     l3=l*3;
     if(l>2)
     {
         bez[l3-4]=( (knot[l]-knot[l-1])*bspl[l-1]
            + (knot[l-1]-knot[l-3])*bspl[l]  )/(knot[l]-knot[l-3]);
     }
     if(l>1)
     {
         bez[l3-2]=( (knot[l]-knot[l-1])*bspl[l]
            + (knot[l-1]-knot[l-2])*bspl[l+1]  )/(knot[l]-knot[l-2]);

         bez[l3-3]=( (knot[l]-knot[l-1])*bez[l3-4]
            + (knot[l-1]-knot[l-2])*bez[l3-2]   )/(knot[l]-knot[l-2]);
     }
     bez[l3-1]= bspl[l+1];
     bez[l3]  = bspl[l+2];        /* careful: dimensioning  for bspl must
                                    be from 0 to l+2!                   */

}
```

Both routines have to be called for each coordinate (i.e., two or three times). Speedups are therefore possible.

7.13   Problems

1. If we write the de Casteljau algorithm in the form of a triangular array as in equation (3.3), subdivision tells us how the three "sides" of that array are related to each other. Write out explicitly how to generate the elements of one side from those of any other one.

2. Consider two Bézier curves with polygons $\mathbf{b}_0, \ldots, \mathbf{b}_n$ and $\mathbf{b}_n, \ldots, \mathbf{b}_{2n}$. Let $\mathbf{b}_{n-r} = \ldots = \mathbf{b}_n = \ldots \mathbf{b}_{n+r}$, so that both curves form one (degenerate) C^r curve. Under what conditions on $\mathbf{b}_{n-r-1}$ and $\mathbf{b}_{n+r+1}$ is that curve also C^{r+1}?

3. We are given a closed polygon. Suppose we want to make the polygon vertices the inner Bézier points $\mathbf{b}_{2i+1}$ of a piecewise quadratic and that we pick arbitrary points on the polygon legs to become the junction

Bézier points $\mathbf{b}_{2i}$. Can we always find a C^1 parametrization for this (tangent continuous) piecewise quadratic curve?

4. Describe the chord length parametrization for closed B-spline curves.

5. Explain which edge of the tetrahedron in Figure 7.3 corresponds to which of the six intervals mentioned in Section 7.3.

6. The following amusing error occurred during the generation of the programs for this book: in the definition of decas, omit the auxiliary array. The routine will then destroy the input array. However, when used in bez_to_points, the curve was plotted correctly. Why?

8

Piecewise Cubic Interpolation

Polynomial interpolation is a fundamental theoretical tool, but for practical purposes, better methods exist. The most popular class of methods is that of piecewise polynomial schemes. All these methods construct curves that consist of polynomial pieces of the same degree and that are of a prescribed overall smoothness. The given data are usually points and parameter values; sometimes, tangent information is added as well.

In practice, one mostly encounters the use of piecewise cubic curves. They may be C^2 – the next chapter is dedicated to that case. If they are only C^1, the tradeoff for the lower differentiability class is *locality*: if a data point is changed, the interpolating curve only changes in the vicinity of that data point.

This chapter can only cover the basic ideas behind piecewise cubic interpolation. A large variety of interpolation methods exists that are designed to cope with special problems. Most such methods try to preserve shape features inherent in the given data, for example convexity or monotonicity. We mention the work by Fritsch and Carlson [162], McLaughlin [254], Foley [154], [153], McAllister and Roulier [251], Schumaker [321].

8.1 C^1 Piecewise Cubic Hermite Interpolation

This is conceptually the simplest of all interpolants, although not the most practical one. It solves the following problem:

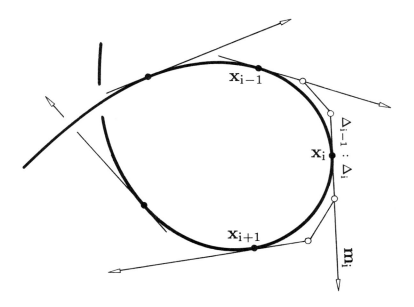

Figure 8.1. Piecewise cubic Hermite interpolation: the Bézier points are obtained directly from the data.

Given: Data points $\mathbf{x}_0, \ldots, \mathbf{x}_L$, corresponding parameter values $u_0, \ldots, u_L$, and corresponding tangent vectors $\mathbf{m}_0, \ldots, \mathbf{m}_L$.

Find: A C^1 piecewise cubic polynomial $\mathbf{s}$ that interpolates to the given data, i.e.,

$$\mathbf{s}(u_i) = \mathbf{x}_i, \quad \frac{\mathrm{d}}{\mathrm{d}u}\mathbf{s}(u_i) = \mathbf{m}_i; \quad i = 0, \ldots, L. \tag{8.1}$$

We construct the solution as a piecewise Bézier curve, as illustrated in Figure 8.1. We find the junction Bézier points immediately: $\mathbf{b}_{3i} = \mathbf{x}_i$. In order to obtain the inner Bézier points, we recall the derivative formula for Bézier curves from Section 7.5:

$$
\begin{aligned}
\frac{\mathrm{d}}{\mathrm{d}u}\mathbf{s}(u_i) &= \frac{3}{\Delta_{i-1}}(\mathbf{b}_{3i} - \mathbf{b}_{3i-1}) \\
&= \frac{3}{\Delta_i}(\mathbf{b}_{3i+1} - \mathbf{b}_{3i}),
\end{aligned}
$$

where $\Delta_i = \Delta u_i$. Thus the inner Bézier points $\mathbf{b}_{3i+1}; i = 0, \ldots, L-1$ are given by

$$\mathbf{b}_{3i+1} = \mathbf{b}_{3i} + \frac{\Delta_i}{3}\mathbf{m}_i \qquad (8.2)$$

and the inner Bézier points $\mathbf{b}_{3i-1}, i = 1, \ldots, L$ are

$$\mathbf{b}_{3i-1} = \mathbf{b}_{3i} - \frac{\Delta_{i-1}}{3}\mathbf{m}_i. \qquad (8.3)$$

What we have done so far is to construct the piecewise Bézier form of the C^1 piecewise cubic Hermite interpolant. Of course, we can utilize the material on cubic Hermite interpolation from Section 6.5 as well. Over the interval $[u_i, u_{i+1}]$, the interpolant $\mathbf{s}$ can be expressed in terms of the cubic Hermite polynomials $\hat{H}_i^3(u)$ that were defined by (6.16). In the situation at hand, the definitions become:

$$\begin{aligned}
\hat{H}_0^3(u) &= B_0^3(t) + B_1^3(t), \\
\hat{H}_1^3(u) &= \tfrac{\Delta_i}{3} B_1^3(t), \\
\hat{H}_2^3(u) &= -\tfrac{\Delta_i}{3} B_2^3(t), \\
\hat{H}_3^3(u) &= B_2^3(t) + B_3^3(t),
\end{aligned} \qquad (8.4)$$

where $t = (u - u_i)/\Delta_i$ is the local parameter of the interval $[u_i, u_{i+1}]$. The interpolant can now be written as

$$\mathbf{s}(u) = \mathbf{x}_i \hat{H}_0^3(u) + \mathbf{m}_i \hat{H}_1^3(u) + \mathbf{m}_{i+1} \hat{H}_2^3(u) + \mathbf{x}_{i+1} \hat{H}_3^3(u). \qquad (8.5)$$

This interpolant is important for some theoretical developments; of more practical value are those developed in the following sections.

8.2 C^1 Piecewise Cubic Interpolation I

The title of this section is not very different from the one of the preceding section, and indeed the problems addressed in both sections differ only by a subtle nuance. Here, we try to solve the following problem:

Given: Data points $\mathbf{x}_0, \ldots, \mathbf{x}_L$ and tangent directions $\mathbf{l}_0, \ldots, \mathbf{l}_L$ at those data points.

Find: A C^1 piecewise cubic polynomial that passes through the given data points and is tangent to the given tangent directions there.

Comparing this problem to the one in the previous section, we find that it is more vaguely formulated: the "Find" part does not contain a single formula. This reflects a typical practical situation: one is not always given

Figure 8.2. C^1 piecewise cubics: example data set.

parameter values u_i or tangent vectors $\mathbf{m}_i$; very often, the only available information is data points and tangent directions, as illustrated in Figure 8.2. It is important to note that we only have tangent *directions*, i.e., we have no vectors with a prescribed length. We can assume without loss of generality that the tangent directions $\mathbf{l}_i$ have been normalized to be of unit length:

$$||\mathbf{l}_i|| = 1.$$

The easiest step in finding the desired piecewise cubic is the same as before: the junction Bézier points $\mathbf{b}_{3i}$ are again given by $\mathbf{b}_{3i} = \mathbf{x}_i$, $i = 0, \ldots, L$.

For each inner Bézier point, we have a one-parameter family of solutions: we only have to ensure that each triple $\mathbf{b}_{3i-1}, \mathbf{b}_{3i}, \mathbf{b}_{3i+1}$ is collinear on the tangent at $\mathbf{b}_{3i}$ and ordered by increasing subscript in the direction of $\mathbf{l}_i$. We can then find a parametrization with respect to which the generated curve is C^1. (See equation 7.20.)

In general, we must determine the inner Bézier points from

$$\mathbf{b}_{3i+1} = \mathbf{b}_{3i} + \alpha_i \mathbf{l}_i \qquad (8.6)$$
$$\mathbf{b}_{3i-1} = \mathbf{b}_{3i} - \beta_i \mathbf{l}_i, \qquad (8.7)$$

so that the problem boils down to finding reasonable values for α_i and β_i. While any nonnegative value for these numbers is a formally valid solution, too small values for α_i and β_i cause the curve to have a corner at $\mathbf{x}_i$, while too large values can create loops. There is probably no optimal choice for α_i and β_i that holds up in every conceivable application – an optimal choice must depend on the desired application.

A "quick and easy" solution that has performed decently many times (but also failed sometimes) is simply to set

$$\alpha_i = \beta_i = 0.4||\Delta \mathbf{x}_i||. \qquad (8.8)$$

(The factor 0.4 is, of course, heuristic.)

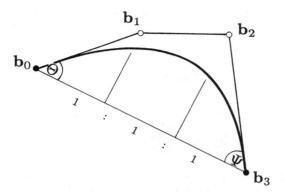

Figure 8.3. Inner Bézier points: this planar curve can be interpreted as a *function* in an oblique coordinate system with $\mathbf{b}_0, \mathbf{b}_3$ as the x-axis.

The parametrization with respect to which this interpolant is a C^1 is the *chord length parametrization*: it is characterized by

$$\frac{\Delta_i}{\Delta_{i+1}} = \frac{||\Delta\mathbf{x}_i||}{||\Delta\mathbf{x}_{i+1}||}. \tag{8.9}$$

A more sophisticated solution is the following: if we consider the planar curve in Figure 8.3, we see that it can be interpreted as a function, where the parameter t varies along the straight line through $\mathbf{b}_0$ and $\mathbf{b}_3$. Then

$$||\Delta\mathbf{b}_0|| = \frac{||\mathbf{b}_3 - \mathbf{b}_0||}{3\cos\Theta}$$

$$||\Delta\mathbf{b}_2|| = \frac{||\mathbf{b}_3 - \mathbf{b}_0||}{3\cos\Psi}.$$

We are dealing with parametric curves, however, which are in general not planar and for which the angles Θ and Ψ could be close to 90 degrees, causing the above expressions to be undefined. But for curves with Θ, Ψ smaller than, say, 60 degrees, the above could be utilized to find reasonable values for α_i and β_i:

$$\alpha_i = \frac{1}{3\cos\Theta}||\Delta\mathbf{x}_i||$$

$$\beta_i = \frac{1}{3\cos\Psi}||\Delta\mathbf{x}_i||.$$

Since $\cos 60° = 1/2$, we can now make a case distinction:

$$\alpha_i = \begin{cases} \frac{||\Delta \mathbf{x}_i||^2}{3\mathbf{l}_i \mathbf{x}_i} & \text{if } |\Theta| \leq 60° \\ \frac{2}{3}||\Delta \mathbf{x}_i|| & \text{otherwise} \end{cases} \qquad (8.10)$$

and

$$\beta_i = \begin{cases} \frac{||\Delta \mathbf{x}_i||^2}{3\mathbf{l}_{i+1} \mathbf{x}_i} & \text{if } |\Psi| \leq 60° \\ \frac{2}{3}||\Delta \mathbf{x}_i|| & \text{otherwise.} \end{cases} \qquad (8.11)$$

This method has the advantage of having *linear precision*.

Note that neither of these two methods is affinely invariant: the first method – equation (8.8) – does not preserve the ratios of the three points $\mathbf{b}_{3i-1}, \mathbf{b}_{3i}, \mathbf{b}_{3i+1}$ since the ratios $||\Delta \mathbf{x}_{i-1}|| : ||\Delta \mathbf{x}_i||$ are not generally invariant under affine maps.[1] The second method uses angles, which are not preserved under affine transformations. However, both methods are invariant under euclidean transformations.

8.3 C^1 Piecewise Cubic Interpolation II

Continuing with the relaxation of given constraints for the interpolatory C^1 cubic spline curve, we now address the following problem:

Given: Data points $\mathbf{x}_0, \ldots, \mathbf{x}_L$ together with corresponding parameter values $u_0, \ldots, u_L$.

Find: A C^1 piecewise cubic polynomial that passes through the given data points.

One solution to this problem is provided by C^2 (and hence also C^1) cubic splines; they will be discussed in Chapter 9. We will here determine tangent directions $\mathbf{l}_i$ or tangent vectors $\mathbf{m}_i$ and then apply the methods from the previous two sections.

Probably the simplest method for tangent estimation is known under the name FMILL. It constructs the tangent direction $\mathbf{l}_i$ at $\mathbf{x}_i$ to be parallel to the chord through $\mathbf{x}_{i-1}$ and $\mathbf{x}_{i+1}$:

$$\mathbf{l}_i = \frac{\mathbf{x}_{i+1} - \mathbf{x}_{i-1}}{||\mathbf{x}_{i+1} - \mathbf{x}_{i-1}||}; \quad i = 1, \ldots, L-1. \qquad (8.12)$$

Once the tangent direction $\mathbf{l}_i$ has been found, the inner Bézier points are

---

[1]Recall that only the ratio of three *collinear* points is preserved under affine maps!

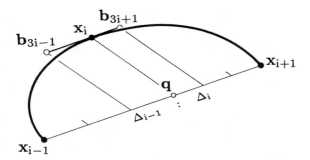

Figure 8.4. FMILL tangents: the tangent at $\mathbf{x}_i$ is parallel to the chord through $\mathbf{x}_{i-1}$ and $\mathbf{x}_{i+1}$.

placed on it according to Figure 8.4:

$$\mathbf{b}_{3i-1} \;=\; \mathbf{b}_{3i} - \frac{\Delta_{i-1}}{3(\Delta_{i-1} + \Delta_i)}\mathbf{l}_i, \qquad (8.13)$$

$$\mathbf{b}_{3i+1} \;=\; \mathbf{b}_{3i} + \frac{\Delta_i}{3(\Delta_{i-1} + \Delta_i)}\mathbf{l}_i. \qquad (8.14)$$

This interpolant is also known as a Catmull-Rom spline.

This construction of the inner Bézier points does not work at $\mathbf{x}_0$ and $\mathbf{x}_L$. One way to pick the tangents there is to use Bessel tangents, as described below.

The idea behind *Bessel tangents*[2] is as follows: in order to find the tangent vector $\mathbf{m}_i$ at $\mathbf{x}_i$, pass the interpolating parabola $\mathbf{q}_i(u)$ through $\mathbf{x}_{i-1}, \mathbf{x}_i, \mathbf{x}_{i+1}$ with corresponding parameter values u_{i-1}, u_i, u_{i+1} and let $\mathbf{m}_i$ be the derivative of $\mathbf{q}_i$. We differentiate $\mathbf{q}_i$ at u_i:

$$\mathbf{m}_i = \frac{\mathrm{d}}{\mathrm{d}u}\mathbf{q}_{\mathbf{i}}(u_i).$$

Written out in terms of the given data, this gives

$$\mathbf{m}_i = \frac{(1 - \alpha_i)}{\Delta_{i-1}}\Delta\mathbf{x}_{i-1} + \frac{\alpha_i}{\Delta_i}\Delta\mathbf{x}_i; \qquad i = 1, \dots, L-1, \qquad (8.15)$$

where

$$\alpha_i = \frac{\Delta_{i-1}}{\Delta_{i-1} + \Delta_i}.$$

---

[2]They are sometimes attributed to Ackland [2].

The endpoints are treated in the same way: $\mathbf{m}_0 = \mathrm{d}/\mathrm{d}u\mathbf{q}_1(u_0), \mathbf{m}_L = \mathrm{d}/\mathrm{d}u\mathbf{q}_{L-1}(u_L)$, which gives

$$\mathbf{m}_0 = 2\frac{\Delta\mathbf{x}_0}{\Delta_0} - \mathbf{m}_1,$$

$$\mathbf{m}_L = 2\frac{\Delta\mathbf{x}_{L-1}}{\Delta_{L-1}} - \mathbf{m}_{L-1}.$$

Another interpolant that makes use of the parabolas $\mathbf{q}_i$ is known as an *Overhauser spline*, after work by A. Overhauser [271] (see also [63]). The ith segment $\mathbf{s}_i$ of such a spline is defined by

$$\mathbf{s}_i(u) = \frac{u_{i+1} - u}{\Delta_i}\mathbf{q}_i(u) + \frac{u - u_i}{\Delta_i}\mathbf{q}_{i+1}(u); \quad i = 1, \ldots, L - 2.$$

In other words, each $\mathbf{s}_i$ is a linear blend between $\mathbf{q}_i$ and $\mathbf{q}_{i+1}$. At the ends, one sets $\mathbf{s}_0(u) = \mathbf{q}_0(u)$ and $\mathbf{s}_{L-1}(u) = \mathbf{q}_{L-1}(u)$.

Upon closer inspection it turns out that the last two interpolants are not different at all: they both yield the same C^1 piecewise cubic interpolant – see Problems. A similar way of determining tangent vectors was developed by McConalogue [253], [252].

Finally, we mention a method created by H. Akima [4]. It sets

$$\mathbf{m}_i = (1 - c_i)\mathbf{a}_{i-1} + c_i\mathbf{a}_i$$

where

$$\mathbf{a}_i = \frac{\Delta\mathbf{x}_i}{\Delta_i}$$

and

$$c_i = \frac{||\Delta\mathbf{a}_{i-2}||}{||\Delta\mathbf{a}_{i-2}|| + ||\Delta\mathbf{a}_i||}.$$

This interpolant appears fairly involved. It generates very good results, however, in situations where one needs curves that oscillate only minimally.

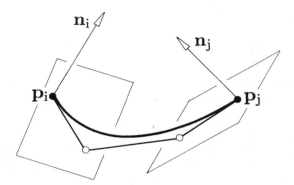

Figure 8.5. Finding cubic boundaries: while the endpoints of a boundary curve is fixed, its end tangents only have to lie in specified planes.

8.4 Point-Normal Interpolation

In a surface generation environment, one is often given a set of points $\mathbf{p}_i \in I\!\!E^3$ and a surface normal vector $\mathbf{n}_i$ at each data point as illustrated in Figure 8.5. Thus we only know the tangent plane of the desired surface at each data point, not the actual endpoint derivatives of the patch boundary curves.

If we know that two points $\mathbf{p}_i$ and $\mathbf{p}_j$ have to be connected, then we must construct a curve leading from $\mathbf{p}_i$ to $\mathbf{p}_j$ that is normal to $\mathbf{n}_i$ at $\mathbf{p}_i$ and to $\mathbf{n}_j$ at $\mathbf{p}_j$. A cubic will suffice to solve this generalized Hermite interpolation problem. In Bézier form, we already have $\mathbf{b}_0 = \mathbf{p}_i$ and $\mathbf{b}_3 = \mathbf{p}_j$. We still need to find $\mathbf{b}_1$ and $\mathbf{b}_2$.

There are infinitely many solutions, so we may try to pick one that is both convenient to compute and of reasonable shape in most cases. Two approaches to this problem appear in Piper [285], page 229 and Nielson [268], page 238.

Piper obtains $\mathbf{b}_1$ in two steps: as a first approximation to $\mathbf{b}_1$, project $\mathbf{b}_3$ into the plane defined by $\mathbf{b}_0 = \mathbf{p}_i$ and $\mathbf{n}_i$. This defines a tangent at $\mathbf{b}_0$. Place the final $\mathbf{b}_1$ anywhere on this tangent, using some of the methods described in Section 8.2. The remaining point $\mathbf{b}_2$ is then obtained analogously.

Nielson defines the tangent at $\mathbf{b}_0$ to be the intersection of the plane defined by $\mathbf{b}_0 = \mathbf{p}_i$ and $\mathbf{n}_i$ and the plane through $\mathbf{b}_0$ containg both $\mathbf{n}_i$ and $\mathbf{p}_j - \mathbf{p}_i$. Again, $\mathbf{b}_1$ would be placed on this tangent according to some measure of optimality. The same procedure is then repeated for $\mathbf{b}_2$.

8.5   Problems

1. Show that Overhauser splines are piecewise cubics with Bessel tangents at the junction points.

2. Show that Akima's interpolant always passes a straight line segment through three subsequent points if they happen to lie on a straight line.

3. One can generalize the quintic Hermite interpolants from Section 6.6 to piecewise quintic Hermite interpolants. These curves need as input positions, first and second derivatives. Devise ways to generate second derivative information from data points and parameter values.

9

Cubic Spline Interpolation

In this chapter, we discuss what is probably *the* most popular curve scheme: C^2 cubic interpolatory splines. We have seen how polynomial Lagrange interpolation fails to produce acceptable results. On the other hand, we saw that cubic B-spline curves are a powerful modeling tool; they are able to model complex shapes easily. This "modeling" is carried out as an *approximation* process, manipulating the control polygon until a desired shape is achieved. We will see how cubic splines can also be used to fulfill the task of *interpolation*, the task of finding a spline curve passing through a given set of points. Cubic spline interpolation was introduced into the CAGD literature by J. Ferguson [148] in 1964, while the mathematical theory was studied in approximation theory (see de Boor [95] or Holladay [208]). For an outline of the history of splines, see Schumaker [322].

Because of the subject's importance, we present two entirely independent derivations of cubic interpolatory splines: the B-spline form and the Hermite form.

9.1 The B-spline Form

We are given a set of data points $\mathbf{x}_0, \ldots, \mathbf{x}_L$ and corresponding parameter values (or knots or breakpoints) $u_0, \ldots, u_L$.[1] We want a cubic B-

---

[1] The knots are in general *not* given – see Section 9.4 on how to generate them.

spline curve $\mathbf{s}$, determined by the same knots and unknown control vertices $\mathbf{d}_{-1}, \ldots, \mathbf{d}_{L+1}$ such that $\mathbf{s}(u_i) = \mathbf{x}_i$; in other words, such that $\mathbf{s}$ *interpolates* to the data points.

The solution to this problem becomes obvious once one realizes the relationship between the data points $\mathbf{x}_i$ and the control vertices $\mathbf{d}_i$. Recall that we can write every B-spline curve as a piecewise Bézier curve (see Section 7.9). In that form, we have

$$\mathbf{x}_i = \mathbf{b}_{3i}; \quad i = 0, \ldots, L.$$

The inner Bézier points $\mathbf{b}_{3i \pm 1}$ are related to the $\mathbf{x}_i$ by

$$\mathbf{x}_i = \frac{\Delta_i \mathbf{b}_{3i-1} + \Delta_{i-1} \mathbf{b}_{3i+1}}{\Delta_{i-1} + \Delta_i} \quad i = 1, \ldots, L - 1, \tag{9.1}$$

where we have set $\Delta_i = \Delta u_i$. Finally, the $\mathbf{b}_{3i \pm 1}$ are related to the control vertices $\mathbf{d}_i$ by

$$\mathbf{b}_{3i-1} = \frac{\Delta_i \mathbf{d}_{i-1} + (\Delta_{i-2} + \Delta_{i-1}) \mathbf{d}_i}{\Delta_{i-2} + \Delta_{i-1} + \Delta_i}; \quad i = 2, \ldots L - 1 \tag{9.2}$$

and

$$\mathbf{b}_{3i+1} = \frac{(\Delta_i + \Delta_{i+1}) \mathbf{d}_i + \Delta_{i-1} \mathbf{d}_{i+1}}{\Delta_{i-1} + \Delta_i + \Delta_{i+1}}; \quad i = 1, \ldots L - 2. \tag{9.3}$$

Near the endpoints of the curve, the situation is somewhat special:

$$\mathbf{b}_2 = \frac{\Delta_1 \mathbf{d}_0 + \Delta_0 \mathbf{d}_1}{\Delta_0 + \Delta_1}, \tag{9.4}$$

$$\mathbf{b}_{3L-2} = \frac{\Delta_{L-1} \mathbf{d}_{L-2} + \Delta_{L-2} \mathbf{d}_{L-1}}{\Delta_{L-2} + \Delta_{L-1}}. \tag{9.5}$$

We can now write down the relationships between the unknown $\mathbf{d}_i$ and the known $\mathbf{x}_i$, i.e., we can eliminate the $\mathbf{b}_i$:

$$(\Delta_{i-1} + \Delta_i) \mathbf{x}_i = \alpha_i \mathbf{d}_{i-1} + \beta_i \mathbf{d}_i + \gamma_i \mathbf{d}_{i+1}, \tag{9.6}$$

where we have set (with $\Delta_{-1} = \Delta_L = 0$):

$$\alpha_i = \frac{\Delta_i^2}{\Delta_{i-2} + \Delta_{i-1} + \Delta_i},$$

$$\beta_i = \frac{\Delta_i(\Delta_{i-2} + \Delta_{i-1})}{\Delta_{i-2} + \Delta_{i-1} + \Delta_i} + \frac{\Delta_{i-1}(\Delta_i + \Delta_{i+1})}{\Delta_{i-1} + \Delta_i + \Delta_{i+1}},$$

$$\gamma_i = \frac{\Delta_{i-1}^2}{\Delta_{i-1} + \Delta_i + \Delta_{i+1}}.$$

If we choose the two Bézier points $\mathbf{b}_1$ and $\mathbf{b}_{3L-1}$ arbitrarily, we obtain a linear system of the form

$$
\begin{bmatrix}
1 & & & & & \\
\alpha_1 & \beta_1 & \gamma_1 & & & \\
& & \ddots & & & \\
& & & \alpha_{L-1} & \beta_{L-1} & \gamma_{L-1} \\
& & & & & 1
\end{bmatrix}
\begin{bmatrix}
\mathbf{d}_0 \\
\mathbf{d}_1 \\
\vdots \\
\mathbf{d}_{L-1} \\
\mathbf{d}_L
\end{bmatrix}
=
\begin{bmatrix}
\mathbf{r}_0 \\
\mathbf{r}_1 \\
\vdots \\
\mathbf{r}_{L-1} \\
\mathbf{r}_L
\end{bmatrix}.
$$

$$(9.7)$$

Here we set

$$\mathbf{r}_0 = \mathbf{b}_1,$$
$$\mathbf{r}_i = (\Delta_{i-1} + \Delta_i)\mathbf{x}_i$$
$$\mathbf{r}_L = \mathbf{b}_{3L-1}.$$

The first and last polygon vertices do not cause much of a problem:

$$\mathbf{d}_{-1} = \mathbf{x}_0, \qquad \mathbf{d}_{L+1} = \mathbf{x}_L.$$

Some discussion about the solution of this tridiagonal system is provided in the next section. Note that an affine parameter transformation does not affect the linear system. Therefore it would not matter if we rescaled our parameter values u_i.

In the special case of all Δ_i being equal, that is, for an equidistant parametrization, the system becomes even simpler:

$$
\begin{bmatrix}
1 & & & & & & \\
\frac{3}{2} & \frac{7}{2} & 1 & & & & \\
& 1 & 4 & 1 & & & \\
& & & \ddots & & & \\
& & & 1 & 4 & 1 & \\
& & & & 1 & \frac{7}{2} & \frac{3}{2} \\
& & & & & & 1
\end{bmatrix}
\begin{bmatrix}
\mathbf{d}_0 \\
\mathbf{d}_1 \\
\mathbf{d}_2 \\
\vdots \\
\mathbf{d}_{L-2} \\
\mathbf{d}_{L-1} \\
\mathbf{d}_L
\end{bmatrix}
=
\begin{bmatrix}
\mathbf{b}_1 \\
6\mathbf{x}_1 \\
6\mathbf{x}_2 \\
\vdots \\
6\mathbf{x}_{L-1} \\
6\mathbf{x}_{L-2} \\
\mathbf{b}_{3L-1}
\end{bmatrix}. \quad (9.8)
$$

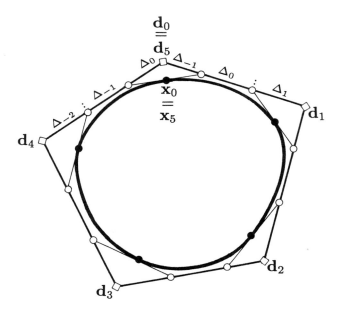

Figure 9.1. Closed curves: the interpolation problem becomes periodic.

Frequently one must deal with *closed* curves; see Figure 9.1. The number of equations is reduced since the C^2 condition at $\mathbf{x}_0 = \mathbf{x}_L$ should not be listed twice in the linear system. It now takes the form:

$$
\begin{bmatrix}
\beta_0 & \gamma_0 & & & & & \alpha_0 \\
\alpha_1 & \beta_1 & \gamma_1 & & & & \\
& & \ddots & & & & \\
& & & \alpha_{L-2} & \beta_{L-2} & \gamma_{L-2} & \\
\gamma_{L-1} & & & & \alpha_{L-1} & \beta_{L-1}
\end{bmatrix}
\begin{bmatrix}
\mathbf{d}_0 \\
\mathbf{d}_1 \\
\vdots \\
\mathbf{d}_{L-2} \\
\mathbf{d}_{L-1}
\end{bmatrix}
=
\begin{bmatrix}
\mathbf{r}_0 \\
\mathbf{r}_1 \\
\vdots \\
\mathbf{r}_{L-2} \\
\mathbf{r}_{L-1}
\end{bmatrix}.
$$

$$(9.9)$$

Here, the right hand sides are of the form

$$
\mathbf{r}_i = (\Delta_{i-1} + \Delta_i)\mathbf{x}_i.
$$

In order for these equations to make sense, we define a *periodic continuation* of the knot sequence:

$$
\Delta_{-1} = \Delta_{L-1}, \Delta_{-2} = \Delta_{L-2}.
$$

The matrix of this system is no longer tridiagonal; yet one does not have to resort to solving a full linear system. For details, see Ahlberg, Nilson, Walsh [3], p. 15.

We conclude with a method for B-spline interpolation that occasionally appears in the literature (e.g., in Yamaguchi [352]). It is possible to solve the interpolation problem without setting up a linear system! Just do the following: construct an initial control polygon – by setting $\mathbf{d}_i = \mathbf{x}_i$, for example. This initial polygon will not define an interpolating curve. So, for i from 0 to L, correct $\mathbf{d}_i$ such that the corresponding curve passes through $\mathbf{x}_i$. Repeat until the solution is found.

This method will always converge, and will not need many steps in order to do so. So why bother with linear systems? The reason is that tridiagonal diagonally dominant linear systems are most effectively solved by a direct method, whereas the above iterative method amounts to solving the system via Gauss-Seidel iteration. So while geometrically appealing, the iterative method loses due to the theorems of numerical analysis.

9.2 The Hermite Form

An interpolatory C^2 piecewise cubic spline may also be written in piecewise cubic Hermite form: for $u \in (u_i, u_{i+1})$, the interpolant is of the form

$$\mathbf{x}(u) = \mathbf{x}_i H_0^3(r) + \mathbf{m}_i \Delta_i H_1^3(r) + \Delta_i \mathbf{m}_{i+1} H_2^3(r) + \mathbf{x}_{i+1} H_3^3(r), \qquad (9.10)$$

where the H_j^3 are cubic Hermite polynomials from equation (6.14) and $r = (u - u_i)/\Delta_i$ is the local parameter of the interval (u_i, u_{i+1}). In (9.10), the $\mathbf{x}_i$ are the known data points, while the $\mathbf{m}_i = \dot{\mathbf{x}}(u_i)$ are the unknown tangent vectors. The interpolant is supposed to be C^2; therefore,

$$\ddot{\mathbf{x}}_+(u_i) - \ddot{\mathbf{x}}_-(u_i) = \mathbf{0}. \qquad (9.11)$$

We insert (9.10) into (9.11) and obtain

$$\Delta_i \mathbf{m}_{i-1} + 2(\Delta_{i-1} + \Delta_i)\mathbf{m}_i + \Delta_{i-1}\mathbf{m}_{i+1} = 3(\tfrac{\Delta_i \Delta \mathbf{x}_{i-1}}{\Delta_{i-1}} + \tfrac{\Delta_{i-1}\Delta \mathbf{x}_i}{\Delta_i});$$

$$i = 1, \ldots, L - 1. \qquad (9.12)$$

Together with two end conditions, (9.12) can be used to compute the unknown tangent vectors $\mathbf{m}_i$. Note that this formulation of the spline interpolation problem depends on the scale of the u_i; it is not invariant under affine parameter transformations. This is due to the use of the Hermite form.

The simplest end condition would be to prescribe $\mathbf{m}_0$ and $\mathbf{m}_L$, a method known as *clamped end condition*. In that case, the matrix of our linear system takes the form

$$
\begin{bmatrix}
1 & & & & \\
\alpha_1 & \beta_1 & \gamma_1 & & \\
& & \ddots & & \\
& & \alpha_{L-1} & \beta_{L-1} & \gamma_{L-1} \\
& & & & 1
\end{bmatrix}
\begin{bmatrix}
\mathbf{m}_0 \\
\mathbf{m}_1 \\
\vdots \\
\mathbf{m}_{L-1} \\
\mathbf{m}_L
\end{bmatrix}
=
\begin{bmatrix}
\mathbf{r}_0 \\
\mathbf{r}_1 \\
\vdots \\
\mathbf{r}_{L-1} \\
\mathbf{r}_L
\end{bmatrix}
\tag{9.13}
$$

where

$$
\begin{aligned}
\alpha_i &= \Delta_i, \\
\beta_i &= 2(\Delta_{i-1} + \Delta_i), \\
\gamma_i &= \Delta_{i-1}
\end{aligned}
$$

and

$$
\begin{aligned}
\mathbf{r}_0 &= \mathbf{m}_0, \\
\mathbf{r}_i &= 3\left(\frac{\Delta_i \Delta \mathbf{x}_{i-1}}{\Delta_{i-1}} + \frac{\Delta_{i-1} \Delta \mathbf{x}_i}{\Delta_i}\right); \quad i = 1, \dots, L-1, \\
\mathbf{r}_L &= \mathbf{m}_L.
\end{aligned}
$$

Having found the $\mathbf{m}_i$, we can easily retrieve the piecewise Bézier form of the curve according to (8.2) and (8.3).

When dealing with linear systems, it is a good idea to make sure that a solution exists and that it is unique. In our case, the coefficient matrix is *diagonally dominant*, which means that the absolute value of any diagonal element is larger than the sum of the absolute values of the remaining elements on the same row:

$$
|\beta_i| > |\alpha_i| + |\gamma_i|.
$$

Such matrices are always invertible; moreover, they allow Gauss elimination without pivoting (see any advanced text on numerical analysis or the fundamental spline text by Ahlberg, Nilson, and Walsh [3]). Thus the spline interpolation problem always possesses a unique solution (after the prescription of two consistent end conditions).

Since the coefficient matrix is *tridiagonal* (only the diagonal element and its two neighbors are nonzero), we do not have to solve a full $(L+1) \times (L+1)$ linear system; one forward substitution sweep and one for backward substitution is sufficient, as implemented in the programs l_u_system and solve_system below. All our remarks about the linear system hold for the B-spline form as well.

9.3 End Conditions

We may have the interpolation routine select the end tangents $\mathbf{m}_0$ and $\mathbf{m}_L$ automatically instead of prescribing it ourselves. One such selection is called the *Bessel end condition*. Here, the end tangent vector $\mathbf{m}_0$ is set equal to the tangent vector at $\mathbf{x}_0$ of the interpolating parabola through the first three data points. Similarly, $\mathbf{m}_L$ is set equal to the tangent vector at $\mathbf{x}_L$ of the interpolating parabola through the last three data points. Now the right hand side changes to

$$\mathbf{r}_0 = -\frac{2(2\Delta_0 + \Delta_1)}{\Delta_0 \beta_1} \mathbf{x}_0 + \frac{\beta_1}{2\Delta_0 \Delta_1} \mathbf{x}_1 - \frac{2\Delta_0}{\Delta_1 \beta_1} \mathbf{x}_2, \qquad (9.14)$$

and

$$\mathbf{r}_L = \frac{2\Delta_{L-1}}{\Delta_{L-2}\beta_{L-1}} \mathbf{x}_{L-2} - \frac{\beta_{L-1}}{2\Delta_{L-2}\Delta_{L-1}} \mathbf{x}_{L-1} + \frac{2(2\Delta_{L-1} + \Delta_{L-2})}{\beta_{L-1}\Delta_{L-1}} \mathbf{x}_L. \quad (9.15)$$

Of course, this condition may also be formulated in terms of the B-spline representation. This is done in the routine `bessel_ends` below

Another possibility is the *quadratic end condition*: it sets $\ddot{\mathbf{x}}(u_0) = \ddot{\mathbf{x}}(u_1)$ and $\ddot{\mathbf{x}}(u_{L-1}) = \ddot{\mathbf{x}}(u_L)$. Now the linear system changes to

$$\begin{bmatrix} 1 & 1 & & & & \\ \alpha_1 & \beta_1 & \gamma_1 & & & \\ & & \ddots & & & \\ & & & \alpha_{L-1} & \beta_{L-1} & \gamma_{L-1} \\ & & & & 1 & 1 \end{bmatrix} \begin{bmatrix} \mathbf{m}_0 \\ \mathbf{m}_1 \\ \vdots \\ \mathbf{m}_{L-1} \\ \mathbf{m}_L \end{bmatrix} = \begin{bmatrix} \mathbf{r}_0 \\ \mathbf{r}_1 \\ \vdots \\ \mathbf{r}_{L-1} \\ \mathbf{r}_L \end{bmatrix}$$

$$\tag{9.16}$$

and

$$\mathbf{r}_0 = \frac{2}{\Delta_0} \Delta \mathbf{x}_0, \quad \mathbf{r}_L = \frac{2}{\Delta_{L-1}} \Delta \mathbf{x}_{L-1}.$$

A slightly more complicated end condition is provided by the *not-a-knot condition*. Using it, we force the first two and the last two polynomial segments to merge into *one* cubic piece. This means that the third derivative of $\mathbf{x}(u)$ is continuous at u_1. Writing down the conditions leads to a non-tridiagonal system which can, however, be transformed into a tridiagonal one. Its first equation is

$$\Delta_1 \beta_1 \mathbf{m}_0 + \beta_1^2 \mathbf{m}_1 =$$
$$\frac{(\Delta_0)^2}{\Delta_1} \Delta \mathbf{x}_1 + \frac{\Delta_1}{\Delta_0} (3\Delta_0 + 2\Delta_1) \Delta \mathbf{x}_0; \qquad (9.17)$$

Figure 9.2. Exact clamped end condition spline.

the last one is

$$\beta^2_{L-1}\mathbf{m}_{L-1} + \Delta_{L-2}\beta_{L-1}\mathbf{m}_L =$$
$$\frac{(\Delta_{L-1})^2}{\Delta_{L-2}}\Delta\mathbf{x}_{L-2} + \frac{\Delta_{L-2}}{\Delta_{L-1}}(3\Delta_{L-1} + 2\Delta_{L-2})\Delta\mathbf{x}_{L-1}. \qquad (9.18)$$

Finally, we mention an end condition that bears the name "natural." The term stems from the fact that this condition arises "naturally" in the context of the minimum property for spline curves, as described below. The natural end condition is defined by $\ddot{\mathbf{x}}(u_0) = \ddot{\mathbf{x}}(u_L) = \mathbf{0}$. The linear system becomes

$$\begin{bmatrix} 2 & 1 & & & & \\ \alpha_1 & \beta_1 & \gamma_1 & & & \\ & & \ddots & & & \\ & & & \alpha_{L-1} & \beta_{L-1} & \gamma_{L-1} \\ & & & & 1 & 2 \end{bmatrix} \begin{bmatrix} \mathbf{m}_0 \\ \mathbf{m}_1 \\ \vdots \\ \mathbf{m}_{L-1} \\ \mathbf{m}_L \end{bmatrix} = \begin{bmatrix} \mathbf{r}_0 \\ \mathbf{r}_1 \\ \vdots \\ \mathbf{r}_{L-1} \\ \mathbf{r}_L \end{bmatrix}$$
$$\qquad (9.19)$$

and

$$\mathbf{r}_0 = \frac{3}{\Delta_0}\Delta\mathbf{x}_0, \quad \mathbf{r}_L = \frac{3}{\Delta_{L-1}}\Delta\mathbf{x}_{L-1}.$$

This end condition forces the curve to behave like a straight line near the endpoints; usually, this results in a poor shape of the spline curve.

$$\kappa = 1$$

$$\kappa = 0$$

Figure 9.3. Curvature plot of exact clamped end condition spline.

The spline system becomes especially simple if the knots u_i are uniformly spaced; for example, the clamped end condition system becomes

$$
\begin{bmatrix}
1 & & & & & \\
1 & 4 & 1 & & & \\
& & \ddots & & & \\
& & & 1 & 4 & 1 \\
& & & & 1 &
\end{bmatrix}
\begin{bmatrix}
\mathbf{m}_0 \\
\mathbf{m}_1 \\
\vdots \\
\mathbf{m}_{L-1} \\
\mathbf{m}_L
\end{bmatrix}
=
\begin{bmatrix}
\mathbf{r}_0 \\
\mathbf{r}_1 \\
\vdots \\
\mathbf{r}_{L-1} \\
\mathbf{r}_L
\end{bmatrix}
\tag{9.20}
$$

where

$$
\begin{aligned}
\mathbf{r}_0 &= \mathbf{m}_0, \\
\mathbf{r}_i &= 3(\mathbf{x}_{i+1} - \mathbf{x}_{i-1}); \quad i = 1, \ldots, L - 1, \\
\mathbf{r}_L &= \mathbf{m}_L.
\end{aligned}
$$

We finish this section with a few examples, using uniform parameter values in all examples.[2] Figure 9.2 shows equally spaced data points read off from a circle and the cubic spline interpolant obtained with clamped end conditions, using the exact end derivatives of the circle (the figure is scaled down in the y-direction). Figure 9.3 shows the curvature plot[3] of the spline curve. Ideally, the curvature should be constant, and the spline curvature is quite close to this ideal.

---

[2] Due to the symmetry inherent in the data points, all parametrizations discussed below yield the same knot spacing.

[3] The graph of curvature *vs* arc length; see also Chapter 23.

Figure 9.4. Bessel end condition spline.

Figure 9.4 shows the same data, but now using Bessel end conditions. Near the endpoints, the curvature deviates from the ideal value, as shown in Figure 9.5.

Finally, Figure 9.6 shows the curve that is obtained using natural end conditions. The end curvatures are forced to be zero, causing considerable deviation from the ideal value, as shown in Figure 9.7.

9.4 The Parametrization

The spline interpolation problem is usually stated as "given data points $\mathbf{x}_i$ and parameter values $u_i, \ldots$." Of course, this is the mathematician's way of describing a problem. In practice, parameter values are rarely given and therefore must be made up somehow. The easiest way to determine the u_i is simply to set $u_i = i$. This is called *uniform* or *equidistant* parametrization. This method is too simplistic to cope with most practical situations. The reason for the overall poor[4] performance of the uniform parametrization can be blamed on the fact that it "ignores" the geometry of the data points.

The following is a heuristic explanation of this fact. We can interpret the parameter u of the curve as time: as time passes from time u_0 to time u_L, the point $\mathbf{x}(u)$ traces out the curve from point $\mathbf{x}(u_0)$ to point $\mathbf{x}(u_L)$. With uniform parametrization, $\mathbf{x}(u)$ spends the same amount of

---

[4]There are cases in which the uniform parametrization fares better than other methods. An interesting example is in Foley [153], page 86.

$\kappa = 1$

$\kappa = 0$

Figure 9.5. Curvature plot of Bessel end condition spline.

time between any two adjacent data points, irrespective of their relative distances. A good analogy is a car driving along the interpolating curve. We have to spend the same amount of time between any two data points. If the distance between two data points is large, we must move with a high speed. If the next two data points are close to each other, we will overshoot since we cannot abruptly change our speed – we are moving with continuous speed and acceleration, which are the physical counterparts of a C^2 parametrization of a curve. It would clearly be more reasonable to adjust speed to the distribution of the data points.

One way of achieving this is to have the knot spacing proportional to the distances of the data points:

$$\frac{\Delta_i}{\Delta_{i+1}} = \frac{||\Delta \mathbf{x}_i||}{||\Delta \mathbf{x}_{i+1}||}. \tag{9.21}$$

A parametrization of the form (9.21) is called *chord length parametrization*. Equation (9.21) does not uniquely define a knot sequence; it rather defines a whole family of parametrizations which are related to each other by affine parameter transformations. In practice, the choices $u_0 = 0$ and $u_L = 1$ or $u_0 = 0$ and $u_L = L$ are reasonable options.

Chord length usually produces better results than uniform knot spacing does, although not in all cases. It has been proven (Epstein [119]) that chord length parametrization (in connection with natural end conditions)

Figure 9.6. Natural end condition spline.

cannot produce curves with corners[5] at the data points, which gives it some
theoretical advantage over the uniform choice.

Another parametrization has been named "centripetal" by E. Lee [237].
It is derived from the physical heuristics presented above. If we set

$$\frac{\Delta_i}{\Delta_{i+1}} = \left[\frac{||\Delta\mathbf{x}_i||}{||\Delta\mathbf{x}_{i+1}||}\right]^{1/2}, \tag{9.22}$$

the resulting motion of a point on the curve will "smooth out" variations
in the centripetal force acting on it.

Yet another parametrization was developed by T. Foley [269]. It sets

$$\Delta_i = d_i\left[1 + \frac{3}{2}\frac{\hat{\Theta}_i d_{i-1}}{d_{i-1} + d_i} + \frac{3}{2}\frac{\hat{\Theta}_{i+1} d_{i+1}}{d_i + d_{i+1}}\right], \tag{9.23}$$

where $d_i = ||\Delta x_i||$ and

$$\hat{\Theta}_i = \min(\pi - \Theta_i, \frac{\pi}{2}),$$

and Θ_i is the angle formed by $\mathbf{x}_{i-1}, \mathbf{x}_i, \mathbf{x}_{i+1}$. Thus $\hat{\Theta}_i$ is the "adjusted"
exterior angle formed by the vectors $\Delta\mathbf{x}_i$ and $\Delta\mathbf{x}_{i-1}$. As the exterior angle

---

[5]A corner is a point on a curve where the tangent (not necessarily the tangent vector!)
changes in a discontinuous way. The special case of a change in 180 degrees is called a
cusp; it may occur even with chord length parametrization.

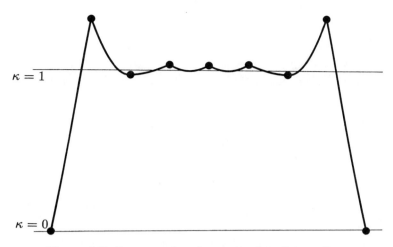

Figure 9.7. Curvature plot of natural end condition spline.

$\hat{\Theta}_i$ increases, the interval Δ_i increases from the minimum of its chord length value up to a maximum of four times its chord length value.

We note one property that distinguishes the uniform parametrization from its competitors: it is the only one that is invariant under affine transformations of the data points. Chord length, centripetal, and the Foley methods all involve length measurements, and lengths are not preserved under affine maps. One solution to this dilemma is the introduction of a modified length measure, as described in Nielson [263].[6]

For more literature on parametrizations, see McConalogue [253], Hartley and Judd [201], [200] and Foley [153].

Figures 9.8 to 9.15[7] show the performance of the discussed parametrization methods for one sample data set. For each method, the interpolant is shown together with its curvature plot. For all methods, Bessel end conditions were chosen.

While the figures are self explanatory, some comments are in place. Note the very uneven spacing of the data points at the marked area of the curves. Of all methods, Foley's copes best with that situation (although we add that many examples exist where the simpler centripetal method wins out). The uniform spline curve seems to have no problems there, if one just inspects the plot of the curve itself. However, the curvature plot reveals a cusp in that region! The huge curvature at the cusp causes a scaling in

---

[6]The Foley parametrization was in fact first formulated in terms of that modified length measure.

[7]kindly provided by T. Foley.

Figure 9.8. Chord length spline.

the curvature plot that annihilates all other information. Also note how
the chord length parametrization yields the "roundest" curve, having the
smallest curvature values, but exhibiting the most marked inflection points.

There is probably no "best" parametrization, since any method can be
defeated by a suitably chosen data set. The following is a (personal) rec-
ommendation. You may improve the shape of the curve, at an increase of
computation time, by the following hierarchy of methods: uniform, chord
length, centripetal, Foley. The best compromise between cost and result is
probably achieved be the centripetal method.

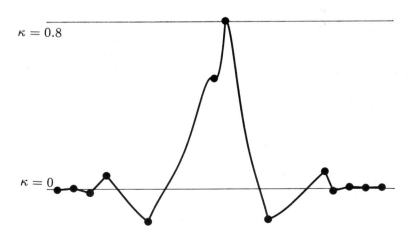

Figure 9.9. Curvature plot of chord length spline.

Figure 9.10. Foley spline.

9.5 The Minimum Property

In the early days of design, say ship design in the eighteen hundreds, the problem had to be handled of how to draw (manually) a smooth curve through a given set of points. One way to obtain a solution was the following: place metal weights (called "ducks") at the data points, and then pass a thin, elastic wooden beam (called a "spline") between the ducks. The resulting curve is always very smooth and usually esthetically pleasing. The same principle is used today, when an appropriate design program is not available, or for manual verification of a computer result; see Figure 9.16.

The plastic or wooden beam assumes a position which minimizes its strain energy. The mathematical model of the beam is a curve **s**, and its strain

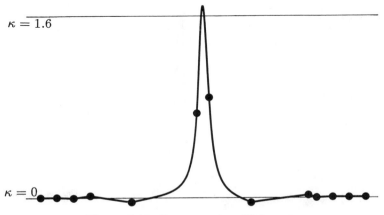

Figure 9.11. Curvature plot of Foley spline.

Figure 9.12. Centripetal spline.

energy E is given by

$$E = \int (\kappa(s))^2 \mathrm{d}s,$$

where κ denotes the curvature of the curve. The curvature of most curves involves integrals and is cumbersome to handle – therefore, one often approximates the above integral by a simpler one:

$$\hat{\mathbf{E}} = \int \left(\frac{\mathrm{d}^2}{\mathrm{d}u^2}\mathbf{s}(u)\right)^2 \mathrm{d}u. \tag{9.24}$$

Note that $\hat{\mathbf{E}}$ is a vector; it is obtained by performing the integration on each component of $\mathbf{s}$.

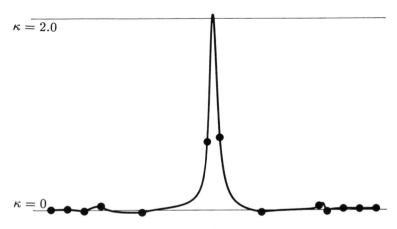

Figure 9.13. Curvature plot of centripetal spline.

Figure 9.14. Uniform spline.

C^2 cubic interpolatory splines have the following nice property: among all C^2 functions that interpolate the given data points at the given parameter values and satisfy the same end conditions, the cubic spline yields the smallest value for each component of $\hat{\mathbf{E}}$. Let $\mathbf{s}(u)$ be the C^2 cubic spline and let $\mathbf{y}(u)$ be another C^2 interpolating curve. We can write $\mathbf{y}$ as

$$\mathbf{y}(u) = \mathbf{s}(u) + [\mathbf{y}(u) - \mathbf{s}(u)].$$

The above integrals are defined componentwise; we will show the minimum property for one component only. Let $s(u)$ and $y(u)$ be the first component of $\mathbf{s}$ and $\mathbf{y}$, respectively.

The "energy integral" $\hat{E}$ of $\mathbf{y}$'s first component becomes

$$\hat{E} = \int_{u_0}^{u_L} (\ddot{s})^2 du + 2 \int_{u_0}^{u_L} \ddot{s}(\ddot{y} - \ddot{s}) du + \int_{u_0}^{u_L} (\ddot{y} - \ddot{s})^2 du.$$

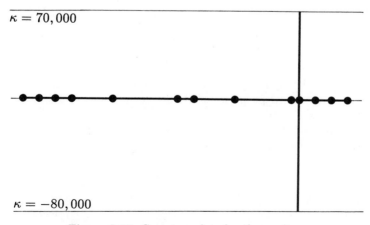

$\kappa = 70,000$

$\kappa = -80,000$

Figure 9.15. Curvature plot of uniform spline.

Figure 9.16. Spline interpolation: A plastic beam, the "spline," is forced to pass through data points, marked by metal weights, the "ducks."

We may integrate the middle term by parts:

$$2 \int_{u_0}^{u_L} \ddot{s}(\ddot{y} - \ddot{s})\mathrm{d}u = \ddot{s}(\dot{y} - \dot{s}) \Big|_{u_0}^{u_L} - \int_{u_0}^{u_L} \dddot{s}(\dot{y} - \dot{s})\mathrm{d}u.$$

The first expression vanishes because of the common end conditions. In the second expression, $\dddot{s}$ is piecewise constant:

$$\int_{u_0}^{u_L} \dddot{s}(\dot{y} - \dot{s})\mathrm{d}u = \sum_{j=0}^{L-1} \dddot{s}_j (y - s) \Big|_{u_0}^{u_L}.$$

All terms in the sum vanish because both **s** and **y** interpolate. Since

$$\int_{u_0}^{u_L} (\ddot{y} - \ddot{s})^2 \mathrm{d}u > 0$$

for continuous $\ddot{y} \neq \ddot{s}$,

$$\int_{u_0}^{u_L} (\ddot{y})^2 \mathrm{d}u \geq \int_{u_0}^{u_L} (\ddot{s})^2 \mathrm{d}u, \qquad (9.25)$$

we have proved the claimed minimum property.

While the minimum property of splines is important – it has spurred substantial research activity – one should not overlook that it is artificial: the replacement of the actual strain energy measure E by $\hat{E}$ is motivated by the desire for mathematical simplicity. The curvature of a curve is given by

$$\kappa(u) = \frac{||\dot{\mathbf{x}} \wedge \ddot{\mathbf{x}}||}{||\dot{\mathbf{x}}||^3}.$$

If $||\dot{\mathbf{x}}|| \approx 1$, then $||\ddot{\mathbf{x}}||$ is a good approximation to κ. This means, however, that the curve must be parametrized according to arc length; see (11.7). This assumption is not very realistic for cubic splines; see Problems.

```
        beta[2] =1.0;
        alpha[2]=0.0;
        gamma[2]=0.0;
        return;
}
/* the rest does the cases l>2.  */

delta_im1=(knot[1]-knot[0]);
delta_i  =(knot[2]-knot[1]);
delta_ip1=(knot[3]-knot[2]);
sum = delta_im1+delta_i;

beta[0]=1.0; gamma[0]=0.0;    /*  this gives first row of matrix. */

alpha[1]=delta_i*delta_i/sum;
beta[1] =(delta_i*delta_im1)/sum
        + delta_im1*(delta_i+delta_ip1)
        / (sum+delta_ip1);
gamma[1]=delta_im1*delta_im1/(sum+delta_ip1);

alpha[1]=alpha[1]/sum;       /* This creates the second  */
beta[1] =beta[1]/sum;        /* row in the matrix.       */
gamma[1]=gamma[1]/sum;

/*Now for the main loop:    */
for(i=2; i<l1; i++)
{
    delta_im2=(knot[i-1]-knot[i-2]);    /* delta_i_minus_2 */
    delta_im1=(knot[i]  -knot[i-1]);    /* delta_i_minus_1 */
    delta_i  =(knot[i+1]-knot[i]);      /* delta_i         */
    delta_ip1=(knot[i+2]-knot[i+1]);    /* delta_i_plus_1  */

    sum = delta_im1+delta_i;

    alpha[i]=delta_i*delta_i/(delta_im2 +sum);
    beta[i] =delta_i*(delta_im2+delta_im1)
        /(delta_im2 + sum)
        +
         delta_im1*(delta_i+delta_ip1)
        /(sum + delta_ip1);
    gamma[i]=delta_im1*delta_im1
        /(sum + delta_ip1);

    alpha[i]=alpha[i]/sum;       /* This creates the i-th  */
    beta[i] =beta[i]/sum;        /* row of the matrix.     */
```

```
        gamma[i]=gamma[i]/sum;
    }


    /*   special care at the end:   */
    delta_im2=knot[1-2]-knot[1-3];
    delta_im1=knot[11]-knot[1-2];
    delta_i  =knot[1]-knot[11];
    sum      =delta_im1+delta_i;

    alpha[11]=delta_i*delta_i/(delta_im2+sum);
    beta[11] =delta_i*(delta_im2+delta_im1)/(delta_im2   + sum)
              +
             delta_im1*delta_i / sum;
    gamma[11]=delta_im1*delta_im1/sum;

    alpha[11]=alpha[11]/sum;
    beta[11] =beta[11]/sum;
    gamma[11]=gamma[11]/sum;

    alpha[1]=0.0; beta[1]=1.0; gamma[1]=0.0;   /* last row.  */
}
```

The next routine performs the LU-decomposition of the matrix from the previous routine. (Note that we do not generate a full matrix but rather three linear arrays!)

```
void l_u_system(alpha,beta,gamma,l,up,low)
/*      perform LU decomposition of tridiagonal system with
    lower diagonal alpha, diagonal beta, upper diagonal gamma.

Input: alpha,beta,gamma: the coefficient matrix entries
       l:                matrix size [0,l]x[0,l]
Output:low:              L-matrix entries
       up:               U-matrix entries
*/
    float alpha[],beta[],gamma[],low[],up[];
    int l;
{
    int i;

    up[0]=beta[0];
    for(i=1; i<=l; i++)
    {
        low[i]=alpha[i]/up[i-1];
        up[i] =beta[i]-low[i]*gamma[i-1];
    }
}
```

Finally, the routine that solves the system for the B-spline coefficients $\mathbf{d}_i$:

```
solve_system(up,low,gamma,l,rhs,d)
/*   solve  tridiagonal linear system
     of size (l+1)(l+1) whose LU decomposition has entries up and low,
     and whose right hand side is rhs, and whose original matrix
     had gamma as  its upper diagonal. Solution is d[0],...,d[l+2].
Input: up,low,gamma:  as above.
       l:             size of system: l+1 eqs in l+1 unknowns.
       rhs:           right hand side, i.e, data points with end
                      'tangent Bezier points' in rhs[1] and rhs[l+1].
Output:d:             solution vector.
Note shift in indexing from text! Both rhs and d are from 0 to l+2.
*/
     float up[],low[],gamma[],rhs[],d[];
     int l;
{
     int i;
     float aux[20];

     d[0] = rhs[0];  /* first data point = first  B-spline vertex */
     d[1] = rhs[1];  /* second data point= second B-spline vertex */

     /* forward substitution:  */
     aux[0]=rhs[1];
     for(i=1; i<=l; i++) aux[i]=rhs[i+1]-low[i]*aux[i-1];

     /* backward substitution:  */
     d[l+1]=aux[l]/up[l];
     for(i=l-1; i>0; i--) d[i+1]=(aux[i]-gamma[i]*d[i+2])/up[i];

                       /* last two data points = last two */
     d[l+2]=rhs[l+2]; /* B-spline vertices.              */
}
```

In case Bessel ends are desired instead of clamped ends, here is the code:

```
void bessel_ends(data,knot,l)
/*     Computes B-spline points data[1] and data[l+1]
       according to bessel end condition.

Input: data:  sequence of data coordinates data[0] to data[l+2].
              Note that data[1] and data[l+1] are expected to
              be empty, as they will be filled by this routine.
              They correspond to the Bezier points bez[1] and bez[31-1].
```

```
            knot: knot sequence
            l:    number of intervals
Output: data: now including ''tangent Bezier points'' data[1], data[l+1].
*/
      float data[], knot[];
      int l;
{
      float alpha, beta; int i;

      if (l==1)
      {/*  This is not really Bessel, but then what do you do
           when you have only one interval? -- make it linear!
       */
           data[1]= (2.0*data[0] + data[3])/3.0;
           data[2]= (2.0*data[3] + data[0])/3.0;
      }
      else if (l==2)
      {
           /* beginning:   */
           alpha= (knot[2]-knot[1])/(knot[2]-knot[0]);
           beta = 1.0 - alpha;

           data[1]=(data[2]-alpha*alpha*data[0]-beta*beta*data[4])
           /(2.0*alpha*beta);
           data[1]=2.0*(alpha*data[0]+beta*data[1])/3.0 + data[0]/3.0;

           /* end:  */
           alpha= (knot[2]-knot[1])/(knot[2]-knot[0]);
           beta = 1.0 - alpha;

           data[3]=(data[2]-alpha*alpha*data[0]-beta*beta*data[4])
           /(2.0*alpha*beta);

           data[3]=2.0*(alpha*data[3]+beta*data[4])/3.0+data[4]/3.0
      }

      else    /* the general case */

      {
           /* beginning:    */
           alpha= (knot[2]-knot[1])/(knot[2]-knot[0]);
           beta = 1.0 - alpha;

           data[1]=(data[2]-alpha*alpha*data[0]-beta*beta*data[3])
           /(2.0*alpha*beta);
           data[1]=2.0*(alpha*data[0]+beta*data[1])/3.0 + data[0]/3.0;
```

```
      /* end:   */
      alpha= (knot[1]-knot[1-1])/(knot[1]-knot[1-2]);
      beta = 1.0 - alpha;

      data[1+1]=(data[1]-alpha*alpha*data[1-1]-beta*beta*data[1+2])
      /(2.0*alpha*beta);

      data[1+1]=2.0*(alpha*data[1+1]+beta*data[1+2])/3.0+data[1+2]/3.0
   }


}
```

The centripetal parametrization is achieved by the following routine:

```
void parameters(data_x,data_y,l,knot)
/*   Finds a centripetal parametrization for a given set
     of 2D data points.
Input:     data_x, data_y: input points, numbered from 0 to l+2.
     l:                     number of intervals.
Output:    knot:            knot sequence. Note: not (knot[l]=1.0)!
Note:      data_x[1], data_x[l+1] are not used! Same for data_y.
*/
     float data_x[], data_y[],knot[];
     int l;
{
     int i,  l1,l2;   /*In the following, special care must be taken */
     float delta;     /* at the ends because of the data structure   */
                      /* used. See note above.                       */
     l1= l-1; l2 = l+2;
     knot[0] = 0.0;      /* initialize -- arbitrary */

     delta=sqrt((data_x[2]-data_x[0])*(data_x[2]-data_x[0])
               +(data_y[2]-data_y[0])*(data_y[2]-data_y[0]));
     knot[1]= sqrt(delta);                /* leave out this sqrt
                                          if you want chord length.*/

     for(i=2; i<l; i++)
     {
         delta=sqrt((data_x[i+1]-data_x[i])*(data_x[i+1]-data_x[i])
                   +(data_y[i+1]-data_y[i])*(data_y[i+1]-data_y[i]));

         knot[i]=knot[i-1]+sqrt(delta);/*leave out this sqrt
                                       if you want chord length.*/
     }
```

```
delta=sqrt((data_x[12]-data_x[1])*(data_x[12]-data_x[1])
            +(data_y[12]-data_y[1])*(data_y[12]-data_y[1]));
knot[l]= knot[l-1]+sqrt(delta);        /* leave out this sqrt
                                          if you want chord length.*/

}
```

A calling sequence that utilizes the above programs might look like this:

```
parameters(data_x,data_y,l,knot);

set_up_system(knot,l,alpha,beta,gamma);

l_u_system(alpha,beta,gamma,l,up,low);

bessel_ends(data_x,knot,l);
bessel_ends(data_y,knot,l);

solve_system(up,low,gamma,l,data_x,bspl_x);
solve_system(up,low,gamma,l,data_y,bspl_y);
```

Here, we solved the 2D-interpolation problem with given data points in data_x, data_y, a knot sequence knot, and the resulting B-spline polygon in bspl_x, bspl_y.

9.7   Problems

1. Show that interpolating splines reproduce straight lines – that they have *linear precision*. (Provided the end conditions are clamped and the tangents are read off the straight line.)

2. Show that they also have quadratic and cubic precision.

3. Try the following: instead of prescribing end conditions at both ends, prescribe first and second derivative at u_0. The interpolant can then be built up segment by segment. Discuss the numerical aspects of this method.

4. Any curve may be reparametrized in terms of its arc length s. Show that a polynomial curve of degree $n > 1$ cannot be polynomial in terms of its arc length s. (See Chapter 11 for the arc length parametrization.)

5. What happens if you replace the knot sequence $u_0, u_1, \ldots, u_L$ by the reversed knot sequence $u_L, u_{L-1}, \ldots, u_0$ but leave the data points in their original ordering? Explain.

10

B-splines

B-splines were investigated as early as the nineteenth century by N. Loba-chevsky (see Renyi [296], p. 165); they were constructed as convolutions of certain probability distributions.[1] In 1946, I.J. Schoenberg [318] used B-splines for statistical data smoothing, and his paper started the modern theory of spline approximation. For the purposes of this book, the discovery of the recurrence relations for B-splines by C. de Boor [97], M. Cox [89], and L. Mansfield was one of the most important developments in this theory. The recurrence relations were first used by Gordon and Riesenfeld [181] in the context of parametric B-spline curves.

This chapter presents a theory for arbitrary degree B-spline curves. The original development of these curves makes use of divided differences and is mathematically involved (see de Boor [98]). A different approach to B-splines was taken by de Boor and Hollig [100]; they used the recurrence relations for B-splines as the starting point for the theory. In this chapter, the theory of B-splines is based on an even more fundamental concept: the Boehm knot insertion algorithm [54]. Another interesting new approach to B-splines is the *blossoming* method proposed by L. Ramshaw [293] and, in a different form, by P. de Casteljau [104].

Warning: *subscripts in this chapter differ from those in Chapter 7! For*

---

[1] However, those were only defined over a very special knot sequence.

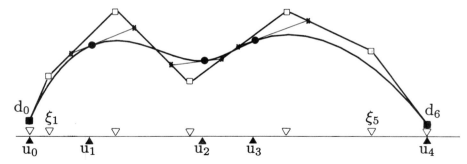

Figure 10.1. B-splines: a nonparametric C^2 cubic spline curve with its B-spline polygon. (In the context of this chapter, the end knots are of multiplicity three.)

the cubic and quadratic cases special subscripts are useful, but the general theory is easier to explain with the notation used here.[2]

10.1 Motivation

Figure 10.1 shows a C^2 cubic spline (nonparametric) with its B-spline polygon. The relationship between the polygon and the curve was discussed in Section 7.9. In that section, we were interested in the parametric case, whereas now we will restrict ourselves to nonparametric (functional) curves of the form $y = f(u)$. The reason is that much of the B-spline theory is explained more naturally in this setting.

In Section 5.5, we considered nonparametric Bézier curves. Recall that over the interval $[u_i, u_{i+1}]$, the abscissae of the Bézier points are $u_i + j\Delta u_i/n$; $j = 0, \ldots, n$. Two cubic Bézier functions that are defined over $[u_{i-1}, u_i]$ and $[u_i, u_{i+1}]$ are C^2 at u_i if an auxiliary point $\mathbf{d}_i$ can be constructed from both curve segments as discussed in Section 7.6. Some of the points $\mathbf{d}_i$ are shown in Figure 10.1. Section 7.6 tells us how to compute the $y-$ values of these points. Using the same reasoning for the $u-$ coordinate $d_i^{(u)}$ (see Problems), we find the abscissae value ξ_i for $\mathbf{d}_i$ to be

$$\xi_i = d_i^{(u)} = \frac{1}{3}(u_{i-1} + u_i + u_{i+1}); \quad i = 1, 2, 3.[3] \tag{10.1}$$

We can now give an algorithm for the "design" of a cubic B-spline function:

---

[2]In terms of this chapter, we used end knots of multiplicity two (quadratic case) or three (cubic case) in Chapter 7. The coefficients there started with the subscript $i = -1$; here, they will start with $i = 0$.

[3]This notation is in harmony with the cubic case of Section 7.6; we will change notation for the general case soon!

1. **Given** knots u_i.

2. **Find** abscissae $\xi_i = \frac{1}{3}(u_{i-1} + u_i + u_{i+1})$.

3. **Define** real numbers d_i to obtain a polygon with vertices (ξ_i, d_i).

4. **Evaluate** this polygon (= piecewise linear function) at the abscissae of the inner Bézier points. This produces a refined polygon, consisting of the inner Bézier points.

5. **Evaluate** the refined polygon at the knots u_i, the abscissae for the junction Bézier points. We now have the junction Bézier points.

After step 5, we have generated a C^2 piecewise cubic Bézier function. In a similar manner, we could generate a C^1 piecewise quadratic Bézier function. In this chapter, we will aim for a generalization of the above definition of piecewise polynomials to include arbitrary degrees and arbitrary differentiability classes.

10.2   Knot Insertion

We will now define an algorithm to "refine" a piecewise linear function. Later, this piecewise linear function will be interpreted as a B-spline polygon, but at this point, we shall only discuss an algorithm that produces one piecewise linear function from another.

Suppose that we are given a number n (later the degree of the B-spline curve) and a number L (later related to the number of polynomial segments of the B-spline curve). Suppose also that we are given a nondecreasing *knot sequence*

$$u_0, \ldots, u_{L+2n-2}.$$

Not all of the u_i have to be distinct. If $u_i = \cdots = u_{i+r-1}$, i.e., if r successive knots coincide, we say that u_i has *multiplicity* r. If a knot does not coincide with any other knot, we say that it is *simple*, or that it has multiplicity one.

When we define B-spline curves later, we will use only the interval $[u_{n-1}, \ldots, u_{L+n-1}]$ as their domain. These knots are the "domain knots." We call L the potential number of curve segments — if all domain knots are simple, L denotes the number of domain intervals; for each domain knot multiplicity, the number of domain intervals drops by one. The sum of all domain knot multiplicities is related to L by

$$\sum_{i=n-1}^{L+n-1} r_i = L + 1,$$

where r_i is the multiplicity of the domain knot u_i.

We shall illustrate the interplay between knot multiplicities and the number of domain intervals by the following examples:

Let $n = 3$, $L = 3$, and

$$\{u_0, ..., u_7\} = \{0, 1, 2, 3, 4, 5, 6, 7\}.$$

All knots are simple, so the number of domain intervals is three.

Leaving n and L unchanged, consider

$$\{u_0, ..., u_7\} = \{0, 1, 2, 3, 3, 5, 6, 7\}.$$

In this knot sequence, $u_3 = u_4$, thus $r_3 = 2$, and we only have two domain intervals.

The multiplicities of the non-domain knots do not affect the number of domain intervals: If we set

$$\{u_0, ..., u_7\} = \{0, 0, 0, 3, 4, 7, 7, 7\},$$

then u_0 and u_5 both have multiplicity three; but they are listed only once each in the domain knot sequence, which is

$$\{u_2, u_3, u_4, u_5\} = \{0, 3, 4, 7\}.$$

Thus we have three domain intervals.

We now define $n + L$ *Greville abscissae* ξ_i by

$$\xi_i = \frac{1}{n}(u_i + \ldots + u_{i+n-1}); \quad i = 0, \ldots, L + n - 1. \tag{10.2}$$

The Greville abscissae are averages of the knots. The number of Greville abscissae equals the number of successive n−tuples of knots in the knot sequence.

We next assume that we are given ordinates d_i, also called *de Boor ordinates*, over the Greville abscissae and hence a polygon P consisting of the points (ξ_i, d_i); $i = 0, \ldots, L + n - 1$. This polygon is a piecewise linear function with breakpoints at the Greville abscissae.Figure 10.2 shows

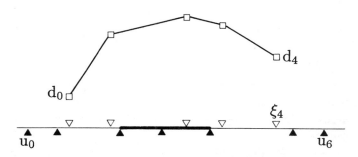

Figure 10.2. Greville abscissae: for various knot sequences and degrees, the corresponding Greville abscissae together with the polygon P are shown. Top left: $n = 1, L = 1$. Top right, $n = 2, L = 2$. Bottom: $n = 3, L = 2$.

some examples. Note how the polygon is not defined over the original knot sequence, but rather over the Greville abscissae.

We will now define our basic polygon manipulation technique, the knot insertion algorithm. As before, at this point we are only concerned with polygons, not with B-spline curves! Suppose a real number $u \in [u_{n-1}, \ldots, u_{L+n-1}]$ is given and we want to *insert* it into the knot sequence. We call the new knot sequence a *refined* knot sequence. It defines a new set of Greville abscissae, called ξ_i^u. Each ξ_i^u will be the abscissa for a vertex (ξ_i^u, d_i^u) of the new polygon P^u. Here is the knot insertion algorithm:

Knot insertion, informal: compute the Greville abscissae ξ_i^u for the refined knot sequence. Evaluate P there to obtain new ordinates $d_i^u = P(\xi_i^u)$. The *refined polygon* P^u is then formed by the points (ξ_i^u, d_i^u). The d_i^u are given by (10.4) below.

Figure 10.3 shows an example of the knot insertion procedure for the quadratic case. It is possible to insert the knot u again – it will then become a *double knot*, or a knot of multiplicity two, which simply means it

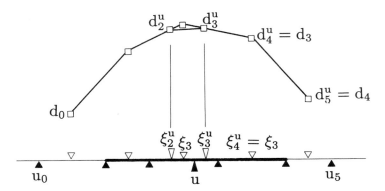

Figure 10.3. Knot insertion: the new knot is u; the new Greville abscissae are marked by larger icons. Old knot sequence: $u_0, u_1, u_2, u_3, u_4, u_5$. New sequence: $u_0, u_1, u_2, u, u_3, u_4, u_5$. In this example, $n = 2, L = 3$.

is listed twice in the knot sequence. As another example of knot insertion, Figure 10.4 shows how the knot u is inserted again.

We shall formalize the knot insertion algorithm soon, but we can already deduce some properties:

- The polygon P^u is obtained from P by *piecewise linear interpolation* (see Section 2.4).

- As a consequence, knot insertion is a *variation diminishing* process: no straight line intersects P^u more often than P.

- As a further consequence, knot insertion is *convexity preserving*: if P is convex, so is P^u.

- Knot insertion is a *local* process: P differs from P^u only in the vicinity of u. (The exact definition of vicinity being a function of the degree n.)

We are now ready for an algorithmic definition of knot insertion. It is mostly intended for use in coding. The informal description above conveys the same information.

Knot insertion algorithm:

Given: $u \in [u_{n-1}, \ldots, u_{L+n-1}]$.

Find: refined polygon P^u, defined over the refined knot sequence that includes u.

1. Find the largest I with $u_I \leq u < u_{I+1}$. If $u = u_I$ and u_I is of multiplicity n : **stop**. Else:

2. For $i = 0, \ldots, I - n + 1$, set $\xi_i^u = \xi_i$.

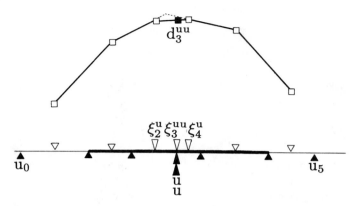

Figure 10.4. Knot insertion: the knot u is inserted again. Old knot sequence: $u_0, u_1, u_2, u, u_3, u_4, u_5$. New sequence: $u_0, u_1, u_2, u, u, u_3, u_4, u_5$.

3. For $i = I - n + 2, \ldots, I + 1$, set

$$\xi_i^u = \frac{1}{n}(u_i + \ldots + u_{i+n-2}) + \frac{1}{n}u.$$

4. For $i = I + 2, \ldots, L + n$, set $\xi_i^u = \xi_{i-1}$.

5. For $i = 0, \ldots, L + n$, set $d_i^u = P(\xi_i^u)$.

6. Renumber the knot sequence to include u as u_{I+1}.

7. Replace L by $L + 1$.

Step 5 only involves actual computation for $i = I - n + 2, \ldots, I + 1$. A formula for $P(\xi_i^u)$ is provided by (10.4). Before we can proceed further, we must verify that we have defined a *consistent* knot insertion process. If we insert two knots, the final result must be independent of the order in which the knots were inserted. More precisely: let u and v be knots to be inserted. Inserting u yields P^u; then, inserting v yields P^{uv}. Inserting v first and u second yields a polygon P^{vu}. We need to establish that $P^{uv} = P^{vu}$. The following outlines the main steps of the proof of that statement.

Let u be in the interval $[u_I, u_{I+1}]$. First, one establishes that $\xi_{i-1} \le \xi_i^u \le \xi_i$. Thus d_i^u is obtained by linear interpolation

$$d_i^u = \frac{\xi_i - \xi_i^u}{\xi_i - \xi_{i-1}} d_{i-1} + \frac{\xi_i^u - \xi_{i-1}}{\xi_i - \xi_{i-1}} d_i; \quad i = I - n + 2, \ldots, I + 1. \qquad (10.3)$$

We invoke (10.2):

$$d_i^u = \frac{\sum_{j=i}^{i+n-1} u_j - \sum_{j=i}^{i+n-2} u_j - u}{u_{i+n-1} - u_{i-1}} d_{i-1} + \frac{\sum_{j=i}^{i+n-2} u_j + u - \sum_{j=i-1}^{i+n-2} u_j}{u_{i+n-1} - u_{i-1}} d_i$$

and simplify:

$$d_i^u = \frac{u_{i+n-1} - u}{u_{i+n-1} - u_{i-1}} d_{i-1} + \frac{u - u_{i-1}}{u_{i+n-1} - u_{i-1}} d_i; \quad i = I - n + 2, \dots, I + 1.$$
(10.4)

As for the second knot v, assume that it is in the interval $[u_J, u_{J+1}]$. We obtain for the d_i^v:

$$d_i^v = \frac{u_{i+n-1} - v}{u_{i+n-1} - u_{i-1}} d_{i-1} + \frac{v - u_{i-1}}{u_{i+n-1} - u_{i-1}} d_i; \quad i = J - n + 2, \dots, J + 1.$$

If u and v are far enough apart – more precisely if the two intervals $[u_{I-n+2}, u_{I+1}]$ and $[u_{J-n+2}, u_{J+1}]$ are disjoint – the two insertion processes do not interfere with each other and there is nothing to prove.

Otherwise, we compute

$$d_{i+1}^{uv} = \frac{u_{i+n-1} - v}{u_{i+n-1} - u_i} d_i^u + \frac{v - u_i}{u_{i+n-1} - u_i} d_{i+1}^u$$

and

$$d_{i+1}^{vu} = \frac{u_{i+n-1} - u}{u_{i+n-1} - u_i} d_i^v + \frac{u - u_i}{u_{i+n-1} - u_i} d_{i+1}^v.$$

We must show that these two expressions are equal. The proof is an exercise in algebra and is omitted here. For the more geometrically inclined, the use of Menelaos' Theorem as mentioned in Section 7.3 will also produce a proof.

In summary, we have shown that the knot insertion algorithm is *order independent*. This fact will be needed throughout our development of B-splines.

10.3   The de Boor Algorithm

In the previous section, we described an operation to manipulate polygons. We shall now use this operation for the definition of B-spline curves. Recall Figure 10.4. There, a knot u was reinserted so that its multiplicity was raised to two. What happens if we reinsert u again? The answer is: nothing. No new Greville abscissae are generated.

In general, for degree n, repeated insertion of a knot u no longer changes the polygon after the multiplicity of u has reached n. We use this fact in the algorithmic definition of a special function, called a B-spline curve.[4] The algorithm used in this definition is called the de Boor algorithm:

---

[4] We use the term "curve" in a loose way; this is to emphasize that the theory developed here carries over to parametric curves easily.

Figure 10.5. The de Boor algorithm: example with $n = 3, L = 2$.

de Boor algorithm, informal: To evaluate an nth degree B-spline curve (given by its de Boor ordinates and knot sequence) at a parameter value u, insert u into the knot sequence until it has multiplicity n. The corresponding polygon vertex is the desired function value.

Before we proceed further, one comment should be made. What is meant by "corresponding polygon vertex?" If a knot u_i is of multiplicity n, then one of the Greville abscissae coincides with u_i, namely $\xi_i = \frac{1}{n}(u_i + \cdots + u_{i+n-1}) = u_i$. Consequently, the polygon has a vertex (u_i, d_i), and d_i is the function value of the B-spline curve at u_i. Figure 10.5 gives an illustration. We now realize that we have encountered an example of the de Boor algorithm earlier: see Figure 10.4 for the case $n = 2$.

Note that the de Boor algorithm needs fewer insertions if the parameter value u is already an element of the knot sequence. If it has multiplicity r, then only $n - r$ reinsertions are necessary to make u a knot of multiplicity n.

We are now ready for a formal definition. Let us denote a B-spline curve of degree n with control polygon P by B_nP, and its value at parameter value u by $[B_nP](u)$. We will only define the curve for values of u between u_{n-1} and u_{L+n-1}.

de Boor algorithm: Let $u \in [u_I, u_{I+1}) \subset [u_{n-1}, u_{L+n-1}]$. Define

$$d_i^k(u) = \frac{u_{i+n-k} - u}{u_{i+n-k} - u_{i-1}} d_{i-1}^{k-1}(u) + \frac{u - u_{i-1}}{u_{i+n-k} - u_{i-1}} d_i^{k-1}(u) \quad (10.5)$$

for $k = 1, \ldots, n - r$, and $i = I - n + k + 1, \ldots, I + 1$. Then

$$s(u) = [B_nP](u) = d_{I+1}^{n-r}(u) \quad (10.6)$$

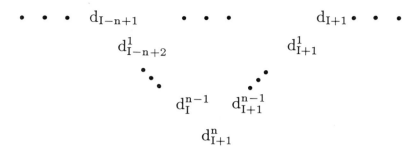

Figure 10.6. The de Boor algorithm: for $u \in [u_I, u_{I+1}]$, the scheme of generated intermediate points is shown.

is the value of the B-spline curve at parameter value u. Here, r denotes the multiplicity of u in case it was already one of the knots. If it was not, set $r = 0$. As usual, we set $d_i^0(u) = d_i$.

C. de Boor [97] published this algorithm in 1972. It is the B-spline analog of the de Casteljau algorithm. Figure 10.6 shows schematically which d_i are involved in (10.5).

In our description of the de Boor algorithm, we did not renumber the knot sequence and the control points at each level, since our interest is only in the final result $d_{I+1}^{n-r}(u)$. Of course, at each level k, we generate a new control polygon that describes the same B-spline curve as the previous control polygon did. In particular, for $k = 1$, we obtain the knot insertion algorithm.

Figure 10.5 shows an example. We can also view that example as a case of multiple knot insertion. In that context, we have constructed several polygons that describe the same B-spline curve:

k=1: the de Boor ordinates $d_0, d_1^1, d_2^1, d_3^1, d_3, d_4$ corresponding to the knot sequence $u_0, u_1, u_2, u, u_3, u_4, u_5, u_6$;

k=2: the de Boor ordinates $d_0, d_1^1, d_2^2, d_3^2, d_3^1, d_3, d_4$ corresponding to the knot sequence $u_0, u_1, u_2, u, u, u_3, u_4, u_5, u_6$;

k=3: the de Boor ordinates $d_0, d_1^1, d_2^2, d_3^3, d_3^2, d_3^1, d_3, d_4$ corresponding to the knot sequence $u_0, u_1, u_2, u, u, u, u_3, u_4, u_5, u_6$.

Let us next examine an important special case. Consider the knot sequence

$$0 = u_0 = u_1 = \cdots = u_{n-1} < u_n = u_{n+1} = \cdots = u_{2n-1} = 1.$$

Here, both u_0 and u_n have multiplicity n. We note that the Greville abscissae are given by

$$\xi_i = \frac{1}{n} \sum_{j=i}^{i+n-1} u_i = \frac{i}{n}; \quad i = 0, \ldots, n.$$

For $0 \leq u \leq 1$, the de Boor algorithm sets $I = n - 1$ and

$$d_i^k(u) = \frac{u_{i+n-k} - u}{u_{i+n-k} - u_{i-1}} d_{i-1}^{k-1} + \frac{u - u_{i-1}}{u_{i+n-k} - u_{i-1}} d_i^{k-1}.$$

Since $n - 1 \geq i - k \geq 0$, we have $u_{i+n-k} = 1, u_{i-1} = 0$ for all i, k; thus

$$d_i^k(u) = (1 - u)d_{i-1}^{k-1} + ud_i^{k-1}; \quad k = 1, \ldots, n. \tag{10.7}$$

This is the de Casteljau algorithm![5] Schoenberg [319] first observed this in 1967, although in a different context. Riesenfeld [299] and Gordon and Riesenfeld [181] are more accessible references. We will be able to draw several important conclusions from this special case. First, we note that the restriction to the interval $[0, 1]$ is not essential: all our constructions are invariant under affine parameter transformations.

Thus, if two adjacent knots in any knot sequence both have multiplicity n, the corresponding B-spline curve is a Bézier curve between those two knots. The B-spline control polygon is the Bézier polygon; the Greville abscissae are equally spaced between the two knots.

After we inserted u until it was of multiplicity n, the initial de Boor polygon (or Bézier polygon, in this case,) was transformed into two Bézier polygons, defining the same curve as did the initial polygon. Thus we have another proof for the fact that the de Casteljau algorithm subdivides Bézier curves.

For a B-spline curve over an arbitrary knot vector, we can always reinsert the given knots into the knot sequence until each knot is of multiplicity n. The B-spline polygon corresponding to that knot sequence is the *piecewise Bézier polygon* of the curve. We have thus shown that *B-spline curves are piecewise polynomial over* $[u_{n-1}, u_{L+n-1}]$. The method of constructing the piecewise Bézier polygon from the B-spline polygon via knot insertion was developed by W. Boehm [53]. A different method was created by P. Sablonnière [313].

---

[5]The subscripts are different – this is simply a matter of notation, however.

10.4   Smoothness of B-spline Curves

Now that we know that B-spline curves are piecewise polynomials of degree n each, we shall investigate their smoothness: how often is a B-spline curve differentiable at a point u? Obviously, we only need to consider the breakpoints – the curve is infinitely often differentiable at all other points.

In order to answer this question, simply reconsider the above example (10.7). Now, let u be an existing knot of multiplicity r. Our knot sequence is:

$$\begin{aligned}
0 &= u_0 = u_1 = \cdots = u_{n-1} \\
&< u_n = u_{n+1} = \ldots = u_{n+r-1} \\
&< u_{n+r} = u_{n+r+1} = \ldots = u_{2n+r-1} = 1;
\end{aligned}$$

the knot to be reinserted is $u = u_n$. The de Boor algorithm only consists of $n - r$ levels. Taking into account the multiplicities of the end knots, we have

$$d_i^k(u) = (1 - u)d_{i-1}^{k-1} + u d_i^{k-1}; \quad k = 1, \ldots, n - r. \tag{10.8}$$

These are the $n - r$ last levels in a de Casteljau algorithm. Therefore the two polynomial curve segments meeting at u are at least $n - r$ times differentiable there (see Sections 4.5 and 7.2).

As above, we note that the restriction to the interval $[0, 1]$ is not essential. If we want to investigate the smoothness of an arbitrary B-spline curve at a knot, we can always force its two neighbors to be of multiplicity n (without changing the curve!) and apply our arguments.

Thus *a B-spline curve is (at least) C^{n-r} at knots with multiplicity r*. In particular, the curve is $n - 1$ times continuously differentiable if all knots are simple, i.e., of multiplicity one. Figure 10.7 shows a cubic $(n = 3)$ B-spline curve over a knot sequence that has several multiple entries. The triple knots at the ends force d_0 and d_{10} to be on the curve.

10.5   The B-spline Basis

Consider a knot sequence $u_0, \ldots, u_K$ and the set of piecewise polynomials of degree n defined over it, where each function in that set is $n - r_i$ times continuously differentiable at knot u_i. All these piecewise polynomials form a linear space. Its dimension is

$$\dim = (n + 1) + \sum_{i=1}^{K-1} r_i. \tag{10.9}$$

For a proof, suppose we want to construct an element of our piecewise polynomial linear space. The number of independent constraints that we

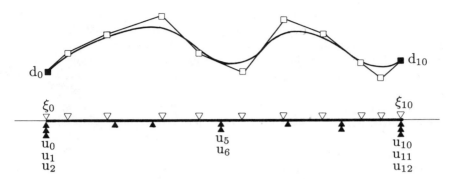

Figure 10.7. Multiple knots: the effects of multiple knots on the curve. Here, $n = 3, L = 8$.

can impose on an arbitrary element, or its number of *degrees of freedom*, is equal to the dimension of the considered linear space. We may start by completely specifying the first polynomial segment, defined over $[u_0, u_1]$; we can do this in $n + 1$ ways, which is the number of coefficients that we can specify for a polynomial of degree n. The next polynomial segment, defined over $[u_1, u_2]$, must agree with the first segment in position and $n - r_1$ derivatives at u_1, thus leaving only r_1 coefficients to be chosen for the second segment. Continuing further, we obtain (10.9).

We are interested in B-spline curves that are piecewise polynomials over the special knot sequence $[u_{n-1}, u_{L+n-1}]$. The dimension of the linear space that they form is $L + n$, which also happens to be the number of B-spline vertices for a curve in this space. If we can define $L + n$ linearly independent piecewise polynomials in our linear function space, we have found a basis for this space. We proceed as follows.

Define functions $N_i^n(u)$, called *B-splines* by defining their de Boor ordinates to satisfy $d_i = 1$ and $d_j = 0$ for all $j \neq i$. The $N_i^n(u)$ are clearly elements of the linear space formed by all piecewise polynomials over $[u_{n-1}, u_{L+n-1}]$. They have *local support*:

$$N_i^n(u) \neq 0 \quad \text{only if} \quad u \in [u_{i-1}, u_{i+n}].$$

This follows because knot insertion, and hence the de Boor algorithm, is a local operation; if a new knot is inserted, only those Greville abscissae that are "close" will be affected.

B−splines also have *minimal support:* if a piecewise polynomial with the same smoothness properties over the same knot vector has less support than

N_i^n, it must be the zero function. All piecewise polynomials defined over $[u_{i-1}, u_{i+n}]$, the support region of N_i^n, are elements of a function space of dimension $2n+1$, according to (10.9). A support region that is one interval "shorter" defines a function space of dimension $2n$. The requirement of vanishing $n-r_{i-1}$ derivatives at u_{i-1} and of vanishing $n-r_{i+n}$ derivatives at u_{i+n} imposes $2n$ conditions on any element in the linear space of functions over $[u_{i-1}, u_{i+n-1}]$. The additional requirement of assuming a nonzero value at some point in the support region raises the number of independent constraints to $2n+1$, too many to be satisfied by an element of the function space with dimension $2n$.

Another important property of the N_i^n is their *linear independence*. In order to show this, we must verify that

$$\sum_{j=0}^{L+n-1} c_j N_j^n(u) \equiv 0 \qquad (10.10)$$

implies $c_j = 0$ for all j. It is sufficient to concentrate on one interval $[u_I, u_{I+1}]$ with $u_I < u_{I+1}$. Because of the local support property of B-splines, (10.10) reduces to

$$\sum_{j=I-n+1}^{I+1} c_j N_j^n(u) \equiv 0 \text{ for } u \in [u_I, u_{I+1}].$$

We have completed our proof if we can show that the linear space of piecewise polynomials defined over $[u_{I-n}, u_{I+n+1}]$ does not contain a nonzero element that vanishes over $[u_I, u_{I+1}]$. Such a piecewise polynomial cannot exist: it would have to be a nonzero local support function over $[u_{I+1}, u_{I+n+1}]$. The existence of such a function would contradict the fact that $B-$splines are of *minimal* local support.

Because the $B-$splines N_i^n are linearly independent, every piecewise polynomial s over $[u_{n-1}, u_{L+n-1}]$ may be written uniquely in the form

$$s(u) = \sum_{j=0}^{L+n-1} d_i N_i^n(u). \qquad (10.11)$$

The $B-$splines thus form a *basis* for this space. This reveals the origin of their name, which is short for *Basis* splines.

10.6   Two Recursion Formulas

We have defined B-spline basis functions in a constructive way: the B-spline N_i^n is defined by the knot sequence and the Greville abscissa ξ_i. The function N_i^n is given by its B-spline control polygon with de Boor ordinates $d_j = \delta_{i,j}$; $j = 0, \ldots, L + n - 1$. From it, we can construct the piecewise Bézier polygon by inserting every knot until it is of multiplicity n. We can then compute values of $N_i^n(u)$ by applying the de Casteljau algorithm to the Bézier polygon corresponding to the interval that u is in. There is a more direct way, which we shall discuss now.

In order to further explore B−splines, let us investigate how they "react" to knot insertion. Let $\hat{u}$ be a new knot inserted into a given knot sequence. Denote the B-splines over the "old" knot sequence by N_i^n, those over the "new" knot sequence by $\hat{N}_i^n$. Note that there is one more element in the set of $\hat{N}_i^n$ than in that of the N_i^n. In fact, the linear space of all piecewise polynomials over the old knot sequence is a subspace of the linear space of all piecewise polynomials over the new sequence. Let N_l^n be an "old" basis function that has $\hat{u}$ in its support. Its B-spline polygon is defined by $d_j = \delta_{j,l}$, where j ranges from 0 to $L + n - 1$ and δ denotes the Kronecker Delta. Its B-spline polygon with respect to the new knot sequence is obtained by the knot insertion process. Only two of the new de Boor ordinates will be different from zero. Equation (10.4) yields

$$\hat{d}_l = \frac{u_{l+n-1} - \hat{u}}{u_{l+n-1} - u_{l-1}} \cdot 0 + \frac{\hat{u} - u_{l-1}}{u_{l+n-1} - u_{l-1}} \cdot 1$$

$$\hat{d}_{l+1} = \frac{u_{l+n} - \hat{u}}{u_{l+n} - u_l} \cdot 1 + \frac{\hat{u} - u_l}{u_{l+n} - u_l} \cdot 0.$$

(Recall that $d_l = 1$, whereas all other $d_j = 0$.) Hence

$$\hat{d}_l = \frac{\hat{u} - u_{l-1}}{u_{l+n-1} - u_{l-1}}$$

$$\hat{d}_{l+1} = \frac{u_{l+n} - \hat{u}}{u_{l+n} - u_l}.$$

Thus we can write N_l^n in terms of $\hat{N}_l^n$ and $\hat{N}_{l+1}^n$:

$$N_l^n(u) = \frac{\hat{u} - u_{l-1}}{u_{l+n-1} - u_{l-1}} \hat{N}_l^n(u) + \frac{u_{l+n} - \hat{u}}{u_{l+n} - u_l} \hat{N}_{l+1}^n(u). \qquad (10.12)$$

This result is due to W. Boehm [54]. It allows us to write B-splines as linear combinations of B-splines over a refined knot sequence.

For the second important recursion formula, we must define an additional B-spline function,[6] N_i^0:

$$N_i^0(u) = \begin{cases} 1 & \text{if } u_{i-1} \le u < u_i \\ 0 & \text{else} \end{cases} \tag{10.13}$$

The announced recursion formula relates B-splines of degree n to B-splines of degree $n - 1$:

$$N_l^n(u) = \frac{u - u_{l-1}}{u_{l+n-1} - u_{l-1}} N_l^{n-1}(u) + \frac{u_{l+n} - u}{u_{l+n} - u_l} N_{l+1}^{n-1}(u). \tag{10.14}$$

In order to prove (10.14), we shall prove the following more general statement:

$$s(u) = \sum_{j=i+r-n+1}^{i+1} d_j^r N_j^{n-r}(u) \tag{10.15}$$

for all $r \in [0, n]$. For its proof, we first check that it is true for $r = n$; this follows from (10.13). By the de Boor algorithm, (10.15) is equivalent to

$$s(u) = \sum_{j=i-n+1+r}^{i+1} (1 - \alpha_j^r) d_{j-1}^{r-1} N_j^{n-r}(u) + \sum_{j=i-n+1+r}^{i+1} \alpha_j^r d_j^{r-1} N_j^{n-r}(u)$$

where

$$\alpha_j^r = \frac{u - u_{i-1}}{u_{i+n-r} - u_{i-1}}.$$

An index transformation yields

$$s(u) = \sum_{j=i-n+r}^{i} (1 - \alpha_{j+1}^r) d_j^{r-1} N_{j+1}^{n-r}(u) + \sum_{j=i-n+1+r}^{i+1} \alpha_j^r d_j^{r-1} N_j^{n-r}(u).$$

Because of the local support of the N_j^{n-r}, this may be changed to

$$s(u) = \sum_{j=i-n+r}^{i+1} (1 - \alpha_{j+1}^r) d_j^{r-1} N_{j+1}^{n-r}(u) + \sum_{j=i-n+r}^{i+1} \alpha_j^r d_j^{r-1} N_j^{n-r}(u).$$

---

[6]See Problem 4!

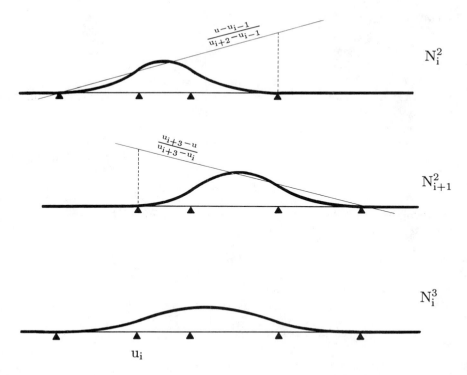

$$N_i^2$$

$$N_{i+1}^2$$

$$N_i^3$$

$$u_i$$

Figure 10.8. The B-spline recursion: two B-splines are combined to form a B-spline of one higher degree.

Hence, by the inductive hypothesis,

$$s(u) = \sum_{j=i-n+r}^{i+1} [\alpha_j^r N_j^{n-r}(u) + (1 - \alpha_{j+1}^r) N_{j+1}^{n-r}(u)] d_j^{r-1}.$$

This step completes the proof of (10.15), since we have now shown that (10.15) holds for $r - 1$ provided that it holds for r. The recurrence (10.14) now follows from comparing (10.15) and (10.6). The development of equation (10.14) is due to L. Mansfield, C. de Boor and M. Cox; see de Boor [97] and [89]. For an illustration of (10.14), see Figure 10.8.

The recursion formula (10.14) shows that a B-spline of degree n is a strictly convex combination of two lower degree ones; it is therefore a very stable formula from a numerical viewpoint. If B-spline curves must be evaluated repeatedly at the same parameter values u_k, it is a good idea to compute the values for $N_i^n(u_k)$ using (10.14) and then to store them.

10.7   Repeated Knot Insertion

We may insert more and more knots into the knot sequence; let us now investigate the effect of such a process. A B-spline curve of degree n is defined over $u_{n-1}, \ldots, u_{L+n-1}$. Let us set $a = u_{n-1}$, $b = u_{L+n-1}$. Let us now insert more knots u_i^r; here r counts the overall number of insertions and i denotes the number of u_i^r in the new knot sequence. After r knot insertions, we have a new polygon P^r that describes the same curve as did the original polygon P. As we insert more and more knots, so as to become dense in $[a, b]$, the sequence of polygons P^r converges to the curve that they all define:

$$\lim_{r \to \infty} P^r = [B_n P]. \tag{10.16}$$

To begin, we recall that a B-spline curve depends only on $d_k, \ldots, d_{k+n}$ over the interval $[u_k, u_{k+1}]$. Then for $u \in [u_k, u_{k+1}]$,

$$\min(d_k, \ldots, d_{k+n}) \leq [B_n P](u) \leq \max(d_k, \ldots, d_{k+n})$$

by the strong convex hull property.

We need to show that for any ϵ, we can find an r such that

$$|P^r(u) - [B_n P](u)| \leq \epsilon \quad \text{for all } u.$$

We know that for any ϵ, we can find an r such that

$$|\xi_{i+1}^r - \xi_i^r| \leq \delta$$

and

$$|P^r(\xi_{i+1}^r) - P^r(\xi_i^r)| \leq \epsilon,$$

since each P^r is continuous. Thus

$$\max[P^r(\xi_i^r), \ldots, P^r(\xi_{i+n}^r)] - \min[P^r(\xi_i^r), \ldots, P^r(\xi_{i+n}^r)] \leq n\epsilon$$

for those i that are relevant to the interval $[u_k, u_{k+1}]$. But we also know that

$$\min(d_i^r) \leq [B_n P](u) \leq \max(d_i^r).$$

Thus,

$$|[B_n P](u) - P_j^r| \leq n\epsilon; \quad j \in [i, \ldots, i+n],$$

which finally yields

$$|[B_n P](u) - P^r(u)| \leq n\epsilon,$$

proving our convergence claim.

The use of repeated knot insertion lies in the *rendering* of B-spline curves. If sufficiently many knots have been inserted into the knot sequence, the resulting control polygon will be arbitrarily close to the curve. Then, instead of plotting the curve directly, one simply plots the refined polygon. In order to have an *adaptive* rendering method, one would control the knot insertion process by inserting more knots where the curve is of high curvature and fewer knots where it is flat.

Of course, B-spline curves may also be *parametric*. All we have to do is use functional B-spline curves (all over the same knot vector) for each component of the parametric curve:

$$\mathbf{x}(u) = \sum_{i=0}^{L+n-1} \mathbf{d}_i N_i^n(u) = \sum_{i=0}^{L+n-1} \begin{bmatrix} d_i^x \\ d_i^y \\ d_i^z \end{bmatrix} N_i^n(u).$$

For $n = 2$ and $n = 3$, these curves have already been described in Chapter 7, although with a different notation that especially suited those cases. General degree B-spline curves enjoy all the properties of the lower degree ones, such as affine invariance and the convex hull property.

An interesting application of repeated knot insertion is due to G. Chaikin [72]. Although this scheme may be described in the context of functional curves, we prefer the more intuitive parametric version. Consider a quadratic B-spline curve over a uniform knot sequence. Insert a new knot at the midpoint of every interval of the knot sequence. If the "old" curve had control vertices $\mathbf{d}_i$ and those of the new one are $\mathbf{d}_i^{(1)}$, it is easy to show that

$$\mathbf{d}_{2i-1}^{(1)} = \frac{3}{4}\mathbf{d}_i + \frac{1}{4}\mathbf{d}_{i-1} \quad \text{and} \quad \mathbf{d}_{2i+1}^{(1)} = \frac{3}{4}\mathbf{d}_i + \frac{1}{4}\mathbf{d}_{i+1}.$$

If this procedure is repeated infinitely often, the resulting sequence of polygons will converge to the original curve, as follows from our previous considerations. Figure 10.9 shows the example of a closed quadratic B-spline curve; two levels of the iteration are shown.

Chaikin's algorithm may be described as *corner-cutting*: At each step, we chisel away the corners of the initial polygon. This process is, on a high level, similar to that of degree elevation for Bézier curves, which is also a convergent process (see Section 5.2). One may ask if corner-cutting processes will always converge to a smooth curve. The answer is "yes," with some mild stipulations on the corner-cutting process, and was first proved by de Boor [96]. One may thus use a corner-cutting procedure to *define* a curve – and only very few of the curves thus generated are piecewise polynomial! Recent work has been carried out by Prautzsch and Micchelli [291] and [256], based on earlier results by de Rham [106], [105].

Figure 10.9. Chaikin's algorithm: starting with the (closed) control polygon of a quadratic B-spline curve, two levels of the Chaikin iteration are shown.

R. Riesenfeld [300] realized that Chaikin's algorithm actually generates uniform quadratic B-spline curves. A general algorithm for the simultaneous insertion of several knots into a B-spline curve has been developed by Cohen, Lyche, and Riesenfeld [83]. This so-called "Oslo algorithm" needs a theory of discrete B-splines for its development (see Bartels *et al.* [34]). The knot insertion algorithm as developed in this chapter is more intuitive and equally powerful.

10.8   Additional Material

After the more theoretical developments of the previous two sections, let us examine some of the properties that we can now derive for B-spline curves.

Linear precision: If $l(u)$ is a straight line of the form $l = au + b$, and if we read off values at the Greville abscissae, the resulting B-spline curve reproduces the straight line:

$$\sum l(\xi_i) N_i^n(u) = l(u).$$

This property is a direct consequence of the de Boor algorithm. It was originally obtained by E. Greville [189], [190] in a different context. The original Greville result is the motivation for the term "Greville abscissae."

Strong convex hull property: Each point on the curve lies in the convex hull of no more than $n + 1$ nearby control points.

Variation diminishing property: The curve is not intersected by any straight line more often than the polygon is. This result has a very simple proof, presented by Lane and Riesenfeld [232]: we may insert every knot until it is of full multiplicity. This is a variation diminishing process, since it is piecewise linear interpolation. Once all knots are of full multiplicity, the B-spline control polygon is the piecewise Bézier polygon, for which we showed the variation diminishing property in Section 5.3.

The parametric case In the parametric case, it is desirable to have u_0 and u_{L+n-1} both of full multiplicity n. This condition forces the first and last control points $\mathbf{d}_0$ and $\mathbf{d}_{L+n-1}$ to lie on the endpoints of the curve. In this way, one has better control of the behavior of the curve at the ends. The spline curves that we discussed in Chapter 7 are all described in this form, although we did not formally make use of knot multiplicities there. If the end knots are allowed to be of lower (even simple) multiplicity, the first and last control vertices do not lie on the curve, and are called "phantom vertices" by Barsky and Thomas [33].

The de Boor algorithm allows a nice geometric description in parametric form. Formally, we perform the algorithm for all components of the control polygon. Geometrically, we may "engrave" parts of the knot sequence on each polygon leg; map the first $n + 1$ subsequent knots onto $\mathbf{d}_0\mathbf{d}_1$, the next subsequent $n + 1$ knots onto $\mathbf{d}_1\mathbf{d}_2$, and so on, until the last subsequent $n + 1$ knots are mapped to the last polygon leg. For example, in Figure 10.10, with $n = 3$ and $L = 5$, the knots $[u_2, u_3, u_4, u_5]$ are mapped to $\mathbf{d}_2\mathbf{d}_3$, whereas $[u_0, u_1, u_2, u_3]$ are mapped to $\mathbf{d}_0\mathbf{d}_1$. The interval $[u_I, u_{I+1}]$ that contains the evaluation parameter u is thus mapped to n polygon legs by n affine maps, which are equivalent to linear interpolation as outlined in Section 2.3. These affine maps take u to the $\mathbf{d}_j^1(u)$. The same procedure is then repeated: consider all sets of subsequent n knots that contain u_I, u_{I+1}. Map them by affine maps to the polygon formed by the $\mathbf{d}_j^1$ and denote the images of u by $\mathbf{d}_j^2$ etc. The final step is to map the interval u_I, u_{I+1} onto $\mathbf{d}_I^{n-1}, \mathbf{d}_{I+1}^{n-1}$ to obtain the point $\mathbf{d}_{I+1}^n$ on the curve.

Finally, a note on how to *store* B-spline curves. It is not convenient to store the knot sequence $\{u_i\}$ and simply list multiple knots as often as indicated by their multiplicity. Roundoff may produce knots that are a small distance apart, yet meant to be identical. It is wiser to store only distinct knots and to note their multiplicities in a second array. From these two arrays, one may compute the original knot sequence when required, e.g., by the de Boor algorithm.

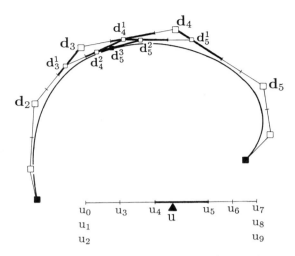

Figure 10.10. The de Boor algorithm in parametric form: all groups of $n + 1 - r$ intervals that contain $[u_4, u_5]$ are mapped onto polygon legs.

10.9 B-spline Basics

Here, we present a collection of the most important formulas and definitions of this chapter. As before, n is the (maximal) degree of each polynomial segment, L is the number of curve segments if all knots in the domain are simple, and, more generally, $L + 1$ is the sum of all domain knot multiplicities.

Knot sequence: $\{u_0, \ldots, u_{L+2n-2}\}$.

Domain: Curve is only defined over $[u_{n-1}, \ldots, u_{L+n-1}]$.

Greville abscissae: $\xi_i = \frac{1}{n}(u_i + \cdots + u_{i+n-1})$.

Support: N_i^n is nonnegative over $[u_{i-1}, u_{i+n}]$.

Control polygon P: $(\xi_i, d_i); \quad i = 0, \ldots, L + n - 1$.

Knot insertion: To insert $u_I \leq u < u_{I+1}$: 1. Find new Greville abscissae $\hat{\xi}_i$. 2. Set new $d_i = P(\hat{\xi}_i)$.

de Boor algorithm: Given $u_I \leq u < u_{I+1}$, set

$$d_i^k(u) = \frac{u_{i+n-k} - u}{u_{i+n-k} - u_{i-1}} d_{i-1}^{k-1}(u) + \frac{u - u_{i-1}}{u_{i+n-k} - u_{i-1}} d_i^{k-1}(u)$$

for $k = 1, \ldots, n - r$, and $i = I - n + k + 1, \ldots, I + 1$. Here, r denotes the multiplicity of u. (Normally, u is not already in the knot sequence; then, $r = 0$.)

Boehm recursion: Let $\hat{u}$ be a new knot; then,

$$N_l^n(u) = \frac{\hat{u} - u_{l-1}}{u_{l+n-1} - u_{l-1}} \hat{N}_l^n(u) + \frac{u_{l+n} - \hat{u}}{u_{l+n} - u_l} \hat{N}_{l+1}^n(u).$$

Mansfield, de Boor, Cox recursion:

$$N_l^n(u) = \frac{u - u_{l-1}}{u_{l+n-1} - u_{l-1}} N_l^{n-1}(u) + \frac{u_{l+n} - u}{u_{l+n} - u_l} N_{l+1}^{n-1}(u).$$

Derivative:

$$\frac{\mathrm{d}}{\mathrm{d}u} N_l^n(u) = \frac{n}{u_{n+l-1} - u_{l-1}} N_l^{n-1}(u) - \frac{n}{u_{l+n} - u_l} N_{l+1}^{n-1}.$$

Derivative of B-spline curve:

$$\frac{\mathrm{d}}{\mathrm{d}u} s(u) = n \sum_{i=1}^{L+n-1} \frac{\Delta d_{i-1}}{u_{n+i-1} - u_{i-1}} N_i^{n-1}(u).$$

Degree elevation:

$$N_i^n(u) = \frac{1}{n} \sum_{j=i-1}^{n+i} N_i^{n+1}(u|u_j),$$

where $N_i^{n+1}(u|u_j)$ is defined over the original knot sequence except that the knot u_j has its multiplicity increased by one. This identity was discovered by H. Prautzsch in 1984, see [290]. Another reference is Barry and Goldman [25].

10.10   Implementation

Here is C code for the de Boor algorithm:

```
float deboor(degree,coeff,knot,u,i)
/*    uses de Boor algorithm to compute one
      coordinate on B-spline curve for param. value u in interval i.
Input: degree:        polynomial degree of each piece of curve
       coeff:         B-spline control points
       knot:          knot sequence
       u:             evaluation abscissa
       i:             u's interval: u[i]<= u < u[i+1]
Output:               coordinate value.
*/
      float coeff[],knot[];
      float u;
      int degree,i;
{
      int k,j;
      float t1,t2;
      float coeffa[30]; /* auxiliary array */

      for (j=i-degree+1; j<=i+1; j++)coeffa[j]=coeff[j]; /* save data */

      for (k=1; k<= degree; k++)
      for ( j=i+1 ;j>=i-degree+k+1; j--)
      {
          t1= (knot[j+degree-k] - u )/(knot[j+degree-k]-knot[j-1]);
          t2= 1.0-t1;

          coeffa[j]=t1* coeffa[j-1]+t2* coeffa[j];
      }
      return (coeffa[i+1]);
}
```

Note that this program does not need to know about L. The next program generates a set of coordinates for a whole B-spline curve – for one coordinate, to be honest — so it has to be called twice for a 2D curve and three times for a 3D curve.

```
bspl_to_points(degree,l,coeff,knot,dense,points,point_num)
/*    generates points on B-spline curve. (one coordinate)
Input: degree:        polynomial degree of each piece of curve
       l:             number of active  intervals
       coeff:         B-spline control points
       knot:          knot sequence: knot[0]...knot[l+2*degree-2]
```

```
          dense:              how many points per segment
Output:points:                output array with function values.
          point_num:          how many points are generated. That number is
                              easier computed here than in the calling program:
                              no points are generated between multiple knots.
*/
     float coeff[],knot[],points[];
     int degree,l,dense,*point_num;
{
     int i,ii,kk;
     float u;
     float deboor();
                                  /* If you want to translate  */
     *point_num=0;                /* this to another language: */
                                  /* just omit the * here and  */
                                  /* below.                    */
     for (i=degree-1; i<l+degree-1; i++)
     {
     if(knot[i+1]>knot[i])                /* skip zero length intervals*/
          for(ii=0; ii<=dense; ii++)
          {
               u=knot[i]+ii*(knot[i+1]-knot[i])/dense;
               points[*point_num]=deboor(degree,coeff,knot,u,i);
               *point_num= (*point_num)+1;
          }
     }
}
```

As an example, the input data for the $y-$ values of the curve in Figure 10.1 are:

degree = 3; l = 4; coeff = 0.8, 2.8, 5.7, 2.6, 5.7, 4.0, 0.6; knot = 0.0, 0.0, 0.0, 2.6, 7.7, 9.9, 17.8, 17.8, 17.8; dense = 10.

10.11   Problems

1. Prove (10.1). Hint: use similar triangles.

2. Find the Bézier points of the closed B-spline curves of degree four whose control polygons consist of the edges of a square and have a) uniform knot spacing and simple knots, b) uniform knot spacing and knots all with multiplicity two.

3. For the case of a planar parametric B-spline curve, does symmetry of the polygon with respect to the $y-$axis imply that same symmetry for the curve?

4. If one uses the recursive relation (10.14) for the evaluation of the B-spline curve, it appears that one needs two additional knots u_{-1} and u_{L+2n-1}. Why does this not really pose a problem?

11

W. Boehm: Differential Geometry I

Differential geometry is based largely on the pioneering work of L. Euler (1707 - 1783), C. Monge (1746 - 1818), and C. F. Gauss (1777 - 1855). One of their concerns was the description of local curve and surface properties such as curvature. These concepts are also of interest in modern Computer Aided Geometric Design. The main tool for the development of general results is the use of local coordinate systems, in terms of which geometric properties are easily described and studied. This introduction discusses local properties of curves independent of a possible imbedding into a surface.

11.1   Parametric Curves and Arc Length

A curve in $I\!R^3$ is given by the parametric representation

$$\mathbf{x} = \mathbf{x}(t) = \begin{bmatrix} x(t) \\ y(t) \\ z(t) \end{bmatrix}, \quad t \in [a, b] \subset I\!R, \tag{11.1}$$

where its cartesian coordinates x, y, z are differentiable functions of t. (We have encountered a variety of such curves already, among them Bézier and

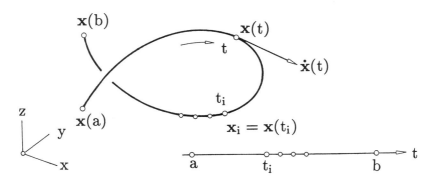

Figure 11.1. Parametric curve in space.

B-spline curves.) To avoid potential problems concerning the parametrization of the curve, we shall assume that

$$\dot{\mathbf{x}}(t) = \begin{bmatrix} \dot{x}(t) \\ \dot{y}(t) \\ \dot{z}(t) \end{bmatrix} \neq \mathbf{0}, \quad t \in [a, b], \tag{11.2}$$

where dots denote derivatives with respect to t. Such a parametrization is called *regular*.

A change $\tau = \tau(t)$ of the parameter, where τ is a differentiable function of t, will not change the shape of the curve. This *reparametrization* will be regular if $\dot{\tau} \neq 0$ for all $t \in [a, b]$, i.e., we can find the inverse $t = t(\tau)$. Let

$$s = s(t) = \int_a^t ||\dot{\mathbf{x}}|| dt \tag{11.3}$$

be such a parametrization. Because

$$\dot{\mathbf{x}} dt = \frac{d\mathbf{x}}{d\tau} \frac{d\tau}{dt} dt = \frac{d\mathbf{x}}{d\tau} d\tau,$$

s is independent of any regular reparametrization. It is an invariant parameter and is called *arc length* parametrization of the curve. One also calls $ds = ||\dot{\mathbf{x}}|| dt$ the *arc element* of the curve.

Remark 1:   Arc length may be introduced more intuitively as follows: let $t_i = a + i\Delta t$, $\Delta t > 0$ be an equidistant partition of the t-axis. Let $\mathbf{x}_i = \mathbf{x}(t_i)$ be the corresponding sequence of points on the curve. *Chord* *length* is then defined by

$$S = \sum_i ||\Delta \mathbf{x}_i|| = \sum_i ||\frac{\Delta \mathbf{x}_i}{\Delta t}|| \Delta t, \qquad (11.4)$$

where $\Delta \mathbf{x}_i = \mathbf{x}_{i+1} - \mathbf{x}_i$. It is easy to check that for $\Delta t \to 0$, chord length S converges to arc length s, while $\Delta \mathbf{x}_i / \Delta t$ converges to the tangent vector $\dot{\mathbf{x}}_i$ at $\mathbf{x}_i$.

Remark 2: Although arc length is an important concept, it is used mostly for theoretical considerations and for the development of curve algorithms. If, for some application, computation of the arc length is unavoidable, it may be approximated by the chord length (11.4).

11.2 The Frenet Frame

We will now introduce a special local coordinate system, linked to a point $\mathbf{x}(t)$ on the curve, that will significantly facilitate the description of local curve properties at that point. Let us assume that all derivatives needed below do exist. The first terms of the Taylor expansion of $\mathbf{x}(t + \Delta t)$ at t are given by

$$\mathbf{x}(t + \Delta t) = \mathbf{x} + \dot{\mathbf{x}} \Delta t + \ddot{\mathbf{x}} \frac{1}{2} \Delta t^2 + \dddot{\mathbf{x}} \frac{1}{6} \Delta t^3 + \ldots .^{[1]}$$

Let us assume that the first three derivatives are linearly independent. Then $\dot{\mathbf{x}}, \ddot{\mathbf{x}}, \dddot{\mathbf{x}}$ form a local affine coordinate system with origin $\mathbf{x}$. In this system, $\mathbf{x}(t)$ is represented by its *canonical coordinates*

$$\begin{bmatrix} \Delta t + \ldots \\ \frac{1}{2} \Delta t^2 + \ldots \\ \frac{1}{6} \Delta t^3 + \ldots \end{bmatrix},$$

where"..." denotes terms of degree four and higher in Δt.

From this local affine coordinate system, one easily obtains a local cartesian (orthonormal) system with origin $\mathbf{x}$ and axes $\mathbf{t}, \mathbf{m}, \mathbf{b}$ by the Gram-Schmidt process of orthonormalization, as shown in Figure 11.2:

$$\mathbf{t} = \frac{\dot{\mathbf{x}}}{||\dot{\mathbf{x}}||}, \quad \mathbf{m} = \mathbf{b} \wedge \mathbf{t}, \quad \mathbf{b} = \frac{\dot{\mathbf{x}} \wedge \ddot{\mathbf{x}}}{||\dot{\mathbf{x}} \wedge \ddot{\mathbf{x}}||}, \qquad (11.5)$$

where "$\wedge$" denotes the cross product.

---

[1] We use the abbreviation $\Delta t^2 = (\Delta t)^2$.

Figure 11.2. Local affine system (left) and Frenet frame (right).

The vector **t** is called *tangent vector* (see Remark 1), **m** is called *main normal vector*,[2] and **b** is called *binormal vector*. The frame (or trihedron) **t**, **m**, **b** is called the *Frenet frame*; it varies its orientation as *t* traces out the curve.

The plane spanned by the point **x** and the two vectors **t**, **m** is called the *osculating plane* **O**. Its equation is

$$\det \begin{bmatrix} \mathbf{y} & \mathbf{x} & \dot{\mathbf{x}} & \ddot{\mathbf{x}} \\ 1 & 1 & 0 & 0 \end{bmatrix} = \det[\mathbf{y} - \mathbf{x}, \dot{\mathbf{x}}, \ddot{\mathbf{x}}] = 0,$$

where **y** denotes any point on **O**. Its parametric form is

$$\mathbf{O}(u, v) = \mathbf{x} + u\dot{\mathbf{x}} + v\ddot{\mathbf{x}}.$$

Remark 3:   The process of orthonormalization yields

$$\mathbf{m} = \frac{\dot{\mathbf{x}}\dot{\mathbf{x}} \cdot \ddot{\mathbf{x}} - \dot{\mathbf{x}}\ddot{\mathbf{x}} \cdot \dot{\mathbf{x}}}{||\dot{\mathbf{x}}\dot{\mathbf{x}} \cdot \ddot{\mathbf{x}} - \dot{\mathbf{x}}\ddot{\mathbf{x}} \cdot \dot{\mathbf{x}}||}.$$

This equation may also be used in the case of planar curves, where the binormal vector $\mathbf{b} = \mathbf{t} \wedge \mathbf{m}$ agrees with the normal vector of the plane.

11.3   Moving the Frame

Letting the Frenet frame vary with *t* provides a good idea of the curve's behavior in space. It is a fundamental idea in differential geometry to express the local change of the frame in terms of the frame itself. The resulting formulas are particularly simple if one uses arc length parametrization. We

---

[2]Warning: one often sees the notation **n** for this vector. We use **m** to avoid confusion with surface normals, to be discussed later.

denote differentiation with respect to arc length by a prime "'". Since
$\mathbf{x}' = \mathbf{t}$ is a unit vector, one finds the following two identities:

$$\mathbf{x}' \cdot \mathbf{x}' = 1 \quad \text{and} \quad \mathbf{x}' \cdot \mathbf{x}'' = 0.$$

The first identity states that the curve is traversed with *unit speed*, the
second one states that the tangent vector is perpendicular to the second
derivative vector, provided the curve is parametrized with respect to arc
length.

Some simple calculations yield the so-called *Frenet-Serret* formulas:

$$\begin{aligned}
\mathbf{t}' &= &+\kappa\mathbf{m} & \\
\mathbf{m}' &= -\kappa\mathbf{t} & &+\tau\mathbf{b}, \\
\mathbf{b}' &= &-\tau\mathbf{m} &
\end{aligned} \tag{11.6}$$

where the terms κ and τ, called *curvature* and *torsion*, may be defined both
in terms of arc length s and in terms of the actual parameter t. We give
both definitions:

$$\begin{aligned}
\kappa &= \kappa(s) = ||\mathbf{x}''||, \\
\kappa &= \kappa(t) = \frac{||\dot{\mathbf{x}} \wedge \ddot{\mathbf{x}}||}{||\dot{\mathbf{x}}||^3},
\end{aligned} \tag{11.7}$$

$$\begin{aligned}
\tau &= \tau(s) = \frac{1}{\kappa^2}\det[\mathbf{x}',\mathbf{x}'',\mathbf{x}'''], \\
\tau &= \tau(t) = \frac{\det[\dot{\mathbf{x}}, \ddot{\mathbf{x}}, \dddot{\mathbf{x}}]}{||\dot{\mathbf{x}} \wedge \ddot{\mathbf{x}}||^2}.
\end{aligned} \tag{11.8}$$

Figure 11.3 illustrates formulas (11.6).

Curvature and torsion have an intuitive geometric meaning: consider a
point $\mathbf{x}(s)$ on the curve and a "consecutive" point $\mathbf{x}(s + \Delta s)$. Let $\Delta\alpha$
denote the angle between the two tangent vectors $\mathbf{t}$ and $\mathbf{t}(s + \Delta s)$ and let
$\Delta\beta$ denote the angle between the two binormal vectors $\mathbf{b}$ and $\mathbf{b}(s + \Delta s)$,
both angles measured in radians. It is easy to verify that $\Delta\alpha = \kappa\Delta s + \dots$
and $\Delta\beta = -\tau\Delta s + \dots$, where "..." denotes terms of higher degree in Δs.
Thus, when $\Delta s \to \mathrm{d}s$, one finds that

$$\kappa = \frac{\mathrm{d}\alpha}{\mathrm{d}s}, \quad \tau = -\frac{\mathrm{d}\beta}{\mathrm{d}s}.$$

In other words, κ and $-\tau$ are the angular velocities of $\mathbf{t}$ and $\mathbf{b}$, respectively,
as the frame is moved according to the parameter s.

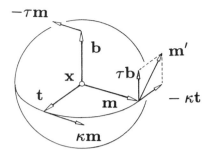

Figure 11.3. The geometric meaning of the Frenet-Serret formulas.

Remark 4:   Note that κ and τ are independent of the current parametrization of the curve. They are euclidean invariants of the curve, i.e., they are not changed by a rigid body motion of the curve. Moreover, any two continuous functions $\kappa = \kappa(s) > 0$ and $\tau = \tau(s)$ define uniquely (except for rigid body motions) a curve that has curvature κ and torsion τ.

Remark 5:   The curve may be written in canonical form in terms of the Frenet frame. Then it has the form

$$
\mathbf{x}(s + \Delta s) = \left[\begin{array}{l} \Delta s \\[4pt] \frac{1}{2}\kappa \Delta s^2 \\[4pt] \end{array} \quad \begin{array}{l} -\frac{1}{6}\kappa^2 \Delta s^3 + \dots \\[2pt] +\frac{1}{6}\kappa' \Delta s^3 + \dots \\[2pt] \frac{1}{6}\kappa\tau \Delta s^3 + \dots \end{array}\right] ,
$$

where "..." again denotes terms of higher degree in Δs.

11.4   The Osculating Circle

The circle that has second order contact with the curve at $\mathbf{x}$ is called the *osculating circle*. Its center is $\mathbf{c} = \mathbf{x} + \rho\mathbf{m}$, and its radius $\rho = \frac{1}{\kappa}$ is called the *radius of curvature*. We shall provide a brief development of these facts. Using the Frenet-Serret formulas (11.6), the Taylor expansion of $\mathbf{x}(s + \Delta s)$ can be written as

$$
\mathbf{x}(s + \Delta s) = \mathbf{x}(s) + \mathbf{t}\Delta s + \frac{1}{2}\kappa\mathbf{m}\Delta s^2 + \dots .
$$

Let ρ^* be the radius of the circle that is tangent to $\mathbf{t}$ at $\mathbf{x}$ and passes through the point $\mathbf{y} = \mathbf{x} + \Delta\mathbf{x}$, where $\Delta\mathbf{x} = \mathbf{t}\Delta s + \frac{1}{2}\kappa\mathbf{m}\Delta s^2$ (see Figure 11.5). Note

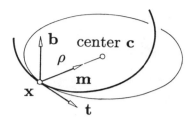

Figure 11.4. The Osculating Circle.

that $\mathbf{y}$ lies in the osculating plane $\mathbf{O}$. Inspection of the figure reveals that $(\frac{1}{2}\Delta\mathbf{x} - \rho^*\mathbf{m})\Delta\mathbf{x} = 0$, i.e., one obtains

$$\rho^* = \frac{1}{2}\frac{(\Delta\mathbf{x})^2}{\mathbf{m}\Delta\mathbf{x}}.$$

From the definition of $\Delta\mathbf{x}$ one obtains $(\Delta\mathbf{x})^2 = \Delta s^2 + \dots$ and $\mathbf{m}\Delta\mathbf{x} = \frac{1}{2}\kappa(\Delta s)^2$. Thus $\rho^* = \frac{1}{\kappa} + \dots$. In particular, $\rho = \frac{1}{\kappa}$ as $\Delta s \to 0$. Obviously, this circle lies in the osculating plane.

Remark 6: Let $\mathbf{x}$ be a rational Bézier curve of degree n as defined in Chapter 15. Its curvature and torsion at $\mathbf{b}_0$ are given by

$$\kappa = \frac{n-1}{n}\frac{w_0 w_2}{w_1^2}\frac{b}{a^2}, \quad \tau = \frac{n-2}{n}\frac{w_0 w_3}{w_1 w_2}\frac{c}{ab}, \tag{11.9}$$

where a is the distance between $\mathbf{b}_0$ and $\mathbf{b}_1$, b is the distance of $\mathbf{b}_2$ to the tangent spanned by $\mathbf{b}_0$ and $\mathbf{b}_1$, and c is the distance of $\mathbf{b}_3$ from the osculating plane spanned by $\mathbf{b}_0, \mathbf{b}_1,$ and $\mathbf{b}_2$, see Figure 11.6. Note that

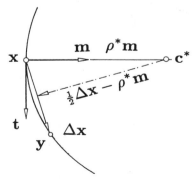

Figure 11.5. Construction of the osculating circle.

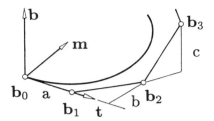

Figure 11.6. Frenet frame and geometric meaning of a, b, c.

these formulas can be used to calculate curvature and torsion at arbitrary points $\mathbf{x}(t)$ of a Bézier curve after subdividing it there (see Section 15.2).

Remark 7: An immediate application of (11.9) is the following: Let $\mathbf{x}$ be a point on an integral quadratic Bézier curve i.e., a parabola. Let 2δ denote the length of a chord parallel to the tangent at $\mathbf{x}$, and let ϵ be the distance between the chord and the tangent. The radius of curvature at $\mathbf{x}$ is then $\rho = \frac{\delta^2}{2\epsilon}$; see Figure 11.7.

Remark 8 An equivalent way to formulate (11.9) is given by

$$\kappa = 2\frac{n-1}{n}\frac{w_0 w_2}{w_1^2}\frac{\text{area}[\mathbf{b}_0, \mathbf{b}_1, \mathbf{b}_2]}{\text{dist}^3[\mathbf{b}_0, \mathbf{b}_1]} \tag{11.10}$$

and

$$\tau = \frac{3}{2}\frac{n-2}{n}\frac{w_0 w_3}{w_1 w_2}\frac{\text{volume}[\mathbf{b}_0, \mathbf{b}_1, \mathbf{b}_2, \mathbf{b}_3]}{\text{area}^2[\mathbf{b}_0, \mathbf{b}_1, \mathbf{b}_2]}. \tag{11.11}$$

The advantage of this formulation is that it can be generalized to "higher order curvatures" of curves that span $I\!\!R^d$, $3 < d \le n$ (see Remark 12 below). An application of this possible generalization will be addressed in Remark 13.

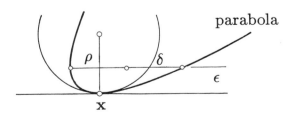

Figure 11.7. Curvature of a parabola.

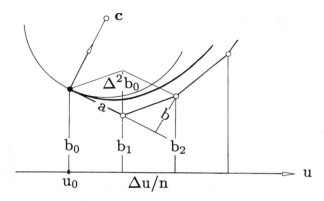

Figure 11.8. Curvature of nonparametric Bézier curve.

11.5   Nonparametric Curves

Let $y = y(t)$; $t \in [a, b]$ be a function. The planar curve $\begin{bmatrix} t \\ y(t) \end{bmatrix}$ is called the graph of $y(t)$ or a *nonparametric curve*. From the above, one derives the following:

the arc element:

$$ds = \sqrt{1 + \dot{y}^2}dt,$$

the tangent vector:

$$\mathbf{t} = \frac{1}{\sqrt{1 + \dot{y}^2}} \begin{bmatrix} 1 \\ \dot{y} \end{bmatrix},$$

the curvature:

$$\kappa = \frac{\ddot{y}}{[1 + \dot{y}^2]^{\frac{3}{2}}},$$

and the center of curvature:

$$\mathbf{c} = \mathbf{x} + \frac{1 + \dot{y}^2}{\ddot{y}} \begin{bmatrix} -\dot{y} \\ 1 \end{bmatrix}.$$

Remark 9:   Note that κ has a sign here. Any planar parametric curve can be given a *signed curvature*, for instance, by using the sign of $\det(\dot{\mathbf{x}}, \ddot{\mathbf{x}})$ (see also (23.1)).

Remark 10:   For a nonparametric Bézier curve (see Section 5.5),

$$y(u) = b_0 B_0^n(t) + \cdots + b_n B_n^n(t);$$

where $u = u_0 + t\Delta u$ is a global parameter, we obtain

$$a = \frac{1}{n}\sqrt{\Delta u^2 + n^2(\Delta b_0)^2}, \quad b = -\frac{\Delta u}{n}\frac{\Delta^2 b_0}{a},$$

as illustrated in Figure 11.8.

11.6   Composite Curves

A curve can be composed of several segments; we have seen spline curves as an example. Let $\mathbf{x}_-$ denote the right endpoint of a segment and $\mathbf{x}_+$ the left endpoint of the adjacent segment. (We will consider only continuous curves, so that $\mathbf{x}_- = \mathbf{x}_+$ always.) Let t be a global parameter of the composite curve and let dots denote derivatives with respect to t. Obviously, the curve is tangent continuous if

$$\dot{\mathbf{x}}_+ = \alpha\dot{\mathbf{x}}_-. \tag{11.12}$$

Moreover, it follows from (11.9) that it is curvature and osculating plane continuous if in addition

$$\ddot{\mathbf{x}}_+ = \alpha^2\ddot{\mathbf{x}}_- + \alpha_{21}\dot{\mathbf{x}}_-, \tag{11.13}$$

and it is torsion continuous if in addition

$$\dddot{\mathbf{x}}_+ = \alpha^3\dddot{\mathbf{x}}_- + \alpha_{32}\ddot{\mathbf{x}}_- + \alpha_{31}\dot{\mathbf{x}}_- \tag{11.14}$$

and vice versa. Since we require the parametrization to be regular, it follows that $\alpha > 0$, while the α_{ij} are arbitrary parameters.

It is interesting to note that curvature and torsion continuous curves exist that are not κ' continuous[3] (see Remark 4). Conversely,

$$\mathbf{x}''' = \mathbf{t}'' = \kappa'\mathbf{m} + \kappa(-\kappa\mathbf{t} + \tau\mathbf{b})$$

implies that $\mathbf{x}'''$ is continuous if κ' is and vice versa. In order to ensure $\mathbf{x}'''_- = \mathbf{x}'''_+$, the coefficients α and α_{ij} must be the result of the application of the chain rule; i.e., with $\alpha_{21} = \beta$ and $\alpha_{31} = \gamma$, one finds that $\alpha_{32} = 3\alpha\beta$. Now, as above, the curve is tangent continuous if

$$\dot{\mathbf{x}}_+ = \alpha\dot{\mathbf{x}}_-, \quad \alpha > 0,$$

---

[3]Recall that $\kappa' = \mathrm{d}\kappa(s)/\mathrm{d}s$, where the prime $'$ denotes differentiation with respect to arc length s of the (composite) curve. A formula for κ' is provided by equation (23.2).

it is curvature and osculating plane continuous if in addition

$$\ddot{\mathbf{x}}_+ = \alpha^2 \ddot{\mathbf{x}}_- + \beta \dot{\mathbf{x}}_-,$$

but it is κ' continuous if in addition

$$\dddot{\mathbf{x}}_+ = \alpha^3 \dddot{\mathbf{x}}_- + 3\alpha\beta\ddot{\mathbf{x}}_- + \gamma\dot{\mathbf{x}}_-$$

and vice versa.

Remark 11:   For planar curves, torsion continuity is a vacuous condition, but κ' continuity is meaningful.

Remark 12: The above results may be used for the definition of higher order *geometric continuity*. A curve is said to be G^r, or r^{th} order geometrically continuous, if there exists a regular reparametrization after which it is C^r. This definition is obviously equivalent to the requirement of C^{r-2} continuity of κ and C^{r-3} continuity of τ. As a consequence, geometric continuity may be defined by using the chain rule, as in the example $r = 3$ above.

Remark 13:   The geometric invariants curvature and torsion may be generalized for higher dimensional curves. Continuing the process mentioned in Remark 8, one finds that a $d-$dimensional curve has $d - 1$ geometric invariants. Continuity of these invariants only makes sense in $\mathbb{E}^d$, as was demonstrated for $d = 2$ in Remark 11.

Remark 14:   Note that although curvature and torsion are euclidean invariants, curvature and torsion continuity (as well as the generalizations discussed in Remarks 12 and 13) are affinely invariant properties of a curve. Both are also projectively invariant properties; see Boehm [56] and Goldman and Micchelli [171].

Remark 15:   If two curve segments meet with a continuous tangent and have (possibly different) curvatures κ_- and κ_+ at the common point, then the ratio κ_-/κ_+ is also a projectively invariant quantity. This is known as Memke's Theorem, see Bol [62].

12

Geometric Continuity I

12.1 Motivation

Before we explain in detail the concept of geometric continuity, we will give an example of a curve that is *curvature continuous* yet *not twice differentiable*. Such curves (and, later, surfaces) are the objects that we will label *geometrically continuous*.

Let us consider Figure 12.1. It shows two symmetric parabolas that are combined to form a composite curve c. This curve is C^1 over the knot sequence $\{0, 1, 2\}$ (or any affine map thereof). However, it does not form a C^2 piecewise polynomial curve over those two intervals: for two parabolas to form a C^2 piecewise quadratic curve, they must both be part of *one* global parabola (see 7.2). That cannot be the case here, since c has parallel tangents at b_0 and b_4, an impossibility for parabolas.

Now let us check for c's curvature at b_2. The two parabolic arcs are symmetric with respect to the perpendicular bisector of b_1 and b_3. They are also tangent continuous at b_2; hence, their centers of curvature at b_2 agree. It follows that c is curvature continuous at b_2. In fact, it is more than that: it possesses a continuously varying normal vector. Another example of a curve that is not C^2 yet has continuously varying curvature and normal vector is the rational representation of the circle as shown in Figure 14.11.

Differential geometry teaches us that c can be *reparametrized* so that the

Figure 12.1. Geometric continuity: a curve **c** is shown that consists of two parabolic arcs, both shown with their Bézier polygons. This curve has continuous curvature but is not twice differentiable at $\mathbf{b}_2$.

new parameter is arc length. With that new parametrization, the curve will actually be C^2. Details are explained in Chapter 11.

We shall adopt the term G^2 curves (second order geometrically continuous) for curves that are *twice differentiable with respect to arc length but not necessarily twice differentiable with respect to their current parametrization*. Note that curves with a zero tangent vector cannot be G^2 under this definition.

12.2   A Characterization of G^2 Curves

We shall give a general characterization of G^2 curves. We make no assumptions about the actual form of **x** (piecewise polynomial, piecewise trigonometric, ...); we assume only that **x** has a global parameter u and that **x** is a C^1 curve with respect to that parametrization. We also make the assumption that $\dot{\mathbf{x}}(u) \neq \mathbf{0}$.

Let "+" and "−" as subscripts denote right and left limits respectively. Differentiation with respect to arc length s will be denoted by a prime " ′ ," differentation with respect to the given parameter u will be denoted by a dot " ˙ ."

In order for **x** to be G^2 at a parameter value u, we must have

$$\mathbf{x}''_{+}(s) - \mathbf{x}''_{-}(s) = \mathbf{0}.$$

Since the parameter u can be viewed as a function of arc length s, a change of variable and application of the chain rule yields

$$(u')^2\ddot{\mathbf{x}}_{+}(u) + u''_{+}\dot{\mathbf{x}}(u) - (u')^2\ddot{\mathbf{x}}_{-}(u) - u''_{-}\dot{\mathbf{x}}(u) = \mathbf{0}. \tag{12.1}$$

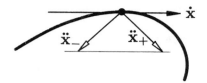

Figure 12.2. G^2 continuity: a curve is not C^2 at a point if its right and left second derivatives do not agree there. It is G^2 if their difference is parallel to the tangent vector.

Let us introduce a function $\nu(u)$ by

$$\nu(u) = \frac{u''_- - u''_+}{(u')^2}. \tag{12.2}$$

Note that the denominator in the definition of $\nu(u)$ does not vanish, since we excluded curves with zero tangent vectors from our considerations.

We can now formulate our characterization: a C^1 curve $\mathbf{x}(u)$ is G^2 if and only if there exists a function $\nu(u)$ such that

$$\ddot{\mathbf{x}}_+(u) - \ddot{\mathbf{x}}_-(u) = \nu(u)\dot{\mathbf{x}}(u). \tag{12.3}$$

The function $\nu(u)$ is uniquely determined by the parametrization $s(u)$. The essence of (12.3) is presented in Figure 12.2.

Every C^2 curve (with nonvanishing tangent vectors) is also G^2, and for C^2 curves the function $\nu(u)$ is seen to be identically zero. Of more interest in this context are G^2 piecewise polynomial curves, which are piecewise analytic, and hence certainly piecewise C^2. For these curves, real numbers ν_i must exist such that

$$\ddot{\mathbf{x}}_+(u_i) - \ddot{\mathbf{x}}_-(u_i) = \nu_i\dot{\mathbf{x}}(u_i). \tag{12.4}$$

To see how this ties in with (12.3), we simply define the function $\nu(u)$ as

$$\nu(u) = \begin{cases} \nu_i & u = u_i \\ 0 & \text{else} \end{cases}. \tag{12.5}$$

A warning concerning (12.4): the ν_i in this equation are not invariant under affine parameter transformations. If we reparametrize a curve by $v = au + b$, then $\nu(v) = a\nu(u)$, as can be seen from (12.3).

Equation (12.4) was derived by Nielson [267] in 1974 as a property of ν-splines, C^1 piecewise cubic interpolatory splines that are G^2 but generally (for $\nu_i \neq 0$) not C^2. But actually (12.4) holds for any piecewise polynomial

G^2 curve, that is, we can find the ν_i from any particular representation of the curve.

Equation (12.1) provides one handy characterization for G^2 curves. It is worthwhile to point out that the use of *arc length* is not at all important for this purpose; it is used for its proximity to differential geometry. In fact, we can say that a curve is G^2 if it is C^2 with respect to *some* parametrization, a definition used by several authors. See Barsky [26], Farin [132], and Manning [247].

12.3   Nu-splines

Nielson [267] derived the equations that determine a G^2 interpolating spline from a particular variational formulation of the interpolation problem (see the end of this section). The characterization (12.4) allows a more straight-forward derivation of the defining equations.

Let $L + 1$ data points $\mathbf{x}_i$; $i = 0, \ldots, L$ be given together with $L + 1$ distinct parameter values u_i. We could pass the unique (except for end conditions) interpolating C^2 spline through the data points, as described in Chapter 9. Knowing that G^2 curves are more general than C^2 ones, we could exploit the added generality to define a wider class of interpolating curves. With some luck, this class will contain interpolants that are more attractive in some sense than C^2 splines are.

An interpolatory G^2 piecewise cubic spline may be written in piecewise cubic Hermite form: for $u \in (u_i, u_{i+1})$, the interpolant can be written as

$$\mathbf{x}(u) = \mathbf{x}_i H_0^3(r) + \mathbf{m}_i \Delta_i H_1^3(r) + \Delta_i \mathbf{m}_{i+1} H_2^3(r) + \mathbf{x}_{i+1} H_3^3(r), \qquad (12.6)$$

where the H_j^3 are cubic Hermite polynomials from equation (6.14) and $r = (u - u_i)/\Delta_i$ is the local parameter of the interval (u_i, u_{i+1}). In (12.6), the $\mathbf{x}_i$ are the known data points, while the $\mathbf{m}_i$ are as yet unknown tangent vectors. The interpolant is supposed to be G^2; it is therefore characterized by (12.4), more specifically,

$$\ddot{\mathbf{x}}_+(u_i) - \ddot{\mathbf{x}}_-(u_i) = \nu_i \mathbf{m}_i \qquad (12.7)$$

for some constants ν_i, where $\mathbf{m}_i = \dot{\mathbf{x}}(u_i)$. The ν_i are constants that can be used to manipulate the shape of the interpolant; they will be discussed soon.

We insert (12.6) into (12.7) and obtain

$$3(\tfrac{\Delta \mathbf{x}_{i-1}}{\Delta_{i-1}} + \tfrac{\Delta \mathbf{x}_i}{\Delta_i}) = \quad \Delta_i \mathbf{m}_{i-1} + (2\Delta_{i-1} + 2\Delta_i + \tfrac{1}{2}\Delta_{i-1}\Delta_i \nu_i)\mathbf{m}_i$$
$$+\Delta_{i-1}\mathbf{m}_{i+1}; i = 1, \ldots, L-1 \qquad (12.8)$$

Together with two end conditions, (12.8) can be used to compute the unknown tangent vectors $\mathbf{m}_i$. The simplest end condition is prescribing $\mathbf{m}_0$ and $\mathbf{m}_L$, but any other end condition from Chapter 9 may be used as well. Note that this formulation of the $\nu-$spline interpolation problem depends on the scale of the u_i; it is not invariant under affine parameter transformations. This results from the use of the Hermite form.

It is now time to investigate the advantages of ν-spline interpolation over standard C^2 spline interpolation. We have created an interpolating piecewise polynomial curve that is more general than the C^2 interpolating spline; setting all ν_i equal to zero reduces the ν-spline system (12.8) to the tridiagonal system for C^2 splines (see Chapter 9). Letting some of the ν_i differ from zero will produce a different curve.

The effect of the ν_i on the shape of the interpolant is best studied by considering a limiting case. Suppose we let the kth of the ν_i tend to $+\infty$. Then the kth equation in (12.8) reduces to $\mathbf{m}_k = \mathbf{0}$. The effect of increasing the value of ν_k is therefore a reduction in length of the tangent vector $\mathbf{m}_k$. If we let all ν_i tend to infinity, all tangent vectors will converge to zero length, and the interpolant will look like a piecewise linear curve through the data points. This limiting case is not G^2, since we did not admit curves with zero tangent vectors into the class of G^2 curves. Figure 12.3 shows that although the limiting $\nu-$spline interpolant *looks* like a piecewise linear curve, it is actually C^1.

The effect of the ν_i on the shape of the interpolating ν-spline curve leads to their description as *tension parameters*. The higher the values of the tension parameters, the "tighter" the curve. Figure 12.4 gives an example. Nu-spline curves are best used in an interactive computer graphics environment: as a first pass, the interpolating C^2 spline to a given data set is computed. Next, one might increase tension values in regions where the spline curve exhibits unwanted undulations. This process is interactive and must be repeated until a satisfactory shape is obtained.

While the original development of $\nu-$splines considered only nonnegative tension values, it seems that negative ν_i can also influence the shape of an interpolating ν-spline curve in a beneficial way (Farin [129]). Finding "good" tension values is not easy, however, and an automatic method for doing so is not yet known.

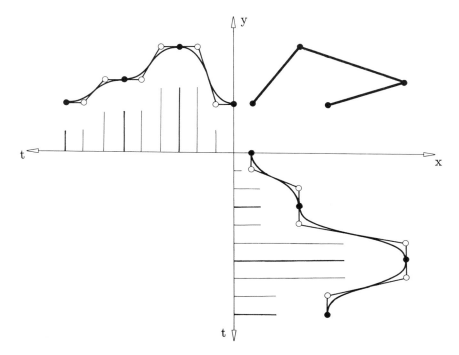

Figure 12.3. Nu-splines: in the limiting case $\nu_i \to \infty$, the interpolant approaches the polygon through the data points. The cross plot shows that it is still C^1.

We have neglected the question of whether the linear system (12.8) always possesses a solution. For the case of all ν_i being zero, we know that the coefficient matrix is positive definite, since this is simply the case of C^2 cubic splines. For that case, we always have a unique solution. If all ν_i are greater than zero, the diagonal elements of the coefficient matrix become larger, and positive definiteness – and thus the existence of a unique solution – is maintained. If some of the ν_i become negative, however, we cannot make a statement about the existence of a solution (or of a unique solution).

A theoretical analysis of the solvability of (12.8) involves the eigenvalues of the coefficient matrix: if they are nonzero, then it is nonsingular. A preliminary analysis using Gershgorin's Circle Theorem is presented by Barsky [28]. At the time this book is being written, no general *a priori* check is known that determines if a given set of tension parameters will cause the matrix to be singular.

We finish our discussion of ν−spline interpolation with a minimum property that was the starting point for this theory. Standard C^2 splines

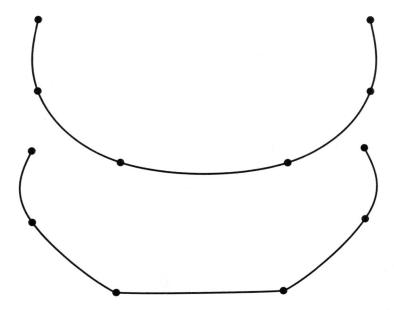

Figure 12.4. Nu-splines: the top curve is a C^2 cubic spline interpolant to the data points. The bottom curve results from selecting high values for ν_2 and ν_3.

minimize the functional

$$\int_{u_0}^{u_L} [\ddot{\mathbf{x}}(t)]^2 \mathrm{d}t,$$

as explained in Section 9.5. The $\nu-$spline interpolant minimizes the more general functional

$$\int_{u_0}^{u_L} [\ddot{\mathbf{x}}(t)]^2 \mathrm{d}t + \sum \nu_i [\mathbf{m}_i]^2. \tag{12.9}$$

If several ν_i are chosen to be very large, this functional forces the corresponding tangent vectors $\mathbf{m}_i$ to become small.

12.4 G^2 Piecewise Bézier Curves

Equation (12.4) provides the condition for a general piecewise polynomial to be G^2. Let us now investigate what happens if we represent such a curve in piecewise Bézier form.

It will be useful to rewrite (12.4). We cross-product both sides with $\dot{\mathbf{x}}$ and obtain

$$\ddot{\mathbf{x}}_+ \wedge \dot{\mathbf{x}} = \ddot{\mathbf{x}}_- \wedge \dot{\mathbf{x}} \tag{12.10}$$

as another characterization of G^2 continuity. In terms of differential geometry, this equation states that $\mathbf{x}$ possesses both continuously varying curvature and binormal vector.

Now let $\mathbf{b}_0, \ldots, \mathbf{b}_n$ and $\mathbf{c}_0, \ldots, \mathbf{c}_n$ be the Bézier polygons of two n^{th} degree polynomials. We assume that both curve segments form a C^1 curve[1] over a knot partition u_0, u_1, u_2, implying

$$\text{ratio}(\mathbf{b}_{n-1}, \mathbf{b}_n, \mathbf{c}_1) = \frac{\Delta_0}{\Delta_1} \tag{12.11}$$

where $\Delta_0 = u_1 - u_0$, $\Delta_1 = u_2 - u_1$. Recalling the formulas for first and second derivatives of Bézier curves, we can express (12.10) in terms of the Bézier points that are involved:

$$\frac{1}{\Delta_0^3} \Delta^2 \mathbf{b}_{n-2} \wedge \Delta \mathbf{b}_{n-1} = \frac{1}{\Delta_1^3} \Delta^2 \mathbf{c}_0 \wedge \Delta \mathbf{c}_0. \tag{12.12}$$

Invoking the geometric interpretation of the second difference vector Δ^2 (see Figure 4.3), we can rewrite (12.12) and obtain a *characterization of G^2 continuity for Bézier curves* (following Farin [132]):

$$\frac{1}{\Delta_0^3} \Delta \mathbf{b}_{n-2} \wedge \Delta \mathbf{b}_{n-1} = \frac{1}{\Delta_1^3} \Delta \mathbf{c}_0 \wedge \Delta \mathbf{c}_1, \tag{12.13}$$

now only using first differences. A useful modification, utilizing (12.11), is the following:

$$\frac{1}{\Delta_0^2} \Delta \mathbf{b}_{n-2} \wedge (\mathbf{c}_1 - \mathbf{b}_{n-1}) = \frac{1}{\Delta_1^2} (\mathbf{c}_1 - \mathbf{b}_{n-1}) \wedge \Delta \mathbf{c}_1. \tag{12.14}$$

The absolute value of the cross product of two vectors equals the area of the parallelogram spanned by the two vectors. Thus the two preceding formulas yield:

$$\frac{\text{area}(\mathbf{b}_{n-2}, \mathbf{b}_{n-1}, \mathbf{b}_n)}{\text{area}(\mathbf{c}_0, \mathbf{c}_1, \mathbf{c}_2)} = \frac{\Delta_0^3}{\Delta_1^3} \tag{12.15}$$

and

$$\frac{\text{area}(\mathbf{b}_{n-2}, \mathbf{b}_{n-1}, \mathbf{c}_1)}{\text{area}(\mathbf{b}_{n-1}, \mathbf{c}_1, \mathbf{c}_2)} = \frac{\Delta_0^2}{\Delta_1^2}. \tag{12.16}$$

---

[1] Remember that one can always find a knot partition such that a tangent continuous piecewise polynomial becomes a C^1 curve!

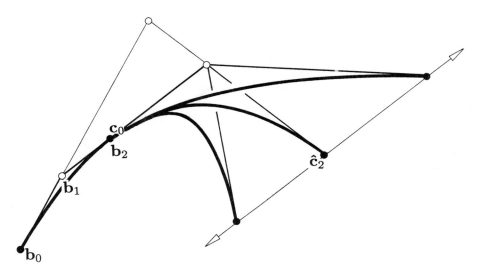

Figure 12.5. G^2 continuity: a family of curvature continuous piecewise quadratic Bézier curves. The point $\hat{\mathbf{c}}_2$ may vary parallel to the tangent.

In both cases, we denote by area$(\mathbf{a}, \mathbf{b}, \mathbf{c})$ the area of the triangle with vertices $\mathbf{a}, \mathbf{b}, \mathbf{c}$. These two formulas are a characterization for *curvature continuity* of two Bézier curves. This is a weaker requirement than G^2 continuity, since it does not guarantee continuity of the osculating plane.

Note that, since $\mathbf{b}_{n-2}, \mathbf{b}_{n-1}, \mathbf{b}_n = \mathbf{c}_0, \mathbf{c}_1, \mathbf{c}_2$ have to be coplanar for (12.12) to hold, it makes sense to assign a *sign* to the above areas. A consequence of G^2 continuity is then that $\mathbf{b}_{n-2}$ and $\mathbf{c}_2$ must be on the same side of the tangent through $\mathbf{b}_{n-1}$ and $\mathbf{c}_1$. Otherwise, (12.16) would involve square roots of negative numbers.

Another consequence of the coplanarity of $\mathbf{b}_{n-2}, \mathbf{b}_{n-1}, \mathbf{b}_n = \mathbf{c}_0, \mathbf{c}_1, \mathbf{c}_2$ is *affine invariance* of the G^2 condition (12.16). The area ratio of two coplanar triangles is not affected by affine maps, and so the left hand side of (12.16) is not affected by an affine map: *affine maps take G^2 curves to G^2 curves.*

In order to see that G^2 continuity is a genuine generalization of the concept of second order differentiability, let us consider two examples.

Figure 12.5 shows two adjacent Bézier curves. They form a C^1 curve over the knot partition determined by the ratio of the three collinear points $\mathbf{b}_2, \mathbf{b}_3 = \mathbf{c}_0, \mathbf{c}_1$. The location of $\mathbf{b}_1$ would uniquely determine $\hat{\mathbf{c}}_2$ if we wanted our two quadratics to form one C^2 curve (see the C^r condition in Section 7.4). If we relax that requirement and are content with G^2

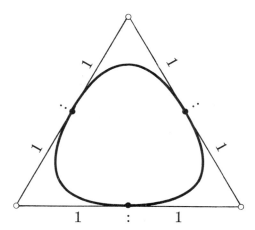

Figure 12.6. G^2 curves: a closed quadratic G^2 spline.

continuity, we may place $\mathbf{c}_2$ anywhere on the straight line through $\hat{\mathbf{c}}_2$ and parallel to the tangent through $\mathbf{b}_3$.

The next example: let $\mathbf{a}$, $\mathbf{b}$, $\mathbf{c}$ be the vertices of a triangle and let $\mathbf{d}$, $\mathbf{e}$, $\mathbf{f}$ be the edge midpoints as in Figure 12.6. We can interpret these points as Bézier points of a piecewise quadratic curve (Figure 12.6). This closed curve is G^2. It is a C^1 curve over any uniform knot sequence, for example $0, 1, 2$. However, one easily verifies that it is not a twice differentiable piecewise quadratic with respect to any knot sequence.

12.5   Direct G^2 Cubic Splines

We have seen in Section 7.9 how to construct the piecewise Bézier polygon of a C^2 cubic spline from a given knot sequence $u_0, \ldots, u_L$ and a given polygon $\mathbf{d}_{-1}, \ldots, \mathbf{d}_{L+1}$. The procedure was to find the inner Bézier points $\mathbf{b}_{3i\pm1}$ on the control polygon using the C^2 conditions and then find the junction points $\mathbf{b}_{3i}$ from the C^1 conditions. The analogous construction for a G^2 spline is less restricted. In particular, one does not have to prescribe a knot sequence in addition to the control polygon. It will be selected automatically by the following algorithm.

We are given a control polygon $\mathbf{d}_{-1}, \ldots, \mathbf{d}_{L+1}$, called the G^2 control polygon. We want to construct a G^2 piecewise cubic Bézier curve with L segments and so must determine $\mathbf{b}_0, \mathbf{b}_1, \ldots \mathbf{b}_{3L}$. We proceed as follows:

- In the case of an open polygon, set
  $\mathbf{b}_0 = \mathbf{d}_{-1}, \mathbf{b}_1 = \mathbf{d}_0, \mathbf{b}_{3L-1} = \mathbf{d}_L, \mathbf{b}_{3L} = \mathbf{d}_{L+1}$.
- Next, select $\mathbf{b}_2$ anywhere on the polygon leg $\mathbf{d}_0, \mathbf{d}_1$ and
  select $\mathbf{b}_{3L-2}$ anywhere on the polygon leg $\mathbf{d}_{L-1}, \mathbf{d}_L$.
- Choose the inner points $\mathbf{b}_{3i-2}, \mathbf{b}_{3i-1}$
  anywhere on the polygon leg $\mathbf{d}_{i-1}, \mathbf{d}_i$.
- Find the junction points $\mathbf{b}_{3i}$ from (12.16).

For the last step, we must compute a ratio Δ_0/Δ_1 for each junction point. It is computable from the inner Bézier points. We may set $\Delta_0 = 1$ without loss of generality, and obtain

$$\Delta_1 = \sqrt{\frac{\mathrm{area}(\mathbf{b}_{3i-2}, \mathbf{b}_{3i-1}, \mathbf{b}_{3i+1})}{\mathrm{area}(\mathbf{b}_{3i-1}, \mathbf{b}_{3i+1}, \mathbf{b}_{3i+2})}},$$

and finally the desired junction point $\mathbf{b}_{3i}$:

$$\mathbf{b}_{3i} = \frac{\Delta_1 \mathbf{b}_{3i-1} + \mathbf{b}_{3i+1}}{1 + \Delta_1}. \tag{12.17}$$

This construction yields the piecewise Bézier polygon of a G^2 cubic spline curve. We note that the osculating plane (see Chapter 11) at $\mathbf{b}_{3i}$ is spanned by $\mathbf{d}_{i-1}, \mathbf{d}_i, \mathbf{d}_{i+1}$. For closed polygons, the first two steps in the above construction are omitted. Numbering would then be mod L.

In interactive design, one would utilize G^2 cubic splines in a two-step procedure. The design of the G^2 control polygon may be viewed as a rough sketch. The program would estimate the inner Bézier points automatically, and the designer could fine-tune the curve shape by readjusting them where necessary. At no time does he or she have to worry about the knot sequence – it is computed automatically from the G^2 conditions.

There is one interesting difference between the above construction for a G^2 spline and the corresponding construction for a C^2 spline: every cubic C^2 possesses a B-spline control polygon – but not every G^2 piecewise cubic curve possesses a G^2 control polygon. The two cubics in Figure 12.7 are curvature continuous, yet they cannot be obtained with the above construction: the control point $\mathbf{d}_1$ would have to be at infinity.

12.6 Implementation

We give a short program that utilizes equation (12.17). It assumes that the piecewise Bézier polygon has been determined except for the junction points $\mathbf{b}_{3i}$, which will be computed:

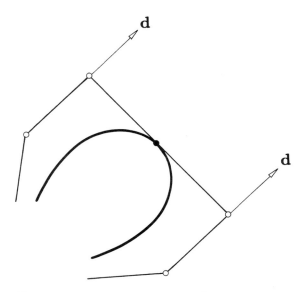

Figure 12.7. G^2 splines: these two cubics are a G^2 spline but do not possess a G^2 control polygon.

```
void direct_gspline(l,bez_x,bez_y)
/* From given interior Bezier points,
   the junction Bezier points b3i are found from the G2 conditions.
Input: l:             no of cubic pieces.
       bez_x,bez_y:   interior Bezier points b_{3i+1}, b_{3i-1}.
Output:bez_x,bez_y:   completed piecewise Bezier polygon.
Note:                 b_0 and b_{3l+3} should be provided, too!
*/
     int l;
     float bez_x[],bez_y[];
{
     int i,i3;
     float h_minus,h_plus;
     float height();

     for(i=1; i<l; i++)
     {
         i3=i*3;
         h_minus=height(bez_x[i3-2],bez_y[i3-2],bez_x[i3-1],
                     bez_y[i3-1],bez_x[i3+1],bez_y[i3+1]);
         h_plus =height(bez_x[i3+2],bez_y[i3+2],bez_x[i3-1],
                     bez_y[i3-1],bez_x[i3+1],bez_y[i3+1]);
```

```
        h_minus=sqrt(abs(h_minus));    /* needs an abs function, */
        h_plus =sqrt(abs(h_plus));     /* which is not included  */

        bez_x[i3]=(h_plus*bez_x[i3-1]+h_minus*bez_x[i3+1])/
                 (h_minus + h_plus);
        bez_y[i3]=(h_plus*bez_y[i3-1]+h_minus*bez_y[i3+1])/
                 (h_minus + h_plus);
    }
}
```

The routine **height** is given by

```
float height(px,py,ax,ay,bx,by)
/* find the height of point (px,py) over
   straight line thru (ax,ay) and (bx,by)
*/
     float px,py,ax,ay,bx,by;
{
     float det,length;
     det = px*ay + ax*by + bx*py -ay*bx - by*px - py*ax;

     length = sqrt( (bx-ax)*(bx-ax) + (by-ay)*(by-ay) );

     return (det/length);
}
```


12.7   Problems

1. Figure 12.6 shows a triangle and an inscribed piecewise quadratic curve. Find the ratio of the areas enclosed by the curve and the triangle.

2. G^2 piecewise cubics, when constructed as direct G^2 splines, may contain straight line segments that are written as cubics. Discuss osculating plane continuity for such curves.

3. The G^2 piecewise cubic from Figure 12.7 cannot be represented as a direct G^2 spline. Can it be obtained from a $\nu-$spline interpolation problem?

4. Find cases where the solution to a $\nu-$spline interpolation problem is not a G^2 curve, even for finite values of ν_i.

13

Geometric Continuity II

The preceding chapter contained the basic algorithms for G^2 curves: an interpolation algorithm (ν−splines) and a design algorithm (direct G^2 splines). In this chapter, we shall add a theoretical framework to these algorithms. See also the Remarks in Chapter 11 concerning geometric continuity.

13.1   Gamma-splines

The direct G^2 cubic splines from Section 12.5 may be a handy tool in interactive design, but they are not amenable to mathematical analysis. A more formal description reveals the relationship between G^2 splines and classical B-splines, as described in Chapter 7. This formalization, developed by W. Boehm [52], is concerned with the same G^2 curves as above, but because of the different treatment, G^2 splines in this context are called γ-splines.

Consider Figure 13.1. The two points $\mathbf{d}_-$ and $\mathbf{d}_+$ are the auxiliary points for the C^2 condition of standard cubic B-spline curves (see Section 7.6). Since they do not agree, the curve is not twice differentiable at $\mathbf{b}_{3i}$. Some notation:

$$A_- = \text{area}(\mathbf{b}_{3i-2}, \mathbf{b}_{3i-1}, \mathbf{b}_{3i+1}),$$
$$A_+ = \text{area}(\mathbf{b}_{3i-1}, \mathbf{b}_{3i+1}, \mathbf{b}_{3i+2}),$$
$$A = \text{area}(\mathbf{b}_{3i-1}, \mathbf{d}_-, \mathbf{b}_{3i+1}) = \text{area}(\mathbf{b}_{3i-1}, \mathbf{d}_+, \mathbf{b}_{3i+1}).$$

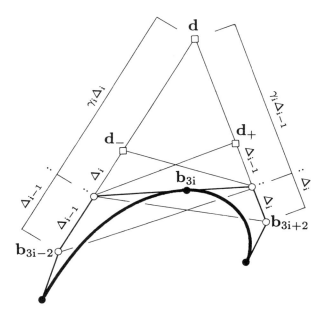

Figure 13.1. Gamma-splines: the G^2 conditions can be formulated in terms of triangle areas.

The last statement needs justification; it is provided through

$$A_- \frac{\Delta_i}{\Delta_{i-1}} = A_+ \frac{\Delta_{i-1}}{\Delta_i} = A,$$

which follows directly from (12.16).

Let $\mathbf{d}_i$ be the intersection of the two straight lines through $\mathbf{b}_{3i-2}, \mathbf{d}_-$ and $\mathbf{d}_+, \mathbf{b}_{3i+2}$. A number γ_i exists then such that

$$\text{area}(\mathbf{b}_{3i-1}, \mathbf{d}_i, \mathbf{b}_{3i+1}) = \gamma_i A.$$

It follows that

$$\text{ratio}(\mathbf{b}_{3i-2}, \mathbf{b}_{3i-1}, \mathbf{d}_i) \;\;=\;\; \frac{\Delta_{i-1}}{\gamma_i \Delta_i}, \tag{13.1}$$

$$\text{ratio}(\mathbf{d}_i, \mathbf{b}_{3i+1}, \mathbf{b}_{3i+2}) \;\;=\;\; \frac{\gamma_i \Delta_{i-1}}{\Delta_i}. \tag{13.2}$$

We can now formulate an algorithm for γ-spline curves: given a control polygon $\mathbf{d}_{-1}, \ldots, \mathbf{d}_{L+1}$, a knot sequence $u_0, \ldots, u_L$, and a set of *shape*

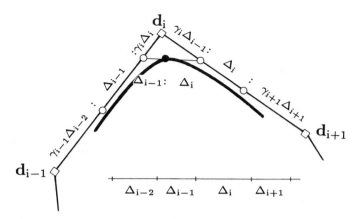

Figure 13.2. Gamma-splines: the Bézier points are connected to the G^2 control polygon by the shown ratios.

parameters $\gamma_1, \ldots, \gamma_{L-1}$, find the piecewise Bézier polygon of the corresponding γ-spline curve. We proceed as indicated in Figure 13.2. We first determine the inner Bézier points $\mathbf{b}_{3i\pm1}$ and then find the junction points $\mathbf{b}_{3i}$.

For the inner Bézier points we get:

$$\mathbf{b}_{3i-2} = \frac{\Delta_{i-1} + \gamma_i \Delta_i}{\Delta} \mathbf{d}_{i-1} + \frac{\gamma_{i-1}\Delta_{i-2}}{\Delta}\mathbf{d}_i \qquad (13.3)$$

$$\mathbf{b}_{3i-1} = \frac{\gamma_i \Delta_i}{\Delta}\mathbf{d}_{i-1} + \frac{\gamma_{i-1}\Delta_{i-2} + \Delta_{i-1}}{\Delta}\mathbf{d}_i, \qquad (13.4)$$

where

$$\Delta = \gamma_{i-1}\Delta_{i-2} + \Delta_{i-1} + \gamma_i \Delta_i. \qquad (13.5)$$

For the junction points we find

$$\mathbf{b}_{3i} = \frac{\Delta_i}{\Delta_{i-1} + \Delta_i}\mathbf{b}_{3i-1} + \frac{\Delta_{i-1}}{\Delta_{i-1} + \Delta_i}\mathbf{b}_{3i+1}. \qquad (13.6)$$

This equation is identical with the corresponding one for C^2 cubic B-spline curves, equation (7.22).

For $\gamma_i = 1$, we recapture the familiar construction for C^2 cubic splines. The value for γ_i may also be negative, giving rise to curves that may have loops. In these cases, the curve does not necessarily stay within the convex hull of the G^2 control polygon (see Farin, Hansford, and Worsey [135] for more details). Typically, one would use values for the γ_i that are between

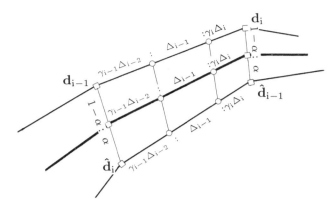

Figure 13.3. γ–splines: a barycentric combination of two γ–splines is obtained by forming the barycentric combination of their G^2 control polygons.

0 and 1. As $\gamma_i \to 0$, the curve comes closer to $\mathbf{d}_i$, giving it a sharper bend there. If we let all γ_i approach zero, the resulting curves will converge to the control polygon, a situation comparable to letting all ν_i tend to infinity in ν–spline interpolation.

13.2   Local Basis Functions for G^2 Splines

In the previous sections, we developed two methods for the generation of G^2 splines: the direct construction from Section 12.5 and the γ-spline development. Clearly, the direct approach is superior for design in that it is based only on geometric entities, whereas for γ-splines, one needs to specify a knot sequence and a sequence of γ_i, both being numerical input. The strength of the γ-spline approach is not in the design field but in the analysis of G^2 splines.

The following property is easy to prove for γ-spline curves, but it is not obvious how to even formulate it for the direct G^2 approach. Consider two γ-spline curves $\mathbf{g}$ and $\hat{\mathbf{g}}$ over the same knot sequence and with the same γ_i. Denote the G^2 control vertices of $\mathbf{g}$ by $\mathbf{d}_i$, those of $\hat{\mathbf{g}}$ by $\hat{\mathbf{d}}_i$. We observe that the barycentric combination

$$\mathbf{h}(u) = (1 - \alpha)\mathbf{g}(u) + \alpha\hat{\mathbf{g}}(u)$$

is again a γ-spline curve. Moreover, the G^2 control polygon for $\mathbf{h}$ consists of the points $(1 - \alpha)\mathbf{d}_i + \alpha\hat{\mathbf{d}}_i$. A glance at Figure 13.3 reveals the truth of this statement: the points $\mathbf{d}_{i-1}, \mathbf{d}_i, \hat{\mathbf{d}}_{i-1}, \hat{\mathbf{d}}_i$ form a bilinear surface. Thus the Bézier points and the G^2 control vertices of $\mathbf{h}$ are related to each other in the same ratios as those of $\mathbf{g}$ and $\hat{\mathbf{g}}$, assuring that $\mathbf{h}$ is again a $\gamma-$spline curve.

A consequence of this linearity property is that all γ-splines over the same knot sequence and with the same γ_i form a linear space whose dimension, $L+3$, equals the number of control vertices of each γ-spline in that space. Each element of that space then has a basis representation

$$\mathbf{x}(u) = \sum_{i=-1}^{L+1} \mathbf{d}_i M_i(u). \tag{13.7}$$

We are slightly negligent here: actually, the M_i do not only depend on u but also on the u_i and the γ_i.

We shall now develop several properties of the M_i until we are finally able to give an explicit form for them. As the geometry of the $\gamma-$spline construction reveals, they have the following properties:

Partition of unity: This follows since the affine invariance of the γ-spline construction implies that (13.7) is a barycentric combination:

$$\sum_{i=-1}^{L+1} M_i(u) \equiv 1. \tag{13.8}$$

Positivity: For $\gamma_i \geq 0$, the γ-spline curve lies in the convex hull of the control polygon. Thus (13.7) is a convex combination:

$$M_i(u) \geq 0. \tag{13.9}$$

Local support: If we change one $\mathbf{d}_i$, the curve is only changed over the four intervals $(u_{i-2}, \ldots, u_{i+2})$. This is illustrated in Figure 7.17 in the context of C^2 B-spline curves. Thus the corresponding basis function $M_i(u)$ must vanish outside this region:

$$M_i(u) = 0 \quad \text{for} \quad u \notin [u_{i-2}, u_{i+2}]. \tag{13.10}$$

Equation (13.10) is a consequence of the fact that a change in $\mathbf{d}_i$ does not affect $\mathbf{b}_j$ with $j \leq 3i - 6$ or with $j \geq 3i + 6$. That change does not affect $\mathbf{b}_{3i\pm5}$ and $\mathbf{b}_{3i\pm4}$ either – therefore, the first and second derivatives of the curve at u_{i-2} and u_{i+2} remain unchanged. As a consequence,

$$\frac{\mathrm{d}}{\mathrm{d}u} M_i(u_{i\pm2}) = \frac{\mathrm{d}^2}{\mathrm{d}u^2} M_i(u_{i\pm2}) = 0. \tag{13.11}$$

With these properties at hand, we can now construct M_i. Consider the

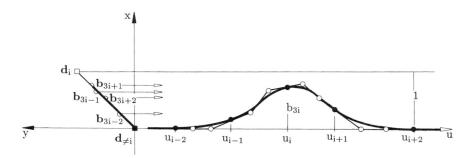

Figure 13.4. Local basis for G^2 splines: a basis function M_i is obtained through the cross plot technique. Only the plot for $x(u)$ is shown, the one for $y(u)$ being identical.

control polygon that is obtained by setting $\mathbf{d}_i = \begin{bmatrix} 1 \\ 1 \end{bmatrix}$ while setting all other vertices $\mathbf{d}_j = \mathbf{0}$. The graph of this polygon is quite degenerate – only one control point is nonzero. Its usefulness stems from the fact that the cross plot of the corresponding γ-spline curve consists of $\begin{bmatrix} M_i(u) \\ M_i(u) \end{bmatrix}$, in other words, it singles out exactly one basis function. We can therefore construct the Bézier points of M_i by the use of a cross plot (see Figure 13.4); if necessary, consult Sections 5.5 and 5.6. The Bézier ordinates of M_i are now a simple consequence of (13.3), (13.4), and (13.6):

$$b_{3i-2} = \frac{\gamma_{i-1}\Delta_{i-2}}{\Gamma_1}, \tag{13.12}$$

$$b_{3i-1} = \frac{\gamma_{i-1}\Delta_{i-2} + \Delta_{i-1}}{\Gamma_1}, \tag{13.13}$$

$$b_{3i+1} = \frac{\Delta_i + \gamma_{i+1}\Delta_{i+1}}{\Gamma_2}, \tag{13.14}$$

$$b_{3i+2} = \frac{\gamma_{i+1}\Delta_{i+1}}{\Gamma_2}, \tag{13.15}$$

where

$$\Gamma_1 = \gamma_{i-1}\Delta_{i-2} + \Delta_{i-1} + \gamma_i\Delta_i$$

and

$$\Gamma_2 = \gamma_i\Delta_{i-1} + \Delta_i + \gamma_{i+1}\Delta_{i+1}.$$

For the junction ordinate b_{3i} we find

$$b_{3i} = \frac{\Delta_i}{\Delta_{i-1} + \Delta_i}b_{3i-1} + \frac{\Delta_{i-1}}{\Delta_{i-1} + \Delta_i}b_{3i+1}. \tag{13.16}$$

All remaining Bézier ordinates of M_i are zero.

The basis functions M_i are C^1 by construction. They are not twice differentiable, not even G^2. It seems a bit of a miracle, then, that a linear combination of *curvature discontinuous* functions can generate a parametric curve that is *curvature continuous*.[1] Let us investigate this phenomenon more closely. A γ-spline, being a G^2 curve, must satisfy the G^2 condition (12.4). This condition must hold for both the $x-$ and the $y-$ component of the curve (and for the z-component if it happens to be a space curve). For the special example in Figure 13.4, both components are given by $M_i(u)$. Thus

$$\frac{\mathrm{d}^2}{\mathrm{d}u^2} M_i(u_j+) - \frac{\mathrm{d}^2}{\mathrm{d}u^2} M_i(u_j-) = \nu_j \frac{\mathrm{d}}{\mathrm{d}u} M_i(u_j), \quad \text{all } j \qquad (13.17)$$

for some ν_j, which are nonzero in the general case.

When we talk about G^2 continuity of M_i, we really mean G^2 continuity of its graph, which is a 2D curve $\begin{bmatrix} u \\ M_i(u) \end{bmatrix}$. In order to be G^2, both components of this curve must satisfy (12.4). The second one does because of (13.17), but the first one, u, does not if the ν_j are allowed to be nonzero, as in this case. The graph of M_i is therefore not curvature continuous.

Equation (13.17) may be used to derive a connection between the γ_j and the ν_j. One obtains (Boehm [52]):

$$\nu_j = 2\left[\frac{1}{\Delta_{j-1}} + \frac{1}{\Delta_j}\right]\left[\frac{1}{\gamma_j} - 1\right]. \qquad (13.18)$$

Let us summarize the historical development of these splines. The first local basis for G^2 splines was developed by G. Nielson and J. Lewis [241] in 1975. In 1981, B. Barsky [26] developed a local basis for so-called β-splines, which are, in the context of this chapter, γ-splines with constant $\gamma_i = \gamma$ and a distorted knot sequence with $\Delta_i = \beta\Delta_{i-1}$. Later, local bases were developed for $\beta-$spline curves that are equivalent to $\gamma-$splines (Bartels and Beatty [35]).

13.3   Beta-splines

Our derivation of $\gamma-$splines was partly based on the fact that every tangent continuous piecewise cubic may be endowed with a knot sequence such that

---

[1] As long as $\dot{\mathbf{x}}(u) \neq \mathbf{0}$ for any u.

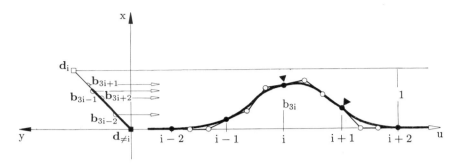

Figure 13.5. β–splines: a basis function is shown. It is defined over a uniform knot partition and is potentially tangent discontinuous. Here, tangent discontinuities occur at the marked points.

it becomes a C^1 piecewise cubic curve (see Section 7.7). In particular, the γ–splines $M_i(u)$ are C^1 piecewise cubics.

A slight modification of the γ– splines M_i gives rise to so-called β–splines $\hat{M}_i$. The modification is not to the function values of M_i but rather to the knot sequence. The idea is to rescale each interval so that it is of unit length. As an example, consider Figures 7.9 and 7.10. The coordinate function $x(u)$ of a C^1 piecewise cubic $\mathbf{x}(u)$ is itself a C^1 piecewise cubic over the u–axis, as shown in Figure 7.9. Rescaling each interval so that it is of unit length causes the graph of $x(u)$ to become tangent discontinuous. Given the tangent discontinuous graph $x(u)$ of Figure 7.10, we can only recover the parametric curve in the cross plot if we know the rescaling factors that made each interval of unit length. These rescaling factors are called $\beta_{1,i}$ and are defined by

$$\beta_{1,i} = \frac{\Delta_{i+1}}{\Delta_i}.$$

In order to obtain β–splines $\hat{M}_i$ from γ–splines M_i, we thus have to rescale the u–axis so that each interval Δ_i is scaled to be of unit length. The resulting β–spline may be tangent discontinuous; see Figure 13.5.

In the context of β–splines, the shape parameters γ_i are replaced by the ν_i from the G^2 condition (12.4) and called $\beta_{2,i}$:

$$\beta_{2,i} = \nu_i.$$

Since the γ_i and the ν_i are related by (13.18), we can now write a piecewise cubic G^2 curve in either γ–spline or β–spline form. More material

Figure 13.6. G^r continuity: a segment of a C^r curve may be reparametrized. The resulting curve is not C^r any more, but still G^r.

about this relationship is presented in DeRose and Barsky [111]. Additional information on $\beta-$splines can be found in Goodman and Unsworth [176], [175].

It should be noted that several definitions of $\beta-$spline curves exist. The above one is the only one that is capable of modeling the full variety of G^2 piecewise cubics. Another kind of $\beta-$spline is obtained by setting all $\beta_{1,i} = \beta_1$ and all $\beta_{2,i} = \beta_2$, thus reducing the number of shape parameters available for the whole curve to two *global* shape parameters. This approach to G^2 piecewise cubics, as described in Barsky [26], [27], has gained popularity in the graphics community. For the purpose of designing real objects, however, these curves are not flexible enough: instead of being a true generalization of B-spline curves, they abandon the most useful property of B-spline curves, namely *local control*.

13.4   Higher Order Geometric Continuity

Just as we can define higher order parametric continuity C^r, we may also define higher order geometric continuity. We say that a curve is r^{th} order geometrically continuous, or G^r, at a given point, if it can be reparametrized such that it will become C^r(see Remark 12 in Section 11.6). In particular, the new parameter might be arc length.

In order to derive conditions for G^r continuity, we start with a composite C^r curve $\mathbf{x}(u)$ with a global parameter u. At a given parameter value u, derivatives from the left and from the right agree:

$$\frac{\mathrm{d}^i}{\mathrm{d}u^i}\mathbf{x}_- = \frac{\mathrm{d}^i}{\mathrm{d}u^i}\mathbf{x}_+; \quad i = 0, \ldots, r. \tag{13.19}$$

Now let us reparametrize the right segment by introducing a new parameter $t = t(u)$, see Figure 13.6. By our above definition, the resulting composite curve will be G^r, while it is clearly not C^r any more. We will now study the conditions for G^r continuity using this composite G^r curve.

Modifying equation (13.19) such as to incorporate the new parametrization yields:

$$\frac{d^i}{du^i}\mathbf{x}_- = \frac{d^i}{du^i}\mathbf{x}(t)_+; \quad i = 0,\ldots,r. \tag{13.20}$$

The terms on the right-hand side of this equation may be expanded using the chain rule. For $i = 1$, we obtain

$$\mathbf{x}'_- = \dot{\mathbf{x}}_+\frac{dt}{du}, \tag{13.21}$$

where a prime denotes differentiation with respect to u, and a dot denotes differentiation with respect to t. For $i = 2$, we have to apply both the chain and the product rule to the right hand side of (13.21):

$$\mathbf{x}_-'' = \ddot{\mathbf{x}}_+\left[\frac{dt}{du}\right]^2 + \dot{\mathbf{x}}_+\frac{d^2t}{du^2}. \tag{13.22}$$

The case $i = 3$:

$$\mathbf{x}_-''' = \dddot{\mathbf{x}}_+\left[\frac{dt}{du}\right]^3 + 3\ddot{\mathbf{x}}_+\frac{dt}{du}\frac{d^2t}{du^2} + \dot{\mathbf{x}}_+\frac{d^3t}{du^3} \tag{13.23}$$

Let us define $\alpha_i = d^it/du^i$. Then the above equations may be written in matrix form:

$$\begin{bmatrix} \mathbf{x}'_- \\ \mathbf{x}_-'' \\ \mathbf{x}_-''' \end{bmatrix} = \begin{bmatrix} \alpha_1 & 0 & 0 \\ \alpha_2 & \alpha_1^2 & 0 \\ \alpha_3 & 3\alpha_1\alpha_2 & \alpha_1^3 \end{bmatrix} \begin{bmatrix} \dot{\mathbf{x}}_+ \\ \ddot{\mathbf{x}}_+ \\ \dddot{\mathbf{x}}_+ \end{bmatrix}. \tag{13.24}$$

The lower triangular matrix in (13.24) is called *connection matrix*; it connects the derivatives of one segment to that of the other. For r^{th} order geometric continuity, the connection matrix is a lower triangular $r \times r$ matrix; for more details see Gregory[188] or Goodman [173]. See also the related discussion in Section 11.6. The connection matrix is a powerful theoretical tool, and has been used to derive variation diminishing properties of geometrically continuous curves (Dyn and Micchelli [118]), to show the projective invariance of torsion continuity (Boehm [56]), and for other theoretical pursuits (Goldman and Micchelli [171]).

The above definition of geometric continuity has been used by Manning [247], Barsky [26], Barsky and DeRose [31] and Farin [132]. In terms of classical differential geometry, the concept of "G^2" is called "order two of contact," see do Carmo [114]. It has been used in a constructive context by G. Geise [164] as early as 1962.

An interesting phenomenon arises if we consider geometric continuity of order higher than two. Consider a G^3 space curve. It is easy to verify that it possesses continuous curvature and torsion. But the converse is not true: there are space curves with continuous curvature and torsion that are not G^3 (Farin [132]). This more general class of curves, called *Frenet frame continuous*, has been studied by Boehm [59]; see also Section 11.6 and Hagen [193], [192]. They are characterized by a more general connection matrix than that for G^3 continuity; it is given by

$$\begin{bmatrix} \alpha_1 & 0 & 0 \\ \alpha_2 & \alpha_1^2 & 0 \\ \alpha_3 & \beta & \alpha_1^3 \end{bmatrix},$$

where β is an arbitrary constant. For higher order Frenet frame continuity, one has to resort to higher-dimensional spaces; this has been carried out by Dyn and Micchelli [118], Goodman [173], Goldman and Micchelli [171], and Pottmann [287]; see also the survey by Gregory [188]. An even more general concept than that of Frenet frame continuity has recently been discussed by H. Pottmann [288].

A condition for torsion continuity of two adjacent Bézier curves with polygons $\mathbf{b}_0, \ldots, \mathbf{b}_n$ and $\mathbf{c}_0, \ldots, \mathbf{c}_n$ is given by

$$\frac{\text{volume}[\mathbf{b}_{n-3}, \ldots, \mathbf{b}_n]}{\|\Delta \mathbf{b}_{n-1}\|^6} = \frac{\text{volume}[\mathbf{c}_0, \ldots, \mathbf{c}_3]}{\|\Delta \mathbf{c}_0\|^6}. \tag{13.25}$$

See Boehm [58], Farin [132], or Hagen [193]. Note the similarity to (12.15)!

A nice geometric interpretaion of the fact that torsion continuity is more general than G^3 continuity is due to W. Boehm [58]: If $\mathbf{b}_{n-3}, \ldots, \mathbf{b}_n$ and $\mathbf{c}_0, \ldots, \mathbf{c}_3$ are given such that the two curves are G^3, can we vary $\mathbf{c}_3$ and still maintain G^3 continuity? The answer is yes, and $\mathbf{c}_3$ may be displaced by any vector parallel to the tangent spanned by $\mathbf{b}_{n-1}$ and $\mathbf{c}_1$ – very similar, in other words, to the situation depicted in Figure 12.5. But we may displace $\mathbf{c}_3$ by any vector parallel to the osculating plane spanned by $\mathbf{b}_{n-2}, \mathbf{b}_n, \mathbf{c}_2$ and still maintain torsion continuity!

13.5 Implementation

The following program incorporates equations (13.3) and (13.4) (using uniform Δ_i), and has to be called once for each coordinate. It does *not* compute the $\mathbf{b}_{3i}$ from (13.6). The idea is that a user might still want to adjust the $\mathbf{b}_{3i\pm1}$ further before computing the junction points. They can be computed using the procedure `direct_gspline` from Section 12.5.

```
void  gamma_spline(bspl,l,gamma,bez)
/*    from B-spline polygon and gammas, find interior
      Bezier points b3i+-1.
Input: bspl:      control polygon (one coordinate only).
       l:         number of cubic pieces.
       gamma:     gamma_i's.
Output:bez:       piecewise Bezier polygon,  but without the
                  junction points b3i.
*/
      int l;
      float bspl[],gamma[],bez[];
{
      int i,i3,l3;

      bez[0]=bspl[0];
      bez[1]=bspl[1];
      if(l>1)
      {
          bez[2]=(gamma[2]*bspl[1]
                  +bspl[2]    )/(gamma[2]+1.0);
      }
      if(l>2)
      {
          bez[4]=(  (1.0+gamma[3])*bspl[2]
                  +gamma[2]*bspl[3]  )/(1.0+gamma[2]+gamma[3]);
      }
/* Now the main part:   */

      for(i=2; i<l-1; i++)
      {
      i3=3*i;
          bez[i3-1]=( gamma[i+1]*bspl[i]
               +  (gamma[i]+1.0)*bspl[i+1])/(1.0+gamma[i]+gamma[i+1]);

          bez[i3+1]=(  (gamma[i+2]+1.0)*bspl[i+1]
               +  gamma[i+1]*bspl[i+2]   )/(1.0+gamma[i+1]+gamma[i+2]);

      }

/* The last points need special attention:  */

      l3=l*3;
      if(l>2)
      {
          bez[l3-4]=( gamma[l]*bspl[l-1]
                  +(1.0+gamma[l-1])*bspl[l]   )/(1.0+gamma[l-1]+gamma[l]);
```

```
    }
    if(l>1)
    {
        bez[13-2]=( bspl[l]
                   + gamma[l]*bspl[l+1]   )/(gamma[l]+1.0);
    }
    bez[13-1]= bspl[l+1];
    bez[13]   = bspl[l+2];

}
```

13.6   Problems

1. Prove (13.18).

2. Suppose two cubic segments form a G^2 curve, but are not C^2 cubics with respect to their parametrization. We know that we can reparametrize both so that they are C^2 afterwards. In particular, that reparametrization may be piecewise polynomial. What is the minimum degree?

3. We derived B-spline interpolation from the C^2 conditions in Section 9.1. Derive interpolatory $\gamma-$ splines from equations (13.3), (13.4), and (13.6).

4. Show that the average of two G^2 piecewise cubics over the same knot sequence is in general not a G^2 curve, i.e., if $\mathbf{x}_1(u)$ and $\mathbf{x}_2(u)$ are two G^2 cubics over the same knot sequence (but possibly with different shape parameters), then $(1-\alpha)\mathbf{x}_1(u) + \alpha\mathbf{x}_2(u)$ is in general not G^2.

5. Find an example of a torsion continuous curve that is not G^3.

6. Let a G^3 curve consist of two cubic Bézier curves. The derivatives of the two curves at the junction point are related by a connection matrix. Work out the corresponding connection matrix for the Bézier points.

14

Conic Sections

Conic sections (short: conics) have received the most attention throughout the centuries of all known curve types. Today, they are an important design tool in the aircraft industry; they are also used in areas like font design. A great many algorithms for the use of conics in design were developed in the 1940s; Liming [244] and [243] are two books with detailed descriptions of those methods.

The first person to consider conics in a CAD environment was S. Coons [87]. Later, R. Forrest [155] further investigated conics and also rational cubics. We shall treat conics in the rational Bézier form; a good reference for this approach is Lee [238]. We present conics partly as a subject in its own right, but also as a first instance of rational Bézier and B-spline curves, to be discussed later.

14.1   Projective Maps of the Real Line

Polynomial curves, as studied before, bear a close relationship to affine geometry. Consequently, the de Casteljau algorithm makes use of ratios, which are the fundamental invariant of affine maps. Thus the class of polynomial curves is invariant under affine transformations: an affine map maps a polynomial curve onto another polynomial curve.

Conic sections, and later rational polynomials, are invariant under a more

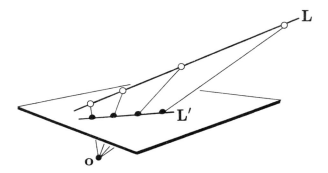

Figure 14.1. Projections: a straight line **L** is mapped onto another straight line **L'** by a projection. Note how ratios of corresponding triples of points are distorted.

general type of maps: the so-called *projective maps*. These maps are studied in *projective geometry*. This is not the place to outline the ideas of that kind of geometry; the interested reader is referred to the recent text by Penna and Patterson [276]. All we will need here is the concept of a projective map.

We start with a map that is familiar to everybody with a background in computer graphics: the *projection*. Consider a plane (called image plane) **P** and a point **o** (called center or origin of projection) in $\mathbb{E}^3$. A point **p** is projected onto **P** through **o** by finding the intersection $\hat{\mathbf{p}}$ between the straight line through **o** and **p** with **P**. For a projection to be well-defined it is necessary that **o** is not in **P**. Any object in $\mathbb{E}^3$ can be projected into **P** in this manner.

In particular, we can project a straight line, **L**, say, onto **P**, as shown in Figure 14.1. We clearly see that our projection is not an affine map: the ratios of corresponding points on **L** and **L'** are not the same. But a projection leaves another geometric property unchanged: the *cross ratio* of four collinear points.

The cross ratio, cr, of four collinear points is defined as a ratio of ratios (ratios are defined by Equation (2.6)):

$$\mathrm{cr}(\mathbf{a}, \mathbf{b}, \mathbf{c}, \mathbf{d}) = \frac{\mathrm{ratio}(\mathbf{a}, \mathbf{b}, \mathbf{d})}{\mathrm{ratio}(\mathbf{a}, \mathbf{c}, \mathbf{d})}. \tag{14.1}$$

This particular definition is only one of several equivalent ones; any permutation of the four points gives rise to a new (equivalent) definition. Our convention (14.1) has the advantage of being symmetric: $\mathrm{cr}(\mathbf{a}, \mathbf{b}, \mathbf{c}, \mathbf{d}) = \mathrm{cr}(\mathbf{d}, \mathbf{c}, \mathbf{b}, \mathbf{a})$. Cross ratios were first studied by C. Brianchon and F. Moebius, who proved their invariance under projective maps in 1827, see [258].

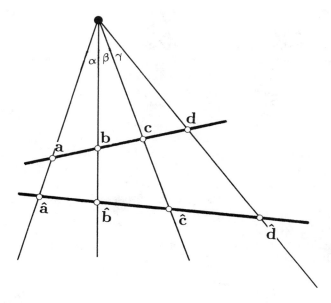

Figure 14.2. Cross ratios: the cross ratios of $\mathbf{a}, \mathbf{b}, \mathbf{c}, \mathbf{d}$ and $\hat{\mathbf{a}}, \hat{\mathbf{b}}, \hat{\mathbf{c}}, \hat{\mathbf{d}}$ only depend on the angles shown and are thus equal.

Let us now prove the above invariance claim. We have to show, with the notation from Figure 14.2, that

$$\mathrm{cr}(\mathbf{a}, \mathbf{b}, \mathbf{c}, \mathbf{d}) = \mathrm{cr}(\hat{\mathbf{a}}, \hat{\mathbf{b}}, \hat{\mathbf{c}}, \hat{\mathbf{d}}). \qquad (14.2)$$

This fact is called the Cross Ratio Theorem.

For a proof, consider Figure 14.2. Denote the area of a triangle with vertices $\mathbf{p}$, $\mathbf{q}$, $\mathbf{r}$ by $\Delta(\mathbf{p}, \mathbf{q}, \mathbf{r})$. We note that for instance

$$\mathrm{ratio}(\mathbf{a}, \mathbf{b}, \mathbf{c}) = \Delta(\mathbf{a}, \mathbf{b}, \mathbf{o})/\Delta(\mathbf{b}, \mathbf{c}, \mathbf{o}).$$

This gives

$$
\begin{aligned}
\mathrm{cr}(\mathbf{a}, \mathbf{b}, \mathbf{c}, \mathbf{d}) &= \frac{\Delta(\mathbf{a}, \mathbf{b}, \mathbf{o})/\Delta(\mathbf{b}, \mathbf{d}, \mathbf{o})}{\Delta(\mathbf{a}, \mathbf{c}, \mathbf{o})/\Delta(\mathbf{c}, \mathbf{d}, \mathbf{o})} \\[2mm]
&= \frac{l_1 l_2 \sin\alpha / l_2 l_4 \sin(\beta + \gamma)}{l_1 l_3 \sin(\alpha + \beta)/l_3 l_4 \sin\gamma} \\[2mm]
&= \frac{\sin\alpha / \sin(\beta + \gamma)}{\sin(\alpha + \beta)/\sin\gamma}.
\end{aligned}
$$

Thus the cross ratio of the four points **a**, **b**, **c**, **d** only depends on the angles at **o**. The four rays emanating from **o** may therefore be intersected by any straight line; the four points of intersection will have the same cross ratio, regardless of the choice of the straight line. All such straight lines are related by projections, and we can therefore say that projections leave the cross ratio of four collinear points invariant. Since the cross ratio is the same for any straight line intersecting the given four straight lines, one also calls it the cross ratio of the four given lines.

A concept that is slightly more abstract than that of projections is that of *projective maps*. Going back to Figure 14.1, we can interpret both **L** and **L′** as copies of the real line. Then the projection of **L** onto **L′** can be viewed as a map of the real line onto itself. With this interpretation a projection defines a projective map of the real line onto itself. On the real line, a point is given by a real number, so we can assume a correspondence between the point **a** and a real number a.

An important observation about projective maps of the real line to itself is that they are defined by three preimage and three image points. To see this, we inspect Figure 14.2. The claim is that **a**, **b**, **d** and their images $\hat{\mathbf{a}}, \hat{\mathbf{b}}, \hat{\mathbf{d}}$ determine a projective map. It is true since if we pick an arbitrary fourth point **c** on **L**, its image $\hat{\mathbf{c}}$ on **L′** is determined by the Cross Ratio Theorem.

A projective map of the real line onto itself is thus determined by three preimage numbers a, b, c and three image numbers $\hat{a}, \hat{b}, \hat{c}$. The projective image $\hat{t}$ of a point t can then be computed from

$$\mathrm{cr}(a, b, t, c) = \mathrm{cr}(\hat{a}, \hat{b}, \hat{t}, \hat{c}).$$

Setting $\rho = (b - a)/(c - b)$ and $\hat{\rho} = (\hat{b} - \hat{a})/(\hat{c} - \hat{b})$, this is equivalent to

$$\frac{\rho}{(t - a)/(c - t)} = \frac{\hat{\rho}}{(\hat{t} - \hat{a})/(\hat{c} - \hat{t})}.$$

Solving for $\hat{t}$:

$$\hat{t} = \frac{(t - a)\hat{\rho}\hat{c} + (c - t)\hat{a}\rho}{\rho(c - t) + \hat{\rho}(t - a)}. \tag{14.3}$$

A convenient choice for the image and preimage points is $a = \hat{a} = 0, c = \hat{c} = 1$. Equation (14.3) then takes on the simpler form

$$\hat{t} = \frac{t\hat{\rho}}{\rho(1 - t) + \hat{\rho}t}. \tag{14.4}$$

Thus a projective map of the real line onto itself corresponds to a *rational linear transformation*. It is left for the reader to verify that the projective map becomes an affine map in the special case that $\rho = \hat{\rho}$.

14.2   Conics as Rational Quadratics

Many equivalent ways exist to define a conic section; for our purposes the following one is very useful: *A conic section in $I\!\!E^2$ is the projection of a parabola in $I\!\!E^3$ into a plane.*

When it comes to the formulation of conics as rational curves, it is customary to abandon the principle of being independent of a fixed coordinate system. One typically chooses the center of the projection to be the origin **0** of a 3D cartesian coordinate system. The plane into which one projects is taken to be the plane $z = 1$. Since we will study planar curves in this section, we may think of this plane as a copy of $I\!\!E^2$, thus identifying points $\begin{bmatrix} x & y \end{bmatrix}^T$ with $\begin{bmatrix} x & y & 1 \end{bmatrix}^T$. Our special projection is characterized by

$$\begin{bmatrix} x \\ y \\ z \end{bmatrix} \;\longrightarrow\; \begin{bmatrix} x/z \\ y/z \\ 1 \end{bmatrix}.$$

Note that a point $\begin{bmatrix} x & y \end{bmatrix}^T$ is the projection of a whole family of points: every point on the straight line $\begin{bmatrix} wx & wy & w \end{bmatrix}^T$ projects to $\begin{bmatrix} x & y \end{bmatrix}^T$. In the following, we will use the shorthand notation $\begin{bmatrix} w\mathbf{x} & w \end{bmatrix}^T$ with $\mathbf{x} \in I\!\!E^2$ for $\begin{bmatrix} wx & wy & w \end{bmatrix}^{T}$.[1] An illustration of this special projection is given in Figure 14.3.

Figure 14.4 gives an example of how to obtain a conic using the projection method.

Back to conics: let $\mathbf{c}(t) \in I\!\!E^2$ be a point on a conic. Then there exist numbers $w_0, w_1, w_2 \in I\!\!R$ and points $\mathbf{b}_0, \mathbf{b}_1, \mathbf{b}_2 \in I\!\!E^2$ such that

$$\mathbf{c}(t) = \frac{w_0 \mathbf{b}_0 B_0^2(t) + w_1 \mathbf{b}_1 B_1^2(t) + w_2 \mathbf{b}_2 B_2^2(t)}{w_0 B_0^2(t) + w_1 B_1^2(t) + w_2 B_2^2(t)}. \tag{14.5}$$

Let us prove (14.5). We may identify $\mathbf{c}(t) \in I\!\!E^2$ with $\begin{bmatrix} \mathbf{c}(t) & 1 \end{bmatrix}^T \in I\!\!E^3$. This point is the projection of a point $\begin{bmatrix} w(t)\mathbf{c}(t) & w(t) \end{bmatrix}^T$ which lies on a 3D parabola. The third component $w(t)$ of this 3D point must be a quadratic function in t, and may be expressed in Bernstein form:

$$w(t) = w_0 B_0^2(t) + w_1 B_1^2(t) + w_2 B_2^2(t).$$

---

[1]Sometimes the set of all points $\begin{bmatrix} wx & wy & w \end{bmatrix}^T$ is called the *homogeneous form* or *homogeneous coordinates* of $\begin{bmatrix} x & y \end{bmatrix}^T$.

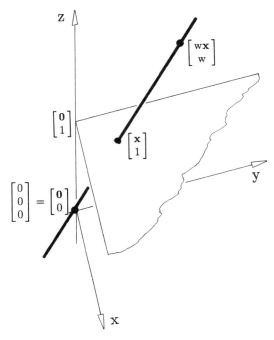

Figure 14.3. Projections: the special projection that is used to write objects in the plane $z = 1$ as projections of objects in $I\!\!E^3$.

Having determined $w(t)$, we may now write

$$w(t) \left[\begin{array}{c} \mathbf{c}(t) \\ 1 \end{array} \right] = \left[\begin{array}{c} \mathbf{c}(t) \sum w_i B_i^2(t) \\ \sum w_i B_i^2(t) \end{array} \right].$$

Since the left hand side of this equation denotes a parabola, we may write

$$\sum_{i=0}^{2} \left[\begin{array}{c} \mathbf{p}_i \\ w_i \end{array} \right] B_i^2(t) = \left[\begin{array}{c} \mathbf{c}(t) \sum w_i B_i^2(t) \\ \sum w_i B_i^2(t) \end{array} \right]$$

with some points $\mathbf{p}_i \in I\!\!E^2$. Thus

$$\sum_{i=0}^{2} \mathbf{p}_i B_i^2(t) = \mathbf{c}(t) \sum_{i=0}^{2} w_i B_i^2(t), \tag{14.6}$$

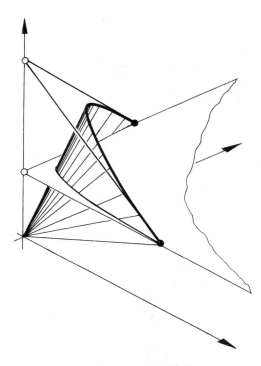

Figure 14.4. Conic sections: a parabolic arc in 3-space is projected into the plane
$z = 1$; the result, in this example, is part of a hyperbola.

and hence
$$\mathbf{c}(t) = \frac{\mathbf{p}_0 B_0^2(t) + \mathbf{p}_1 B_1^2(t) + \mathbf{p}_2 B_2^2(t)}{w_0 B_0^2(t) + w_1 B_1^2(t) + w_2 B_2^2(t)}.$$

Setting $\mathbf{p}_i = w_i \mathbf{b}_i$ now proves (14.5).

We call the points $\mathbf{b}_i$ the *control polygon* of the conic $\mathbf{c}$; the numbers w_i
are called *weights* of the corresponding control polygon vertices. Thus the
conic control polygon is the projection of the control polygon with vertices
$\begin{bmatrix} w_i \mathbf{b}_i & w_i \end{bmatrix}^{\mathrm{T}}$, which is the control polygon of the 3D parabola that we
projected onto $\mathbf{c}$.

The form (14.5) is called the *rational quadratic form* of a conic section.
If all weights are equal, we recover nonrational quadratics, i.e., parabolas.
The influence of the weights on the shape of the conic is illustrated in Figure
14.5. In that figure, we have chosen
$$\mathbf{b}_0 = \begin{bmatrix} 0 \\ 1 \end{bmatrix}, \mathbf{b}_1 = \begin{bmatrix} 0 \\ 0 \end{bmatrix}, \mathbf{b}_2 = \begin{bmatrix} 1 \\ 0 \end{bmatrix}.$$

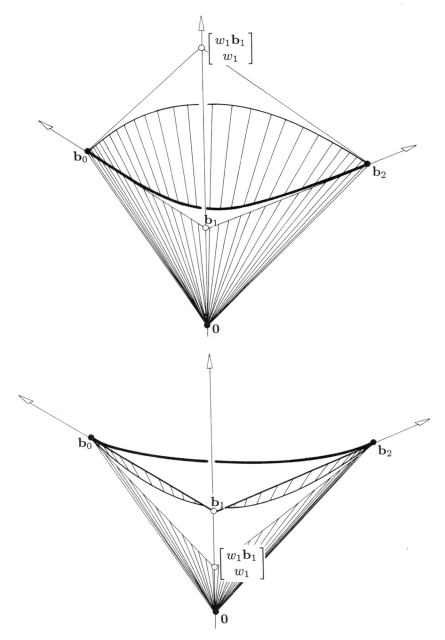

Figure 14.5. Conic sections: in the two shown examples, $w_0 = w_2 = 1$. As w_1 becomes larger, i.e., as $[w_1 \mathbf{b}_1, w_1]$ moves "up" on the z−axis, the conic is "pulled" towards $\mathbf{b}_1$.

Note that a common nonzero factor in the w_i does not affect the conic at all. If $w_0 \neq 0$, one may therefore always achieve $w_0 = 1$ by a simple scaling of all w_i. There are other changes of the weights that leave the curve shape unchanged: these correspond to *rational linear parameter transformations*. Let us set

$$t = \frac{\hat{t}}{\hat{\rho}(1 - \hat{t}) + \hat{t}}, \quad (1 - t) = \frac{\hat{\rho}(1 - \hat{t})}{\hat{\rho}(1 - \hat{t}) + \hat{t}}$$

(corresponding to the choice $\rho = 1$ in (14.4)). We may insert this into (14.5) and obtain:

$$\mathbf{c}(\hat{t}) = \frac{\hat{\rho}^2 w_0 \mathbf{b}_0 B_0^2(\hat{t}) + \hat{\rho} w_1 \mathbf{b}_1 B_1^2(\hat{t}) + w_2 \mathbf{b}_2 B_2^2(\hat{t})}{\hat{\rho}^2 w_0 B_0^2(\hat{t}) + \hat{\rho} w_1 B_1^2(\hat{t}) + w_2 B_2^2(\hat{t})}. \quad (14.7)$$

Thus the curve shape is not changed if each weight w_i is replaced by $\hat{w}_i = \hat{\rho}^{2-i} w_i$. If, for a given set of weights w_i, we select

$$\hat{\rho} = \sqrt{\frac{w_2}{w_0}},$$

we obtain $\hat{w}_0 = w_2$, and, after dividing all three weights through by w_2, we even have $\hat{w}_0 = \hat{w}_2 = 1$. A conic that satisfies this condition is said to be in *standard form*. All conics with $w_0, w_2 \neq 0$ may be rewritten in standard form with the above choice of $\hat{\rho}$.

If in standard form, i.e., $w_0 = w_2 = 1$, the point $\mathbf{s} = \mathbf{c}(\frac{1}{2})$ is called *shoulder point*. The shoulder point tangent is parallel to $\mathbf{b}_0 \mathbf{b}_2$. If we set $\mathbf{m} = (\mathbf{b}_0 + \mathbf{b}_2)/2$, then the ratio of the three collinear points $\mathbf{m}, \mathbf{s}, \mathbf{b}_1$ is given by

$$\mathrm{ratio}(\mathbf{m}, \mathbf{s}, \mathbf{b}_1) = w_1.$$

We finish this section with a theorem that will be useful in the later development of rational curves: *Any four tangents to a conic intersect each other in the same cross ratio.* The theorem is illustrated in Figure 14.6. The proof of this Four Tangent Theorem is simple: one shows that it is true for parabolas (see Problems). It then follows for all conics by their definition as a projection of a parabola and by the fact that cross ratios are invariant under projections. This theorem is due to J. Steiner. It is a projective version of the Three Tangent Theorem from Section 3.1.

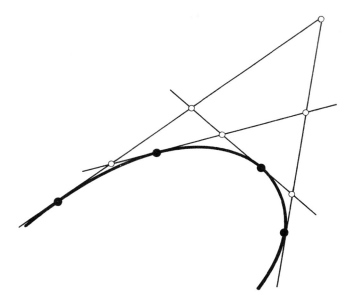

Figure 14.6. The Four Tangent Theorem: there are four points marked on each of the four tangents to the shown conic. The four cross ratios generated by them are all equal.

14.3 A de Casteljau Algorithm

We may evaluate (14.5) by evaluating the numerator and the denominator separately and then dividing through. A more geometric algorithm is obtained by projecting each intermediate de Casteljau point $\begin{bmatrix} w_i^r \mathbf{b}_i^r & w_i^r \end{bmatrix}^{\mathrm{T}}$ into $I\!\!E^2$:

$$\mathbf{b}_i^r(t) = (1-t)\frac{w_i^{r-1}}{w_i^r}\mathbf{b}_i^{r-1} + t\frac{w_{i+1}^{r-1}}{w_i^r}\mathbf{b}_{i+1}^{r-1}, \tag{14.8}$$

where

$$w_i^r(t) = (1-t)w_i^{r-1}(t) + tw_{i+1}^{r-1}(t). \tag{14.9}$$

This algorithm has a strong connection to the Four Tangent Theorem above: if we introduce auxiliary points

$$\mathbf{q}_i^r(t) = \frac{w_i^r\mathbf{b}_i^r + w_{i+1}^r\mathbf{b}_{i+1}^r}{w_i^r + w_{i+1}^r}, \tag{14.10}$$

then

$$\mathrm{cr}(\mathbf{b}_i^r, \mathbf{q}_i^r, \mathbf{b}_i^{r+1}, \mathbf{b}_{i+1}^r) = \frac{1-t}{t} \tag{14.11}$$

assumes the same value for all r, i. While computationally more involved than the straightforward algebraic approach, this generalized de Casteljau algorithm has the advantage of being numerically stable: it uses only convex combinations, provided the weights are positive and $t \in [0, 1]$.

14.4 Derivatives

In order to find the derivative of a conic section, i.e., the vector $\dot{\mathbf{c}}(t) = \mathrm{d}\mathbf{c}/\mathrm{d}t$, we may employ the quotient rule. For a simpler derivation, let us rewrite (14.6) as

$$\mathbf{p}(t) = w(t)\mathbf{c}(t).$$

We apply the product rule:

$$\dot{\mathbf{p}}(t) = \dot{w}(t)\mathbf{c}(t) + w(t)\dot{\mathbf{c}}(t)$$

and solve for $\dot{\mathbf{c}}(t)$:

$$\dot{\mathbf{c}}(t) = \frac{1}{w(t)}[\dot{\mathbf{p}}(t) - \dot{w}(t)\mathbf{c}(t)]. \tag{14.12}$$

We may evaluate (14.12) at the endpoint $t = 0$:

$$\dot{\mathbf{c}}(0) = \frac{2}{w_0}[w_1\mathbf{b}_1 - w_0\mathbf{b}_0 - (w_1 - w_0)\mathbf{b}_0].$$

After some simplifications we obtain

$$\dot{\mathbf{c}}(0) = \frac{2w_1}{w_0}\Delta\mathbf{b}_0. \tag{14.13}$$

Similarly, we obtain

$$\dot{\mathbf{c}}(1) = \frac{2w_1}{w_2}\Delta\mathbf{b}_1. \tag{14.14}$$

Let us now consider two conics, one defined over the interval $[u_0, u_1]$ with control polygon $\mathbf{b}_0, \mathbf{b}_1, \mathbf{b}_2$ and weights w_0, w_1, w_2 and the other defined over the interval $[u_1, u_2]$ with control polygon $\mathbf{b}_2, \mathbf{b}_3, \mathbf{b}_4$ and weights w_2, w_3, w_4. Both segments form a C^1 curve if

$$\frac{w_1}{\Delta_0}\Delta\mathbf{b}_1 = \frac{w_3}{\Delta_1}\Delta\mathbf{b}_2, \tag{14.15}$$

where the appearance of the interval lengths Δ_i is due to the application of the chain rule, which is necessary since we now consider a composite curve with a global parameter u; see also Section 7.1.

14.5   The Implicit Form

Every conic $\mathbf{c}(t)$ has an *implicit representation* of the form

$$f(x,y) = 0,$$

where f is a quadratic polynomial in x and y. In order to find this representation, recall that $\mathbf{c}(t)$ may be written in terms of barycentric coordinates of the polygon vertices $\mathbf{b}_0, \mathbf{b}_1, \mathbf{b}_2$:

$$\mathbf{c}(t) = \tau_0 \mathbf{b}_0 + \tau_1 \mathbf{b}_1 + \tau_2 \mathbf{b}_2; \qquad (14.16)$$

see Section 18.1. Since $\mathbf{c}(t)$ may also be written as a rational Bézier curve (14.5), and since both representations are unique, we may compare the coefficients of the $\mathbf{b}_i$:

$$
\begin{aligned}
\tau_0 &= [w_0(1-t)^2]/D, & (14.17) \\
\tau_1 &= [2w_1 t(1-t)]/D, & (14.18) \\
\tau_2 &= [w_2 t^2]/D, & (14.19)
\end{aligned}
$$

where $D = \sum w_i B_i^2$. We may solve (14.17) and (14.19) for $(1-t)$ and t, respectively. Inserting both expressions into (14.18) yields

$$\tau_1^2 = 4\frac{\tau_0 \tau_2 w_1^2}{w_0 w_2}.$$

This may be written more symmetrically as

$$\frac{\tau_1^2}{\tau_0 \tau_2} = \frac{4w_1^2}{w_0 w_2}. \qquad (14.20)$$

This is the desired implicit form, since the barycentric coordinates u, v, w of $\mathbf{c}(t)$ are given by

$$
\tau_0 = \frac{\begin{vmatrix} c^x & b_1^x & b_2^x \\ c^y & b_1^y & b_2^y \\ 1 & 1 & 1 \end{vmatrix}}{\begin{vmatrix} b_0^x & b_1^x & b_2^x \\ b_0^y & b_1^y & b_2^y \\ 1 & 1 & 1 \end{vmatrix}}, \quad
\tau_1 = \frac{\begin{vmatrix} b_0^x & c^x & b_2^x \\ b_0^y & c^y & b_2^y \\ 1 & 1 & 1 \end{vmatrix}}{\begin{vmatrix} b_0^x & b_1^x & b_2^x \\ b_0^y & b_1^y & b_2^y \\ 1 & 1 & 1 \end{vmatrix}}, \quad
\tau_2 = \frac{\begin{vmatrix} b_0^x & b_1^x & c^x \\ b_0^y & b_1^y & c^y \\ 1 & 1 & 1 \end{vmatrix}}{\begin{vmatrix} b_0^x & b_1^x & b_2^x \\ b_0^y & b_1^y & b_2^y \\ 1 & 1 & 1 \end{vmatrix}}.
$$

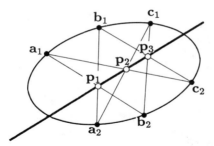

Figure 14.7. Pascal's Theorem: the intersections points $\mathbf{p}_1, \mathbf{p}_2, \mathbf{p}_3$ of the indicated pairs of straight lines are collinear.

The implicit form has an important application: suppose we are given a conic section $\mathbf{c}$ and an arbitrary point $\mathbf{x} \in I\!\!E^2$. Does $\mathbf{x}$ lie on $\mathbf{c}$? This question is hard to answer if $\mathbf{c}$ is given in the parametric form (14.5). Using the implicit form, this question is answered easily. First, compute the barycentric coordinates τ_0, τ_1, τ_2 of $\mathbf{x}$ with respect to $\mathbf{b}_0, \mathbf{b}_1, \mathbf{b}_2$. Then insert τ_0, τ_1, τ_2 into (14.20). If (14.20) is satisfied, $\mathbf{x}$ lies on the conic.

Any conic section is uniquely determined by five distinct points in the plane. If the points have coordinates $(x_1, y_1), \ldots, (x_5, y_5)$, the implicit form of the interpolating conic is given by

$$f(x,y) = \begin{vmatrix} x^2 & xy & y^2 & x & y & 1 \\ x_1^2 & x_1y_1 & y_1^2 & x_1 & y_1 & 1 \\ x_2^2 & x_2y_2 & y_2^2 & x_2 & y_2 & 1 \\ x_3^2 & x_3y_3 & y_3^2 & x_3 & y_3 & 1 \\ x_4^2 & x_4y_4 & y_4^2 & x_4 & y_4 & 1 \\ x_5^2 & x_5y_5 & y_5^2 & x_5 & y_5 & 1 \end{vmatrix} = 0.$$

The fact that five points are sufficient to determine a conic is a consequence of the most fundamental theorem in the theory of conics, *Pascal's Theorem*. Consider six points on a conic, arranged as in Figure 14.7. If we connect points as shown, we form six straight lines. Pascal's theorem states that the three intersection points $\mathbf{p}_1, \mathbf{p}_2, \mathbf{p}_3$ are always collinear.

It can be used to *construct* a conic through five points: referring to Figure 14.7 again, let $\mathbf{a}_1, \mathbf{b}_1, \mathbf{c}_1, \mathbf{a}_2, \mathbf{b}_2$ be given (no three of them collinear). Let $\mathbf{p}_1$ be the intersection of the two straight lines through $\mathbf{a}_1, \mathbf{b}_2$ and $\mathbf{a}_2, \mathbf{b}_1$. We may now fix a line l through $\mathbf{p}_1$, thus obtaining $\mathbf{p}_2$ and $\mathbf{p}_3$. The sixth point on the conic is then determined as the intersection of the two straight lines through $\mathbf{a}_1, \mathbf{p}_2$ and $\mathbf{b}_1, \mathbf{p}_3$. We may construct arbitrarily many points on the conic by letting the straight line l vary.

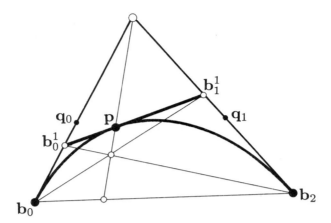

Figure 14.8. Conic constructions: given are $\mathbf{b}_0, \mathbf{b}_1, \mathbf{b}_2$, and the tangent through $\mathbf{b}_0^1$ and $\mathbf{b}_1^1$.

14.6   Two Classic Problems

A large number of methods exists to construct conic sections from given pieces of information, most based on Pascal's Theorem. A nice collection is in the book by R. Liming [243]. An in-depth discussion of those methods is beyond the scope of this book; we restrict ourselves to the solution of two problems.

1. Conic from two points and tangents plus another point. The given data amount to prescribing $\mathbf{b}_0, \mathbf{b}_1, \mathbf{b}_2$. The missing weight w_1 must be determined from the point $\mathbf{p}$, which is assumed to be on the conic. We assume, without loss of generality, that the conic is in standard form ($w_0 = w_2 = 1$).

For the solution, we make use of the implicit form (14.20). We can easily determine the barycentric coordinates τ_0, τ_1, τ_2 of $\mathbf{p}$ with respect to the triangle formed by the three $\mathbf{b}_i$. We can then solve (14.20) for the unknown weight w_1:

$$w_1 = \frac{\tau_1}{2\sqrt{\tau_0 \tau_2}}. \tag{14.21}$$

If $\mathbf{p}$ is inside the triangle formed by $\mathbf{b}_0, \mathbf{b}_1, \mathbf{b}_2$, equation (14.21) always has a solution. Otherwise, problems might occur; see Problems.

2. Conic from two points and tangents plus a third tangent. Again, we are given the Bézier polygon of the conic plus a tangent, which passes through two points that we call $\mathbf{b}_0^1$ and $\mathbf{b}_1^1$. We have to find the interior weight w_1, assuming the conic will be in standard form. The un-

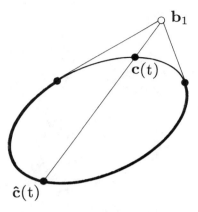

Figure 14.9. The complementary segment: the original conic segment and the complementary segment, both evaluated for all parameter values $t \in [0,1]$, comprise the whole conic section.

known weight w_1 determines the two auxiliary points $\mathbf{q}_0$ and $\mathbf{q}_1$, with $\overline{\mathbf{q}_0, \mathbf{q}_1}$ parallel to $\overline{\mathbf{b}_0, \mathbf{b}_1}$, see Figure 14.8.

We compute the ratios $r_0 = \mathrm{ratio}(\mathbf{b}_0, \mathbf{b}_0^1, \mathbf{b}_1)$ and $r_1 = \mathrm{ratio}(\mathbf{b}_1, \mathbf{b}_1^1, \mathbf{b}_2)$. From the definition of the $\mathbf{q}_i$ (14.10), it follows that $\mathrm{ratio}(\mathbf{b}_0, \mathbf{q}_0, \mathbf{b}_1) = w_1$ and $\mathrm{ratio}(\mathbf{b}_1, \mathbf{q}_1, \mathbf{b}_2) = 1/w_1$. The cross ratio property (14.11) now yields

$$\frac{r_0}{w_1} = r_1 w_1, \qquad (14.22)$$

from which we easily determine $w_1 = \sqrt{r_0/r_1}$. The number under the square root must be nonnegative for this to be meaningful – see Problems.

14.7 Classification

In a projective environment, all conics are equivalent: projective maps map conics to conics. In affine geometry, conics fall into three classes, namely hyperbolas, parabolas, and ellipses. Thus: ellipses are mapped to ellipses under affine maps, parabolas to parabolas, and hyperbolas to hyperbolas. How can we tell of what type a given conic is?

Before we answer that question (following Lee [238]), let us consider the *complementary segment* of a conic. If the conic is in standard form, it is obtained by reversing the sign of w_1. Note that the implicit form (14.20) is not affected by this; hence we still have the same conic, but with a different representation. If $\mathbf{c}(t)$ is a point on the original conic and $\hat{\mathbf{c}}(t)$ is a point

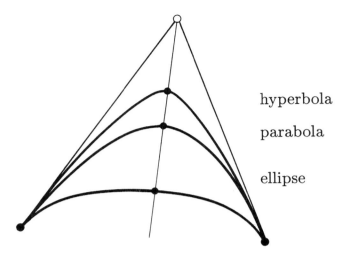

Figure 14.10. Conic classification: the three types of conics are obtained by varying the center weight w_1, assuming $w_0 = w_2 = 1$.

on the complementary segment, one easily verifies that $\mathbf{b}_1, \mathbf{c}(t)$, and $\hat{\mathbf{c}}(t)$ are collinear, as shown in Figure 14.9. If we assume that $w_1 > 0$, then the behavior of $\hat{\mathbf{c}}(t)$ determines of what type the conic is: if $\hat{\mathbf{c}}(t)$ has no singularities in $[0, 1]$, it is an ellipse, if it has one singularity, it is a parabola, and if it has two singularities, it is a hyperbola.

The singularities, corresponding to points at infinity of $\hat{\mathbf{c}}(t)$, are determined by the real roots of the denominator $\hat{w}(t)$ of $\hat{\mathbf{c}}(t)$. There are at most two real roots, and they are given by

$$t_{1,2} = \frac{1 - w_1 \pm \sqrt{w_1^2 - 1}}{2 - 2w_1}.$$

Thus, a conic is an ellipse if $w_1 < 1$, a parabola if $w_1 = 1$, and a hyperbola if $w_1 > 1$. The three types of conics are shown in Figure 14.10. See also Figure 14.5.

The circle is one of the more important conic sections; let us now pay some special attention to it. So let our rational quadratic (with $w_1 < 1$) describe an arc of a circle. Because of the symmetry properties of the circle, the control polygon must form an isosceles triangle. If we know the angle $\alpha = \angle(\mathbf{b}_2, \mathbf{b}_0, \mathbf{b}_1)$, we should be able to determine the weight w_1.[2] We may

---

[2]The actual size of the control polygon does not matter, of course: it can be changed by a scaling to any size we want, and scalings do not affect the weights!

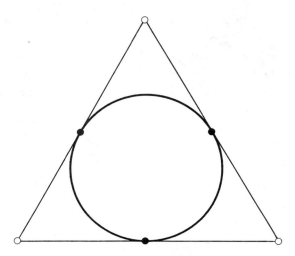

Figure 14.11. Circles: an arc of a circle may be written as three rational Bézier quadratics.

utilize the solution to the second problem in Section 14.6 together with some elementary trigonometry and obtain

$$w_1 = \cos\alpha.$$

A whole circle is representable by piecing several such arcs together. For example, we might choose to represent a circle by three equal arcs, resulting in a configuration as shown in Figure 14.11. The angles α equal 60 degrees, and so the weights of the inner Bézier points is $1/2$, whereas the junction Bézier points have weights of unity, since each arc is in standard form.

Note that we have a representation of the circle that is C^1, assuming uniform parameter intervals. It is not C^2, however! Still we have an *exact* representation of the circle, not an approximation. Thus this particular representation of the circle is an example of a G^2 curve.

14.8   Problems

1. Equation (14.21) does not always have a solution. Identify the "forbidden" regions for the third point **p** on the conic.

2. In the same manner, investigate equation (14.22).

3. Prove that the Four Tangent Theorem holds for parabolas. Hint: use the de Casteljau algorithm and consider Figure 7.4.

4. Establish the connection between (14.11) and the four tangent theorem.

5. In Problem 2 from Section 14.6, find a geometric construction for the point on the conic corresponding to the given tangent.

6. Interpret the solutions to the "classical problems" (Section 14.6) as an application of Pascal's Theorem.

15

Rational Bézier and B-spline Curves

Rational B-spline curves[1] are becoming the standard curve and surface description in the field of CAD and graphics. The growing number of articles concerned with them includes those by Vesprille [345], Tiller [337], and Piegl and Tiller [284]. The use of rational curves in CAGD may be traced back to Coons [87], [85], and Forrest [155].

15.1   Rational Bézier Curves

In the previous chapter, we obtained a conic section in $I\!\!E^2$ as the projection of a parabola (a quadratic) in $I\!\!E^3$. Conic sections may be expressed as rational quadratic (Bézier) curves, and their generalization to higher degree rational curves is quite straightforward: a rational Bézier curve of degree n in $I\!\!E^3$ is the projection of an nth degree Bézier curve in $I\!\!E^4$ into the hyperplane $w = 1$. We may view this 4D hyperplane as a copy of $I\!\!E^3$; we assume that a point in $I\!\!E^4$ is given by its coordinates $\begin{bmatrix} x & y & z & w \end{bmatrix}^{\text{T}}$. Proceeding in exactly the same way as we did for conics, we can show that

---

[1] Often called NURBS for *nonuniform rational B-splines*.

an nth degree rational Bézier curve is given by

$$\mathbf{x}(t) = \frac{w_0\mathbf{b}_0 B_0^n(t) + \cdots + w_n\mathbf{b}_n B_n^n(t)}{w_0 B_0^n(t) + \cdots + w_n B_n^n(t)}; \quad \mathbf{x}(t), \mathbf{b}_i \in I\!\!E^3. \tag{15.1}$$

The w_i are again called *weights*; the $\mathbf{b}_i$ form the control polygon. It is the projection of the 4D control polygon $\begin{bmatrix} w_i\mathbf{b}_i & w_i \end{bmatrix}^{\text{T}}$ of the nonrational 4D preimage of $\mathbf{x}(t)$.

If all weights equal one,[2] we obtain the standard nonrational Bézier curve; in that case, the denominator is identically equal to one. If some w_i are negative, singularities may occur; we will therefore only deal with nonnegative w_i. Rational Bézier curves enjoy all the properties that their nonrational counterparts possess; for example, they are affinely invariant. We can see this by rewriting (15.1) as

$$\mathbf{x}(t) = \sum_{i=0}^{n} \mathbf{b}_i \frac{w_i B_i^n(t)}{\sum_{i=0}^{n} w_i B_i^n(t)}.$$

We see that the basis functions

$$\frac{w_i B_i^n(t)}{\sum_{i=0}^{n} w_i B_i^n(t)}$$

sum to one identically, thus asserting affine invariance. If all w_i are nonnegative, we have the convex hull property. We also have symmetry, invariance under affine parameter transformations, endpoint interpolation, and the variation diminishing property. Obviously, the conic sections from the preceding section are included in the set of all rational Bézier curves, further justifying their increasing popularity.

The w_i are typically used as *shape parameters*. If we increase one w_i, the curve is pulled toward the corresponding $\mathbf{b}_i$, as illustrated in Figure 15.1. Note that the effect of changing a weight is different from that of moving a control vertex, illustrated in Figure 15.1. If we let all weights tend to infinity at the same rate, we do *not* approach the control polygon since a common (if large) factor in the weights does not matter – the rational Bézier curve shape parameters behave differently from $\gamma-$ or $\nu-$spline shape parameters.

---

[2]It is sufficient to set them all equal – a common factor does not matter.

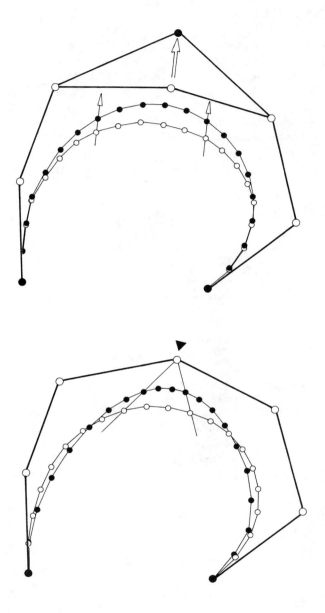

Figure 15.1. Influence of the weights: top, a nonrational curve with a change in one control point. Bottom, with one weight changed.

15.2   The de Casteljau Algorithm

A rational Bézier curve may be evaluated by applying the de Casteljau algorithm to both numerator and denominator and finally dividing through. A warning is in place: while simple and usually effective, this method is not numerically stable. If some of the w_i are large, the 3D intermediate control points $[w_i \mathbf{b}_i]^r$ are no longer in the convex hull of the original control polygon $\{\mathbf{b}_i\}$; this may result in a loss of accuracy.[3]

An expensive yet more accurate technique is to project every intermediate de Casteljau point $\begin{bmatrix} w_i\mathbf{b}_i & w_i \end{bmatrix}^{\mathrm{T}}$; $\mathbf{b}_i \in I\!\!E^3$ into the hyperplane $w = 1$. This yields the rational de Casteljau algorithm (see Farin [120]):

$$\mathbf{b}_i^r(t) = (1-t)\frac{w_i^{r-1}}{w_i^r}\mathbf{b}_i^{r-1} + t\frac{w_{i+1}^{r-1}}{w_i^r}\mathbf{b}_{i+1}^{r-1}, \qquad (15.2)$$

with

$$w_i^r(t) = (1-t)w_i^{r-1}(t) + tw_{i+1}^{r-1}(t). \qquad (15.3)$$

An explicit form for the intermediate points $\mathbf{b}_i^r$ is given by

$$\mathbf{b}_i^r(t) = \frac{\sum_{j=0}^r w_{i+j}\mathbf{b}_{i+j}B_j^r(t)}{\sum_{j=0}^r w_{i+j}B_j^r(t)}.$$

Note that for positive weights, the $\mathbf{b}_i^r$ are all in the convex hull of original $\mathbf{b}_i$, thus assuring numerical stability.

The rational de Casteljau algorithm allows a nice geometric interpretation. While the standard de Casteljau algorithm makes use of ratios of three points, this one makes use of the *cross ratio of four points*. Let us define auxiliary points $\mathbf{q}_i^r(t)$ that are located on the straight lines joining $\mathbf{b}_i^r$ and $\mathbf{b}_{i+1}^r$, subdividing them in the ratio

$$\mathrm{ratio}(\mathbf{b}_i^r, \mathbf{q}_i^r, \mathbf{b}_{i+1}^r) = \frac{w_{i+1}^r}{w_i^r}.$$

Then all of the following cross ratios are equal:

$$\mathrm{cr}(\mathbf{b}_i^r, \mathbf{q}_i^r, \mathbf{b}_i^{r+1}, \mathbf{b}_{i+1}^r) = \frac{1-t}{t} \quad \text{for all } r, i.$$

---

[3]These points are obtained by applying the de Casteljau algorithm to the control points $w_i\mathbf{b}_i$ of the numerator of (15.1).

For $r = 0$, the auxiliary points

$$\mathbf{q}_i = \mathbf{q}_i^0 = \frac{w_i \mathbf{b}_i + w_{i+1} \mathbf{b}_{i+1}}{w_i + w_{i+1}}$$

are directly related to the weights w_i: given the weights, we can find the $\mathbf{q}_i$, and given the $\mathbf{q}_i$, we can find the weights w_i.[4] Thus the $\mathbf{q}_i$ may be used as *shape parameters*: moving a $\mathbf{q}_i$ along the polygon leg $\mathbf{b}_i, \mathbf{b}_{i+1}$ influences the shape of the curve. It may be preferable to let a designer use these geometric handles rather than requiring him or her to input numbers for the weights.[5]

As in the nonrational case, the de Casteljau algorithm may be used to *subdivide* a curve. The de Casteljau algorithm subdivides the 4D preimage of our 3D rational Bézier curve $\mathbf{x}(t)$, see Section 7.2. The intermediate 4D points $\begin{bmatrix} w_i^r \mathbf{b}_i^r & w_i^r \end{bmatrix}^{\mathrm{T}}$; $\mathbf{b}_i^r \in \mathbb{E}^3$, may be projected into the hyperplane $w = 1$ to provide us with the control polygons for the "left" and "right" curve segment: the control vertices and weights corresponding to the interval $[0, t]$ are given by

$$\mathbf{b}_i^{\text{left}} = \mathbf{b}_0^i(t), \quad w_i^{\text{left}} = w_0^i, \tag{15.4}$$

where the $\mathbf{b}_0^i(t)$ and the w_0^i are computed from (15.2). The control points and weights corresponding to the interval $[t, 1]$ are given by

$$\mathbf{b}_i^{\text{right}} = \mathbf{b}_{n-i}^i(t), \quad w_i^{\text{right}} = w_{n-i}^i. \tag{15.5}$$

15.3 Derivatives

For the first derivative of a rational Bézier curve, we obtain

$$\dot{\mathbf{x}}(t) = \frac{1}{w(t)} [\dot{\mathbf{p}}(t) - \dot{w}(t)\mathbf{x}(t)], \tag{15.6}$$

where we have set

$$\mathbf{p}(t) = w(t)\mathbf{x}(t); \quad \mathbf{p}(t), \mathbf{x}(t) \in \mathbb{E}^3 \tag{15.7}$$

---

[4]To be precise, we can only find them modulo an – immaterial – common factor.
[5]This situation is similar to the way curves are generated using the direct G^2 spline algorithm from Chapter 12 as compared to the generation of γ–splines.

in complete analogy to the development in Section 14.4. For higher derivatives, we differentiate (15.7) r times:

$$\mathbf{p}^{(r)}(t) = \sum_{j=0}^{r} \binom{r}{j} w^{(j)}(t)\mathbf{x}^{(r-j)}(t).$$

We can solve for $\mathbf{x}^{(r)}(t)$:

$$\mathbf{x}^{(r)}(t) = \frac{1}{w(t)}[\mathbf{p}^{(r)} - \sum_{j=1}^{r} \binom{r}{j} w^{(j)}(t)\mathbf{x}^{(r-j)}(t)]. \tag{15.8}$$

This is a recursive formula for the rth derivative of a rational Bézier curve. It only involves taking derivatives of polynomial curves.

For the first derivative at the endpoint of a rational Bézier curve, we find

$$\dot{\mathbf{x}}(0) = \frac{n w_1}{w_0}\Delta\mathbf{b}_0.$$

Let us now consider two rational Bézier curves, one defined over the interval $[u_0, u_1]$ with control polygon $\mathbf{b}_0, \ldots, \mathbf{b}_n$ and weights $w_0, \ldots, w_n$ and the other defined over the interval $[u_1, u_2]$ with control polygon $\mathbf{b}_n, \ldots, \mathbf{b}_{2n}$ and weights $w_n, \ldots, w_{2n}$. Both segments form a C^1 curve if

$$\frac{w_{n-1}}{\Delta_0}\Delta\mathbf{b}_{n-1} = \frac{w_{n+1}}{\Delta_1}\Delta\mathbf{b}_n, \tag{15.9}$$

where the appearance of the interval lengths Δ_i is due to the application of the chain rule, which is necessary since we now consider a composite curve with a global parameter u; as explained in Section 7.1.

While the computation of higher order derivatives is quite involved in the case of rational Bézier curves, we note that the computation of curvature or torsion may be simplified by the application of formula 11.9 or 11.10 and 11.11.

15.4   Osculatory Interpolation

With rational cubics, it is easy to solve an interesting kind of interpolation problem: given a Bézier polygon $\mathbf{b}_0, \mathbf{b}_1, \mathbf{b}_2, \mathbf{b}_3$ and a curvature value at each endpoint, find a set of weights w_0, w_1, w_2, w_3 such that the corresponding rational cubic assumes the given curvatures at $\mathbf{b}_0$ and $\mathbf{b}_1$. The following method is very similar to one developed by T. Goodman in 1988; see [174]. We assume without loss of generality that $w_0 = w_3 = 1$.[6] The given curvatures κ_0 and κ_3 are then related to the unknown weights by (11.10):

$$\kappa_0 = \frac{4}{3} \frac{w_2}{w_1^2} c_0, \quad \kappa_3 = \frac{4}{3} \frac{w_1}{w_2^2} c_1, \tag{15.10}$$

where

$$c_0 = \frac{\text{area}[\mathbf{b}_0, \mathbf{b}_1, \mathbf{b}_2]}{\text{dist}^3[\mathbf{b}_0, \mathbf{b}_1]}, \quad c_1 = \frac{\text{area}[\mathbf{b}_1, \mathbf{b}_2, \mathbf{b}_3]}{\text{dist}^3[\mathbf{b}_2, \mathbf{b}_3]}.$$

Equations(15.10) decouple nicely, so that we can determine our unknowns w_1 and w_2:

$$w_1 = \frac{4}{3} \Big[\frac{c_0^2}{\kappa_0^2} \frac{c_1}{\kappa_1} \Big]^{\frac{1}{3}}, \quad w_2 = \frac{4}{3} \Big[\frac{c_0}{\kappa_0} \frac{c_1^2}{\kappa_1^2} \Big]^{\frac{1}{3}}. \tag{15.11}$$

For planar control polygons, the quantities c_0 or c_1 may be negative – this happens when a control polygon is S-shaped. This is meaningful since curvature may be defined as *signed curvature* for 2D curves, as defined in (23.1). Of course, one should then also prescribe the corresponding κ_0 and κ_1 as being negative, so that one ends up with positive weights.

A similar interpolation problem was addressed by Klass [228] and de Boor, Hollig, and Sabin for the nonrational case: they prescribe two points and corresponding tangent directions and curvatures [101]. The solution (when it exists) can only be obtained using an iterative method.

15.5   Reparametrization and Degree Elevation

Arguing exactly as in the conic case (see the end of Section 14.2), we may *reparametrize* a rational Bézier curve by changing the weights according to

$$\hat{w}_i = c^i w_i; \quad i = 0, \ldots, n,$$

---

[6]Goodman [174] assumes that $w_1 = w_2 = 1$.

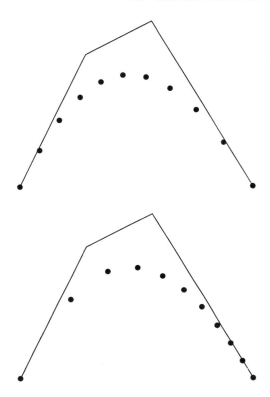

Figure 15.2. Reparametrizations: top, a rational Bézier curve evaluated at parameter values $0, 0.1, 0.2, \ldots, 1$. Bottom, the same curve and parameter values but after a reparametrization with $c = 3$.

where c is any nonzero constant. Figure 15.2 shows how the reparametrization affects the parameter spacing on the curve; note that the curve shape remains the same. We may always transform a rational Bézier curve to *standard form* by using the rational linear parameter transformation resulting from the choice

$$c = \sqrt[n]{\frac{w_0}{w_n}}.$$

This results in $\hat{w}_n = w_0$; after dividing all weights through by w_0, we have the standard form $\hat{w}_0 = \hat{w}_n = 1$. A different derivation of this result is in Patterson [272].

How can rational Bézier curvesin non-standard form arise? A common case occurs in connection with rational Bézier surfaces, as discussed in Section 17.7: the end weights of an isoparametric curve will in general not

Figure 15.3. Ambiguous curve representations: the two heavy polygons represent the same rational quartic. Also indicated is the rational cubic representation that they were both obtained from.

be unity. Such curves are often "extracted" from a surface and then treated as entities in their own right.

We may perform *degree elevation* (in analogy to Section 5.1) by degree elevating the 4D polygon with control vertices $\begin{bmatrix} w_i \mathbf{b}_i & w_i \end{bmatrix}^T$ and projecting the resulting control vertices into the hyperplane $w = 1$. Let us denote the control vertices of the degree elevated curve by $\mathbf{b}_i^{(1)}$; they are given by

$$\mathbf{b}_i^{(1)} = \frac{w_{i-1}\alpha_i \mathbf{b}_{i-1} + w_i(1-\alpha_i)\mathbf{b}_i}{w_{i-1}\alpha_i + w_i(1-\alpha_i)}; \quad i = 0, \ldots, n+1 \qquad (15.12)$$

and $\alpha_i = i/(n+1)$. The weights $w_i^{(1)}$ of the new control vertices are given by

$$w_i^{(1)} = w_{i-1}\alpha_i + w_i(1-\alpha_i); \quad i = 0, \ldots, n+1.$$

The connection of reparametrization and degree elevation may lead to surprising situations. Consider the following procedure: take any rational Bézier curve in standard form and degree elevate it. Next, take the original curve, reparametrize it, then degree elevate it and bring it to standard form. We end up with two different polygons (and two different sets of standardized weights) that both describe the same rational curve. This situation is very different from the nonrational case! It is illustrated in Figure 15.3.

For the sake of completeness, we should mention that other ways exist to reparametrize rational curves than just by rational linear reparametrizations. For example, the reparametrization $t \leftarrow \alpha t(1-t)$ does not change the curve, but it raises the degree from n to $2n$. As long as the reparametrization is of the form $t \leftarrow r(t)$, where $r(t)$ is a rational polynomial, we do not leave the class of rational curves. It is an interesting task to determine if a rational curve has been "degree elevated" in this way. For a solution, consult Sederberg [325].

15.6 Rational Cubic B-spline Curves

In this section, we take advantage of the special notation from Chapter 7. A 3D rational cubic B-spline curve is the projection through the origin of a 4D nonrational cubic B-spline curve into the hyperplane $w = 1$. The control polygon of the rational B-spline curve is given by vertices $\mathbf{d}_{-1}, \ldots, \mathbf{d}_{L+1}$; each vertex $\mathbf{d}_i \in I\!\!E^3$ has a corresponding weight w_i. The rational B-spline curve has a piecewise rational cubic Bézier representation. It may be obtained by projecting the corresponding 4D Bézier points into the hyperplane $w = 1$. Thus we obtain

$$\mathbf{b}_{3i-2} = \frac{w_{i-1}(1 - \alpha_i)\mathbf{d}_{i-1} + w_i \alpha_i \mathbf{d}_i}{v_{3i-2}} \tag{15.13}$$

$$\mathbf{b}_{3i-1} = \frac{w_{i-1}\beta_i \mathbf{d}_{i-1} + w_i(1 - \beta_i)\mathbf{d}_i}{v_{3i-1}}, \tag{15.14}$$

where all points $\mathbf{b}_j, \mathbf{d}_k$ are in $I\!\!E^3$ and

$$\Delta = \Delta_{i-2} + \Delta_{i-1} + \Delta_i,$$
$$\alpha_i = \frac{\Delta_{i-2}}{\Delta},$$
$$\beta_i = \frac{\Delta_i}{\Delta}.$$

The weights of these Bézier points are given by

$$v_{3i-2} = w_{i-1}(1 - \alpha_i) + w_i \alpha_i, \tag{15.15}$$
$$v_{3i-1} = w_{i-1}\beta_i + w_i(1 - \beta_i). \tag{15.16}$$

For the junction points, we obtain

$$\mathbf{b}_{3i} = \frac{\gamma_i v_{3i-1}\mathbf{b}_{3i-1} + (1 - \gamma_i)v_{3i+1}\mathbf{b}_{3i+1}}{v_{3i}}. \tag{15.17}$$

where

$$\gamma_i = \frac{\Delta_i}{\Delta_{i-1} + \Delta_i}$$

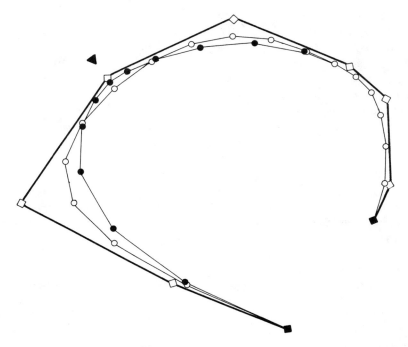

Figure 15.4. Rational B-splines: the weight of the indicated control point is changed. The curve is only affected locally.

and

$$v_{3i} = \gamma_i v_{3i-1} + (1 - \gamma_i)v_{3i+1}$$

is the weight of the junction point $\mathbf{b}_{3i}$.

Another way to generate the piecewise rational Bézier polygon is by taking the control polygon $[w_i \mathbf{d}_i, w_i]^{\mathrm{T}}$, converting it to Bézier form, and then dividing through by the Bézier weights. This is less geometric, but was still chosen as the basis for the C procedure `ratbspline_to_bezier` at the end of this section, simply because it is more efficient.

Designing with rational B-spline curves is not very different from designing with their nonrational counterparts. We now have the added freedom of being able to change weights. A change of only one weight affects a rational B-spline curve only locally, as shown in Figure 15.4.

This development follows the general philosophy of computing with rational curves: we are given 3D points $\mathbf{x}_i$ and their weights w_i. Transform them to 4D points $\begin{bmatrix} w_i \mathbf{x}_i & w_i \end{bmatrix}^{\mathrm{T}}$ and perform 4D nonrational algorithms (for example, finding the Bézier points of a B-spline curve). The result of these operations will be a set of 4D points $\begin{bmatrix} \mathbf{y}_i & v_i \end{bmatrix}^{\mathrm{T}}$. From these, obtain 3D points $\mathbf{y}_i/v_i$. The weights of these 3D points are the numbers v_i.

Let us close this section with a result that somewhat limits the use of C^2 rational B-spline curves. *There is no symmetric periodic representation of a circle as a C^2 rational cubic B-spline curve.*

If such a representation existed, it would be of the form

$$\mathbf{x}(u) = \sum w_i \mathbf{d}_i N_i^3(u) / \sum w_i N_i^3(u),$$

where all w_i are equal by symmetry. Then the w_i cancel out, leaving us with an integral B-spline curve, which is not capable of representing a circle. Note, however, that we can represent any *open* circular arc by C^2 rational cubics.

15.7 Interpolation with Rational Cubics

The interpolation problem in the context of rational B-splines is the following:

Given: 3D data points $\mathbf{x}_0, \ldots, \mathbf{x}_L$, parameter values $u_0, \ldots, u_L$, and weights $w_0, \ldots, w_L$.

Find: a C^2 rational B-spline curve with control vertices $\mathbf{d}_{-1}, \ldots, \mathbf{d}_{L+1}$ and weights $v_{-1}, \ldots, v_{L+1}$ that interpolates to the given data and weights.

For the solution of this problem, we follow the philosophy outlined at the end of the last section: solve a 4D interpolation problem to the data points $\begin{bmatrix} w_i \mathbf{x}_i & w_i \end{bmatrix}^{\mathrm{T}}$ and parameter values u_i. All we have to do is to solve the linear system (9.7), where input and output is now 4D instead of the usual 3D. We will obtain a 4D control polygon $\begin{bmatrix} \mathbf{e}_i & v_i \end{bmatrix}^{\mathrm{T}}$, from which we now obtain the desired $\mathbf{d}_i$ as $\mathbf{d}_i = \mathbf{e}_i/v_i$. The v_i are the weights of the control vertices $\mathbf{d}_i$.

We have not yet addressed the problem of how to choose the weights w_i for the data points $\mathbf{x}_i$. No known algorithms exist for this problem. It seems reasonable to assign high weights in regions where the interpolant is expected to curve sharply. Yet there is a limit to the assignment of weights: if all of them are very high, this will not have a significant effect on the curve since a common factor in all weights will simply cancel out. Also, care must be taken to prevent the denominator of the interpolant from being zero. This is not a trivial task – for instance, we might assign a very large weight to one data point while keeping all the others at unity. The resulting weight function $w(t)$ will not be positive everywhere, giving rise to singularities at its zeroes.

Integral cubic spline interpolation has *cubic precision*: if the data points and the parameter values come from one global cubic, the interpolant reproduces that cubic. In the context of rational spline interpolation, an analogous question is that of *conic precision*: if the data points and the parameter values come from one global conic, can we reproduce it? We must also require that the data points have weights assigned to them. With them, we may view the rational spline interpolation problem as an integral spline interpolation problem in $I\!E^4$. There, cubic splines have quadratic precision, i.e., we may recapture any parabola. The projection of the parabola yields a conic section; thus if our data – points, parameter values, and weights – were taken from a conic, rational cubic spline interpolation will reproduce the conic.

We should note, however, that this argument is limited to open curves – for closed curves, we have already seen that we cannot represent a circle as a C^2 symmetric periodic B-spline curve.

15.8   Rational B-splines of Arbitrary Degree

It is now straightforward how to generalize the concept of general B-spline curves to the rational case. A 3D rational B-spline curve is the projection through the origin of a 4D nonrational B-spline curve into the hyperplane $w = 1$. It is thus given by

$$\mathbf{s}(u) = \frac{\sum_{j=0}^{L+n-1} w_i \mathbf{d}_i N_i^n(u)}{\sum_{j=0}^{L+n-1} w_i N_i^n(u)}. \tag{15.18}$$

We have chosen the notation from Chapter 10. Thus (15.18) is the generalization of (10.11) to the rational parametric case.

A rational B-spline curve is given by its knot sequence, its 3D control polygon, and its weight sequence. The control vertices $\mathbf{d}_i$ are the projections of the 4D control vertices $\begin{bmatrix} w_i \mathbf{d}_i & w_i \end{bmatrix}^T$.

To evaluate a rational B-spline curve at a parameter value u, we may apply the de Boor algorithm to both numerator and denominator of (15.18) and finally divide through. This corresponds to the evaluation of the 4D nonrational curve with control vertices $\begin{bmatrix} w_i \mathbf{d}_i & w_i \end{bmatrix}^T$ and to projecting the result into $I\!E^3$. Just as in the case of Bézier curves, this may lead to instabilities, and so we give a rational version of the de Boor algorithm that is more stable but also computationally more involved:

de Boor algorithm, rational: Let $u \in [u_I, u_{I+1}) \subset [u_{n-1}, u_{L+n-1}]$. Define

$$\mathbf{d}_i^k(u) = \left[(1 - \alpha_i^k)w_{i-1}^{k-1}\mathbf{d}_{i-1}^{k-1}(u) + \alpha_i^k w_i^{k-1}\mathbf{d}_i^{k-1}(u)\right]/w_i^k \quad (15.19)$$

for $k = 1, \ldots, n - r$, and $i = I - n + k + 1, \ldots, I + 1$, where

$$\alpha_i^k = \frac{u - u_{i-1}}{u_{i+n-k} - u_{i-1}}$$

and

$$w_i^k = (1 - \alpha_i^k)w_{i-1}^{k-1} + \alpha_i^k w_i^{k-1}.$$

Then

$$\mathbf{s}(u) = \mathbf{d}_{I+1}^{n-r}(u) \quad (15.20)$$

is the point on the B-spline curve at parameter value u. Here, r denotes the multiplicity of u in case it was already one of the knots. If it was not, set $r = 0$. As usual, we set $\mathbf{d}_i^0 = \mathbf{d}_i$ and $w_i^0 = w_i$.

The reader is referred to Section 10.3 for the notation.

Knot insertion is, as in the nonrational case, performed by executing just one step of the de Boor algorithm, i.e., by fixing $k = 1$ in the above algorithm. The original polygon vertices $\mathbf{d}_{I-n+2}, \ldots, \mathbf{d}_I$ are replaced by the $\mathbf{d}_{I-n+2}^{(1)}, \ldots, \mathbf{d}_{I+1}^{(1)}$; their weights are the numbers $w_{I-n+2}^{(1)}, \ldots, w_{I+1}^{(1)}$.

A rational B-spline curve, being piecewise rational polynomial, has a piecewise rational Bézier representation. We can find the Bézier points and their weights for each segment by inserting every knot until it has multiplicity n, i.e., by applying the de Boor algorithm to each knot.

15.9   Implementation

The following computes a point on a rational Bézier curve:

```
float ratbez(degree,coeff,weight,t)
/*
     uses rational de casteljau to compute
     point on ratbez curve for param. value t.
Input: degree:   degree of curve
       coeff:    control point coordinates
       weight:   weights
       t:        evaluation paramter
```

```
*/
    float coeff[],weight[];
    float t;
    int degree;
    {
    int r,i;
    float t1,t2,ww1,ww2;
    float coeffa[20], weighta[20];
    t1 = 1.0 - t;


    for (i=0;i<=degree; i++)
    {
        coeffa[i]=coeff[i];
        weighta[i]=weight[i];
    }

    for (r=1; r<= degree; r++)
    for (i=0; i<= degree - r; i++)
    {
        t1= (i+r-degree*t)/(float)r;
        t2= 1.0-t1;

        ww1 = weighta[i]; ww2= weighta[i+1];
        weighta[i] = t1*ww1 + t2*ww2;
        coeffa[i]= ( t1*ww1 * coeffa[i]
                + t2*ww2 * coeffa[i+1] ) / weighta[i];

    }
    return (coeffa[0]);
    }
```

The next routine subdivides a rational Bézier curve at a parameter value t:

```
float   rat_subdiv(degree,coeff,weight,t,bleft,bright,wleft,wright)
/*
    subdivides ratbez curve at parameter value t.
Input: degree: degree of curve
       coeff:  curve coefficients
       weight: weights
       t:      subdivision parameter value
Output: bleft: left subdivided polygon
        bright: right subdivided polygon
        wleft:  weights of left polygon
        wright: weights of right polygon
Note:   Ordering of right polygon is reversed.
*/
```

```
      float coeff[],weight[],bleft[],
          bright[],wleft[],wright[];
      float t;
      int degree;
{
      int r,i;
      float t1,ww1,ww2;
      t1 = 1.0 - t;
/*
      first, obtain right subpolygon from rat de Casteljau
*/
      for (i=0;i <= degree; i++) wright[i] = weight[i];

      for (i=0;i <= degree; i++) bright[i] = coeff[i];

      for (r=1; r<= degree; r++)
      for (i=0; i<= degree - r; i++)
      {
          ww1 = wright[i]; ww2= wright[i+1];
          wright[i] = t1*wright[i] + t*wright[i+1];
          bright[i]= ( t1*ww1 * bright[i]
                  +  t*ww2 * bright[i+1] ) / wright[i];
      }

/*
      use same as above in order to get left half. Idea:
      reverse ordering; then the above yields left half.
*/
      t = 1.0 - t; t1 = 1.0 - t;
      for (i=0;i <= degree; i++) wleft[degree -i] = weight[i];

      for (i=0;i <= degree; i++) bleft[degree-i] = coeff[i];

      for (r=1; r<= degree; r++)
      for (i=0; i<= degree - r; i++)
      {
          ww1 = wleft[i]; ww2= wleft[i+1];
          wleft[i] = t1*wleft[i] + t*wleft[i+1];
          bleft[i]= ( t1*ww1 * bleft[i]
                  +  t*ww2 * bleft[i+1] ) / wleft[i];
      }

}
```

Finally, a program that generates the piecewise rational Bézier form from a rational cubic B-spline curve:

```
void ratbspline_to_bezier(bspl_x,bspl_y,bspl_w,knot,l,bez_x,bez_y,bez_w)
/* converts rational  cubic B-spline polygon into piecewise
rational Bezier polygon
Input: bspl_x, bspl_y: planar B-spline control polygon
       bspl_w:         B-spline weights
       knot:           knot sequence
       l:              no. of intervals

Output: bez_x, bez_y:  planar piecewise Bezier polygon
        bez_w:         Bezier weights (not in piecewise standard form!)
*/
     float bspl_x[],bspl_y[], bspl_w[], knot[];
     float bez_x[], bez_y[], bez_w[];
     int l;
{
     int i, i3, l3, l2;
     float hbez_x[20], hbez_y[20], hbez_w[20];

     l2=l+2; l3=l*3;

     for(i=0; i<= l2; i++)
     {
         bspl_x[i]=bspl_x[i]*bspl_w[i];          /* create 3D preimage */
         bspl_y[i]=bspl_y[i]*bspl_w[i];          /* of B-spline polygon*/
     }

     bspline_to_bezier(bspl_w,knot,l,hbez_w); /* convert bspline to */
     bspline_to_bezier(bspl_x,knot,l,hbez_x); /* Bezier in 3-space  */
     bspline_to_bezier(bspl_y,knot,l,hbez_y);


     for(i=0; i<= l3; i++)
     {
         bez_x[i]=hbez_x[i]/hbez_w[i];           /* project into 2-space */
         bez_y[i]=hbez_y[i]/hbez_w[i];
         bez_w[i]=hbez_w[i];
     }
}
```

15.10   Problems

1. In Section 15.7, we investigated rational C^2 cubic spline interpolants. Investigate rational G^2 cubic $\nu-$spline or $\gamma-$spline interpolants.

2. Suppose you are given two coplanar rational quadratic segments that form a C^1 curve, but not a G^2 curve. Can you adjust the weights (not the control polygons!) such that the resulting segments form a G^2 curve? Hint: use (11.9).

3. Generalize degree elevation for Bézier curves to the rational case.

4. Define a rational Aitken's algorithm, i.e., one where the data points are assigned weights. Try to adjust those weights in an attempt to reduce the oscillatory behavior of the interpolant.

5. In Section 15.4, we said that signed curvature only makes sense in $\mathbb{E}^2$. Why not in $\mathbb{E}^3$?

16

Tensor Product Bézier Surfaces

The first person to consider this class of surfaces for design purposes was probably de Casteljau, who was investigating them between 1959 and 1963. The popularity of this type of surfaces is, however, due to the work of Bézier only slightly later, as documented in Chapter 1. Initially, Bézier patches were only used to approximate a given surface. It took some time until people realized that any B-spline surface can also be written in piecewise Bézier form.

We will use the example of Bézier patches to demonstrate the tensor product approach to surface patches. Once that principle is developed, it will be trivial to generalize other curve schemes to tensor product surfaces.

16.1 Bilinear Interpolation

In Section 2.3 we studied linear interpolation in $\mathbb{E}^3$ and derived properties of this elementary method that we then used for the development of Bézier curves. In an analogous fashion, one can base the theory of *tensor product Bézier surfaces* on the concept of *bilinear interpolation*. While linear interpolation fits the "simplest" *curve* between two points, bilinear interpolation fits the "simplest" *surface* between four points.

To be more precise: Let $\mathbf{b}_{0,0}, \mathbf{b}_{0,1}, \mathbf{b}_{1,0}, \mathbf{b}_{1,1}$ be four distinct points in $\mathbb{E}^3$.

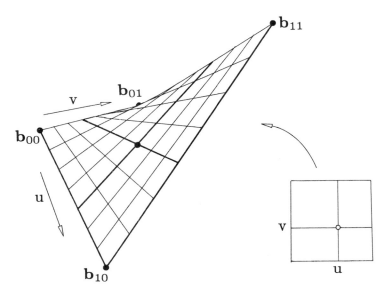

Figure 16.1. Bilinear interpolation: a hyperbolic paraboloid is defined by four points $\mathbf{b}_{i,j}$.

The set of all points $\mathbf{x} \in I\!\!E^3$ of the form

$$\mathbf{x}(u,v) = \sum_{i=0}^{1} \sum_{j=0}^{1} \mathbf{b}_{i,j} B_i^1(u) B_j^1(v) \tag{16.1}$$

is called a *hyperbolic paraboloid* through the four $\mathbf{b}_{i,j}$. In matrix form:

$$\mathbf{x}(u,v) = \begin{bmatrix} 1-u & u \end{bmatrix} \begin{bmatrix} \mathbf{b}_{00} & \mathbf{b}_{01} \\ \mathbf{b}_{10} & \mathbf{b}_{11} \end{bmatrix} \begin{bmatrix} 1-v \\ v \end{bmatrix}. \tag{16.2}$$

Since (16.1) is linear in both u and v and it interpolates to the input points, the surface $\mathbf{x}$ is called the *bilinear interpolant*. An example is shown in Figure 16.1.

The bilinear interpolant can be viewed as a map of the unit square $0 \leq u, v \leq 1$ in the u, v-plane. We say that the unit square is the *domain* of the interpolant, while the surface $\mathbf{x}$ is its *range*. A line parallel to one of the the axes in the domain corresponds to a curve in the range; it is called an *isoparametric curve*. Every isoparametric curve of the hyperbolic paraboloid (16.1) is a straight line, thus, hyperbolic paraboloids are *ruled surfaces*; see also Sections 20.1 and 22.10. In particular, the isoparametric line $u = 0$ is mapped onto the straight line through $\mathbf{b}_{0,0}$ and $\mathbf{b}_{0,1}$; analogous statements hold for the other three boundary curves.

Instead of evaluating the bilinear interpolant directly, one can apply a two-stage process that we will employ later in the context of tensor product interpolation. We can compute two intermediate points

$$
\begin{aligned}
\mathbf{b}_{0,0}^{0,1} &= (1 - v)\mathbf{b}_{0,0} + v\mathbf{b}_{0,1} & (16.3) \\
\mathbf{b}_{1,0}^{0,1} &= (1 - v)\mathbf{b}_{1,0} + v\mathbf{b}_{1,1} & (16.4)
\end{aligned}
$$

and obtain the final result as

$$
\mathbf{x}(u, v) = \mathbf{b}_{0,0}^{1,1}(u, v) = (1 - u)\mathbf{b}_{0,0}^{0,1} + u\mathbf{b}_{1,0}^{0,1}.
$$

This amounts to computing the coefficients of the isoparametric line $v = const$ first and then evaluating this isoparametric line at u. The reader should verify that the other possibility, computing a $u = const$ isoparametric line first and then evaluating it at v, gives the same result.

Since linear interpolation is an affine map, and since we apply linear interpolation (or affine maps) in both the $u-$ and $v-$ direction, one sometimes sees the term "biaffine map" for bilinear interpolation; see Ramshaw [293].

The term "hyperbolic paraboloid" comes from analytic geometry. We shall justify this name by considering the (nonparametric) surface $z = xy$. It can be interpreted as the bilinear interpolant to the four points

$$
\begin{bmatrix} 0 \\ 0 \\ 0 \end{bmatrix}, \begin{bmatrix} 1 \\ 0 \\ 0 \end{bmatrix}, \begin{bmatrix} 0 \\ 1 \\ 0 \end{bmatrix}, \begin{bmatrix} 1 \\ 1 \\ 1 \end{bmatrix}
$$

and is shown in Figure 16.2. If we intersect the surface with a plane parallel to the x, y-plane, the resulting curve is a *hyperbola*; if we intersect it with a plane containing the z-axis, the resulting curve is a *parabola*.

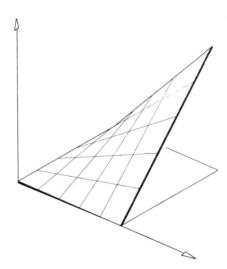

Figure 16.2. Bilinear interpolation: the surface $z = xy$ over the unit square.

16.2   The Direct de Casteljau Algorithm

Bézier curves may be obtained by repeated application of linear interpolation. We shall now obtain surfaces from repeated application of *bilinear interpolation*.

Suppose we are given a rectangular array of points $\mathbf{b}_{i,j}; 0 \leq i, j \leq n$ and parameter values (u, v). The following algorithm generates a point on a surface determined by the array of the $\mathbf{b}_{i,j}$:

Given $\{\mathbf{b}_{i,j}\}_{i,j=0}^{n}$ and $(u, v) \in \mathbb{R}^2$, set

$$
\mathbf{b}_{i,j}^{r,r} = \begin{bmatrix} 1-u & u \end{bmatrix} \begin{bmatrix} \mathbf{b}_{i,j}^{r-1,r-1} & \mathbf{b}_{i,j+1}^{r-1,r-1} \\ \mathbf{b}_{i+1,j}^{r-1,r-1} & \mathbf{b}_{i+1,j+1}^{r-1,r-1} \end{bmatrix} \begin{bmatrix} 1-v \\ v \end{bmatrix} .
$$

$$
r = 1, \ldots, n
$$
$$
i, j = 0, \ldots, n - r
$$

(16.5)

and $\mathbf{b}_{i,j}^{0,0} = \mathbf{b}_{i,j}$. Then $\mathbf{b}_{0,0}^{n,n}$ is the point with parameter values (u, v) on the *Bézier surface* $\mathbf{b}^{n,n}$. (The reason for the somewhat clumsy identical superscripts will be explained in the next section.) The net of the $\mathbf{b}_{i,j}$ is called the *Bézier net* or *control net* of the surface $\mathbf{b}^{n,n}$. The $\mathbf{b}_{i,j}$ are called

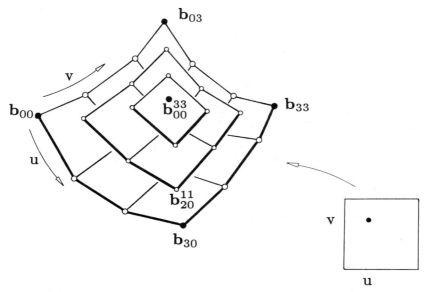

Figure 16.3. The direct de Casteljau algorithm for surfaces: the point on the surface is found from repeated bilinear interpolation.

control points or Bézier points, just as in the curve case. Figure 16.3 shows an example for $n = 3$.

We have defined a surface scheme through a constructive algorithm just as we have done in the curve case. We could now continue to derive analytic properties of these surfaces, again as in the curve case. This is possible without much effort; however, we shall use a different approach in Section 16.3.

In the next section we shall be able to handle surfaces that are of different degrees in u and v. Such surfaces have control nets $\{\mathbf{b}_{i,j}\}$; $i = 0, \ldots, m$, $j = 0, \ldots, n$. The direct de Casteljau algorithm for such surfaces exists, but it needs a case distinction: consulting Figure 16.4, we see that the direct de Casteljau algorithm cannot be performed until the point of the surface is reached. Instead, after $k = \min(m, n)$, the intermediate $\mathbf{b}_{i,j}^{k,k}$ form a curve control polygon. We now must proceed with the univariate de Casteljau algorithm to obtain a point on the surface. This case distinction is awkward and will not be encountered by the tensor product approach in the next section.

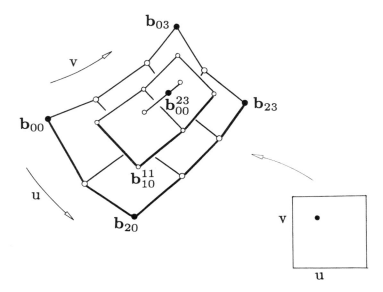

Figure 16.4. The direct de Casteljau algorithm: a surface with $(m, n) = (2, 3)$ proceeds in a univariate manner after no more direct de Casteljau steps can be performed.

16.3 The Tensor Product Approach

We have seen in the introduction by P. Bézier how stylists in the design shop physically created surfaces: templates were used to scrape material off a rough clay model (see Figure 1.12 in Chapter 1). Different templates are used as more and more of the surface is carved out of the clay. Analyzing this process from a theoretical viewpoint, one arrives at the following intuitive definition of a surface: *A surface is the locus of a curve that is moving through space and thereby changing its shape.* See Figure 16.5 for an illustration.

We will now formalize this intuitive concept in order to arrive at a mathematical description of a surface. First, we assume that the moving curve is a Bézier curve of constant degree m. (This assumption is made so that the following formulas will work out; it is actually a serious restriction on the class of surfaces that we can represent using the tensor product approach.) At any time, the moving curve is then determined by a set of control points. Each original control point moves through space on a curve. Our next assumption is that this curve is also a Bézier curve, and that the curves on which the control points move are all of the same degree. An example is given in Figure 16.6.

Figure 16.5. Tensor product surfaces: a surface can be thought of as being swept out by a moving and deforming curve.

This can be formalized as follows: let the initial curve be a Bézier curve of degree m:

$$\mathbf{b}^m(u) = \sum_{i=0}^{m} \mathbf{b}_i B_i^m(u).$$

Let each $\mathbf{b}_i$ traverse a Bézier curve of degree n:

$$\mathbf{b}_i = \mathbf{b}_i(v) = \sum_{j=0}^{n} \mathbf{b}_{i,j} B_j^n(v).$$

We can now combine these two equations and obtain the point $\mathbf{b}^{m,n}(u,v)$ on the surface $\mathbf{b}^{m,n}$ as

$$\mathbf{b}^{m,n}(u,v) = \sum_{i=0}^{m} \sum_{j=0}^{n} \mathbf{b}_{i,j} B_i^m(u) B_j^n(v). \tag{16.6}$$

With this notation, the original curve $\mathbf{b}^m(u)$ now has Bézier points $\mathbf{b}_{i,0}; i = 0, \ldots, m$.

It is not difficult to prove that the definition of a Bézier surface (16.6) and the definition using the direct de Casteljau algorithm are equivalent, see Problems.

Figure 16.6. Tensor product Bézier surfaces: a surface is obtained by moving the control points of a curve (quadratic) along other Bézier curves (cubic). Bottom: the final Bézier net.

We have described the Bézier surface (16.6) as being obtained by moving the isoparametric curve corresponding to $v = 0$. It is an easy exercise to check that the three remaining boundary curves could also have been used as the starting curve.

An arbitrary isoparametric curve $\hat{v} = const$ of a Bézier surface $\mathbf{b}^{m,n}$ is a Bézier curve of degree m in u, and its $m + 1$ Bézier points are obtained by evaluating all rows of the control net at $v = const$. As a formula:

$$\mathbf{b}_{i,0}^{0n}(\hat{v}) = \sum_{j=0}^{n} \mathbf{b}_{ij} B_j^n(\hat{v}); \quad i = 0, \ldots m.$$

This process of obtaining the Bézier points of an isoparametric line is a second possible interpretation of Figure 16.6. The coefficients of the isoparametric line can be obtained by applying $m + 1$ de Casteljau algorithms. A point on the surface is then obtained by performing one more de Casteljau algorithm.

Isoparametric curves $u = const$ are treated analogously.

Note, however, that other straight lines in the domain are mapped to higher degree curves on the patch: they are generally of degree $n + m$. Two special examples of such curves are the two diagonals of the domain rectangle.

16.4   Properties

Most properties of Bézier patches follow in a straightforward way from those of Bézier curves– the reader is referred to sections 3.3 and 4.2. We give a brief listing:

Affine invariance: The direct de Casteljau algorithm consists of repeated bilinear and possibly subsequent repeated linear interpolation. All these operations are affinely invariant; hence, so is their composition. We can also argue that in order for (16.6) to be a barycentric combination (and therefore affinely invariant), we must have

$$\sum_{j=0}^{n}\sum_{i=0}^{m} B_i^m(u)B_j^n(v) \equiv 1. \tag{16.7}$$

This is easily verified algebraically.

Convex hull property: For $0 \leq u, v \leq 1$, the terms $B_i^m(u)B_j^n(v)$ are nonnegative. Then, taking (16.7) into account, (16.6) is a convex combination.

Boundary curves: The boundary curves of the patch $\mathbf{b}^{m,n}$ are polynomial curves. Their Bézier polygons are given by the boundary polygons of the control net. In particular, the four corners of the control net all lie on the patch.

Variation diminishing property: This property is *not* inherited from the univariate case. In fact, it is not at all clear what the definition of variation diminution should be in the bivariate case. Counting intersections with straight lines, as we did for curves, would not make Bézier patches variation diminishing; it is easy to visualize a patch that is intersected by a straight line while its control net is

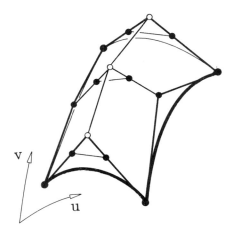

Figure 16.7. Degree elevation: the surface problem can be reduced to a series of univariate problems.

not. (Here, we would view the control net as a collection of bilinear patches.) Other attempts at a suitable definition of a bivariate variation diminishing property have been similarly unsuccessful.

16.5   Degree Elevation

Suppose we want to rewrite a Bézier surface of degree (m, n) as one of degree $(m + 1, n)$. This amounts to finding coefficients $\mathbf{b}_{i,j}^{(1,0)}$ such that

$$\mathbf{b}^{m,n}(u, v) = \sum_{j=0}^{n} \left[\sum_{i=0}^{m+1} \mathbf{b}_{i,j}^{(1,0)} B_i^{m+1}(u) \right] B_j^n(v).$$

The $n+1$ terms in square brackets represent $n+1$ univariate degree elevation problems as discussed in Section 5.1. They are solved by a direct application of (5.2):

$$\mathbf{b}_{i,j}^{(1,0)} = (1 - \frac{i}{m+1})\mathbf{b}_{i,j} + \frac{i}{m+1}\mathbf{b}_{i-1,j}; \left\{ \begin{array}{l} i = 0, \ldots, m + 1 \\ j = 0, \ldots n. \end{array} \right. \qquad (16.8)$$

A tensor product surface is thus degree elevated in the u-direction by treating all columns of the control net as Bézier polygons of m-th degree curves and degree elevating each of them. This is illustrated in Figure 16.7.

Degree elevation in the v−direction works the same way, of course. If we want to degree elevate in both the u− and the v-direction, we can perform the procedure first in the u−direction, then in the v−direction, or we can proceed the other way around. Both approaches yield the same surface of degree $(m + 1, n + 1)$. Its coefficients $\mathbf{b}_{i,j}^{(1,1)}$ may be found in a one-step method:

$$\mathbf{b}_{i,j}^{(1,1)} = \left[\begin{array}{cc} \frac{i}{m+1} & 1 - \frac{i}{m+1} \end{array} \right] \left[\begin{array}{cc} \mathbf{b}_{i-1,j-1} & \mathbf{b}_{i-1,j} \\ \mathbf{b}_{i,j-1} & \mathbf{b}_{i,j} \end{array} \right] \left[\begin{array}{c} \frac{j}{n+1} \\ 1 - \frac{j}{n+1} \end{array} \right] \quad (16.9)$$
$$i = 0, \ldots, m + 1,$$
$$j = 0, \ldots, n + 1.$$

The net of the $\mathbf{b}_{i,j}^{(1,1)}$ is obtained by *piecewise bilinear interpolation* from the original control net.

16.6   Derivatives

In the curve case, taking derivatives was accomplished by differencing the control points. The same will be true here. The derivatives that we will consider are *partial derivatives* $\partial/\partial u$ or $\partial/\partial v$. A partial derivative is the tangent vector of an isoparametric curve, and can be found by a straightforward calculation:

$$\frac{\partial}{\partial u} \mathbf{b}^{m,n}(u, v) = \sum_{j=0}^{n} \left[\frac{\partial}{\partial u} \sum_{i=0}^{m} \mathbf{b}_{i,j} B_i^m(u) \right] B_j^n(v).$$

The bracketed terms depend only on u, and we can apply the formula for the derivative of a Bézier curve (4.16):

$$\frac{\partial}{\partial u} \mathbf{b}^{m,n}(u, v) = m \sum_{j=0}^{n} \sum_{i=0}^{m-1} \Delta^{1,0} \mathbf{b}_{i,j} B_i^{m-1}(u) B_j^n(v).$$

Here we have generalized the standard difference operator in the obvious way: the superscript $(1, 0)$ means that differencing is performed only on the first subscript: $\Delta^{1,0} \mathbf{b}_{i,j} = \mathbf{b}_{i+1,j} - \mathbf{b}_{i,j}$. If we take v−partials, we employ a difference operator that acts only on the second subscripts: $\Delta^{0,1} \mathbf{b}_{i,j} = \mathbf{b}_{i,j+1} - \mathbf{b}_{i,j}$. We then obtain

$$\frac{\partial}{\partial v} \mathbf{b}^{m,n}(u, v) = n \sum_{i=0}^{m} \sum_{j=0}^{n-1} \Delta^{0,1} \mathbf{b}_{i,j} B_j^{n-1}(v) B_i^m(u).$$

Again, a surface problem can be broken down into several univariate problems: to compute a $u-$partial, for instance, interpret all columns of the control net as Bézier curves of degree m and compute their derivatives (evaluated at the desired value of u). Then interpret these derivatives as coefficients of another Bézier curve of degree n and compute its value at the desired value of v.

We can write down formulas for higher order partials:

$$\frac{\partial^r}{\partial u^r} \mathbf{b}^{m,n}(u,v) = \frac{m!}{(m-r)!} \sum_{j=0}^{n} \sum_{i=0}^{m-r} \Delta^{r,0}\mathbf{b}_{i,j} B_i^{m-r}(u) B_j^n(v). \quad (16.10)$$

and

$$\frac{\partial^s}{\partial v^s} \mathbf{b}^{m,n}(u,v) = \frac{n!}{(n-s)!} \sum_{i=0}^{m} \sum_{j=0}^{n-s} \Delta^{0,s}\mathbf{b}_{i,j} B_j^{n-s}(v) B_i^m(u). \quad (16.11)$$

Here, the difference operators are defined by

$$\Delta^{r,0}\mathbf{b}_{i,j} = \Delta^{r-1,0}\mathbf{b}_{i+1,j} - \Delta^{r-1,0}\mathbf{b}_{i,j}$$

and

$$\Delta^{0,s}\mathbf{b}_{i,j} = \Delta^{0,s-1}\mathbf{b}_{i,j+1} - \Delta^{0,s-1}\mathbf{b}_{i,j}.$$

It is not hard now to write down the most general case, namely *mixed partials* of arbitrary order:

$$\frac{\partial^{r+s}}{\partial u^r \partial v^s} \mathbf{b}^{m,n}(u,v) =$$

$$\frac{m!n!}{(m-r)!(n-s)!} \sum_{i=0}^{m-r} \sum_{j=0}^{n-s} \Delta^{r,s}\mathbf{b}_{i,j} B_i^{m-r}(u) B_j^{n-s}(v). \quad (16.12)$$

Before we proceed to consider some special cases, the reader should recall that the coefficients $\Delta^{r,s}\mathbf{b}_{i,j}$ are vectors and therefore do not "live" in $\mathbb{E}^3$. See Section 4.3 for more details.

A partial derivative of a (point-valued) surface is itself a (vector-valued) surface. We can evaluate it along isoparametric lines, of which the four boundary curves are the ones of most interest. Such a derivative, e.g. $\partial/\partial u \mid_{u=0}$ is called a *cross-boundary derivative*. We can thus restrict (16.10) to $u = 0$ and get, with a slight abuse of notation,

$$\frac{\partial^r}{\partial u^r} \mathbf{b}^{m,n}(0,v) = \frac{m!}{(m-r)!} \sum_{j=0}^{n} \Delta^{r,0}\mathbf{b}_{0,j} B_j^n(v). \quad (16.13)$$

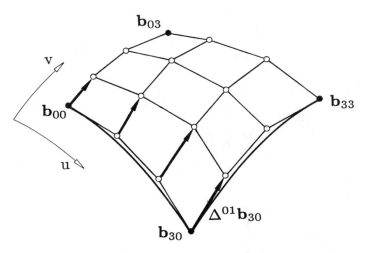

Figure 16.8. Cross boundary derivatives: along the edge $u = 0$, the cross boundary derivative only depends on two rows of control points.

Similar formulas hold for the other three edges. We thus have determined that r-th order cross-boundary derivatives, evaluated along that boundary, depend only on the $r + 1$ rows (or columns) of Bézier points next to that boundary. This will be important when we formulate conditions for C^r continuity between adjacent patches. The case $r = 1$ is illustrated in Figure 16.8.

16.7   Normal Vectors

The *normal vector* $\mathbf{n}$ of a surface is a normalized vector that is normal to the surface at a given point. It can be computed from the cross product of any two vectors that are tangent to the surface at that point. Since the partials $\partial/\partial u$ and $\partial/\partial v$ are two such vectors, we may set

$$\mathbf{n}(u, v) = \frac{\frac{\partial}{\partial u}\mathbf{b}^{m,n}(u, v) \wedge \frac{\partial}{\partial v}\mathbf{b}^{m,n}(u, v)}{||\frac{\partial}{\partial u}\mathbf{b}^{m,n}(u, v) \wedge \frac{\partial}{\partial v}\mathbf{b}^{m,n}(u, v)||}, \qquad (16.14)$$

where "$\wedge$" denotes the cross product.

At the four corners of the patch, the involved partials are simply differences of boundary points, for example

$$\mathbf{n}(0, 0) = \frac{\Delta^{1,0}\mathbf{b}_{0,0} \wedge \Delta^{0,1}\mathbf{b}_{0,0}}{||\Delta^{1,0}\mathbf{b}_{0,0} \wedge \Delta^{0,1}\mathbf{b}_{0,0}||}. \qquad (16.15)$$

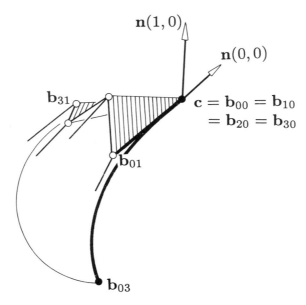

Figure 16.9. Degenerate patches: a "triangular" patch is created by collapsing a whole boundary curve into a point. The normal at that point may be undefined. Normals are shown for $u = 0$ and for $u = 1$.

The normal at one of the corners (we take $\mathbf{b}_{0,0}$ as an example) is undefined if $\Delta^{1,0}\mathbf{b}_{0,0}$ and $\Delta^{0,1}\mathbf{b}_{0,0}$ are linearly dependent: if that were the case, (16.15) would degenerate into an expression of the form $\frac{\mathbf{0}}{0}$. The corresponding patch corner is then called *degenerate*. Two cases of special interest are illustrated in Figures 16.9, 16.10, and 16.11.

In the first of these, a whole boundary curve is collapsed into a single point. As an example, we could set $\mathbf{b}_{00} = \mathbf{b}_{10} = \cdots = \mathbf{b}_{m0} = \mathbf{c}$. Then the boundary $\mathbf{b}(u, 0)$ would degenerate into a single point. In such cases, the normal vector at $v = 0$ may or may not be defined. To examine this in more detail, consider the tangents of the isoparametric lines $u = \hat{u}$, evaluated at $v = 0$. These tangents must be perpendicular to the normal vector, if it exists. So a condition for the existence of the normal vector at $\mathbf{c}$ is that all $v-$partials, evaluated at $v = 0$, are coplanar. But that is equivalent to $\mathbf{b}_{01}, \mathbf{b}_{11}, \ldots, \mathbf{b}_{m1}$ and $\mathbf{c}$ being coplanar.

A second possibility in creating degenerate patches is to allow two corner partials to be collinear, for example, $\partial/\partial u$ and $\partial/\partial v$ at $(0, 0)$, as shown in Figure 16.11. In that case, $\mathbf{b}_{10}, \mathbf{b}_{01}$, and $\mathbf{b}_{00}$ are collinear. Then the normal at $\mathbf{b}_{00}$ is defined, provided that $\mathbf{b}_{11}$ is not collinear with $\mathbf{b}_{10}, \mathbf{b}_{01}$,

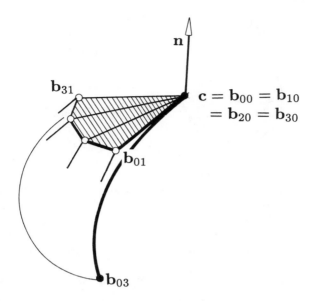

Figure 16.10. Degenerate patches: if all $\mathbf{b}_{i1}$ and $\mathbf{c}$ are coplanar, then the normal vector at $\mathbf{c}$ is perpendicular to that plane.

and $\mathbf{b}_{00}$. Recall that $\mathbf{b}_{00}, \mathbf{b}_{10}, \mathbf{b}_{01}$, and $\mathbf{b}_{11}$ form the osculating paraboloid at $(u, v) = (0, 0)$. Then it follows that the tangent plane at $\mathbf{b}_{00}$ is the plane through the four coplanar points $\mathbf{b}_{00}, \mathbf{b}_{10}, \mathbf{b}_{01}$, and $\mathbf{b}_{11}$. The normal at $\mathbf{b}_{00}$ is perpendicular to it.

A warning: when we say "the normal is defined" then it should be understood that this is a purely mathematical statement. In any of the above degeneracies, a program using (16.14) will crash. A case distinction is necessary, and then the program can branch into the special cases that we just described.

16.8   Twists

The *twist* of a surface[1] is its mixed partial $\partial^2/\partial u \partial v$. According to (16.12), the twist surface of $\mathbf{b}^{m,n}$ is a Bézier surface of degree $(m-1, n-1)$, and its (vector) coefficients have the form $mn\Delta^{1,1}\mathbf{b}_{i,j}$. These coefficients have a nice geometric interpretation. For its discussion, we refer to Figure 16.12.

---

[1]In this chapter, we are only dealing with polynomial surfaces. For these, the twist is uniquely defined. For other surfaces, it may depend on the order in which derivatives are taken; see Section 21.1.

Figure 16.11. Degenerate patches: the normals at all four corners of this patch are determined by the triangles that are formed by the corner subquadrilaterals (one corner highlighted).

The point $\mathbf{p}_{i,j}$ in that figure is the fourth point on the parallelogram defined by $\mathbf{b}_{i,j}, \mathbf{b}_{i+1,j}, \mathbf{b}_{i,j+1}$. It is defined by

$$\mathbf{p}_{i,j} - \mathbf{b}_{i+1,j} = \mathbf{b}_{i,j+1} - \mathbf{b}_{i,j}. \tag{16.16}$$

Since

$$\Delta^{1,1}\mathbf{b}_{i,j} = (\mathbf{b}_{i+1,j+1} - \mathbf{b}_{i+1,j}) - (\mathbf{b}_{i,j+1} - \mathbf{b}_{i,j}), \tag{16.17}$$

it follows that

$$\Delta^{1,1}\mathbf{b}_{i,j} = \mathbf{b}_{i+1,j+1} - \mathbf{p}_{i,j}. \tag{16.18}$$

Thus the terms $\Delta^{1,1}\mathbf{b}_{i,j}$ measure the deviation of each subquadrilateral of the Bézier net from a parallelogram.

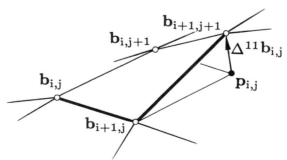

Figure 16.12. Twists: the twist coefficients are proportional to the deviations of the subquadrilaterals from parallelograms.

The twists at the four patch corners determine the deviation of the respective corner subquadrilaterals of the control net from parallelograms. For example,

$$\frac{\partial^2}{\partial u \partial v} \mathbf{b}^{m,n}(0,0) = mn\Delta^{1,1}\mathbf{b}_{00}. \tag{16.19}$$

This twist vector is a measure for the deviation of $\mathbf{b}_{11}$ from the tangent plane at $\mathbf{b}_{00}$.

An interesting class of surfaces is obtained if all subquadrilaterals $\mathbf{b}_{i,j}$, $\mathbf{b}_{i+1,j}$, $\mathbf{b}_{i+1,j}$, $\mathbf{b}_{i+1,j+1}$ are parallelograms; in that case the twist vanishes everywhere. Such surfaces are called *translational surfaces* and will be discussed in Section 21.3; an example is shown in Figure 21.4.

16.9 The Matrix Form of a Bézier Patch

In Section 4.6, we formulated a matrix expression for Bézier curves. This approach carries over well to tensor product patches. We can write:

$$\mathbf{b}^{m,n}(u,v) = $$
$$\begin{bmatrix} B_0^m(u) & \cdots & B_m^m(t) \end{bmatrix} \begin{bmatrix} \mathbf{b}_{00} & \cdots & \mathbf{b}_{0n} \\ \vdots & & \vdots \\ \mathbf{b}_{m0} & \cdots & \mathbf{b}_{mn} \end{bmatrix} \begin{bmatrix} B_0^n(v) \\ \vdots \\ B_n^n(v) \end{bmatrix}. \tag{16.20}$$

The matrix $\{\mathbf{b}_{ij}\}$, defining the control net, is sometimes called the *geometry matrix* of the patch. If we perform a basis transformation and write the Bernstein polynomials in monomial form, we obtain

$$\mathbf{b}^{m,n}(u,v) = \begin{bmatrix} u^0 & \cdots & u^m \end{bmatrix} M^{\mathrm{T}} \begin{bmatrix} \mathbf{b}_{00} & \cdots & \mathbf{b}_{0n} \\ \vdots & & \vdots \\ \mathbf{b}_{m0} & \cdots & \mathbf{b}_{mn} \end{bmatrix} N \begin{bmatrix} v^0 \\ \vdots \\ v^n \end{bmatrix}. \tag{16.21}$$

The square matrices M and N are given by

$$m_{ij} = (-1)^{j-i}\binom{m}{j}\binom{j}{i} \tag{16.22}$$

and

$$n_{ij} = (-1)^{j-i}\binom{n}{j}\binom{j}{i}. \tag{16.23}$$

In the bicubic case, $m = n = 3$, we have

$$M = N = \begin{bmatrix} 1 & -3 & 3 & -1 \\ 0 & 3 & -6 & 3 \\ 0 & 0 & 3 & -3 \\ 0 & 0 & 0 & 1 \end{bmatrix}.$$

For reasons of numerical stability, the use of the monomial form (16.21) is not advisable (see the discussion in Section 24.3). It is included here since it is still in widespread use.

16.10   Nonparametric Patches

This section is the bivariate analog of Section 5.5. Having outlined the main ideas there, we can be brief here. A nonparametric surface is of the form $z = f(x, y)$. It has the parametric representation

$$\mathbf{x}(u, v) = \begin{bmatrix} u \\ v \\ f(u, v) \end{bmatrix},$$

and we restrict both u and v to be between zero and one. We are interested in functions f that are in Bernstein form:

$$f(x, y) = \sum_i^m \sum_j^n b_{ij} B_i^m(x) B_j^n(y).$$

Using the identity (4.13) for both variables u and v, we see that the Bézier points of $\mathbf{x}$ are given by

$$\mathbf{b}_{ij} = \begin{bmatrix} i/m \\ j/n \\ b_{ij} \end{bmatrix}.$$

The points $(i/m, j/n)$ in the (x, y)-plane are called *Bézier abscissae* of the function f; the b_{ij} are called its *Bézier ordinates*. A nonparametric Bézier function is not constrained to be defined over the unit square; if a point $\mathbf{p}$ and two vectors $\mathbf{v}$ and $\mathbf{w}$ define a parallelogram in the (x, y)-plane, then the Bézier abscissae $\mathbf{a}_{ij} \in I\!E^2$ of a nonparametric Bézier function over this domain are given by $\mathbf{a}_{ij} = \mathbf{p} + i\mathbf{v} + j\mathbf{w}$. Figure 16.13 gives an exampple.

Integrals also carry over from the univariate case. With a proof analogous to the one in Section 5.7, one can show that

$$\int_0^1 \int_0^1 \sum_i^m \sum_j^n b_{ij} B_i^m(x) B_j^n(x) = \frac{\sum_i^m \sum_j^n b_{ij}}{(m+1)(n+1)}. \tag{16.24}$$

Figure 16.13. Nonparametric patches: the Bézier points are located over a regular partition of the domain rectangle.

16.11 Implementation

As an example of the tensor product principle, here is a routine that plots isoparametric curves of a Bézier patch. It uses the standard drawing routines **move_abs_2** and **polyline_abs_2** , which might have to be replaced by other routines. Notice that drawing is 2D, i.e., after a viewing transformation (projection into $x, y-$plane) has been applied. The generalization for drawing in 3D should be obvious.

```
void plot_surf(bx,by,degree_u,degree_v,u_points,v_points)
/*      plots v_points isoparametric curves of the  surface,
        each with u_points points on it.

Input: bx, by:             arrays with x- and y- coordinates of control net.
       degree_u,degree_v: degrees in u- and v- direction.
       u_points:           how many points per curve
       v_points:           how many curves to draw
Output:                    Plot of isolines.
*/

       int degree_u,degree_v,u_points,v_points;
```

```
float bx[20][20], by[20][20];

{

    int i,j,u_points1;
    float u,v,del_u,del_v;
    float aux_x[5],aux_y[5], arrax[5],array[5];
    float points_x[100], points_y[100];
    int iv;
    float hornbez();


    del_v= 1.0/((float)v_points);
    u_points1=u_points+1;
    v=0.0;  /* first iso-curve is (bx[u,0],by[u,0])  */

    for(iv=0; iv<= v_points; iv++)/* loop over all curves to be drawn*/
    {
        for(i=0;i<=degree_u; i++)/* create aux. arrays*/
        {
        for(j=0; j<= degree_v; j++)
            {
            arrax[j]=bx[i][j];
            array[j]=by[i][j];
            }

         aux_x[i]=hornbez(degree_v,arrax,v);   /*x-eval. at v*/
         aux_y[i]=hornbez(degree_v,array,v);   /*y-eval. at v*/
        }
        /*
         The Bezier points for the iso-curve are put in aux_x, aux_y:
        */
        bez_to_points(degree_u,u_points,aux_x,points_x);
        bez_to_points(degree_u,u_points,aux_y,points_y);

        move_abs_2(points_x[0],points_y[0]);        /* plotting */
        polyline_abs_2(points_x,points_y,u_points1); /* the point*/
                                                     /* arrays    */
        v = v+del_v;                    /* v-value for next iso-curve */
    }
}
```

16.12 Problems

1. Draw the hyperbolic paraboloid from Figure 16.2 over the square
   (-1,-1), (1,-1), (1,1), (-1,1). Try to do it manually, i.e, without graphics support.

2. Show that the direct de Casteljau algorithm generates surfaces of the
   form (16.6).

3. Show that Bézier surfaces have bilinear precision: if $\mathbf{b}_{i,j} = \mathbf{x}(\frac{i}{m}, \frac{j}{n})$
   and $\mathbf{x}$ is bilinear, then $\mathbf{b}^{m,n}(u,v) = \mathbf{x}(u,v)$ for all u, v and for arbitrary m, n.

4. Give an explicit formula for $\Delta^{r,s} \mathbf{b}_{i,j}$. Hint: use (4.18).

5. If a Bézier surface is given by its control net, we can use the de
   Casteljau algorithm to compute $\mathbf{b}^{m,n}(u,v)$ in three ways: by the
   direct form from Section 16.2, or by the two possible tensor product
   approaches, computing the coefficients of a u (or v) isoparametric
   line, and then evaluating that curve at v (or u). While theoretically
   equivalent, the computation counts for these methods differ. Work
   out the details.

17

Composite Surfaces and Spline Interpolation

Tensor product Bézier patches were under development in the early sixties; at about the same time, people started to think about piecewise surfaces. One of the first publications was de Boor's work on bicubic splines [95] in 1962. Almost simultaneously, and apparently unaware of de Boor's work, J. Ferguson [148] implemented piecewise bicubics at Boeing. His method was used extensively, although it had the serious flaw of using only zero corner twist vectors. An excellent account of the industrial use of piecewise bicubics is the article by G. Peters [277].

17.1 Smoothness and Subdivision

Let $\mathbf{x}(u, v)$ and $\mathbf{y}(u, v)$ be two patches, defined over $[u_{I-1}, u_I] \times [v_J, v_{J+1}]$ and $[u_I, u_{I+1}] \times [v_J, v_{J+1}]$, respectively. They are r times continuously differentiable across their common boundary curve $\mathbf{x}(u_I, v) = \mathbf{y}(u_I, v)$ if all $u-$partials up to order r agree there:

$$\frac{\partial^r}{\partial u^r}\mathbf{x}(u, v)\bigg|_{u=u_I} = \frac{\partial^r}{\partial u^r}\mathbf{y}(u, v)\bigg|_{u=u_I}. \tag{17.1}$$

271

Now suppose both patches are given in Bézier form; let the control net of the "left" patch be $\{\mathbf{b}_{ij}\}; 0 \leq i \leq m, 0 \leq j \leq n$ and $\{\mathbf{b}_{ij}\}; m \leq i \leq 2m, 0 \leq j \leq n$. We can then invoke equation (16.13) for the cross-boundary derivative of a Bézier patch. That formula is in local coordinates, and in order to make the transition to global coordinates (u, v), we must invoke the chain rule, just as we did for composite curves (equation (7.16)):

$$(\frac{1}{\Delta_{I-1}})^r \sum_{j=0}^n \Delta^{r,0} \mathbf{b}_{m-r,j} B_j^n(v) = (\frac{1}{\Delta_I})^r \sum_{j=0}^n \Delta^{r,0} \mathbf{b}_{m,j} B_j^n(v), \qquad (17.2)$$

where $\Delta_I = u_{I+1} - u_I$. Since the $B_j^n(v)$ are linearly independent, we can compare coefficients:

$$(\frac{1}{\Delta_{I-1}})^r \Delta^{r,0} \mathbf{b}_{m-r,j} = (\frac{1}{\Delta_I})^r \Delta^{r,0} \mathbf{b}_{m,j}; \quad j = 0, \ldots, n.$$

This is the C^r condition (7.16) for Bézier curves, applied to all $n + 1$ rows of the composite Bézier net. We thus have the C^r condition for composite Bézier surfaces: *two adjacent patches are C^r across their common boundary if and only if all rows of their control net vertices can be interpreted as polygons of C^r piecewise Bézier curves.* We have again succeeded in reducing a surface problem to several curve problems. The smoothness conditions apply analogously to the v-direction.

The case $r = 1$ is illustrated in Figure 17.1. The C^1 condition states that for every j, the polygon formed by $\mathbf{b}_{0,j}, \ldots, \mathbf{b}_{2m,j}$ is the control polygon of a C^1 piecewise Bézier curve. For this to be the case, the three points $\mathbf{b}_{m-1,j}, \mathbf{b}_{m,j}, \mathbf{b}_{m+1,j}$ must be collinear and in the ratio $\Delta_I : \Delta_{I+1}$. This ratio must be the same for all j. Simple collinearity is *not* sufficient: composite surfaces that have $\mathbf{b}_{m-1,j}, \mathbf{b}_{m,j}, \mathbf{b}_{m+1,j}$ collinear for each j but not in the same ratio will in general not be C^1. Moreover, they will not even have a continuous tangent plane. The rigidity of the C^1 condition can be a serious obstacle in the design of surfaces that consist of a network of Bézier patches (or of piecewise polynomial patches in other representations).

In the univariate case, the de Casteljau algorithm not only provided the point on the curve, but could also be used to *subdivide* the curve. A similar result is true for the surface case. Suppose the domain rectangle of a Bézier patch is subdivided into two subrectangles by a straight line $u = \hat{u}$. That line maps to an isoparametric curve on the patch, which is thus subdivided into two subpatches. We wish to find the control nets for each patch. These two patches, being part of one global surface, meet with C^n continuity. Therefore, all their rows of control points must be control

Figure 17.1. C^1 continuous Bézier patches: the shown control points must be collinear and all be in the same ratio.

polygons of C^n piecewise n^{th} degree curves. Those curves are related to each other by the univariate subdivision process from Section 7.2.

We now have the following subdivision algorithm: interpret all rows of the control net as control polygons of Bézier curves. Subdivide each of these curves at $u = \hat{u}$. The resulting control points form the two desired control nets. For an example, see Figure 17.2.

Subdivision along an isoparametric line $v = \hat{v}$ is treated analogously. If we want to subdivide a patch into four subpatches that are generated by two isoparametric lines $u = \hat{u}$ and $v = \hat{v}$, we apply the subdivision procedure twice. It does not matter in which direction we subdivide first.

17.2 Bicubic B-spline Surfaces

B-spline surfaces (both rational and nonrational) play an important role in current surface design methods and will here be discussed in more detail. Using the notation from Chapter 10 a parametric tensor product B-spline surface may be written as

$$\mathbf{x}(u,v) = \sum_i \sum_j \mathbf{d}_{ij} N_i^3(u) N_j^3(v), \tag{17.3}$$

Figure 17.2. Subdivision of a Bézier patch: all rows are subdivided using the de Casteljau algorithm.

where we assume that one knot sequence in the u−direction and one in the v−direction is given. A typical control net, corresponding to triple end knots[1] and consisting of 5×3 bicubic patches, is shown in Figure 17.3.

Two more bicubic B-spline surfaces, again with triple end knots, are shown in Plates IV, IX, X, and XI. For curves, triple end knots meant that the first and last two B-spline control points were also Bézier control points; the same is true here. The B-spline control points $\mathbf{d}_{ij}$ for which i or j equal 0 or 1, are also control vertices of the piecewise Bézier net of the surface. Thus they determine the boundary curves and the cross-boundary derivatives.

This raises a general question: since a bicubic B-spline surface is a collection of bicubic patches, how can we find the Bézier net of each patch? The answer to this question may be useful for the conversion of a B-spline data format to the piecewise Bézier form. It is also relevant if we decide to evaluate a B-spline surface by first breaking it down into bicubics. The solution arises, as usual for tensor products, from the breakdown of this surface problem into a series of curve problems. If we rewrite (17.3) as

$$\mathbf{x}(u, v) = \sum_i N_i^3(v) \Big[\sum_j \mathbf{d}_{ij} N_j^3(u) \Big],$$

we see that for each i the sum in square brackets describes a B-spline curve in the variable u. We may convert it to Bézier form by

---

[1]This is the notation from Chapter 10. The notation from Chapter 7 is implicitly based on triple end knots.

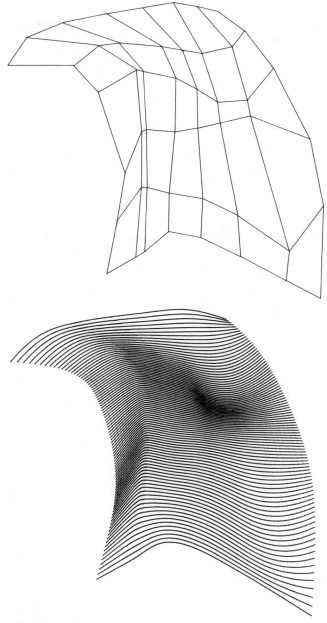

Figure 17.3. Bicubic B-spline surfaces: top: a control net for a bicubic B-spline surface consisting of 5 × 3 patches. Bottom: the corresponding surface.

Figure 17.4. Bringing a bicubic B-spline surface into piecewise bicubic Bézier form: we first perform B-spline–Bézier curve conversion row by row, then column by column.

using the univariate methods described in Chapter 7 or 10. This corresponds to interpreting the B-spline control net row by row as univariate B-spline polygons and then converting them to piecewise Bézier form. The Bézier points thus obtained may – column by column – be interpreted as B-spline polygons, which we may again transform to Bézier form one by one. This final family of Bézier polygons constitutes the piecewise Bézier net of the surface, as illustrated in Figure 17.4. Plate XI shows the piecewise Bézier net obtained from the B-spline net of the surface in Plates IX and X.

Needless to say, we could have started the B-spline-Bézier conversion process column by column. From the Bézier form, we may now transform to any other piecewise polynomial form, such as the piecewise monomial or the piecewise Hermite form.

17.3   Twist Estimation

Suppose that we are given a rectangular network of points $\mathbf{x}_{IJ}$; $0 \leq I \leq M$, $0 \leq J \leq N$ and two sets of parameter values u_I and v_J. We want a C^1 piecewise cubic surface $\mathbf{x}(u, v)$ that interpolates to the data points:

$$\mathbf{x}(u_I, v_J) = \mathbf{x}_{IJ}.$$

For a solution, we utilize curve methods wherever possible. We will first fit piecewise cubics to all rows and columns of data points using methods that were developed in Chapter 8. We must keep in mind, however, that all curves in the u–direction have the same parametrization, given by the u_I; the v–curves are all defined over the v_J.

Figure 17.5. Piecewise bicubic interpolation: after a network of curves has been created, one still must determine four more coefficients per patch.

Creating a network of C^1 piecewise cubics through the data points is only the first step towards a surface, however. Our aim is a piecewise bicubic surface, and so far we have only constructed the boundary curves for each patch. This constitutes twelve data out of the sixteen needed for each patch. Figure 17.5 illustrates the situation. In Bézier form, we are still missing four interior Bézier points per patch, namely $\mathbf{b}_{11}, \mathbf{b}_{21}, \mathbf{b}_{12}, \mathbf{b}_{22}$; in terms of derivatives, we must still determine the *corner twists* of each patch.

We now list a few methods to determine the missing twists.

Zero twists: Historically, this is the first twist estimation "method." It appears, hidden in a set of formulas in pseudo-code, in the paper by Ferguson [148]. Ferguson did not comment on the effects that this choice of twist vectors might have.

As we have seen above, surfaces exist that have identically vanishing twists – these are translational surfaces (see Figure 21.4). If the boundary curves of a patch are pairwise related by translations, then the assignment of zero twists is a good idea, but not otherwise. In these other cases, the boundary curves are *not* the generating curves of a translational surface. If zero twists are assigned, the generated patch *will* locally behave like a translational surface, giving rise to the infamous "flat spots" of zero twists. The effects of zero twists will be illustrated in Chapter 23.

If a network of patches has to be created, this choice of twists automati-

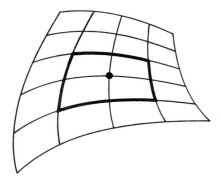

Figure 17.6. Adini's twist: the outer boundary curves of four adjacent patches define a Coons surface; its twist at the "middle" point is Adini's twist.

cally guarantees C^1 continuity of the overall surface. Thus it is mathematically "safe," but does not guarantee "nice" shapes.

Adini's twist: This method has been introduced into the CAGD literature through the paper by Barnhill, Brown, and Klucewicz [19], based on a scheme ("Adini's rectangle") from the finite element literature. The basic idea is this: the four cubic boundary curves define a bilinearly blended Coons patch (see Chapter 20) which happens to be a bicubic patch itself. Take the corner twists of that patch to be the desired twist vectors.

If a network of patches has to be generated, the above Adini's twists would not guarantee a C^1 surface. A simple modification is necessary: let four patches meet at a point, as in Figure 17.6. The four outer boundary curves of the four patches again define a bilinearly blended Coons patch. This Coons patch (consisting of four bicubics) has a well-defined twist at the parameter value where the four bicubics meet. Take that twist to be the desired twist. It is given by

$$\mathbf{x}_{uv}(u_i, v_j) =$$
$$\frac{\mathbf{x}_v(u_{i+1}, v_j) - \mathbf{x}_v(u_{i-1}, v_j)}{u_{i+1} - u_{i-1}}$$
$$+\frac{\mathbf{x}_u(u_i, v_{j+1}) - \mathbf{x}_u(u_i, v_{j-1})}{v_{j+1} - v_{j-1}}$$
$$-\frac{\mathbf{x}(u_{i+1}, v_{j+1}) - \mathbf{x}(u_{i-1}, v_{j+1}) - \mathbf{x}(u_{i+1}, v_{j-1}) + \mathbf{x}(u_{i-1}, v_{j-1})}{(u_{i+1} - u_{i-1})(v_{j+1} - v_{j-1})}.$$

It is easy to check that Adini's method, applied to patch boundaries of a translational surface, yields zero twists, which is desirable for that situation.

Adini's twist is a reasonable choice, because, considered as an interpolant, it reproduces all bivariate polynomials of the form $uv^j, u^iv; i, j \in \{0, 1, 2, 3\}$, which is a surprisingly large set.[2]

Bessel twists: This method estimates the twist at $\mathbf{x}(u_I, v_J)$ to be the twist of the biquadratic interpolant to the nine points $\mathbf{x}(u_{I+r}, v_{J+s}); r, s \in \{-1, 0, 1\}$. Since a biquadratic patch has a bilinear twist, Bessel's twist is the bilinear interpolant to the twists of the four bilinear patches formed by the nine points. Those twists are given by

$$\mathbf{q}_{I,J} = \frac{\Delta^{1,1}\mathbf{x}(u_I, v_J)}{\Delta_I \Delta_J},$$

and Bessel's twist can now be written as

$$\mathbf{x}_{uv}(u_I, v_J) = \begin{bmatrix} 1 - \alpha_I & \alpha_I \end{bmatrix} \begin{bmatrix} \mathbf{q}_{I-1,J-1} & \mathbf{q}_{I-1,J} \\ \mathbf{q}_{I,J-1} & \mathbf{q}_{I,J} \end{bmatrix} \begin{bmatrix} 1 - \beta_J \\ \beta_J \end{bmatrix}$$

where

$$\alpha_I = \frac{\Delta_{I-1}}{u_{I+1} - u_{I-1}}, \quad \beta_J = \frac{\Delta_{J-1}}{v_{J+1} - v_{J-1}}.$$

Selesnick's method (Selesnick [332]): This method requires some of the differential geometry from Chapter 22. The twist normal component $M = \mathbf{n}\mathbf{x}_{uv}$ (see Equation (22.5)) is related to the Gaussian curvature K by equation (22.11). If one has an estimate for the Gaussian curvature (e.g., from surrounding points), one can solve (22.11) for M:

$$M = \pm\sqrt{LN - K(EG - F^2)}.$$

The tangent components of the corner twist, L and N, may be taken to be those of Adini's twist. (Selesnick actually proposes a nonlinear scheme to compute them.)

The sign of the normal component should be chosen such that the interior Bézier points lie above the corner tangent planes ("above" means in the direction of the surface normal). This choice favors the construction of convex patches when the boundary curves are convex and K is estimated to be positive.

If a network of patches is to be constructed, this method requires C^2 patch boundary curves. With that assumption, it provides a twist estimate that yields an overall C^1 surface.

---

[2]and the reason why this twist is called, in the context of finite elements, a "serendipity element."

Energy method: This considers the functional

$$\int_S (\kappa_1^2 + \kappa_2^2) \mathrm{d}S,$$

which is a standard fairness criterion for surfaces in engineering (Nowacki and Reese [270] and Walter [347]). It is used because it measures the strain energy of flexure and torsion in a thin rectangular elastic plate with small deflection.

Hagen and Schulze [196] used this functional for a variational formulation of the twist estimation problem, with the assumption of orthogonal patch boundary curves. One can drop this restriction and obtain an estimate for the normal twist component M (Farin and Hagen [134]):

$$M = \frac{F(EN + GL)}{EG - F^2 + 2F^2}.$$

The tangent components of the twist vector may be computed as in Selesnick's method. For a network of patches, one would have to require C^2 patch boundaries in order to produce an overall C^1 surface.

Brunet's twist: (Brunet [65]) has developed a method different from the previous ones in that it does not start from a network of patch boundary curves, but rather from a C^1 network of bicubic patches. It then tries to modify the existing twist vectors in order to achieve a surface that "wiggles" less than the original surface.

Brunet makes the assumption that the bilinearly blended Coons patch (see Chapter 20) to the given patch boundaries would be 'optimally smooth'. (Note that by our remarks on Adini's twist that surface is the one obtained from applying Adini's method to the curve network.) He then modifies the given surface to come closer to the "Adini surface." Brunet's method, in Bézier terms, is illustrated in Figure 17.7: a convex combination is taken between the interior Bézier points of the given surface and those corresponding to zero twists. Brunet states that

$$\mathbf{b}_{11}^{\mathrm{new}} = .25 \mathbf{b}_{11}^{\mathrm{zero}} + .75 \mathbf{b}_{11}^{\mathrm{old}} \tag{17.4}$$

yields surfaces that exhibit fewer undulations than the original surface.

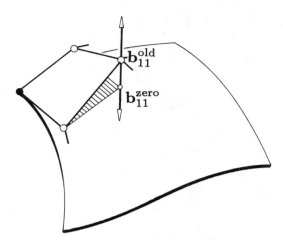

Figure 17.7. Brunet's twist: a convex combination is taken between the given interior Bézier point and the "Adini" Bézier point.

17.4 Tensor Product Interpolants

In Chapter 16, we saw one example of a tensor product patch. We shall now exploit the tensor product method in order to obtain interpolating rectangular surfaces. Let

$$\mathbf{x}(u,v) = \sum_{i=0}^{m} \sum_{j=0}^{n} \mathbf{c}_{ij} A_i(u) B_j(v)$$

be a tensor product surface. The functions A_i and B_j are arbitrary at this point, but for the sake of concreteness, one may think of them as being Bernstein polynomials or B-spline basis functions.[3] This equation may be written in matrix form as

$$\mathbf{x}(u,v) = \begin{bmatrix} A_0(u) & \cdots & A_m(u) \end{bmatrix} \begin{bmatrix} \mathbf{c}_{00} & \cdots & \mathbf{c}_{0n} \\ \vdots & & \vdots \\ \mathbf{c}_{m0} & \cdots & \mathbf{c}_{mn} \end{bmatrix} \begin{bmatrix} B_0(v) \\ \vdots \\ B_n(v) \end{bmatrix}.$$

$$(17.5)$$

Suppose now that we are given an $(m+1) \times (n+1)$ array of data points $\mathbf{x}_{ij}$; $0 \le i \le m$, $0 \le j \le n$. If the surface (17.5) is to interpolate to

---

[3]They may be different basis functions; e.g., B-splines in u and Lagrange polynomials in v.

them, equation (17.5) must be true for each pair (u_i, v_j). We thus obtain $(n + 1) \times (m + 1)$ equations, which we may write concisely as

$$\mathbf{X} = ACB, \tag{17.6}$$

where

$$\mathbf{X} = \begin{bmatrix} \mathbf{x}_{00} & \cdots & \mathbf{x}_{0n} \\ \vdots & & \vdots \\ \mathbf{x}_{m0} & \cdots & \mathbf{x}_{mn} \end{bmatrix},$$

$$A = \begin{bmatrix} A_0(u_0) & \cdots & A_0(u_m) \\ \vdots & & \vdots \\ A_m(u_0) & \cdots & A_m(u_m) \end{bmatrix},$$

$$\mathbf{C} = \begin{bmatrix} \mathbf{c}_{00} & \cdots & \mathbf{c}_{0n} \\ \vdots & & \vdots \\ \mathbf{c}_{m0} & \cdots & \mathbf{c}_{mn} \end{bmatrix},$$

and

$$B = \begin{bmatrix} B_0(v_0) & \cdots & B_0(v_n) \\ \vdots & & \vdots \\ B_n(v_0) & \cdots & B_n(v_n) \end{bmatrix}.$$

The matrices A and B have already appeared in Section 6.3; they are *Vandermonde matrices*.

In an interpolation context, the $\mathbf{x}_{ij}$ are known and the coefficients $\mathbf{c}_{ij}$ are unknown. They are found from (17.6) by setting

$$\mathbf{C} = A^{-1}\mathbf{X}B^{-1}. \tag{17.7}$$

The inverse matrices in (17.7) exist provided that the functions A_i and B_j are linearly independent (which they are in all cases of practical interest).

Equation (17.7) shows how a solution to the interpolation problem *could* be found, but one should not try to invert the matrices A and B explicitly! In order to solve and understand better the tensor product interpolation problem, we rewrite (17.6) as

$$\mathbf{X} = \mathbf{D}B, \tag{17.8}$$

where we have set

$$\mathbf{D} = A\mathbf{C}. \tag{17.9}$$

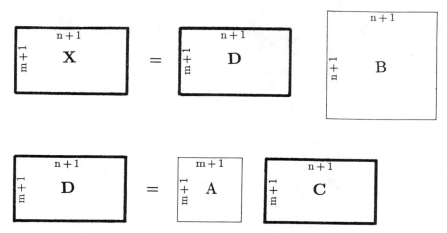

Figure 17.8. Tensor product interpolation: the dimensions of the involved matrices.

Note that $\mathbf{D}$ consists of $(m+1)$ rows and $(n+1)$ columns. Equation (17.8) can be interpreted as a family of (m+1) univariate interpolation problems – one for each row of $\mathbf{X}$ and $\mathbf{D}$, where $\mathbf{D}$ contains the unknowns. Having solved all $(n+1)$ problems (all having the same coefficient matrix B!), we can attack (17.9), since we have just computed $\mathbf{D}$. Equation (17.9) may be interpreted as a family of $(n+1)$ univariate interpolation problems, all having the same coefficient matrix A. Figure 17.8 shows the dimensions of the involved matrices.

We thus see how the tensor product form allows a significant "compactification" of the interpolation process. Without the tensor product structure, we would have to solve a linear system of order $(m+1)(n+1)\times(m+1)(n+1)$. That is an order of magnitude more complex than solving $m+1$ problems with the same $(n+1)\times(n+1)$ matrix and then solving $n+1$ problems with the same $(m+1)\times(m+1)$ matrix. If $m=n$, the naive approach would thus need $O(m^6)$ computations, whereas the tensor product approach just needs $O(m^4)$.

Let us look at one specific example, namely bicubic B-spline interpolation. Suppose we have $(K+1)\times(L+1)$ data points $\mathbf{x}_{IJ}$ and two knot sequences $u_0,\ldots,u_K$ and $v_0,\ldots,v_L$. Our development is illustrated in Figure 17.9. We use the notation from Chapter 9. For each row of data points, we prescribe two end conditions (e.g. by specifying tangent vectors or Bézier points) and solve the univariate B-spline interpolation problem as described in Section 9.1. This produces the elements of the above matrix $\mathbf{D}$, marked by triangles in Figure 17.9. We now take every row of $\mathbf{D}$

Figure 17.9. Tensor product bicubic spline interpolation: the solution is obtained in a two-step process.

and perform univariate B-spline interpolation on it, again by prescribing end conditions such as end tangents[4]. Note that at the four corners, this amounts to the prescription of twist vectors. An example is shown in Figure 17.10. In it, the data points are connected in the $u-$direction – this is just to show the structure of the data.

Although mathematically equivalent, the two processes – first row by row, then column by column; or: first column by column, then row by row – do not yield the same computation count.

17.5   The Parametrization

While tensor product interpolation is very elegant, its use is limited to cases where the data points possess a rectangular structure. When the data points deviate from a "nice" grid, we have to face a problem that is associated with the process of bicubic spline interpolation, in fact, for most kinds of tensor product interpolation: the problem of finding an appropriate parametrization. In the curve case (Section 9.4), we were able to devise several methods that assigned parameter values to the given data points. So why not take those methods and apply them to the tensor product case in much the same way in which we generalized curve methods to their tensor product counterparts? The problem is that we have to produce *one* set of parameter values for *all* isoparametric curves in the $u-$direction; the same holds for the $v-$direction.

We may endow each isoparametric curve (in the $u-$direction, say,) with a parametrization from Section 9.4. In order to arrive at *one* parametrization

---

[4]Note that **D** has two more rows than **X**. This is due to the end conditions; in order to resolve the apparent discrepancy, we may think of **X** as having two additional rows which constitute the end condition data.

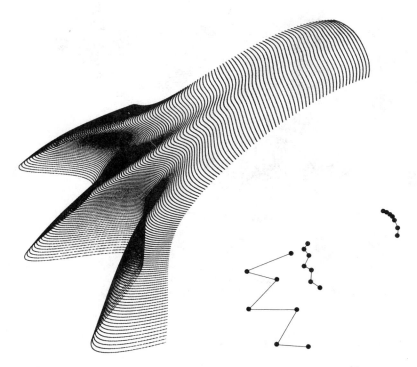

Figure 17.10. Tensor product bicubic spline interpolation: the given data, lower right (scaled down), and the solution, using Bessel end conditions and uniform parametrizations.

for all of them, we may then carry out some averaging process. Such an approach will only produce acceptable results if all our isoparametric curves have the same shape characteristics, i.e., if they essentially yield the same parametrization. This is, however, not always the case, as Figures 17.11, 17.12, 17.13 illustrate.[5]

Are there ways out of the dilemma? Not if one has unevenly distributed data and insists on bicubic spline interpolation. If one is willing to go to higher degrees and to replace C^1 or C^2 continuity by G^1 continuity (see Chpater 19), then several methods exist – see the literature cited in that chapter.

---

[5]Another interesting phenomenon may be observed here: note how the first and the third of this set of surfaces have varying densities in their plots. The reason is that each cubic isoparametric curve was plotted in 90 increments. With very unequal parameter spacing, this generates abruptly varying spacing on the curves.

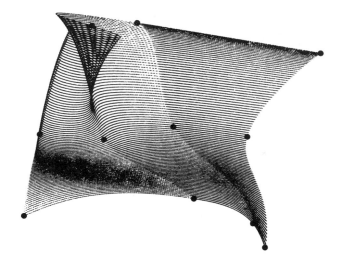

Figure 17.11. Parametrizing a bicubic spline interpolant: all "horizontal" isoparametric curves have the parametrization $u_i = [0, 4, 5.5, 6.0]$. Note that the bottom curve has a reasonable shape.

17.6 Bicubic Hermite Patches

We emphasize the Bézier and B-spline form for composite surfaces, although one can also form the tensor product of the cubic Hermite interpolation scheme (see Section 6.5). The input parameters to this patch representation are points, partials, and mixed partials. A bicubic patch in Hermite form is given by

$$\mathbf{x}(u, v) = \sum_{i=0}^{3} \sum_{j=0}^{3} \mathbf{h}_{i,j} H_i^3(u) H_j^3(v); \quad 0 \le u, v \le 1, \tag{17.10}$$

where the H_i^3 are the cubic Hermite functions from 6.5 and the $\mathbf{h}_{i,j}$ are given by

$$[\mathbf{h}_{i,j}] = \begin{bmatrix} \mathbf{x}(0,0) & \mathbf{x}_v(0,0) & \mathbf{x}_v(0,1) & \mathbf{x}(0,1) \\ \mathbf{x}_u(0,0) & \mathbf{x}_{uv}(0,0) & \mathbf{x}_{uv}(0,1) & \mathbf{x}_u(0,1) \\ \mathbf{x}_u(1,0) & \mathbf{x}_{uv}(1,0) & \mathbf{x}_{uv}(1,1) & \mathbf{x}_u(1,1) \\ \mathbf{x}(1,0) & \mathbf{x}_v(1,0) & \mathbf{x}_v(1,1) & \mathbf{x}(1,1) \end{bmatrix}. \tag{17.11}$$

The coefficients of this form are shown in Figure 17.14. Note how the

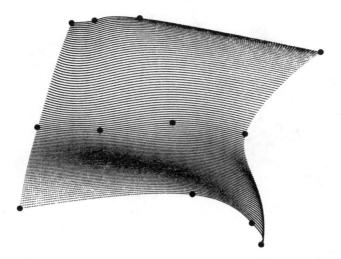

Figure 17.12. Parametrizing a bicubic spline interpolant: all "horizontal" isoparametric curves have the parametrization $u_i = [0, 1, 2, 3]$.

coefficients in the matrix are grouped into four two by two partitions, each holding the data pertaining to one corner.[6]

In the context of composite surfaces, one is given a network of bicubic patches. The equation of patch (I, J) in the network is given by

$$\mathbf{x}(u, v) = \sum_{i=0}^{3} \sum_{j=0}^{3} \mathbf{h}_{i,j} H_i^3(s) H_j^3(t); \quad 0 \le s, t \le 1. \tag{17.12}$$

Here, s and t are local coordinates of the intervals $[u_I, u_{I+1}]$ and $[v_J, v_{J+1}]$. The coefficient matrix now changes:

$$[\mathbf{h}_{i,j}] = \begin{bmatrix} \mathbf{x}(0,0) & \Delta_J\mathbf{x}_v(0,0) & \Delta_J\mathbf{x}_v(0,1) & \mathbf{x}(0,1) \\ \Delta_I\mathbf{x}_u(0,0) & \Delta_I\Delta_J\mathbf{x}_{uv}(0,0) & \Delta_I\Delta_J\mathbf{x}_{uv}(0,1) & \Delta_I\mathbf{x}_u(0,1) \\ \Delta_I\mathbf{x}_u(1,0) & \Delta_I\Delta_J\mathbf{x}_{uv}(1,0) & \Delta_I\Delta_J\mathbf{x}_{uv}(1,1) & \Delta_I\mathbf{x}_u(1,1) \\ \mathbf{x}(1,0) & \Delta_J\mathbf{x}_v(1,0) & \Delta_J\mathbf{x}_v(1,1) & \mathbf{x}(1,1) \end{bmatrix}. \tag{17.13}$$

A composite surface, expressed in piecewise bicubic Hermite form, is C^1 if adjacent patches have coefficient matrices that coincide in the two rows

---

[6]This is a deviation from standard notation. Standard notation groups by order of derivatives, i.e., there is a group of four positions, four u−partials, and so on. The form (17.11) was chosen since it groups coefficients according to their geometric location. Also, it is closer to the Bézier form of a bicubc patch.

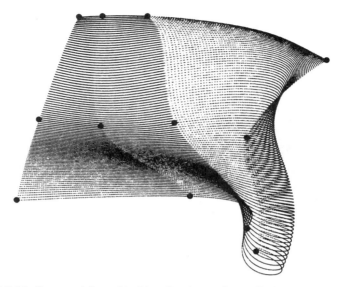

Figure 17.13. Parametrizing a bicubic spline interpolant: all "horizontal" isoparametric curves have the parametrization $u_i = [0, 0.5, 1.5, 6.5]$. Now the top curve has a good shape.

or columns parallel to the common boundary. Thus, storage requirements may be reduced.

Bicubic patches in Hermite form may also be utilized for bicubic spline interpolation as described above for the B-spline form. One solves $(m + 1)$ univariate interpolation problems as outlined in Section 9.2 in order to obtain the v-partials at the data points. Next, one solves $(n + 1)$ interpolation problems to obtain the $u-$partials at the data points. Now one takes the $u-$partials and solves row by row to obtain the twists at the data points. (Or one takes the $v-$partials and solves column by column to obtain the twists.) This is a three-stage process, and does not compare favorably with the two-stage B-spline solution to the same problem.

17.7 Rational Bézier and B-spline Surfaces

We can generalize Bézier and B-spline surfaces to their rational counterparts in much the same way as we did for the curve cases. In other words, we define a rational Bézier or B-spline surface as the projection of a 4D tensor

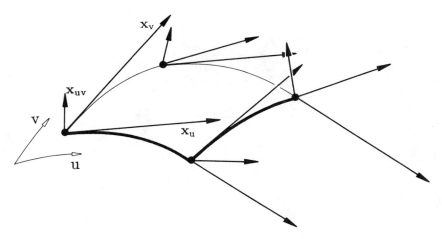

Figure 17.14. Bicubic Hermite patches: the shown points and vectors define a patch.

product Bézier or B-spline surface. Thus, the rational Bézier patch takes the form

$$\mathbf{x}(u,v) = \frac{\sum_i \sum_j w_{i,j} \mathbf{b}_{i,j} B_i^m(u) B_j^n(v)}{\sum_i \sum_j w_{i,j} B_i^m(u) B_j^n(v)},\qquad(17.14)$$

and a rational B-spline surface is written as

$$\mathbf{s}(u,v) = \frac{\sum_i \sum_j w_{i,j} \mathbf{d}_{i,j} N_i^m(u) N_j^n(v)}{\sum_i \sum_j w_{i,j} N_i^m(u) N_j^n(v)}.\qquad(17.15)$$

Figure 17.15 shows an example of a rational B-spline surface. It was obtained from the same control net as the surface in Figure 17.3, but with weights as shown in the figure. Note how the "dip" became more pronounced, as well as the "vertical ridge."

Rational surfaces are obtained as the projections of tensor product patches – but they are not tensor product patches themselves. Recall that a tensor product surface is of the form $\mathbf{x}(u,v) = \sum_i \sum_j \mathbf{c}_{i,j} F_{i,j}(u,v)$, where the basis functions $F_{i,j}$ may be expressed as products $F_{i,j}(u,v) = A_i(u)B_j(v)$. The basis functions for (17.15) are of the form

$$F_{i,j}(u,v) = \frac{w_{i,j} N_i^m(u) N_j^n(v)}{\sum_i \sum_j w_{i,j} N_i^m(u) N_j^n(v)}.$$

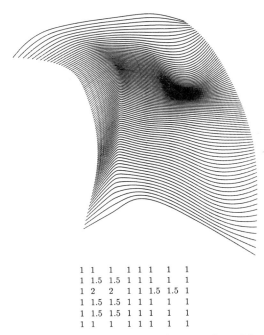

1	1	1	1	1	1	1	1
1	1.5	1.5	1	1	1	1	1
1	2	2	1	1	1.5	1.5	1
1	1.5	1.5	1	1	1	1	1
1	1.5	1.5	1	1	1	1	1
1	1	1	1	1	1	1	1

Figure 17.15. Rational B-spline surfaces: a surface together with the set of weights used to generate it.

Because of the structure of the denominator, this may in general not be factored into the required form $F_{i,j}(u,v) = A_i(u)B_j(v)$.

But even though rational surfaces do not possess a tensor product structure, we may utilize many tensor product algorithms for their manipulation. Consider, for example, the problem of finding the piecewise rational bicubic Bézier form of a rational bicubic B-spline surface. All we have to do is to convert each row of the B-spline control net into piecewise rational Bézier cubics (according to Section 15.6). Then we repeat this process for each column of the resulting net (and the resulting weights!), simply following the principle outlined in Figure 17.4.

As another example, consider the problem of extracting an isoparametric curve from a rational Bézier surface. Suppose the curve corresponds to $v = \hat{v}$. We simply interpret all columns of the control net as control polygons and evaluate each at $\hat{v}$, using the rational de Casteljau algorithm, for example. Keep in mind that we also have to compute a weight in each case. We can now interpret all obtained points together with their weights as the Bézier control polygon of the desired isoparametric curve. In general, its end weights will not be unity, i.e., the curve will not be in standard form (as described in Section 15.5). This situation may be remedied by the use of the reparametrization algorithm which is also described in that section.

Currently, rational B-spline surfaces are used for two reasons: they allow the exact representation of surfaces of revolution and of quadric surfaces. We will briefly describe surfaces of revolution in rational B-spline form here – quadric surfaces will be treated in Section 18.10.

A surface of revolution is given by

$$\mathbf{x}(u, v) = \begin{bmatrix} r(v) \cos u \\ r(v) \sin u \\ z(v) \end{bmatrix}.$$

For fixed v, an isoparametric line $v = const$ traces out a circle of radius $r(v)$, called a *meridian*. Since a circle may be exactly represented by rational quadratic arcs, we may find an exact rational representation of a surface of revolution provided we can represent $r(v), z(v)$ in rational form.

The most convenient way to define a surface of revolution is to prescribe the (planar) generating curve, or generatrix, given by

$$\mathbf{g}(v) = [r(v), 0, z(v)]^{\mathrm{T}}$$

and by the axis of revolution, in the same plane as $\mathbf{g}$. Suppose $\mathbf{g}$ is given by its control polygon, knot sequence, and weight sequence. We can construct a surface of revolution such that each meridian consists of three rational quadratic arcs, as shown in Figure 14.11. For each vertex of the generating polygon, construct an equilateral triangle (perpendicular to the axis of revolution) as in Figure 14.11. Assign the given weights of the generatrix to the three polygons corresponding to the triangle edge midpoints; assign half those weights to the three control polygons corresponding to the triangle vertices. In this way, we represent *exactly* "classical" surfaces such as cylinders, spheres, or tori.

Instead of breaking down each meridian into three arcs, we might have used four or more. This would have resulted in a larger number of patches; for an illustration, see Piegl and Tiller [284].

Note that although the generatrix may be defined over a knot sequence $\{v_j\}$ with only simple knots, this is not possible for the knots of the meridian circles: we have to use double knots, thereby essentially reducing it to the piecewise Bézier form.

17.8 Volume Deformations

Sometimes local control of a surface, nice as it may be, is not what is needed. A typical design request is "stretch this surface in that direction," or "bend that surface like so." These are *global* shape deformations, and the usual tweaking of control polygon vertices is somewhat cumbersome for this task. P. Bézier devised a method to deform a Bézier patch in a manner that would satisfy this global deformation principle. We shall see that it is also applicable to B-spline surfaces. For literature, see Bézier [48], [45], [47]. A more graphics-oriented version of this principle was presented by Sederberg and Parry [330].

To illustrate the principle, let us consider the 2D case first. Let $\mathbf{x}(t)$ be a planar curve (Bézier, B-spline, rational B-spline, etc.) which is, without loss of generality, located within the unit square. Next, let us cover the square with a regular grid of points $\mathbf{b}_{i,j} = [i/m, j/n]^{\mathrm{T}}; i = 0, \ldots, m; j = 0, \ldots, n$. We can now write every point (u, v) as

$$(u, v) = \sum_{i=0}^{m} \sum_{j=0}^{n} \mathbf{b}_{i,j} B_i^m(u) B_j^n(v);$$

this follows from the linear precision property of Bernstein polynomials (4.13).

If we now distort the grid of $\mathbf{b}_{i,j}$ into a grid $\hat{\mathbf{b}}_{i,j}$, the point (u, v) will be mapped to a point $(\hat{u}, \hat{v})$:

$$(\hat{u}, \hat{v}) = \sum_{i=0}^{m} \sum_{j=0}^{n} \hat{\mathbf{b}}_{i,j} B_i^m(u) B_j^n(v),$$

in other words, we are dealing with a mapping of $\mathbb{E}^2$ to $\mathbb{E}^2$.

In particular, the control vertices of the curve $\mathbf{x}(t)$ will be mapped to new control vertices, which in turn determine a new curve $\mathbf{y}(t)$. Note that $\mathbf{y}$ is only an approximation to the image of $\mathbf{x}$ under (17.8).[7] This is highlighted by the fact that the image of $\mathbf{x}$'s control polygon under (17.8) would be a collection of curve arcs, not another piecewise linear polygon.

We now have an *indirect* method for curve design: changing the $\mathbf{b}_{i,j}$ will produce globally deformed curves. This technique may facilitate certain design tasks that are otherwise tedious to perform. Figure 17.16 gives an example of the use of this global design technique.

---

[7] An exact procedure is described be T. DeRose [108].

Figure 17.16. Global curve distortions: A Bézier polygon is distorted into another polygon, resulting in a deformation of the initial curve.

This technique may be generalized. For instance, we may replace the Bézier distortion (17.8) by an analogous tensor product B-spline distortion. This would re-introduce some form of local control into our design scheme.

The next level of generalization is to $I\!\!E^3$: we introduce a *trivariate* Bézier patch by

$$(\hat{u}, \hat{v}, \hat{w}) = \sum_{i=0}^{m} \sum_{j=0}^{n} \sum_{k=0}^{l} \hat{\mathbf{b}}_{i,j,k} B_i^m(u) B_j^n(v) B_k^l(w),$$

which constitutes a deformation of 3D space $I\!\!E^3$. We may use (17.8) to deform the control net of a surface which is embedded in the unit cube. Again, the use of a Bézier patch for the distortion is immaterial; we might have used tricubic B-splines etc. in order to introduce some degree of locality into the method.

An example is shown in Figure 17.17. Part of the mushroom-shaped surface is embedded in a trivariate Bézier volume that is cubic in the vertical direction and linear in the other two. The top layer of control points is moved upwards, leading to a C^2 distortion of the initial object.

Why use deformation methods instead of just manipulating control vertices interactively? Volume deformation methods allow a designer to modify whole assemblies of surfaces at once, in a way that spreads out the changes in each part of the assembly in a very harmonic way. Tweaking control vertices one by one, one has no chance at arriving at a similarly balanced modification.

Figure 17.17. Global surface distortions: part of a surface is embedded in a Bézier volume (top). That volume is distorted (middle), leading to a distorted final object (bottom).

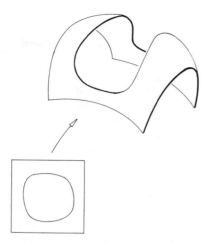

Figure 17.18. Trimmed surfaces: certain parts of a tensor product surface are marked as "invalid."

17.9   Trimmed Surfaces

Tensor product patches (or surfaces) are very handy where they can be applied. They can be applied to data that are inherently rectilinear. Not all situations lend themselves to a rectangular arrangement of patches or surfaces, and we should anticipate problems for such situations.

An example where rectangular topology is not appropriate is given in Plate III. Towards the lower right quadrant of that figure, we see a small "patch" surface that blends the central part of the hood to the part over the fender. (Such surfaces, by the way, are extremely tedious to design.) If you take a close look at Plate III, you will see that the surfaces covered by the patch surface are not drawn where the patch surface is drawn. In fact, they are not defined there. The parts that are occupied by the patch surface are not part of the "regular" surfaces.

Such modification of tensor product surfaces is achieved by a technique known as "trimming." A trimmed tensor product surface is essentially a regular tensor product surface, but with certain areas marked as invalid or invisible. These areas are usually defined by (fairly dense) polygons in the u, v-domain of the patch, as shown in Figure 17.18. Trimmed surfaces should be viewed as an "engineering" extension of tensor product patches. That is to say, they are not a panacea to all surface problems either. Take for example the problem of joining two trimmed surfaces together in a smooth way. If they are to join along trim curves, there is no way of ensuring exact tangent plane continuity between them, as was the case for standard tensor patches. Such smoothness questions must be dealt with on a case by case basis, which is clearly not very desirable. Just consider the problem of fitting the above mentioned blend surface from Plate III between its neighbors!

Literature on trimmed surfaces: Farouki and Hinds [142], Shantz and Chang [333], Casale and Bobrow [69], Miller [257].

17.10   Implementation

The routine that converts a rational bicubic B-spline control net into the piecewise rational bicubic Bézier form:

```
    void ratbspl_to_bez_surf(bspl_x,bspl_y,bspl_w,lu,lv,knot_u,
                             knot_v,bez_x,bez_y,bez_w,aux_x,aux_y,aux_w)
/*    Converts B-spline control net into piecewise
      Bezier control net (bicubic).
Input:       bspl_x,bspl_y:   B-spline control net (one coordinate only)
             bspl_w:          B-spline weights
             lu,lv:           no. of intervals in u- and v-direction
             knot_u, knot_v:  knot vectors in u- and v-direction
Output:      bez_x,bez_y:     piecewise bicubic Bezier net.
             bez_w:           Bezier weights.
Work space:aux_x,aux_y,aux_w: needed to store intermediate results.

Remark:      The  piecewise Bezier net only stores each control point once,
             i.e., neighboring patches share the same boundary.
             Knots are simple (but, in the language of Chapter 10, the
             boundary knots have multiplicity three).
*/
      float bspl_x[20][20],bspl_y[20][20],bspl_w[20][20],bez_x[20][20],
            bez_y[20][20],bez_w[20][20],knot_u[],knot_v[],
            aux_x[20][20],aux_y[20][20],aux_w[20][20];
      int   lu,lv;
{
      int   k,i,j,ii,jj,lu2,lv2,lu3,lv3;
      float help_x[20],help_y[20], help_w[20];
      float  help2_x[20],help2_y[20],help2_w[20];

      lu2=lu+2; lv2=lv+2;  lu3=lu*3; lv3=3*lv;

      for(i=0;  i<= lu2; i++)   /* convert all rows of bspl to bezier */
      {
            for(j=0; j<=lv2; j++)
```

```
                {
                help_x[j]=bspl_x[i][j];
                help_y[j]=bspl_y[i][j];
                help_w[j]=bspl_w[i][j];
                }
           ratbspline_to_bezier(help_x,help_y,help_w,
           knot_v,lv,help2_x,help2_y,help2_w);

           for(j=0; j<=lv3; j++)
                {
                aux_x[i][j]=help2_x[j];
                aux_y[i][j]=help2_y[j];
                aux_w[i][j]=help2_w[j];
                }
      }
   for(ii=0; ii<=lu2; ii++)
   for(jj=0; jj<=lv3; jj++)


   for(j=0;j<=lv3; j++)   /* now convert all columns of aux to bezier */
   {
        for(i=0; i<=lu2; i++)
                {
                help_x[i]=aux_x[i][j];
                help_y[i]=aux_y[i][j];
                help_w[i]=aux_w[i][j];
                }
        ratbspline_to_bezier(help_x,help_y,help_w,
        knot_u,lu,help2_x,help2_y,help2_w);

        for(i=0; i<=lu3; i++)
                {
                bez_x[i][j]=help2_x[i];
                bez_y[i][j]=help2_y[i];
                bez_w[i][j]=help2_w[i];
                }
      }
}
```

Once the piecewise Bézier representation of a bicubic spline surface is achieved, the following routine plots the whole surface:

```
void plot_bez_surfaces(bez_x,bez_y,lu,lv,u_points,v_points)
/*     Plots piecewise bicubic Bezier  surface
Input: bez_x, bez_y:        control nets
       lu,lv:               no. of segments in u- and v- direction
```

```
            u_points,v_p oints: per patch: v_points many
                                isoparametric curves with u_points
                                points on each
*/
      float bez_x[20][20], bez_y[20][20];
      int lu,lv;
{
      int i,j,ii,jj,lu3,lv3;
      float aux_x[20][20], aux_y[20][20];

      lu3=lu*3;  lv3=lv*3;

      for(i=0; i<lu3; i=i+3)
      for(j=0; j<lv3; j=j+3)
      {
            for(ii=0; ii<=3; ii++)
            for(jj=0; jj<=3; jj++)
            {
                  aux_x[ii][jj]=bez_x[i+ii][j+jj];
                  aux_y[ii][jj]=bez_y[i+ii][j+jj];
            }
            plot_surf(aux_x,aux_y,3,3,u_points,v_points);
      }
}
```

Tensor product spline interpolation (bicubic) is carried out by the following routine. It utilizes Bessel end conditions.

```
void spline_surf_int(data_x,data_y,bspl_x,bspl_y,lu,lv,knot_u,
                     knot_v,aux_x,aux_y)
/*     Interpolates to an array of size [0,lu+2]x[0,lv+2]
Input:     data_x, data_y:   data array (one coordinate only)
           lu,lv:            no. of intervals in u- and v-direction
           knot_u, knot_v:   knot vectors in u- and v-direction
Output:    bspl_x,bspl_y:    B-spline control net.

Work space: aux_x, aux_y.

Remark:    On input, it is assumed that data_x and data_y have rows
           1 and lu+1 and columns 1 and lv+1 empty, i.e., they are
           not filled with data points. Example for lu=4, lv=7:

           x0xxxxxx0x
           0000000000
           x0xxxxxx0x             x=data coordinate,
           x0xxxxxx0x             0=unused  input array
```

```
        x0xxxxxx0x                    element.
        0000000000                    The 0's will be filled with
        x0xxxxxx0x                    'tangent Bezier points'.
```

This approach makes it easy to feed in clamped end conditions
if so desired: put in values in the 0's and delete the calls
to bessel_ends below.
```
*/
    float bspl_x[20][20],bspl_y[20][20],
        data_x[20][20],data_y[20][20],
        knot_u[],knot_v[],                  /* If 20 is not your   */
        aux_x[20][20],aux_y[20][20];        /* favorite dimension, */
    int  lu,lv;                             /* some changes will   */
{                                           /* be necessary!       */
    int  i,j,lu2,lv2;
    float help_x[20],help_y[20],alpha[20],
        beta[20],gamma[20],up[20],low[20],
        help2_x[20],help2_y[20];

    lu2=lu+2; lv2=lv+2;
    /* interpolate all rows of data: */

    /*set up system in v-direction:  */

    set_up_system(knot_v,lv,alpha,beta,gamma);/*system setup  happens*/
    l_u_system(alpha,beta,gamma,lv,up,low);   /*outside loop!       */

    for(i=0;  i<= lu2; i++)
    {

        for(j=0;  j<=lv2; j++)
            {
            help_x[j]=data_x[i][j];
            help_y[j]=data_y[i][j];
            }
        bessel_ends(help_x,knot_v,lv);
        bessel_ends(help_y,knot_v,lv);
        solve_system(up,low,gamma,lv,help_x,help2_x);
        solve_system(up,low,gamma,lv,help_y,help2_y);

        for(j=0;  j<=lv2; j++)
            {
            aux_x[i][j]=help2_x[j];
            aux_y[i][j]=help2_y[j];
            }
    }
```

```
/* now interpolate all columns of aux: */

set_up_system(knot_u,lu,alpha,beta,gamma);/*system set up happens*/
l_u_system(alpha,beta,gamma,lu,up,low);    /*outside loop!        */

for(j=0;j<=lv2; j++)
{
    for(i=0; i<=lu2; i++)
        {
        help_x[i]=aux_x[i][j];
        help_y[i]=aux_y[i][j];
        }
    bessel_ends(help_x,knot_u,lu);
    bessel_ends(help_y,knot_u,lu);
    solve_system(up,low,gamma,lu,help_x,help2_x);
    solve_system(up,low,gamma,lu,help_y,help2_y);

    for(i=0; i<=lu2; i++)
        {
        bspl_x[i][j]=help2_x[i];
        bspl_y[i][j]=help2_y[i];
        }
}
}
```

17.11 Problems

1. Justify that in tensor product interpolation (Section 17.4), it does not matter if one starts with the row interpolation process or with the column interpolation process. Give computation counts for both strategies. (They are not equal!)

2. Generalize quintic Hermite and Lagrange interpolation to the tensor product case.

3. Generalize the B-spline knot insertion algorithm to the tensor product case.

4. Show that if two polynomial surfaces are C^1 across a common boundary, then they are also twist continuous across that boundary.

5. We defined a direct de Casteljau algorithm for tensor product Bézier surfaces in Section 16.2. Define a direct de Boor algorithm for tensor product B-spline surfaces.

6. Suppose we want to find a parametrization $\{u_i\}$ for a tensor product interpolant. We may parametrize all rows of data points and then form the averages of the parametrizations thus obtained. Or: we could average all rows of data points, e.g., by setting $\mathbf{p}_i = \sum_j \frac{j}{n} \mathbf{x}_{i,j}$ and we could then parametrize the $\mathbf{p}_i$. Do we get the same result? Discuss both methods.

Plate I.
An automobile.
(Courtesy of Mercedes-Benz, FRG.)

Plate II.
Color rendering of the
hood. *(Courtesy of
Mercedes-Benz, FRG.)*

Plate III.
Wire frame rendering of the
hood *(Courtesy of
Mercedes-Benz, FRG.)*

Plate IV. In a database, the hood is stored as an assembly of bicubic spline surfaces. The B-spline net of one of the surfaces is shown. *(Courtesy of Mercedes-Benz, FRG.)*

Plate V. A wire frame rendering of a surface (top left) and its Gaussian (top right), mean (bottom left), and absolute (bottom right) curvatures.

Plate VI.
The same curvatures
for a different surface.

Plate VII.
The surface from Plate VI,
but now with several twist
vectors. (Also, a different color
map is used.)

Plate VIII.
The surface from Plate VI,
after perturbations have
been applied.

Plate IX.
A bicubic B-spline surface.
(Courtesy of Silicon Graphics.)

Plate X.
The surface from Plate IX,
now with its B-spline net.
(Courtesy of Silicon Graphics.)

Plate XI.
The same surface, now
with the piecewise Bézier net.
(Courtesy of Silicon Graphics.)

18

Bézier Triangles

When de Casteljau invented Bézier curves in 1959, he realized the need for the extension of the curve ideas to surfaces. Interestingly enough, the first surface type that he considered was what we now call Bézier triangles. This historical "first" of triangular patches is reflected by the mathematical statement that they are a more "natural" generalization of Bézier curves than are tensor product patches. We should note that while de Casteljau's work was never published, Bézier's was, therefore the corresponding field now bears Bézier's name. For the placement of triangular Bernstein-Bézier surfaces in the field of CAGD, see Barnhill [16].

While de Casteljau's work (established in two internal Citroën technical reports [103] and [102]) remained unknown until its discovery by W. Boehm around 1975, other researchers realized the need for triangular patches. M. Sabin [307] worked on triangular patches in terms of Bernstein polynomials, unaware of de Casteljau's work. Among the people concerned with the development of triangular patches we name P.J. Davis [93], L. Frederickson [160], P. Sablonnière [309],and D. Stancu [336]. All of their Bézier-type approaches relied on the fact that piecewise surfaces were defined over regular triangulations; arbitrary triangulations were considered by Farin [121]. Two surveys on the field of triangular Bézier patches are now available: Farin [131] and de Boor [94].

18.1   Barycentric Coordinates and Linear Interpolation

Barycentric coordinates were already discussed in Section 2.3. There, they were used in connection with straight lines – now we will use them as coordinate systems when dealing with the plane. Barycentric coordinates are at the origin of affine geometry – they were first introduced by F. Moebius in 1827; see his collected works [258].

Consider a triangle with vertices $\mathbf{a}$, $\mathbf{b}$, $\mathbf{c}$ and a fourth point $\mathbf{p}$, all in $I\!\!E^2$. It is always possible to write $\mathbf{p}$ as a barycentric combination of $\mathbf{a}$, $\mathbf{b}$, $\mathbf{c}$:

$$\mathbf{p} = u\mathbf{a} + v\mathbf{b} + w\mathbf{c}. \tag{18.1}$$

A reminder: in order for (18.1) to be a barycentric combination (and hence to be geometrically meaningful), we require that

$$u + v + w = 1. \tag{18.2}$$

The coefficients $\mathbf{u} := (u, v, w)$ are called *barycentric coordinates* of $\mathbf{p}$ with respect to $\mathbf{a}$, $\mathbf{b}$, $\mathbf{c}$. We will often drop the distinction between the barycentric coordinates of a point and the point itself; we will then speak of "the point $\mathbf{u}$."

If the four points $\mathbf{a}$, $\mathbf{b}$, $\mathbf{c}$, and $\mathbf{p}$ are given, we can always determine $\mathbf{p}$'s barycentric coordinates u, v, w: equations (18.1) and (18.2) can be viewed as a linear system of three equations (recall that (18.1) is shorthand for two scalar equations) in three unknowns u, v, w. The solution is obtained by an application of Cramer's rule:

$$u = \frac{\text{area}(\mathbf{p}, \mathbf{b}, \mathbf{c})}{\text{area}(\mathbf{a}, \mathbf{b}, \mathbf{c})}, \quad v = \frac{\text{area}(\mathbf{a}, \mathbf{p}, \mathbf{c})}{\text{area}(\mathbf{a}, \mathbf{b}, \mathbf{c})}, \quad w = \frac{\text{area}(\mathbf{a}, \mathbf{b}, \mathbf{p})}{\text{area}(\mathbf{a}, \mathbf{b}, \mathbf{c})}. \tag{18.3}$$

Actually, Cramer's rule makes use of determinants; they are related to areas by the identity

$$\text{area}(\mathbf{a}, \mathbf{b}, \mathbf{c}) = \frac{1}{2} \begin{vmatrix} a_x & b_x & c_x \\ a_y & b_y & c_y \\ 1 & 1 & 1 \end{vmatrix}. \tag{18.4}$$

We note that in order for (18.3) to be well defined, we must have $\text{area}(\mathbf{a}, \mathbf{b}, \mathbf{c}) \neq 0$, which means that $\mathbf{a}$, $\mathbf{b}$, $\mathbf{c}$ must not lie on a straight line.

Due to their connection with barycentric combinations, barycentric coordinates are *affinely invariant*: let $\mathbf{p}$ have barycentric coordinates u, v, w with respect to $\mathbf{a}$, $\mathbf{b}$, $\mathbf{c}$. Now map all four points to another set of four points by an affine map Φ. Then $\Phi\mathbf{p}$ has the same barycentric coordinates u, v, w with respect to $\Phi\mathbf{a}$, $\Phi\mathbf{b}$, $\Phi\mathbf{c}$.

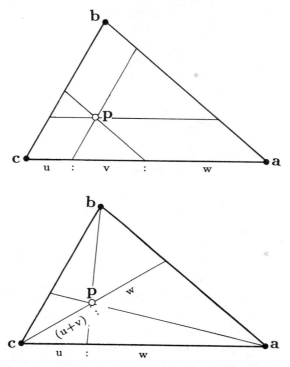

Figure 18.1. Barycentric coordinates: let $\mathbf{p} = u\mathbf{a} + v\mathbf{b} + w\mathbf{c}$. The two figures show some of the ratios that are generated by certain straight lines through $\mathbf{p}$.

Figure 18.1 illustrates more of the geometric properties of barycentric coordinates. An immediate consequence of Figure 18.1 is known as *Ceva's Theorem:*

$$\text{ratio}(\mathbf{a}, \mathbf{p}_c, \mathbf{b}) \cdot \text{ratio}(\mathbf{b}, \mathbf{p}_a, \mathbf{c}) \cdot \text{ratio}(\mathbf{c}, \mathbf{p}_b, \mathbf{a}) = 1.$$

More details on this and related theorems can be found in most geometry books, e.g. Gans [163] or Berger[39].

Any three noncollinear points $\mathbf{a}$, $\mathbf{b}$, $\mathbf{c}$ define a barycentric coordinate system in the plane. The points inside the triangle $\mathbf{a}$, $\mathbf{b}$, $\mathbf{c}$ have positive barycentric coordinates, while the remaining ones have (some) negative barycentric coordinates. Figure 18.2 shows more.

We may use barycentric coordinates to define *linear interpolation.* Suppose we are given three points $\mathbf{p}_1, \mathbf{p}_2, \mathbf{p}_3 \in E^3$. Then any point of the form

$$\mathbf{p} = \mathbf{p}(\mathbf{u}) = \mathbf{p}(u, v, w) = u\mathbf{p}_1 + v\mathbf{p}_2 + w\mathbf{p}_3 \qquad (18.5)$$

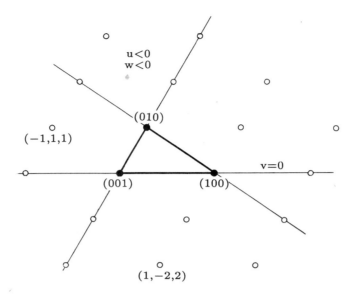

Figure 18.2. Barycentric coordinates: a triangle defines a coordinate system in the plane.

with $u + v + w = 1$ lies in the plane spanned by $\mathbf{p}_1, \mathbf{p}_2, \mathbf{p}_3$. This map from $I\!\!E^2$ to $I\!\!E^3$ is called *linear interpolation*. Since $u + v + w = 1$, we may interpret u, v, w as barycentric coordinates of $\mathbf{p}$ relative to $\mathbf{p}_1, \mathbf{p}_2, \mathbf{p}_3$. We may also interpret u, v, w as barycentric coordinates of a point in $I\!\!E^2$ relative to some triangle $\mathbf{a}, \mathbf{b}, \mathbf{c} \in I\!\!E^2$. Then (18.5) may be interpreted as a map of the triangle $\mathbf{a}, \mathbf{b}, \mathbf{c} \in I\!\!E^2$ onto the triangle $\mathbf{p}_1, \mathbf{p}_2, \mathbf{p}_3 \in I\!\!E^3$. We call the triangle $\mathbf{a}, \mathbf{b}, \mathbf{c}$ the *domain triangle*. Note that the actual location or shape of the domain triangle is totally irrelevant to the definition of linear interpolation. (Of course, we must demand that it be nondegenerate.) Since we can interpret u, v, w as barycentric coordinates in both two and three dimensions, it follows that linear interpolation (18.5) is an affine map.

18.2   The de Casteljau Algorithm

The de Casteljau algorithm for triangular patches is a direct generalization of the corresponding algorithm for curves. The curve algorithm uses repeated linear interpolation, and that process is also the key ingredient in the triangle case. The "triangular" de Casteljau algorithm is completely analogous to the univariate one, the main difference being notation. The control net is now of a triangular structure; in the quartic case, the control net consists of vertices

$$
\begin{array}{c}
\mathbf{b}_{040}\\
\mathbf{b}_{031}\,\mathbf{b}_{130}\\
\mathbf{b}_{022}\,\mathbf{b}_{121}\,\mathbf{b}_{220}\\
\mathbf{b}_{013}\,\mathbf{b}_{112}\,\mathbf{b}_{211}\,\mathbf{b}_{310}\\
\mathbf{b}_{004}\,\mathbf{b}_{103}\,\mathbf{b}_{202}\,\mathbf{b}_{301}\,\mathbf{b}_{400}
\end{array}
$$

Note that all subscripts sum to 4. In general, the control net consists of $\frac{1}{2}(n+1)(n+2)$ vertices. The numbers $\frac{1}{2}(n+1)(n+2)$ are called *triangle numbers*.

Some notation: we denote the point $\mathbf{b}_{ijk}$ by $\mathbf{b_i}$. Also, we use the abbreviations $\mathbf{e1} = (1,0,0), \mathbf{e2} = (0,1,0), \mathbf{e3} = (0,0,1)$ and $|\mathbf{i}| = i+j+k$. When we say $|\mathbf{i}| = n$, we mean $i+j+k = n$, always assuming $i, j, k \geq 0$.

Here is the de Casteljau algorithm:

de Casteljau algorithm:

Given: a triangular array of points $\mathbf{b_i} \in I\!\!E^3; |\mathbf{i}| = n$ and a point in $I\!\!E^2$ with barycentric coordinates $\mathbf{u}$.

Set:

$$
\mathbf{b_i^r}(\mathbf{u}) = u\mathbf{b_{i+e1}^{r-1}}(\mathbf{u}) + v\mathbf{b_{i+e2}^{r-1}}(\mathbf{u}) + w\mathbf{b_{i+e3}^{r-1}}(\mathbf{u}) \tag{18.6}
$$

where

$$
r = 1, \ldots, n \quad \text{and} \quad |\mathbf{i}| = n - r
$$

and $\mathbf{b_i^0}(\mathbf{u}) = \mathbf{b_i}$. Then $\mathbf{b_0^n}(\mathbf{u})$ is the point with parameter value $\mathbf{u}$ on the *Bézier triangle*[1] $\mathbf{b}^n$.

Figure 18.3 illustrates the construction of a point on a cubic Bézier triangle. We give a simple example: for $n = 3, r = 1$, and $\mathbf{i} = (2,0,0)$, we would obtain $\mathbf{b}_{200}^1 = u\mathbf{b}_{300} + v\mathbf{b}_{210} + w\mathbf{b}_{201}$. A complete numerical example is given in Section 18.6. At this point, the reader should compare the "triangular" de Casteljau algorithm with the univariate one, and also have a look at the barycentric form of Bézier curves, see Section 5.9.

Based on the de Casteljau algorithm, we can state many properties of Bézier triangles:

Affine invariance: This property follows since linear interpolation is an affine map and since the de Casteljau algorithm makes use of linear interpolation only.

---

[1] more precisely: triangular Bézier patch.

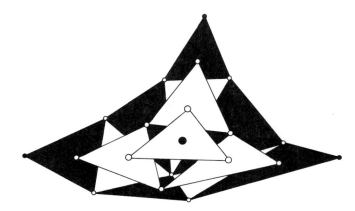

Figure 18.3. The "triangular" de Casteljau algorithm: a point is constructed by repeated linear interpolation.

Invarianceunderaffineparameter transformations: This property is guaranteed since such a reparametrization amounts to choosing a new domain triangle, but we have not even specified any particular domain triangle. More precisely: a point **u** will have the same barycentric coordinates **u** after an affine transformation of the domain triangle.

The convex hull property is guaranteed since for $0 \leq u, v, w \leq 1$, each $\mathbf{b_i^r}$ is a convex combination of the previous $\mathbf{b_i^{r-1}}$.

The boundary curves of a triangular patch are determined by the boundary control vertices (having at least one zero as a subscript). For example, a point on the boundary curve $\mathbf{b}^n(u, 0, w)$ is generated by

$$\mathbf{b_i^r}(u, 0, w) = u\mathbf{b_{i+e1}^{r-1}} + w\mathbf{b_{i+e3}^{r-1}}; \quad u + w = 1,$$

which is the univariate de Casteljau algorithm for Bézier curves.

18.3 Bernstein Polynomials

Univariate Bernstein polynomials are the terms of the binomial expansion of $[t + (1-t)]^n$. In the bivariate case, Bernstein polynomials $B_{\mathbf{i}}^n$ are defined by[2]

$$B_{\mathbf{i}}^n(\mathbf{u}) = \binom{n}{\mathbf{i}} u^i v^j w^k = \frac{n!}{i!j!k!} u^i v^j w^k; \quad |\mathbf{i}| = n. \tag{18.7}$$

---

[2]Keep in mind that although $B_{\mathbf{i}}^n(u, v, w)$ *looks* trivariate, it really is not, since $u + v + w = 1$.

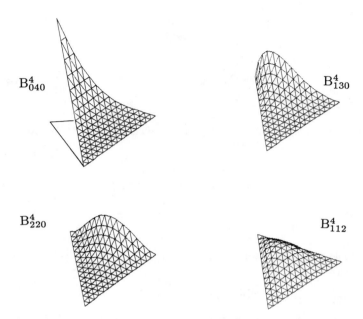

Figure 18.4. Bernstein polynomials: four quartic basis functions are shown; the shapes of the remaining ones follow from symmetry.

We define $B_{\mathbf{i}}^n(\mathbf{u}) = 0$ if some of the (i, j, k) are negative. Some of the quartic Bernstein polynomials are shown in Figure 18.4.

As an example, the quartic Bernstein polynomials could be arranged in the following triangular scheme (corresponding to the control point arrangement in the de Casteljau algorithm):

$$v^4$$
$$4v^3w \quad 4uv^3$$
$$6v^2w^2 \quad 12uv^2w \quad 6u^2v^2$$
$$4vw^3 \quad 12uvw^2 \quad 12u^2vw \quad 4u^3v$$
$$w^4 \quad 4uw^3 \quad 6u^2w^2 \quad 4u^3w \quad u^4$$

Bernstein polynomials satisfy the following recursion:

$$B_{\mathbf{i}}^n(\mathbf{u}) = uB_{\mathbf{i-e1}}^{n-1}(\mathbf{u}) + vB_{\mathbf{i-e2}}^{n-1}(\mathbf{u}) + wB_{\mathbf{i-e3}}^{n-1}(\mathbf{u}); \quad |\mathbf{i}| = n. \qquad (18.8)$$

This follows from their definition (18.7) and the use of the identity

$$\binom{n}{\mathbf{i}} = \binom{n}{i}\binom{n-i}{j}.$$

The intermediate points $\mathbf{b_i^r}$ in the de Casteljau algorithm can be expressed in terms of Bernstein polynomials:

$$\mathbf{b_i^r(u)} = \sum_{|\mathbf{j}|=r} \mathbf{b_{i+j}} B_{\mathbf{j}}^r(\mathbf{u}); \quad |\mathbf{i}| = n - r. \tag{18.9}$$

Setting $r = n$, we see that a triangular Bézier patch can be written in terms of Bernstein polynomials:

$$\mathbf{b^n(u)} = \mathbf{b_0^n(u)} = \sum_{|\mathbf{j}|=n} \mathbf{b_j} B_{\mathbf{j}}^n(\mathbf{u}). \tag{18.10}$$

We still need to prove (18.9). We use induction and the recursive definition of Bernstein polynomials:

$$
\begin{aligned}
\mathbf{b_i^{r+1}} &= u\mathbf{b_{i+e1}^r} + v\mathbf{b_{i+e2}^r} + w\mathbf{b_{i+e3}^r} \\
&= u\sum_{|\mathbf{j}|=r} \mathbf{b_{i+j+e1}} B_{\mathbf{j}}^r + v\sum_{|\mathbf{j}|=r} \mathbf{b_{i+j+e2}} B_{\mathbf{j}}^r + w\sum_{|\mathbf{j}|=r} \mathbf{b_{i+j+e3}} B_{\mathbf{j}}^r \\
&= \sum_{|\mathbf{j}|=r+1} u\mathbf{b_{i+j}} B_{\mathbf{j}-e1}^r + v\mathbf{b_{i+j}} B_{\mathbf{j}-e2}^r + w\mathbf{b_{i+j}} B_{\mathbf{j}-e3}^r \\
&= \sum_{|\mathbf{j}|=r+1} \mathbf{b_{i+j}} B_{\mathbf{j}}^{r+1}.
\end{aligned}
$$

Compare with the similar proof for the univariate case (4.6)!

We can generalize (18.10) just as we could in the univariate case:

$$\mathbf{b^n(u)} = \sum_{|\mathbf{j}|=n-r} \mathbf{b_j^r(u)} B_{\mathbf{j}}^{n-r}(\mathbf{u}); \quad 0 \le r \le n. \tag{18.11}$$

18.4 Derivatives

When we discussed derivatives for tensor product patches (Section 16.6), we considered *partials* because they are easily computed for those surfaces. The situation is different for triangular patches; the appropriate derivative here is the *directional derivative*. Let $\mathbf{u_1}$ and $\mathbf{u_2}$ be two points in the domain. Their difference $\mathbf{d} = \mathbf{u}_2 - \mathbf{u}_1$ defines a vector.[3] The directional derivative of a surface $\mathbf{x}(\mathbf{u})$ with respect to $\mathbf{d}$ is given by

$$D_{\mathbf{d}}\mathbf{x}(\mathbf{u}) = d\mathbf{x}_u(\mathbf{u}) + e\mathbf{x}_v(\mathbf{u}) + f\mathbf{x}_w(\mathbf{u}).$$

This can be written more concisely as

$$D_{\mathbf{d}}\mathbf{x}(\mathbf{u}) = \sum_{|\mathbf{i}|=1} \partial^{\mathbf{i}}\mathbf{x}(\mathbf{u})B_{\mathbf{i}}^1(\mathbf{d}),$$

where

$$\partial^{\mathbf{i}}\mathbf{x}(\mathbf{u}) = \frac{\partial^{|\mathbf{i}|}}{\partial u^i \partial v^j \partial w^k}\mathbf{x}(\mathbf{u})$$

are the partials of $\mathbf{x}$. Note that the terms $B_{\mathbf{i}}^1(\mathbf{d})$ are well-defined, even if $d + e + f = 0$.

A geometric interpretation of the notion of directional derivative shows that a straight line $\mathbf{u}(t) = \mathbf{u} + t\mathbf{d}$ through a point $\mathbf{u}$ in the domain with direction $\mathbf{d}$ is mapped onto a curve $\mathbf{x}(\mathbf{u}(t))$ on the surface $\mathbf{x}$. The tangent vector of this curve at $\mathbf{x}(\mathbf{u})$ is the desired directional derivative. Note that this tangent vector depends on the length of $\mathbf{d}$.

We can also compute higher order directional derivatives :

$$D_{\mathbf{d}}^r\mathbf{x}(\mathbf{u}) = \sum_{|\mathbf{j}|=r} \partial^{\mathbf{j}}\mathbf{x}(\mathbf{u})B_{\mathbf{j}}^r(\mathbf{d}), \tag{18.12}$$

a standard result in multivariate calculus. Equation (18.12) holds for any surface $\mathbf{x}$; the Bernstein polynomials that appear in it are simply a natural way to write down directional derivatives of a surface $\mathbf{x}(\mathbf{u})$ in barycentric form. We write out the case $r = 2$ in detail:

$$D_{\mathbf{d}}^2\mathbf{x}(\mathbf{u}) = \frac{\partial^2\mathbf{x}}{\partial u^2}d^2 + 2\frac{\partial^2\mathbf{x}}{\partial u\partial v}de + 2\frac{\partial^2\mathbf{x}}{\partial u\partial w}df + \frac{\partial^2\mathbf{x}}{\partial v^2}e^2 + 2\frac{\partial^2\mathbf{x}}{\partial v\partial w}ef + \frac{\partial^2\mathbf{x}}{\partial w^2}f^2.$$

This may be written in matrix form:

$$D_{\mathbf{d}}^2\mathbf{x}(\mathbf{u}) = \begin{bmatrix} d & e & f \end{bmatrix} \begin{bmatrix} \frac{\partial^2\mathbf{x}}{\partial u^2} & \frac{\partial^2\mathbf{x}}{\partial u\partial v} & \frac{\partial^2\mathbf{x}}{\partial u\partial w} \\ \frac{\partial^2\mathbf{x}}{\partial u\partial v} & \frac{\partial^2\mathbf{x}}{\partial v^2} & \frac{\partial^2\mathbf{x}}{\partial v\partial w} \\ \frac{\partial^2\mathbf{x}}{\partial u\partial w} & \frac{\partial^2\mathbf{x}}{\partial v\partial w} & \frac{\partial^2\mathbf{x}}{\partial w^2} \end{bmatrix} \begin{bmatrix} d \\ e \\ f \end{bmatrix}.$$

This is a quadratic form, and the matrix is simply the Hessian of $\mathbf{x}(\mathbf{u})$.

---

[3]In barycentric coordinates, a point $\mathbf{u}$ is characterized by $u + v + w = 1$, while a vector $\mathbf{d} = (d, e, f)$ is characterized by $d + e + f = 0$.

Back to the general case: the partials $\partial^{\mathbf{j}}$ of the Bernstein polynomials are given by

$$\partial^{\mathbf{j}} B_{\mathbf{i}}^n(\mathbf{u}) = \frac{n!}{(n-r)!} B_{\mathbf{i}-\mathbf{j}}^{n-r}(\mathbf{u}); \quad |\mathbf{j}| = r. \tag{18.13}$$

We can also apply the operator $D_{\mathbf{d}}^r$ to Bernstein polynomials, i.e., we can combine (18.12) and (18.13):

$$D_{\mathbf{d}}^r B_{\mathbf{i}}^n(\mathbf{u}) = \frac{n!}{(n-r)!} \sum_{|\mathbf{j}|=r} B_{\mathbf{j}}^r(\mathbf{d}) B_{\mathbf{i}-\mathbf{j}}^{n-r}(\mathbf{u}). \tag{18.14}$$

We are now in a position to give the rth directional derivative of a Bézier triangle:

$$D_{\mathbf{d}}^r \mathbf{b}^n(\mathbf{u}) = \frac{n!}{(n-r)!} \sum_{|\mathbf{j}|=r} \mathbf{b}_{\mathbf{j}}^{n-r}(\mathbf{u}) B_{\mathbf{j}}^r(\mathbf{d}). \tag{18.15}$$

For a proof of (18.15), we apply (18.14) to the definition (18.10) and obtain

$$D_{\mathbf{d}}^r \mathbf{b}^n(\mathbf{u}) = \frac{n!}{(n-r)!} \sum_{|\mathbf{i}|=n} \sum_{|\mathbf{j}|=r} \mathbf{b}_{\mathbf{i}} B_{\mathbf{j}}^r(\mathbf{d}) B_{\mathbf{i}-\mathbf{j}}^{n-r}(\mathbf{u}).$$

We rearrange and obtain

$$D_{\mathbf{d}}^r \mathbf{b}^n(\mathbf{u}) = \frac{n!}{(n-r)!} \sum_{|\mathbf{i}|=n-r} \sum_{|\mathbf{j}|=r} \mathbf{b}_{\mathbf{i}+\mathbf{j}} B_{\mathbf{j}}^r(\mathbf{d}) B_{\mathbf{i}}^{n-r}(\mathbf{u}) \tag{18.16}$$

$$= \frac{n!}{(n-r)!} \sum_{|\mathbf{j}|=r} B_{\mathbf{j}}^r(\mathbf{d}) \sum_{|\mathbf{i}|=n-r} \mathbf{b}_{\mathbf{i}+\mathbf{j}} B_{\mathbf{i}}^{n-r}(\mathbf{u}).$$

Application of (18.9) completes the proof.

A dual result is given by

$$D_{\mathbf{d}}^r \mathbf{b}^n(\mathbf{u}) = \frac{n!}{(n-r)!} \sum_{|\mathbf{j}|=n-r} \mathbf{b}_{\mathbf{j}}^r(\mathbf{d}) B_{\mathbf{j}}^{n-r}(\mathbf{u}). \tag{18.17}$$

This is proved by replacing $\mathbf{u}$ by $\mathbf{d}$ in (18.9). Then (18.16) yields (18.17).

Figure 18.5. Directional derivatives: the coefficients of the directional derivative of a triangular patch are the vectors $\mathbf{b}_{\mathbf{j}}^1(\mathbf{d})$.

After this intensive use of algebra, let us slow down and try to interpret our results. First we note that (18.15) is the analog of (4.22) in the univariate case. This sounds surprising at first, since (18.15) does not contain differences. Recall, however, that some of the components of $\mathbf{d}$ must be negative (since $d + e + f = 0$). Then the $B_{\mathbf{j}}^r(\mathbf{d})$ yield positive and negative values. We may therefore view terms involving $B_{\mathbf{j}}^r(\mathbf{d})$ as generalized differences. (In the univariate case, this is easily verified using the barycentric form of a Bézier curve.) Similarly, (18.17) may be viewed as a generalization of the univariate (4.19).

For $r = 1$, the terms $\mathbf{b}_{\mathbf{j}}^1(\mathbf{d})$ in (18.17) have a simple geometric interpretation: since $\mathbf{b}_{\mathbf{j}}^1(\mathbf{d}) = d\mathbf{b}_{\mathbf{j}+\mathbf{e}1} + e\mathbf{b}_{\mathbf{j}+\mathbf{e}2} + f\mathbf{b}_{\mathbf{j}+\mathbf{e}3}$ and $|\mathbf{j}| = n - 1$, they denote the affine map of the vector $\mathbf{d} \in I\!\!E^2$ to the triangle formed by $\mathbf{b}_{\mathbf{j}+\mathbf{e}1}, \mathbf{b}_{\mathbf{j}+\mathbf{e}2}, \mathbf{b}_{\mathbf{j}+\mathbf{e}3}$. The directional derivative of $\mathbf{b}^n$ is thus a triangular patch whose coefficients are the images of $\mathbf{d}$ on each subtriangle in the control net (see Figure 18.5). For computational purposes, we would compute the net of the $n\mathbf{b}_{\mathbf{j}}^1(\mathbf{d})$ and use them as the input for a de Casteljau algorithm of an $(n - 1)^{\text{st}}$ degree Bézier patch.

Similarly, let us set $r = 1$ in (18.15). Then,

$$
\begin{aligned}
D_{\mathbf{d}}\mathbf{b}^n(\mathbf{u}) &= n \sum_{|\mathbf{j}|=1} \mathbf{b}_{\mathbf{j}}^{n-1}(\mathbf{u}) B_{\mathbf{j}}^1(\mathbf{d}) \\
&= n(d\mathbf{b}_{\mathbf{e}1}^{n-1} + e\mathbf{b}_{\mathbf{e}2}^{n-1} + f\mathbf{b}_{\mathbf{e}3}^{n-1}).
\end{aligned}
$$

Since this is true for all directions $\mathbf{d} \in I\!\!E^2$, it follows that $\mathbf{b}_{\mathbf{e}1}^{n-1}, \mathbf{b}_{\mathbf{e}2}^{n-1}, \mathbf{b}_{\mathbf{e}3}^{n-1}$ define the *tangent plane* at $\mathbf{b}^n(\mathbf{u})$. This is the direct generalization of the corresponding univariate result. In particular, the three vertices $\mathbf{b}_{0,n,0}, \mathbf{b}_{0,n-1,1}, \mathbf{b}_{1,n-1,0}$ span the tangent plane at $\mathbf{b}_{0,n,0}$ with analogous

Figure 18.6. Cross-boundary derivatives: any first order cross-boundary directional derivative of a quartic, evaluated along the indicated edge, depends only on the two indicated rows of Bézier points.

results for the remaining two corners. Again, we see that the de Casteljau algorithm produces derivative information as a byproduct of the evaluation process.

The duality of the formulas (18.15) and (18.17) has an interesting computational spinoff. In order to compute the $r-th$ derivative with respect to **d** at $\mathbf{x}(\mathbf{u})$, we must perform r "difference" de Casteljau steps with respect to **d**, and $n - r$ evaluation steps with respect to **u**. It does not matter in which order we perform those steps (Farin [130]), so we have whole variety of possible combinations to compute a directional derivative.

We next discuss *cross-boundary derivatives* of Bézier triangles. Consider the edge $u = 0$ and a direction **d** not parallel to it. The directional derivative with respect to **d**, evaluated along $u = 0$, is the desired cross-boundary derivative. It is given by

$$D_{\mathbf{d}}\mathbf{b}^n(\mathbf{u})\Big|_{u=0} = \frac{n!}{(n-r)!} \sum_{|\mathbf{i}_0|=n-r} \mathbf{b}_{\mathbf{i}_0}^r(\mathbf{d}) B_{\mathbf{i}_0}^{n-r}(\mathbf{u})\Big|_{u=0}, \qquad (18.18)$$

where $\mathbf{i}_0 = (0, j, k)$. Since $\mathbf{u} = (0, v, w) = (0, v, 1 - v)$, this is a univariate expression, a Bézier curve in barycentric form as discussed in Section 5.9. Note that it depends only on the $r + 1$ rows of Bézier points closest to the boundary under consideration. Analogous results hold for the other two boundaries; see Figure 18.6. This result is the straightforward generalization of the corresponding univariate result. We will use it for the construction of composite surfaces, just as we did for curves.

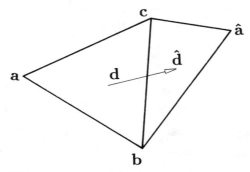

Figure 18.7. Subdivision: the domain geometry.

18.5 Subdivision

We will later study surfaces that consist of several triangular patches forming a C^r overall surface. Now, we start with a surface consisting of just two triangular patches. Let their domain triangles be defined by points $\mathbf{a}, \mathbf{b}, \mathbf{c}, \hat{\mathbf{a}}$, as shown in Figure 18.7. If the common boundary is through $\mathbf{b}$ and $\mathbf{c}$, then the (domain!) point $\hat{\mathbf{a}}$ can be expressed in terms of barycentric coordinates of $\mathbf{a}, \mathbf{b}, \mathbf{c}$:

$$\hat{\mathbf{a}} = v_1 \mathbf{d} + v_2 \mathbf{b} + v_3 \mathbf{c}.$$

Suppose now that a Bézier triangle $\mathbf{b}^n$ is given that has the triangle $\mathbf{a}, \mathbf{b}, \mathbf{c}$ as its domain. Of course it is defined over the whole plane, in particular over $\hat{\mathbf{a}}, \mathbf{c}, \mathbf{b}$. What are the Bézier points of $\mathbf{b}^n$ if we consider only the part of it that is defined over $\hat{\mathbf{a}}, \mathbf{c}, \mathbf{b}$?[4]

Let $\mathbf{u}$ denote the barycentric coordinates in $\mathbf{a}, \mathbf{b}, \mathbf{c}$ and let $\hat{\mathbf{u}}$ denote those in $\hat{\mathbf{a}}, \mathbf{c}, \mathbf{b}$. Then the surface (of which $\mathbf{b}^n$ is just one segment) can be written in two ways:

$$\sum_{|\mathbf{i}|=n} \mathbf{b_i} B_{\mathbf{i}}^n(\mathbf{u}) = \sum_{|\hat{\mathbf{i}}|=n} \hat{\mathbf{b}}_{\mathbf{i}} B_{\mathbf{i}}^n(\hat{\mathbf{u}}).$$

Let $\mathbf{d}$ be the barycentric coordinates (with respect to $\mathbf{a}, \mathbf{b}, \mathbf{c}$) of a direction that is not parallel to the common boundary $\mathbf{b}, \mathbf{c}$. Let $\hat{\mathbf{d}}$ be the barycentric coordinates of the same direction with respect to $\hat{\mathbf{a}}, \mathbf{c}, \mathbf{b}$.

We can now consider directional derivatives by applying (18.17):

$$\sum_{|\mathbf{j}_0|=n-r} \mathbf{b}_{\mathbf{j}_0}^r(\mathbf{d}) B_{\mathbf{j}_0}^{n-r}(\mathbf{u}) \Big|_{u=0} = \sum_{|\mathbf{j}_0|=n-r} \hat{\mathbf{b}}_{\mathbf{j}_0}^r(\hat{\mathbf{d}}) B_{\mathbf{j}_0}^{n-r}(\hat{\mathbf{u}}) \Big|_{\hat{u}=0}; \quad r = 0, \ldots, n.$$

---

[4]Be sure to compare this development with the univariate case from Section 7.2!

Here, $\mathbf{j}_0 = (0, j, k)$. Comparing coefficients yields

$$\mathbf{b}_{\mathbf{j}_0}^r(\mathbf{d}) = \hat{\mathbf{b}}_{\mathbf{j}_0}^r(\hat{\mathbf{d}}) \quad r = 0, \ldots, n.$$

Now $\mathbf{b}_{\mathbf{j}_0}^r$ is itself a polynomial of degree r, formed by a subnet of the original control net; the same is true for $\hat{\mathbf{b}}_{\mathbf{j}_0}^r$. The last set of equations states that for any r, the two polynomials $\mathbf{b}_{\mathbf{j}_0}^r$ and $\hat{\mathbf{b}}_{\mathbf{j}_0}^r$ agree in all derivatives up to order r, evaluated along the common boundary:

$$D_{\mathbf{d}}^r \mathbf{b}_{\mathbf{j}_0}^r(\mathbf{u}) = D_{\hat{\mathbf{d}}}^r \hat{\mathbf{b}}_{\mathbf{j}_0}^r(\hat{\mathbf{u}}).$$

Thus, they are equal for all values of $\mathbf{u}$ and corresponding $\hat{\mathbf{u}}$:

$$\mathbf{b}_{\mathbf{j}_0}^r(\mathbf{u}) = \hat{\mathbf{b}}_{\mathbf{j}_0}^r(\hat{\mathbf{u}}).$$

Let $\mathbf{v}$ be the barycentric coordinates of $\hat{\mathbf{a}}$ with respect to $\mathbf{a}, \mathbf{b}, \mathbf{c}$. The last equation, being satisfied by all $\mathbf{u}$, is also satisfied by $\mathbf{v}$. Noting that $\mathbf{u} = \mathbf{v}$ corresponds to $\hat{\mathbf{u}} = \mathbf{e1}$, we obtain

$$\mathbf{b}_{\mathbf{j}_0}^r(\mathbf{v}) = \hat{\mathbf{b}}_{\mathbf{j}_0}^r(\mathbf{e1}).$$

Since $\hat{\mathbf{b}}_{\mathbf{j}_0}^r(\mathbf{e1}) = \hat{\mathbf{b}}_{(r,j,k)}$, we now have (Farin [121]):

$$\hat{\mathbf{b}}_{(r,j,k)} = \mathbf{b}_{\mathbf{j}_0}^r(\mathbf{v}); r = 0, \ldots, n; \quad j + k = n - r, \tag{18.19}$$

thus constructing the control points $\hat{\mathbf{b}}_{\mathbf{j}}$ row by row, each row corresponding to a different value of r. An numerical example is given in the next section.

We thus have an algorithm that allows us to construct the Bézier points of the "extension" of $\mathbf{b}^n$ to an adjacent patch. It should be noted that this algorithm does not use convex combinations (when $\hat{\mathbf{a}}$ is outside $\mathbf{a}, \mathbf{b}, \mathbf{c}$). It performs piecewise linear extrapolation, and should therefore not be expected to be very stable.

If $\hat{\mathbf{a}}$ is inside $\mathbf{a}, \mathbf{b}, \mathbf{c}$, then we do use convex combinations only, and (18.19) provides a *subdivision algorithm*. Just as $\hat{\mathbf{a}}$ subdivides the triangle $\mathbf{a}, \mathbf{b}, \mathbf{c}$

Figure 18.8. Subdivision: the intermediate points from the de Casteljau algorithm form the three sub-patch control nets.

into three subtriangles, the point $\mathbf{b}^n(\mathbf{v})$ subdivides the triangular patch into three sub-patches. Equation (18.19) provides the Bézier points for each of them. Figure 18.8 gives an illustration.

Just as in the curve case, if we insert a dense sequence of points into the domain triangle, the resulting sequence of control nets will converge to the surface. This fact may be used in rendering techniques or in intersection algorithms.

A special case arises if $\mathbf{v}$ is on one of the edges of the domain triangle $\mathbf{a}, \mathbf{b}, \mathbf{c}$. Then (18.19) generates the Bézier points of the surface curve through $\mathbf{b}^n(\mathbf{v})$ and the opposite patch corner; see Figure 18.9. Such curves, joining a vertex to a point on the opposite edge, are called "radial lines."

18.6 Differentiability

The concept of differentiability is straightforward for tensor product patches: we compare cross-boundary partials. As we have seen, partials are not an adequate tool when dealing with triangular patches. We will use the following generalization. Consider two triangular patches that are maps of two adjacent domain triangles. Any straight line in the domain that crosses the common edge is mapped onto a composite curve in $I\!\!E^3$, having one segment in each patch. If all composite curves that can be obtained in this way are C^r curves, then we say that the two patches are C^r continuous.

Equation (18.19) gives a condition by which two adjacent patches can be part of one global polynomial surface. If we do not let r vary from 0 to n, but from 0 to some $s \leq n$, we have a condition for C^s continuity between

Figure 18.9. Subdivision: the Bézier points of a surface curve that is the image of a straight line through one of the domain triangle vertices.

adjacent patches:

$$\hat{\mathbf{b}}_{(r,j,k)} = \mathbf{b}_{\mathbf{j}_0}^{r}(\mathbf{v}); r = 0, \ldots, s. \tag{18.20}$$

Equation (18.20) is a necessary and sufficient condition for the C^s continuity of two adjacent patches. We can make that claim since cross-boundary derivatives up to order s depend only on the $s+1$ rows of control points "parallel" to the considered boundary.

For $s = 0$, (18.20) states that the two patches must share a common boundary control polygon. The case $s = 1$ is more interesting; there, (18.20) becomes

$$\hat{\mathbf{b}}_{(1,j,k)} = v_1 \mathbf{b}_{1,j,k} + v_2 \mathbf{b}_{0,j+1,k} + v_3 \mathbf{b}_{0,j,k+1}.$$

Thus each $\hat{\mathbf{b}}_{(1,j,k)}$ is obtained as a barycentric combination of the vertices of a boundary subtriangle of the control net of $\mathbf{b}^n$. Moreover, for all $j + k = n - 1$, these barycentric combinations are identical. Thus all pairs of subtriangles shown in Figure 18.10 are coplanar, and each pair is an affine map of the pair of domain triangles of the two patches.[5] We call the pairs of coplanar subtriangles that satisfy this condition *affine pairs*.

To be more specific, we give a numerical example of a C^1 extension of a given cubic patch. Let its Bézier points be given by:

---

[5]It is *not* sufficient that the pairs are coplanar – this does not even guarantee a continuous tangent plane.

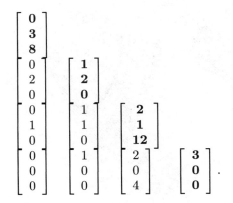

$$
\begin{bmatrix} 0 \\ 3 \\ 8 \end{bmatrix}
\begin{bmatrix} 0 \\ 2 \\ 0 \end{bmatrix}
\begin{bmatrix} 1 \\ 2 \\ 0 \end{bmatrix}
\begin{bmatrix} 0 \\ 1 \\ 0 \end{bmatrix}
\begin{bmatrix} 1 \\ 1 \\ 0 \end{bmatrix}
\begin{bmatrix} 2 \\ 1 \\ 12 \end{bmatrix}
\begin{bmatrix} 0 \\ 0 \\ 0 \end{bmatrix}
\begin{bmatrix} 1 \\ 0 \\ 0 \end{bmatrix}
\begin{bmatrix} 2 \\ 0 \\ 4 \end{bmatrix}
\begin{bmatrix} 3 \\ 0 \\ 0 \end{bmatrix}.
$$

According to our previous development, let $\mathbf{b}_{300} = [0,0,0]^{\mathrm{T}}$ be the image of $\mathbf{a}$, $\mathbf{b}_{030} = [3,0,0]^{\mathrm{T}}$ the image of $\mathbf{b}$, and $\mathbf{b}_{003} = [0,3,8]^{\mathrm{T}}$ the image of $\mathbf{c}$. Now define a fourth point $\hat{\mathbf{a}}$ in the domain by specifying its barycentric coordinates $\mathbf{v} = (-2, 3/2, 3/2)$ with respect to the triangle $\mathbf{a}, \mathbf{b}, \mathbf{c}$. Note that we do not care what the actual values of $\mathbf{a}, \mathbf{b}, \mathbf{c}$, and $\hat{\mathbf{a}}$ are; all we need to know is their geometric relationship, which is captured by the value of $\mathbf{v}$. We can now evaluate our Bézier triangle at the (domain) point $\mathbf{v}$. The de Casteljau steps are as follows: for $r = 1$, the $\mathbf{b}_{\mathbf{i}}^1$ are given by

$$
\begin{bmatrix} 3/2 \\ 7/2 \\ 12 \end{bmatrix}
\begin{bmatrix} 3/2 \\ 5/2 \\ 0 \end{bmatrix}
\begin{bmatrix} 5/2 \\ 5/2 \\ 18 \end{bmatrix}
\begin{bmatrix} 3/2 \\ 3/2 \\ 0 \end{bmatrix}
\begin{bmatrix} 5/2 \\ 3/2 \\ 6 \end{bmatrix}
\begin{bmatrix} 7/2 \\ 3/2 \\ 10 \end{bmatrix}.
$$

The $\mathbf{b}_{\mathbf{i}}^2$ are

$$
\begin{bmatrix} 3 \\ 4 \\ 45 \end{bmatrix}
\begin{bmatrix} 3 \\ 3 \\ 9 \end{bmatrix}
\begin{bmatrix} 4 \\ 3 \\ 30 \end{bmatrix}.
$$

Finally, the result is given by $\mathbf{b}_{\mathbf{0}}^3(\mathbf{v}) = [9/2, 9/2, 189/2]^{\mathrm{T}}$.

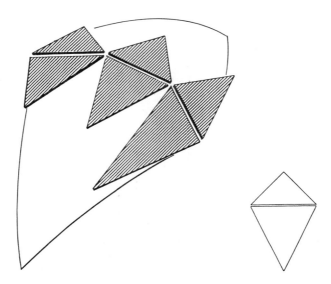

Figure 18.10. C^1-continuity: the shaded pairs of triangles must be coplanar and be an affine map of the two domain triangles.

If we are interested in C^1 continuity of two Bézier triangles, one defined over $\mathbf{a}, \mathbf{b}, \mathbf{c}$ and the other over $\hat{\mathbf{a}}, \mathbf{b}, \mathbf{c}$, then we only need to consider the points $\hat{\mathbf{b}}_{0,j,k} = \mathbf{b}_{0,j,k}; j + k = 3$, and $\hat{\mathbf{b}}_{1,j,k} = \mathbf{b}_{0,j,k}^1; j + k = 2$ from above. They are set boldface. This fixes two rows of Bézier points of the $\hat{\mathbf{a}}, \mathbf{b}, \mathbf{c}$ triangle; the remaining two may be given any values; the two patches would still be C^1.

Of course, having performed the whole de Casteljau algorithm, we may now even collect *all* Bézier points that define the "new" triangle. They are all the boldface points from above, including the point $\hat{\mathbf{b}}_{300} = [9/2, 9/2, 189]^{\mathrm{T}}$.

Figure 18.11 shows a composite C^1 surface that consists of several Bézier triangles. The (wire frame) plot of the surface does not look very smooth. This is due to the different spacing of isoparametric lines in the plot, not to discontinuities in the surface.

18.7 Degree Elevation

It is possible to write $\mathbf{b}^n$ as a Bézier triangle of degree $n + 1$:

$$\sum_{|\mathbf{i}|=n} \mathbf{b_i} B_\mathbf{i}^n(\mathbf{u}) = \sum_{|\hat{\mathbf{i}}|=n+1} \mathbf{b}_\mathbf{i}^{(1)} B_\mathbf{i}^{n+1}(\mathbf{u}). \tag{18.21}$$

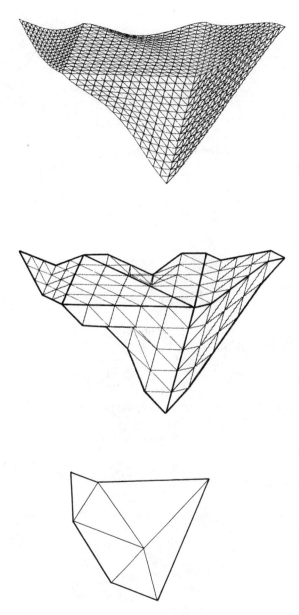

Figure 18.11. Bézier triangles: a composite C^1 surface. Top: the surface; middle: the piecewise quintic control net; bottom: the domain triangles. Note that the "center" patch is actually planar.

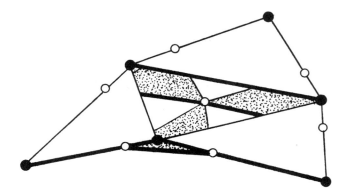

Figure 18.12. Degree elevation: a quadratic control net together with the equivalent cubic net.

The control points $\mathbf{b_i}^{(1)}$ are obtained from

$$\mathbf{b_i}^{(1)} = \frac{1}{n+1}[i\mathbf{b_{i-e1}} + j\mathbf{b_{i-e2}} + k\mathbf{b_{i-e3}}]. \qquad (18.22)$$

For a proof, we multiply the left hand side of (18.21) by $u + v + w$ and compare coefficients of like powers. Figure 18.12 illustrates the case $n = 2$. Degree elevation is performed by piecewise linear interpolation of the original control net. Therefore, the degree elevated control net lies in the convex hull of the original one.

As in the univariate case, degree elevation may be repeated. That process generates a sequence of control nets that have the surface patch as their limit (Farin [130]). More details are in Farin [131].

18.8 Nonparametric Patches

In an analogy to the univariate case, we may write the function

$$z = \sum_{|\mathbf{i}|=n} b_\mathbf{i} B_\mathbf{i}^n(\mathbf{u}) \qquad (18.23)$$

as a surface

$$\begin{bmatrix} u \\ v \\ w \\ z \end{bmatrix} = \sum_{|\mathbf{i}|=n} \begin{bmatrix} i/n \\ j/n \\ k/n \\ b_\mathbf{i} \end{bmatrix} B_\mathbf{i}^n(\mathbf{u}).$$

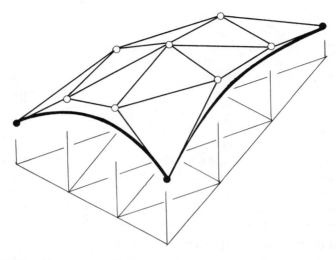

Figure 18.13.   Nonparametric patches: the abscissae of the control net are the n-partition points of the domain triangle.

Thus the abscissae values of the control polygon of a nonparametric patch are given by the triples $\mathbf{i}/n$, as illustrated in Figure 18.13. The last equation holds because of the *linear precision* property of the Bernstein polynomials $B_{\mathbf{i}}^{n}$,

$$u = \sum_{|\mathbf{i}|=n} \frac{i}{n} B_{\mathbf{i}}^{n}(\mathbf{u}),$$

and analogous formulas for v and w. The proof is by degree elevation from one to n of the linear function u.

A triangular patch that can be written as a nonparametric one is given by the example in Section 18.6. Its domain triangle would then be $[0,0,0]^{\mathrm{T}}$, $[3,0,0]^{\mathrm{T}}$, $[0,3,0]^{\mathrm{T}}$.

Nonparametric Bézier triangles play an important role in the investigation of spaces of piecewise polynomials, as studied in approximation theory. Their use has facilitated the investigation of one of the main open questions in that field: what is the dimension of those function spaces? (See, for instance, Alfeld and Schumaker [6]). They have also been useful in defining nonparametric piecewise polynomial interpolants; see, for example, Barnhill and Farin [20], or Sablonniere [311].

Bézier triangles may be generalized to *Bézier tetrahedra* by introducing barycentric coordinates in tetrahedra; see Problem 5.

18.9   Rational Bézier Triangles

Following the familiar theme of generating rational curve and surface schemes, we define a rational Bézier triangle to be the projection of a nonrational 4D Bézier triangle. We thus have:

$$\mathbf{b}^n(\mathbf{u}) = \mathbf{b}_0^n(\mathbf{u}) = \frac{\sum_{|\mathbf{i}|=n} w_{\mathbf{i}}\mathbf{b}_{\mathbf{i}}B_{\mathbf{i}}^n(\mathbf{u})}{\sum_{|\mathbf{i}|=n} w_{\mathbf{i}}B_{\mathbf{i}}^n(\mathbf{u})}, \tag{18.24}$$

where, as usual, the $w_{\mathbf{i}}$ are the weights associated with the control vertices $\mathbf{b}_{\mathbf{i}}$. Needless to say, for positive weights we have the convex hull property, and we have affine and projective invariance.

Rational Bézier triangles may be evaluated by a de Casteljau algorithm in a not too surprising way:

Rational de Casteljau algorithm

Given: a triangular array of points $\mathbf{b}_{\mathbf{i}} \in I\!\!E^3$; $|\mathbf{i}| = n$, corresponding weights $w_{\mathbf{i}}$, and a point in a domain triangle with barycentric coordinates $\mathbf{u}$.

Set:

$$\mathbf{b}_{\mathbf{i}}^r(\mathbf{u}) = \frac{uw_{\mathbf{i+e1}}^{r-1}\mathbf{b}_{\mathbf{i+e1}}^{r-1} + vw_{\mathbf{i+e2}}^{r-1}\mathbf{b}_{\mathbf{i+e2}}^{r-1} + ww_{\mathbf{i+e3}}^{r-1}\mathbf{b}_{\mathbf{i+e3}}^{r-1}}{w_{\mathbf{i}}^r} \tag{18.25}$$

where

$$w_{\mathbf{i}}^r = w_{\mathbf{i}}^r(\mathbf{u}) = uw_{\mathbf{i+e1}}^{r-1}(\mathbf{u}) + vw_{\mathbf{i+e2}}^{r-1}(\mathbf{u}) + ww_{\mathbf{i+e3}}^{r-1}(\mathbf{u})$$

and

$$r = 1,\ldots,n \quad \text{and} \quad |\mathbf{i}| = n - r$$

and $\mathbf{b}_{\mathbf{i}}^0(\mathbf{u}) = \mathbf{b}_{\mathbf{i}}, w_{\mathbf{i}}^0 = w_{\mathbf{i}}$. Then $\mathbf{b}_0^n(\mathbf{u})$ is the point with parameter value $\mathbf{u}$ on the rational Bézier triangle $\mathbf{b}^n$.

This algorithm works since we can interpret each intermediate $\mathbf{b}_{\mathbf{i}}^r$ as the projection of the corresponding point in the de Casteljau algorithm of the nonrational 4D preimage of our patch.

Something surprising happens now, after everything so far was yet another exercise in generating rational schemes. In the case of rational Bézier curves, the initial weights could be used to define auxiliary points $\mathbf{q}_i$, as described in Section 15.2. In the triangle case we can also define auxiliary points $\mathbf{q}_{\mathbf{i}}$, namely by setting

$$\mathbf{q}_{\mathbf{i}} = \frac{w_{\mathbf{i+e1}}\mathbf{b}_{\mathbf{i+e1}} + w_{\mathbf{i+e2}}\mathbf{b}_{\mathbf{i+e2}} + w_{\mathbf{i+e3}}\mathbf{b}_{\mathbf{i+e3}}}{w_{\mathbf{i+e1}} + w_{\mathbf{i+e2}} + w_{\mathbf{i+e3}}}; \quad |\mathbf{i}| = n - 1.$$

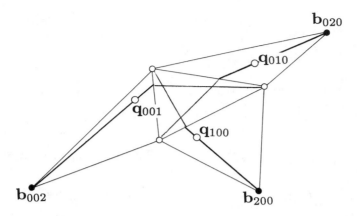

Figure 18.14. Auxiliary points: an arbitrary choice of the three auxiliary points $\mathbf{q_{e1}}, \mathbf{q_{e2}}, \mathbf{q_{e3}}$ would overdetermine the location of $\mathbf{p}$.

The usefulness of the $\mathbf{q}_i$ in the curve case stemmed from the fact that they could be used as a design handle: we could define points $\mathbf{q}_i$ and then retrieve the weights w_i. Now, in the triangle case, this is no longer possible (first noted by Ramshaw [293]). We can see why just by considering the quadratic case $n = 2$, illustrated in Figure 18.14.

If we were given a set of weights $w_\mathbf{i}$; $|\mathbf{i}| = 2$, we would not only generate the auxiliary points $\mathbf{q_i}$, but also the point

$$\mathbf{p} = \frac{w_{011}\mathbf{b}_{011} + w_{101}\mathbf{b}_{101} + w_{110}\mathbf{b}_{110}}{w_{011} + w_{101} + w_{110}}.$$

The point $\mathbf{p}$ is then at the intersection of the three straight lines $\overline{\mathbf{q}_{001}, \ \mathbf{b}_{110}}$, etc. shown in Figure 18.14. If we prescribed the three $\mathbf{q_i}$ arbitrarily (as is actually shown in Figure 18.14), those straight lines would not intersect in one point any more, thus leaving $\mathbf{p}$ overdetermined. Since the existence of a set of weights implied the existence of $\mathbf{p}$, the nonexistence of $\mathbf{p}$ implies that we cannot find a set of weights if we prescribe the $\mathbf{q_i}$ arbitrarily.

For higher degrees, the situation is analogous. So far, no geometric way is known that could define weights similar to the auxiliary point approach for curves (see Problems).

We now give a formula for the *directional derivative* of a rational Bézier triangle. Just as in Section 18.4, let $\mathbf{d}$ denote a direction in the domain triangle, expressed in barycentric coordinates. We are interested in the ceeding exactly as in the curve case (see Section 14.4), we obtain:

$$D_{\mathbf{d}}\mathbf{b}^n(\mathbf{u}) = \frac{1}{w(\mathbf{u})}[\dot{\mathbf{p}}(\mathbf{u}) - D_{\mathbf{d}}(\mathbf{u})\mathbf{b}^n(\mathbf{u})],$$

where we have set

$$\mathbf{p}(\mathbf{u}) = w(\mathbf{u})\mathbf{b}^n(\mathbf{u}) = \sum_{|\mathbf{i}|=n} w_{\mathbf{i}}\mathbf{b}_{\mathbf{i}}B_{\mathbf{i}}^n(\mathbf{u}).$$

Higher derivatives follow the pattern outlined in Section 14.4, i.e.

$$D_{\mathbf{d}}^r\mathbf{b}^n(\mathbf{u}) = \frac{1}{w(\mathbf{u})}\left[D_{\mathbf{d}}^r\mathbf{p}(\mathbf{u}) - \sum_{j=1}^r D_{\mathbf{d}}^j w(\mathbf{u})D_{\mathbf{d}}^{r-j}(\mathbf{u})\right].$$

18.10   Quadrics

There were (at least) two motivations for the use of rational Bézier curves: they are projectively invariant, and they allow us to represent conics, namely in the form of rational quadratics. While the first argument holds trivially for rational Bézier triangles, the second one does not carry over immediately.

The proper generalization of a conic to the case of surfaces is a *quadric surface*, quadric for short. A conic (curve) has the implicit equation $q(x,y) = 0$, where q is a quadratic polynomial in x and y (see Section 14.5). Similarly, a quadric has the implicit equation $q(x,y,z) = 0$, where q is quadratic in x, y, z.

Quadrics are of importance in almost all solid modeling systems – these systems rely heavily on the ability to quickly decide if a given point is inside or outside a given object. If that object is bounded by simple implicit surfaces, such a decision is simple and reliable. If the objects' boundaries are made up from, say, bicubics, the same decision is much more time-consuming and error-prone.

Every finite arc of a conic could be written as a quadratic rational Bézier curve – can we also write every triangle-shaped region on a quadric as a rational quadratic Bézier triangle? Let us try an octant of a sphere. In rational quadratic form, it would have six control net coefficients and six associated weights. Since a rational quadratic has no interior Bézier points, we only have to concentrate on the boundary curve representation. They are quarters of circles, and their representation is given in Section 14.7, see also Figure 18.15. Thus we should be done, but actually, we are stuck: if we try to evaluate our rational quadratic at $\mathbf{u} = [\frac{1}{3},\frac{1}{3},\frac{1}{3}]$, we do not end up

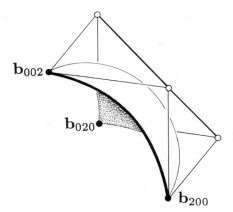

Figure 18.15. The octant of a sphere: an attempt to write it as a quadratic rational Bézier triangle. The weights of the solid control points are unity; the others have weight 1/2.

on the sphere! Thus *not every triangular quadric patch can be represented as a triangular rational quadratic patch.*

We have seen that rational quadratic triangular patches and quadric triangular patches are far from being in a one-to-one relationship. Luckily, this does not mean that we cannot express quadric patches as rational Bézier triangles – we just have to use higher degrees. In fact, rational *quartic* Bézier triangles are always sufficient for this purpose. Our initial example, the octant of the sphere, has the following rational quartic representation (Farin, Piper, Worsey [136]). The control net (for the octant of the *unit sphere*) is given by

$$[0,0,1]$$
$$[\alpha,0,1] \quad [0,\alpha,1]$$
$$[\beta,0,\beta] \quad [\gamma,\gamma,1] \quad [0,\beta,\beta]$$
$$[1,0,\alpha] \quad [1,\gamma,\gamma] \quad [\gamma,1,\gamma] \quad [0,1,\alpha]$$
$$[1,0,0] \quad [1,\alpha,0] \quad [\beta,\beta,0] \quad [\alpha,1,0] \quad [0,1,0]$$

where

$$\alpha = (\sqrt{3}-1)/\sqrt{3}, \quad \beta = (\sqrt{3}+1)/2\sqrt{3}, \quad \gamma = 1 - (5-\sqrt{2})(7-\sqrt{3})/46.$$

The weights are:

$$w_{040} = 4\sqrt{3}(\sqrt{3}-1), w_{031} = 3\sqrt{2}, w_{202} = 4, w_{121} = \frac{\sqrt{2}}{\sqrt{3}}(3+2\sqrt{2}-\sqrt{3}),$$

the other ones following by symmetry.

In order to represent the whole sphere, we would assemble eight copies of this octant patch. Other representations are also possible: each octant may be written as a rational biquadratic patch (introducing singularities at the north and south poles), see [284]. A representation of the whole sphere as two rational bicubics (Piegl [283]) turned out to be incorrect (see Cobb [80]). Quite a different way of representing the sphere is also due to J. Cobb: he covers it with six rational bicubics having a cube-like connectivity [81].

Let us now discuss the following question: given a rational quadratic Bézier triangle, what are the conditions that it represents a quadric patch? The following will be useful for that purpose.

We defined a conic section as the projective map of a parabola, the only conic allowing a polynomial parametrization. For surfaces, we again consider those quadrics that permit polynomial parametrizations: these are the paraboloids, consisting of elliptic and hyperbolic paraboloids and of the parabolic cylinders. Every quadric surface may be defined as a projective image of one of these paraboloids.[6]

A paraboloid may be represented by a parametric polynomial surface of degree two. However, as we have seen, not every parametric quadratic is a paraboloid. We need an extra condition, which is easily formulated if we write the quadratic surface in triangular Bézier form: *A quadratic Bézier triangle is an elliptic or hyperbolic paraboloid if and only if the second derivative vectors of the three boundary curves are parallel to each other. It is a parabolic cylinder if those three vectors are only coplanar.* This statement is due to W. Boehm.

For a proof, we observe that nonparametric or functional quadratic polynomials (i.e., of the form $z = f(x, y)$) include all three types of paraboloids, and all three satisfy the conditions of the theorem. Next, we observe that every paraboloid may be obtained as an affine map of a paraboloid of the same type. Thus every paraboloid may be obtained as an affine map of a functional quadratic surface. Consequently, the control net of any paraboloid must be an affine image of the control net of a functional quadratic Bézier triangle.

We thus obtain the following characterization of quadric surfaces: *A rational quadratic Bézier triangle is a quadric if and only if all three boundary curves meet in a common point and have coplanar tangents there.* This is to be interpreted as a statement in the context of projective geometry, so the common point may also be the point at infinity; see Figure 18.16 for an illustration.

A quadric is determined by nine points. If nine points (x_1, y_1), ..., (x_9, y_0) are given, then their interpolating quadric may be written in im-

---

[6]W. Boehm, private communication.

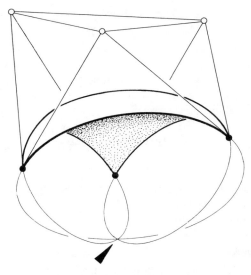

Figure 18.16. Quadrics as rational quadratics: the defining condition is that the extensions of the three boundary curves meet in one point (marked by an arrow) and have coplanar tangents there.

plicit form as follows:

$$
q(x, y, z) =
\begin{vmatrix}
x^2 & y^2 & z^2 & xy & xz & yz & x & y & z & 1 \\
x_1^2 & y_1^2 & z_1^2 & x_1 y_1 & x_1 z_1 & y_1 z_1 & x_1 & y_1 & z_1 & 1 \\
\vdots & \vdots & \vdots & \vdots & \vdots & \vdots & \vdots & \vdots & \vdots & \vdots \\
x_9^2 & y_9^2 & z_9^2 & x_9 y_9 & x_9 z_9 & y_9 z_9 & x_9 & y_9 & z_9 & 1
\end{vmatrix}
= 0.
$$
$$(18.26)$$

18.11 Problems

1. Barycentric coordinates are affinely invariant, being the ratio of two triangle areas in the plane. Prove the more general statement: the ratio of the areas of any two coplanar regions is invariant under affine maps.

2. Find the equation of an edge bisector of a triangle in terms of barycentric coordinates.

3. Work out exactly how terms involving $B_{\mathbf{j}}^r(\mathbf{d})$ generalize the univariate difference operator.

4. Work out a degree reduction procedure for Bézier triangles. (Literature: Petersen [278].)

5. In Section 17.8, we saw how to modify surfaces by embedding them in the unit cube and then to distort it using trivariate tensor product schemes. Experiment with the following: instead of embedding a surface in a cube, embed it in a tetrahedron and distort it using a *Bézier tetrahedron*:

$$\mathbf{b}(\mathbf{u}) = \sum_{|\mathbf{i}|=n} \mathbf{b_i} B_{\mathbf{i}}^n(\mathbf{u}),$$

where now $\mathbf{u} = (u_1, u_2, u_3, u_4)$ are barycentric coordinates in a tetrahedron. Also try to embed the surface into a collection of tetrahedra for more local control. More literature on Bézier tetrahedra: de Boor [94], Farin [131], Hoschek and Lasser [215], Goldman [169], Lasser [234], Worsey and Farin [351].

6. Then experiment with *rational* Bézier tetrahedra.

7. Suppose that in Figure 18.14 we prescribed $\mathbf{p}$ instead of the three $\mathbf{q_i}$. We could then find several sets of weights. Can that idea be generalized to higher degrees?

19

Geometric Continuity for Surfaces

The concept of geometric continuity is not restricted to curves. Surfaces in this regard are much more complex to deal with, so we will restrict ourselves to the case of first order geometric continuity. Here are some pointers to the literature: Boehm [60], Charrot and Gregory [77], DeRose [110], Farin [128], Gregory [188], Hahn [197], Herron [204], Hoschek and Liu [216], Kahmann [223], Jensen [219], Jones [221], Nielson [268], Piper [285], Sarraga [317],[316], Shirman and Séquin [334], Van Wijk [340], Vinacua and Brunet [346], and Veron, Ris, Musse [344].

19.1 Introduction

Let us take a look at Figure 19.1. It shows the (potential) boundary curves of two cubic triangular Bézier patches. In each, the interior control point $\mathbf{b}_{111}$ is missing. Can we determine these two missing points such that the resulting two patches form a C^1 surface? We must thus produce two control nets that satisfy the C^1 condition as illustrated in Figure 18.10. But this is not possible in our example: the two shaded pairs of triangles in Figure 19.1 are not affine pairs in the sense of Section 18.6, i.e., they cannot be obtained as an affine map of *one* pair of domain triangles.

We have a better chance of solving the problem if we relax the requirement of C^1 continuity to that of G^1 continuity: *Two patches with a com-*

Figure 19.1. G^1 continuity: the shown cubic curves cannot be the boundary curves of two C^1 cubic Bézier triangles since no suitable pair of domain triangles can be found.

mon boundary curve are called G^1 if they have continuously varying tangent plane along that boundary curve. The concept of G^1 continuity is a genuine generalization of C^1 continuity: all (nondegenerate) C^1 surfaces are G^1, but not the other way around.

An example (if somewhat simplistic) of a G^1 yet non-C^1 surface is easiliy constructed: take two triangles formed by the diagonal of a square in the $x, y-$plane and interpret them as two linear Bézier triangular patches. They are clearly G^1, but they are not C^1 if we pick as their domain two triangles formed by splitting an arbitrary triangle along one of its medians.

One important aspect of G^1 continuity is that it is completely independent of the domains of the two involved surface patches. For C^1 continuity, the interplay between range and domain geometry was crucial, but now the domains are only needed so that we can evaluate each patch.

We will next discuss the different configurations of G^1 continuity between triangular and rectangular patches.

19.2   Triangle-Triangle

In this section, we shall construct a (sufficient) condition for two adjacent triangular Bézier patches to be G^1. We only have to consider the control polygon of the common boundary curve and the two "parallel" rows of control points in each patch. The situation is illustrated in Figure 19.2, where some suitable abbreviations are introduced.

Let $\mathbf{x}(t)$ be a point on the common boundary curve of the two patches. It may be constructed using the de Casteljau algorithm from either patch since the de Casteljau algorithm yields the tangent plane at a point (see Section 18.4), being spanned by the $\mathbf{b}_{\mathbf{i}}^{n-1}$. These points are labeled $\mathbf{p}(t), \mathbf{q}_b(t), \mathbf{q}_t(t)$,

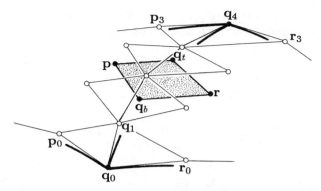

Figure 19.2. G^1 continuity: the G^1 constraints may be expressed in terms of the de Casteljau algorithm. The quartic case is shown.

and $\mathbf{r}(t)$ in Figure 19.2. The two patches are G^1 if these four points are coplanar for all t, i.e. if the lines $\mathbf{pr}$ and $\mathbf{q}_b\mathbf{q}_t$ always intersect.[1] This means that numbers λ and μ exist such that

$$\lambda\mathbf{p}(t) + (1-\lambda)\mathbf{r}(t) = \mu\mathbf{q}_b(t) + (1-\mu)\mathbf{q}_t(t) \tag{19.1}$$

for all t. Of course, $\mu = \mu(t)$ and $\lambda = \lambda(t)$.

We can write out explicitly expressions for $\mathbf{p}(t), \mathbf{q}_b(t), \mathbf{q}_t(t)$, and $\mathbf{r}(t)$:

$$\mathbf{p}(t) = \sum_{i=0}^{n-1} \mathbf{p}_i B_i^{n-1}(t),$$

$$\mathbf{q}_b(t) = \sum_{i=0}^{n-1} \mathbf{q}_i B_i^{n-1}(t),$$

$$\mathbf{q}_t(t) = \sum_{i=0}^{n-1} \mathbf{q}_{i+1} B_i^{n-1}(t),$$

$$\mathbf{r}(t) = \sum_{i=0}^{n-1} \mathbf{r}_i B_i^{n-1}(t).$$

---

[1]To be precise, we must also require that $\mathbf{p}$ and $\mathbf{q}$ be on *different sides* of $\mathbf{q}_t$ and $\mathbf{q}_b$; otherwise we might generate surfaces that double back on themselves along the common boundary curve.

We now attempt to simplify our task of formulating G^1 conditions: we make the assumption that $\lambda(t)$ and $\mu(t)$ are both *linear*, i.e.

$$\lambda(t) = \lambda_0 + \lambda_1 t, \quad \mu(t) = \mu_0 + \mu_1 t.$$

Our G^1 condition (19.1) can then be written as

$$(\lambda_0 + \lambda_1 t) \sum_{i=0}^{n-1} \mathbf{p}_i B_i^{n-1}(t) + (1 - \lambda_0 - \lambda_1 t) \sum_{i=0}^{n-1} \mathbf{r}_i B_i^{n-1}(t)$$

$$= (\mu_0 + \mu_1 t) \sum_{i=0}^{n-1} \mathbf{q}_i B_i^{n-1}(t) + (1 - \mu_0 - \mu_1 t) \sum_{i=0}^{n-1} \mathbf{q}_{i+1} B_i^{n-1}(t).$$

Rearranging:

$$\sum_{i=0}^{n-1} [\lambda_0 \mathbf{p}_i + (1 - \lambda_0)] B_i^{n-1} + \lambda_1 \sum_{i=0}^{n-1} [\mathbf{p}_i - \mathbf{r}_i] \frac{i+1}{n} B_{i+1}^n$$

$$= \sum_{i=0}^{n-1} [\mu_0 \mathbf{q}_i + (1 - \mu_0) \mathbf{q}_{i+1}] B_i^{n-1} + \mu_1 \sum_{i=0}^{n-1} [\mathbf{q}_i - \mathbf{q}_{i+1}] \frac{i+1}{n} B_{i+1}^n.$$

The terms B_{i+1}^n were obtained from equation (5.28). We next perform degree elevation on the B_i^{n-1} terms and compare coefficients of the resulting B_i^n, which yields

$$\frac{i}{n} [(\lambda_0 + \lambda_1) \mathbf{p}_{i-1} + (1 - \lambda_0 - \lambda_1) \mathbf{r}_{i-1} + (1 - \frac{i}{n}) [\lambda_0 \mathbf{p}_i + (1 - \lambda_0) \mathbf{r}_i]$$

$$= \frac{i}{n} [(\mu_0 + \mu_1) \mathbf{q}_{i-1} + (1 - \mu_0 - \mu_1) \mathbf{q}_i] + (1 - \frac{i}{n}) [\mu_0 \mathbf{q}_i + (1 - \mu_0) \mathbf{q}_{i+1}].$$

We may simplify this by setting

$$\alpha_1 = \lambda_0 + \lambda_1, \quad \beta_1 = \mu_0 + \mu_1, \quad \alpha_0 = \lambda_0, \quad \beta_0 = \mu_0$$

and rearranging:

$$\frac{i}{n} \Big[[\alpha_1 \mathbf{p}_{i-1} + (1 - \alpha_1) \mathbf{r}_{i-1}] - [\beta_1 \mathbf{q}_{i-1} + (1 - \beta_1) \mathbf{q}_i] \Big]$$
$$= -(1 - \frac{i}{n}) \Big[[\alpha_0 \mathbf{p}_i + (1 - \alpha_0) \mathbf{r}_i] - [\beta_0 \mathbf{q}_i + (1 - \beta_0) \mathbf{q}_{i+1}] \Big]. \tag{19.2}$$

This is our desired G^1 condition. If it holds for all $i = 0, \ldots, n$, the two patches have a continuous tangent plane all along their common boundary.

In order to arrive at a geometric interpretation of (19.2), we first consider the special cases $i = 0$ and $i = n$. For $i = 0$, we obtain

$$\alpha_0 \mathbf{p}_0 + (1 - \alpha_0)\mathbf{r}_0 = \beta_0 \mathbf{q}_0 + (1 - \beta_0)\mathbf{q}_1, \tag{19.3}$$

and $i = n$ yields

$$\alpha_1 \mathbf{p}_{n-1} + (1 - \alpha_1)\mathbf{r}_{n-1} = \beta_1 \mathbf{q}_{n-1} + (1 - \beta_1)\mathbf{q}_n. \tag{19.4}$$

These equations describe the geometry of the planar quadrilaterals formed by $\mathbf{p}_0, \mathbf{q}_0, \mathbf{r}_0, \mathbf{q}_1$ and $\mathbf{p}_{n-1}, \mathbf{q}_{n-1}, \mathbf{r}_{n-1}, \mathbf{q}_n$, respectively. If we were given the two quadrilaterals in some application, we could then readily determine $\alpha_0, \alpha_1, \beta_0, \beta_1$, namely by interpreting (19.3) and (19.4) as two overdetermined linear systems for those quantities. If the involved quadrilaterals are planar, unique solutions will exist.

Let us concentrate on $\mathbf{p}_0, \mathbf{q}_0, \mathbf{r}_0, \mathbf{q}_1$ for a while. The two numbers α_0 and β_0 tell us how to compute the intersection of the two diagonals: either as $\alpha_0 \mathbf{p}_0 + (1-\alpha_0)\mathbf{r}_0$, or as $\beta_0 \mathbf{q}_0 + (1-\beta_0)\mathbf{q}_1$. In any other quadrilateral, formed by $\mathbf{p}_i, \mathbf{r}_i, \mathbf{q}_i, \mathbf{q}_{i+1}$, the analogous two expressions: $\alpha_0 \mathbf{p}_i + (1 - \alpha_0)\mathbf{r}_i$ and $\beta_0 \mathbf{q}_i + (1-\beta_0)\mathbf{q}_{i+1}$ will in general yield two different points. The difference vector of these two points is an indication of how much the shape of the arbitrary quadrilateral differs from that of $\mathbf{p}_0, \mathbf{q}_0, \mathbf{r}_0, \mathbf{q}_1$. This difference vector may be written as

$$\mathbf{d}_{i,0} = [\alpha_0 \mathbf{p}_i + (1 - \alpha_0)\mathbf{r}_i] - [\beta_0 \mathbf{q}_i + (1 - \beta_0)\mathbf{q}_{i+1}].$$

Similarly, we may measure how the quadrilateral $\mathbf{p}_i, \mathbf{r}_i, \mathbf{q}_i, \mathbf{q}_{i+1}$ differs from $\mathbf{p}_{n-1}, \mathbf{r}_{n-1}, \mathbf{q}_{n-1}, \mathbf{q}_n$:

$$\mathbf{d}_{i,n} = [\alpha_1 \mathbf{p}_{i-1} + (1 - \alpha_1)\mathbf{r}_{i-1}] - [\beta_1 \mathbf{q}_{i-1} + (1 - \beta_1)\mathbf{q}_i].$$

Now our G^1 condition takes on the simple form

$$\frac{i}{n}\mathbf{d}_{i,n} - (1 - \frac{i}{n})\mathbf{d}_{i,0} = \mathbf{0}; \quad i = 0, \ldots, n.$$

The quadratic case is illustrated in Figure 19.3. This case is of special interest: our G^1 condition is only sufficient, not necessary, in general. However, for quadratics, it is both sufficient *and* necessary. [2]

---

[2]This was observed by T. DeRose – private communication.

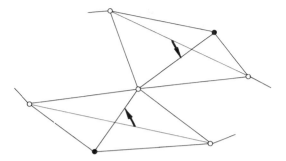

Figure 19.3. G^1 continuity: for two quadratics, the shape difference vectors $\mathbf{d}_{1,2}$ and $\mathbf{d}_{1,0}$ are shown. Note that they sum to $\mathbf{0}$.

19.3   Rectangle-Rectangle

We now consider two tensor product Bézier patches with a common boundary curve of degree n, illustrated in Figure 19.4. Consider any point $\mathbf{x}(t)$ on this curve. It may be constructed using the (univariate) de Casteljau algorithm. The de Casteljau algorithm yields the tangent of a curve as a byproduct (Section 4.5), namely as the difference of the two intermediate points $\mathbf{b}_1^{n-1}$ and $\mathbf{b}_0^{n-1}$. In Figure 19.4, those two points are labeled $\mathbf{q}_b$ and $\mathbf{q}_t$. It now follows that the tangent plane of the left patch in Figure 19.4 is spanned by the points $\mathbf{p}, \mathbf{q}_b, \mathbf{q}_t$ and that of the right patch is spanned by

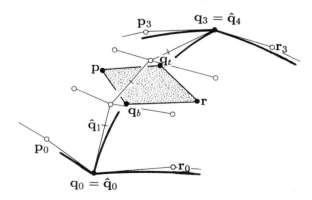

Figure 19.4. G^1 continuity for rectangular patches: the shaded quadrilateral must be planar as it varies along the common boundary. The case of a cubic boundary curve is shown.

$\mathbf{q}_b, \mathbf{q}_t, \mathbf{r}$, where

$$\mathbf{p}(t) = \sum_{i=0}^{n} \mathbf{p}_i B_i^n(t)$$

and

$$\mathbf{r}(t) = \sum_{i=0}^{n} \mathbf{r}_i B_i^n(t).$$

We could now follow a similar development as in the previous section, but a little trick will give us our desired G^1 condition for free. Let us simply degree elevate the common boundary curve from degree n to $n+1$. Call the degree elevated control points $\hat{\mathbf{q}}_0, \ldots, \hat{\mathbf{q}}_{n+1}$ (see Section 5.1 for the degree elevation procedure). Now we are in the situation of the previous section! Namely, we have $n+1$ control points $\mathbf{p}_i$, $n+2$ control points $\hat{\mathbf{q}}_i$, and $n+1$ control points $\mathbf{r}_i$. With other words, our situation is equivalent to that of a G^1 join between two triangular patches of degree $n+1$.

The desired G^1 condition is therefore given by

$$
\begin{aligned}
&\tfrac{i}{n+1}\Big[[\alpha_1 \mathbf{p}_{i-1} + (1-\alpha_1)\mathbf{r}_{i-1}] - [\beta_1 \hat{\mathbf{q}}_{i-1} + (1-\beta_1)\hat{\mathbf{q}}_i] \Big] \\
&= -(1 - \tfrac{i}{n+1})\Big[[\alpha_0 \mathbf{p}_i + (1-\alpha_0)\mathbf{r}_i] - [\beta_0 \hat{\mathbf{q}}_i + (1-\beta_0)\hat{\mathbf{q}}_{i+1}] \Big],
\end{aligned}
\tag{19.6}
$$

where i varies from 0 to $n+1$.

The geometric interpretation is analogous to that of the preceding section.

19.4   Rectangle-Triangle

This situation, illustrated in Figure 19.5, is now treated in a completely analogous way. We assume that both patches have a common boundary curve of degree n. If we degree elevate the triangular patch (Section 18.7), we have the control point rows $\hat{\mathbf{p}}_0, \ldots, \hat{\mathbf{p}}_n$ (from the tensor product patch), $\hat{\mathbf{q}}_0, \ldots, \hat{\mathbf{q}}_{n+1}$ (the degree elevated common boundary curve), and $\mathbf{r}_0, \ldots, \mathbf{r}_n$ (from the degree elevated triangular patch). Thus the G^1 condition is

$$
\begin{aligned}
&\tfrac{i}{n+1}\Big[[\alpha_1 \hat{\mathbf{p}}_{i-1} + (1-\alpha_1)\mathbf{r}_{i-1}] - [\beta_1 \hat{\mathbf{q}}_{i-1} + (1-\beta_1)\hat{\mathbf{q}}_i] \Big] \\
&= -(1 - \tfrac{i}{n+1})\Big[[\alpha_0 \hat{\mathbf{p}}_i + (1-\alpha_0)\mathbf{r}_i] - [\beta_0 \hat{\mathbf{q}}_i + (1-\beta_0)\hat{\mathbf{q}}_{i+1}] \Big],
\end{aligned}
\tag{19.7}
$$

again with i ranging from 0 to n+1.

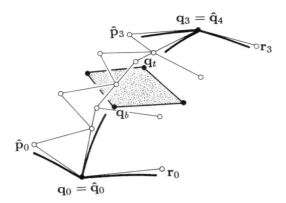

Figure 19.5. G^1 continuity for triangular and rectangular patches: the shaded quadrilateral must be planar as it varies along the common boundary. The case of a cubic boundary curve is shown.

19.5 "Filling in" Rectangular Patches

Suppose that we were given the boundary curves of two bicubic patches, as shown in Figure 19.4. At the endpoints of the common boundary curve, we assume that the three curves meeting there have coplanar tangents. Can we find interior Bézier points $\mathbf{p}_1, \mathbf{p}_2$ and $\mathbf{r}_1, \mathbf{r}_2$ such that the two patches will have a continuously varying tangent plane along the common boundary? We shall employ the G^1 condition (19.6) for this purpose. As a first step, we determine α_0 and β_0 from $\mathbf{p}_0, \hat{\mathbf{q}}_0, \mathbf{r}_0, \hat{\mathbf{q}}_1$ and α_1, β_1 from $\mathbf{p}_3, \hat{\mathbf{q}}_3, \mathbf{r}_3, \hat{\mathbf{q}}_4$.

There are three equations in (19.6) that involve our four unknowns $\mathbf{p}_1, \mathbf{p}_2$ and $\mathbf{r}_1, \mathbf{r}_2$. After some suitable modification, they are of the form

$$\alpha_0 \mathbf{p}_1 + (1 - \alpha_0)\mathbf{r}_1 = \mathbf{rhs1},$$
$$\alpha_1 \mathbf{p}_1 + (1 - \alpha_1)\mathbf{r}_1 + \alpha_0 \mathbf{p}_2 + (1 - \alpha_0)\mathbf{r}_2 = \mathbf{rhs2},$$
$$\alpha_1 \mathbf{p}_2 + (1 - \alpha_1)\mathbf{r}_2 = \mathbf{rhs3}.$$

We have abbreviated the right hand sides of the equations somewhat.

The above may be written matrix form:

$$A\mathbf{x} = \mathbf{b}, \tag{19.8}$$

with

$$A = \begin{bmatrix} \alpha_0 & 1 - \alpha_0 & & \\ \alpha_1 & 1 - \alpha_1 & \alpha_0 & 1 - \alpha_0 \\ & & \alpha_1 & (1 - \alpha_1) \end{bmatrix}$$

$\mathbf{x} = [\mathbf{p}_1, \mathbf{p}_2$ and $\mathbf{r}_1, \mathbf{r}_2]^{\mathrm{T}}$, and $\mathbf{b} = [\mathbf{rhs1}, \mathbf{rhs2}, \mathbf{rhs3}]^{\mathrm{T}}$.

Since the rows of A are linearly independent, the underdetermined system (19.8) always has solutions. One way of finding one is by solving the four by four system

$$A^{\mathrm{T}} A \mathbf{x} = A^{\mathrm{T}} \mathbf{b},$$

which yields the least squares solution.

Another approach would be to try to stay as close as possible to the $\mathbf{r}_i$ and $\mathbf{p}_i$ that are generated by Adini's twists (see Section 17.3). This idea was carried out by Sarraga [317],[316] in a slightly different context.

19.6   "Filling in" Triangular Patches

Let us reconsider Figure 19.1. Do our G^1 conditions allow us to complete the curve network such that the resulting surface will be G^1? In our notation, the undetermined points are $\mathbf{p}_1$ and $\mathbf{r}_1$. There are two G^1 equations that involve these points. They are of the form

$$\begin{aligned} \alpha_1 \mathbf{p}_1 + (1 - \alpha_1)\mathbf{r}_1 &= \mathbf{rhs1}, \\ \alpha_0 \mathbf{p}_1 + (1 - \alpha_0)\mathbf{r}_1 &= \mathbf{rhs2}. \end{aligned}$$

The coefficient matrix of this system:

$$A = \left[\begin{array}{cc} \alpha_1 & 1 - \alpha_1 \\ \alpha_0 & 1 - \alpha_0 \end{array} \right]$$

is singular if $\alpha_0 = \alpha_1$. In this case, we are therefore not guaranteed to have a solution (see Piper [285] for an explicit counterexample).

We can, however, solve the problem if we resort to quartics. After we degree elevate all boundary curves, we now have to determine unknown control points $\mathbf{p}_1, \mathbf{p}_2$ and $\mathbf{r}_1, \mathbf{r}_2$. This is exactly the situation from the preceding section and is solved in exactly the same way. B. Piper [285] first used quartics to solve this kind of Hermite interpolation problem.

19.7   Theoretical Aspects

We have developed an approach to geometric continuity that is powerful enough to solve several application-oriented problems. It is practical, but it is not *general*: there are G^1 surfaces that do not satisfy the condition (19.2); see Problems. T. DeRose has developed conditions that are both necessary and sufficient for G^1 continuity of adjacent Bézier patches.

Several authors (consult the surveys by Boehm [60], Herron [204], and Gregory [188]) define geometric continuity of surfaces in the following way: two surfaces that share a common boundary curve are called G^r if, for every point of the boundary curve, there exists a reparametrization such that both surfaces are C^r in a neighborhood of that point. For the case $r = 1$, this definition yields tangent plane continuity. Its advantage is that it also works for higher orders; the price to be paid is that it is rather abstract. For the case of G^2 continuity, another poular definition is to require a common Dupin's indicatrix along the boundary curve, see Section 22.12 and Kahmann [223] and Pegna and Wolter [274].

19.8   Problems

1. In Section 19.1 we saw an example of triangular patch boundaries that could not be completed to an overall C^1 surface. Find similar examples for tensor product patches.

2. Show that the G^1 conditions (19.2) include the case of strict C^1 continuity.

3. Construct surfaces that are G^1 yet do not satisfy (19.2).

4. Consider eight triangular patches, assembled such as to form eight octants of a sphere-like surface. Show that this closed surface cannot be C^1, i.e., one cannot find a region in the plane that is composed of eight triangles that have a C^1 map that maps them to the surface.

20

Coons Patches

We have already encountered design tools that originated in car companies; Bézier curves and surfaces were developed by Citroën and Renault in Paris. Two other major concepts also emerged from the automotive field: Coons' patches (S. Coons consulted for Ford, Detroit) and Gordon surfaces (W. Gordon worked for General Motors, Detroit).[1] These methods have a different flavor than Bézier or B-spline methods: instead of being described by control nets, they "fill in" curve networks in order to generate surfaces.

Let us review the part of the design process that gave rise to the methods of this chapter. Even in days of CAD/CAM, the first step in the design of a new car is (and certainly was in the sixties) the manual production of a clay or wooden model of that car. The CAD process begins with the task of communicating the form of this model to the CAD database.

This communication process starts with data acquisition; in this case, the model is *digitized*: a digitizing device records points (in a fixed coordinate system) where a sensor touches the model surface. This sensor is moved over the model along certain predefined lines, called *feature lines*. Each of these lines is thus broken down into a sequence of digitized points. Once these are stored, curves are fitted through them, for example, by using interpolating splines. The resulting network of curves now must be completed in order to

---

[1] Just for the record – in the late sixties, Chrysler began to develop a curve and surface scheme that was based on Chebychev polynomials.

generate a full surface description of the model. This process – generating a surface from a network of curves – is solved using Coons and Gordon surfaces.

Additional literature on Coons patches includes: Coons' "little red book" [88] (also available in a French translation [84]) and Barnhill [14],[13].

Before we start with their description, we need to discuss an important "building block."

20.1   Ruled Surfaces

Ruled surfaces, also called "lofted surfaces"[2] are both simple and fundamental to surface design. They are of considerable importance in their own right, in particular for the design of "functional" surfaces in mechanical engineering. Ruled surfaces solve the following problem: given two space curves c_1 and c_2, both defined over the same parameter interval $u \in [0, 1]$, find a surface x that contains both curves as 'opposite' boundary curves. More precisely: find x such that

$$\mathbf{x}(u, 0) = \mathbf{c}_1(u), \quad \mathbf{x}(u, 1) = \mathbf{c}_2(u). \tag{20.1}$$

Clearly, the stated problem has infinitely many solutions, so we pick the "simplest" one:

$$\mathbf{x}(u, v) = (1 - v)\mathbf{c}_1(u) + v\mathbf{c}_2(u), \tag{20.2}$$

or, with (20.1):

$$\mathbf{x}(u, v) = (1 - v)\mathbf{x}(u, 0) + v\mathbf{x}(u, 1). \tag{20.3}$$

Ruled surfaces have the familiar flavor of *linear interpolation*: every isoparametric line $u = const$ is a straight line segment, as illustrated in Figure 20.1.

The difference from earlier occurences of linear interpolation is that now we interpolate to whole *curves*, not just points. This process is still quite manageable, however: note how the linear terms in v are kept separate from the data terms in u.

An important aspect of ruled surfaces of the form (20.3) is the generality that is allowed for the input curves $\mathbf{x}(u, 0)$ and $\mathbf{x}(u, 1)$: there is virtually no restriction on them other than having to be defined over the same parameter interval. (We chose the interval $[0, 1]$, but any other interval $[a, b]$ will do –

---

[2]The word "lofted" has an interesting history: In the days of completely manual ship design, full-scale drawings were difficult to handle in the design office. These drawings were stored and dealt with in large attics, called "lofts."

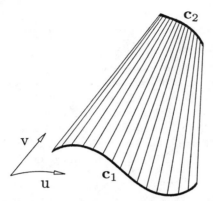

Figure 20.1. Ruled surfaces: two arbitrary curves c_1, c_2 are given. A surface is fitted between them by linear interpolation.

we will then have to use formula 2.9 for general linear interpolation.) For instance, one of the input curves might be a cubic polynomial curve, the other a spline curve or even a polygon. More information on ruled surfaces can be found in Section 22.10.

20.2   Coons Patches: Bilinearly Blended

A ruled surface interpolates to *two* boundary curves – a rectangular surface, however, has *four* boundary curves, and that is precisely to what a Coons patch interpolates. This first instance of Coons patches was also developed first by Coons, see [87].

To be more precise: given are four arbitrary curves $c_1(u), c_2(u)$ and $d_1(v), d_2(v)$, defined over $u \in [0,1]$ and $v \in [0,1]$, respectively. Find a surface $\mathbf{x}$ that has these four curves as boundary curves:

$$\mathbf{x}(u,0) = \mathbf{c}_1(u), \qquad \mathbf{x}(u,1) = \mathbf{c}_2(u), \qquad (20.4)$$
$$\mathbf{x}(0,v) = \mathbf{d}_1(v), \qquad \mathbf{x}(1,v) = \mathbf{d}_2(v). \qquad (20.5)$$

We have just developed ruled surfaces, so let us utilize them for this new problem. The four boundary curves define two ruled surfaces:

$$\mathbf{r}_c(u,v) = (1-v)\mathbf{x}(u,0) + v\mathbf{x}(u,1)$$

and
$$\mathbf{r}_d(u, v) = (1 - u)\mathbf{x}(0, v) + u\mathbf{x}(1, v).$$

Both interpolants are shown in Figure 20.2, and we see that $\mathbf{r}_c$ interpolates
to the **c**-curves, yet fails to reproduce the **d**-curves. The situation for $\mathbf{r}_d$
is similar, and therefore equally unsatisfactory. Both $\mathbf{r}_c$ and $\mathbf{r}_d$ do well on
two sides, yet fail on the other two, where they are *linear*. Our strategy is
therefore as follows: let us try to retain what each ruled surface interpolates
to and let us try to eliminate what it fails to interpolate to. A little thought
reveals that the "interpolation failures" are captured by one surface: the
bilinear interpolant $\mathbf{r}_{cd}$ to the four corners (see also Section 16.1):

$$\mathbf{r}_{cd}(u, v) = \begin{bmatrix} 1 - u & u \end{bmatrix} \begin{bmatrix} \mathbf{x}(0,0) & \mathbf{x}(0,1) \\ \mathbf{x}(1,0) & \mathbf{x}(1,1) \end{bmatrix} \begin{bmatrix} 1 - v \\ v \end{bmatrix}.$$

We are now ready to create a Coons patch **x**. It is given by

$$\mathbf{x} = \mathbf{r}_c + \mathbf{r}_d - \mathbf{r}_{cd}, \tag{20.6}$$

or, in the form of a recipe: "loft$_u$+loft$_v$−bilinear." The involved surfaces
and the solution are illustrated in Figure 20.2. Writing out (20.6) in full
detail gives

$$\begin{aligned}
\mathbf{x}(u, v) = \quad & \begin{bmatrix} 1 - u & u \end{bmatrix} \begin{bmatrix} \mathbf{x}(0, v) \\ \mathbf{x}(1, v) \end{bmatrix} \\
+ & \begin{bmatrix} \mathbf{x}(u,0) & \mathbf{x}(u,1) \end{bmatrix} \begin{bmatrix} 1 - v \\ v \end{bmatrix} \\
- & \begin{bmatrix} 1 - u & u \end{bmatrix} \begin{bmatrix} \mathbf{x}(0,0) & \mathbf{x}(0,1) \\ \mathbf{x}(1,0) & \mathbf{x}(1,1) \end{bmatrix} \begin{bmatrix} 1 - v \\ v \end{bmatrix}.
\end{aligned} \tag{20.7}$$

It is left as an exercise for the reader to verify that (20.7) does indeed
interpolate to all four boundary curves.

We can now justify the name "bilinearly blended" for the above Coons
patch: a ruled surface "blends" together the two defining boundary curves.
Also, this blending takes place in both directions. However, the Coons
patch is *not* generally itself a bilinear surface – the name refers purely to
the method of construction.

The functions $1 - u, u$ and $1 - v, v$ are called *blending functions*. A close
inspection of (20.7) reveals that many other pairs of blending functions, say,
$f_1(u), f_2(u)$ and $g_1(v), g_2(v)$, could also be used to construct a generalized

Figure 20.2. Coons patches: a bilinearly blended Coons patch is composed of two lofted surfaces and a bilinear surface.

Coons patch. It would then be of the general form

$$
\begin{aligned}
\mathbf{x}(u, v) = \quad & \begin{bmatrix} f_1(u) & f_2(u) \end{bmatrix} \begin{bmatrix} \mathbf{x}(0, v) \\ \mathbf{x}(1, v) \end{bmatrix} \\
+ & \begin{bmatrix} \mathbf{x}(u, 0) & \mathbf{x}(u, 1) \end{bmatrix} \begin{bmatrix} g_1(v) \\ g_2(v) \end{bmatrix} \qquad (20.8) \\
- & \begin{bmatrix} f_1(u) & f_2(u) \end{bmatrix} \begin{bmatrix} \mathbf{x}(0, 0) & \mathbf{x}(0, 1) \\ \mathbf{x}(1, 0) & \mathbf{x}(1, 1) \end{bmatrix} \begin{bmatrix} g_1(v) \\ g_2(v) \end{bmatrix}.
\end{aligned}
$$

There are only two restrictions on the f_i and g_i: each pair must sum to one identically: otherwise we would generate non-barycentric combinations of points (see Section 2.1). Also, we must have $f_1(0) = g(0) = 1, f_1(1) = g_1(1) = 0$ in order to actually interpolate. The shape of the blending functions has a predictable effect on the shape of the resulting Coons patch. Typically one requires f_1 and g_1 to be monotonically decreasing; this produces surfaces of predictable shape, but is not necessary for theoretical reasons. Surface modelers that employ Coons patches typically allow designers to change the blending functions as a way to model the interior of the patch.

20.3   Coons Patches: Partially Bicubically Blended

The bilinearly blended Coons patch solves a problem of considerable importance with very little effort, but we pay for that by an annoying drawback. Consider Figure 20.3: it shows two bilinearly blended Coons patches, defined over $u \in [0, 2], v \in [0, 1]$. The boundary curves $v = 0$ and $v = 1$, both composite curves, are differentiable. However, the cross-boundary derivative is clearly discontinuous along $u = 1$; see also Problems.

Analyzing this problem, we see that it can be blamed on the fact that cross-boundary tangents along one boundary depend on *data not pertaining to that boundary*. For example, for any given bilinearly blended Coons patch, a change in the boundary curve $\mathbf{x}(1, v)$ will affect the derivatives across the boundary $\mathbf{x}(0, v)$.

How can we separate the derivatives across one boundary from information along the opposite boundary? The answer: use different blending funtions, namely, some that have zero slopes at the endpoints. Striving for simplicity, as usual, we find two obvious candidates for such blending functions: the cubic Hermite polynomials H_0^3 and H_3^3 from Section 6.5, as defined by (6.14).

Figure 20.3. Coons patches: the input curves for two neighboring patches may have C^1 boundary curves (left), yet the two Coons patches determined by them do not form a smooth surface (right).

Let us investigate the effect of this choice of blending functions: we have set $f_1 = g_1 = H_0^3$ and $f_2 = g_2 = H_3^3$ in (20.8). The cross-boundary derivative along, say, $u = 0$, now becomes:

$$\mathbf{x}_u(0, v) = \begin{bmatrix} \mathbf{x}_u(0,0) & \mathbf{x}_u(0,1) \end{bmatrix} \begin{bmatrix} H_0^3(v) \\ H_3^3(v) \end{bmatrix} ; \qquad (20.9)$$

all other terms vanish since $d/duH_{3i}^3(0) = d/duH_{3i}^3(1) = 0$ for $i = 0$ and $i = 1$. Thus, the only data that influence $\mathbf{x}_u$ along $u = 0$ are the two tangents $\mathbf{x}_u(0,0)$ and $\mathbf{x}_u(0,1)$ – we have achieved our goal to make the cross-boundary derivative along one boundary depend only on information pertaining to that boundary. With our new blending functions, the two patches from Figure 20.3 would now be C^1.

Unfortunately, we have also created a new problem. At the patch corners, these patches often seem to have "flat spots." The reason: partially bicubically blended Coons patches,[3] constructed as above, suffer from *zero corner twists*:

$$\mathbf{x}_{uv}(i, j) = \mathbf{0}; \quad i, j \in \{0, 1\}.$$

This is easily verified by simply taking the u, v−partial of (20.8) and evaluating at the patch corners.

---

[3]We use the term *partially* bicubically blended since only a part of all cubic Hermite basis functions is utilized.

In order to understand this situation better, let us resort to the simpler case of curves – to functional curves for added simplicity. The two graphs $x(u)$ and $y(u)$ in Figure 12.3 illustrate what happens if we replace the linear functions $1 - t, t$ in piecewise linear interpolation by $H_0^3(t), H_3^3(t)$. We clearly see the introduction of "flat spots." The reason for this poor performance lies in the fact that we only use two functions, H_0^3 and H_3^3 from the full set of four Hermite polynomials. Both have zero derivatives at the interval endpoints, and pass that property on to the interpolant.

We will now modify the partially bicubically blended Coons patch to in order avoid the flat spots at the corners.

20.4   Coons Patches: Bicubically Blended

Cubic Hermite interpolation needs more input than positional data – first derivative information is called for. Since our positional input consists of whole curves, not just points, the obvious data to supply are derivatives along those input curves. Our given data now consist of

$$\mathbf{x}(u, 0), \quad \mathbf{x}(u, 1), \quad \mathbf{x}(0, v), \quad \mathbf{x}(1, v)$$

and

$$\mathbf{x}_v(u, 0), \quad \mathbf{x}_v(u, 1), \quad \mathbf{x}_u(0, v), \quad \mathbf{x}_u(1, v).$$

We can think of the now prescribed cross-boundary derivatives as "tangent ribbons," illustrated in Figure 20.4 (only two of the four "ribbons" are shown there).

The derivation of the bicubically blended Coons patch is analogous to the one in Section 20.2: we must simply generalize the concept of a ruled surface appropriately. This is almost trivial; we obtain

$$\mathbf{h}_c(u, v) = H_0^3(u)\mathbf{x}(0, v) + H_1^3(u)\mathbf{x}_u(0, v) + H_2^3(u)\mathbf{x}_u(1, v) + H_3^3(u)\mathbf{x}(1, v)$$

for the u- direction (this surface is shown in Figure 20.4) and

$$\mathbf{h}_d(u, v) = H_0^3(v)\mathbf{x}(u, 0) + H_1^3(v)\mathbf{x}_v(u, 0) + H_2^3(v)\mathbf{x}_v(u, 1) + H_3^3(v)\mathbf{x}(u, 1).$$

Proceeding as in the bilinearly blended case, we define the interpolant to the corner data. This gives the tensor product bicubic Hermite interpolant

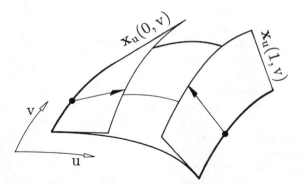

Figure 20.4. Coons patches: for the bicubically blended case, the concept of the lofted surface is generalized. In addition to the given boundary curves, cross-boundary derivatives are supplied.

$\mathbf{h}_{cd}$ from Section 17.6:

$$\mathbf{h}_{cd}(u, v) = \begin{array}{c} \\ \times \end{array} \begin{bmatrix} H_0^3(u) & H_1^3(u) & H_2^3(u) & H_3^3(u) \end{bmatrix} \begin{bmatrix} \mathbf{x}(0,0) & \mathbf{x}_v(0,0) & \mathbf{x}_v(0,1) & \mathbf{x}(0,1) \\ \mathbf{x}_u(0,0) & \mathbf{x}_{uv}(0,0) & \mathbf{x}_{uv}(0,1) & \mathbf{x}_u(0,1) \\ \mathbf{x}_u(1,0) & \mathbf{x}_{uv}(1,0) & \mathbf{x}_{uv}(1,1) & \mathbf{x}_u(1,1) \\ \mathbf{x}(1,0) & \mathbf{x}_v(1,0) & \mathbf{x}_v(1,1) & \mathbf{x}(1,1) \end{bmatrix} \begin{bmatrix} H_0^3(v) \\ H_1^3(v) \\ H_2^3(v) \\ H_3^3(v) \end{bmatrix}.$$

$$(20.10)$$

The bicubically blended Coons patch now becomes

$$\mathbf{x} = \mathbf{h}_c + \mathbf{h}_d - \mathbf{h}_{cd}. \tag{20.11}$$

Before closing this section, we need to take a closer look at the $\mathbf{h}_{cd}$ part of (20.11). Upon closer inspection, we find that it wants data that we were not willing (or able) to provide in our initial problem description, namely the central "twist partition" of the 4×4 matrix in (20.10). The bicubically blended Coons patch needs these quantities as input, and this has caused CAD software developers many headaches since Coons proposed his surface scheme in 1964. The most popular "solution" seems to be to simply define each of the four corner twists to be the zero vector. The drawbacks of that choice have already been discussed in Section 16.8, but alternatives are pointed out in that section, too.

20.5 Piecewise Coons Surfaces

We will now apply the bicubically blended patch to the situation that it was intended to solve: we assume that we are given a network of curves as

shown in Figure 21.5 and that we want to fill in this curve network with
bicubically blended Coons patches. The resulting surface will be C^1.

In order to apply (20.11), we must create twist vectors and cross boundary derivatives (tangent ribbons) from the given curve network. As a pre-
processing step, we estimate a twist vector $\mathbf{x}_{uv}(u_i, v_j)$ at each patch corner.
This can be done by using any of the twist vector estimators discussed in
Section 17.3. In that section, we assumed that the boundary curves of each
patch were cubics; that assumption does not affect the computation of the
twist vectors at all, however.

Having found a twist vector for each data point, we now need to create
cross-boundary derivatives for each boundary curve. Let us focus our attention on one patch of our network, and let us assume for simplicity (but
without loss of generality!) that the parameters u and v vary between 0
and 1. We shall now construct the tangent ribbon $\mathbf{x}_v(u, 0)$. We have four
pieces of information about $\mathbf{x}_v(u, 0)$: the value of $\mathbf{x}_v(u, 0)$ at $u = 0$ and at
$u = 1$, and the derivatives (with respect to u) there, which are the twists
that we made up above, namely $\mathbf{x}_{uv}(0, 0)$ and $\mathbf{x}_{uv}(1, 0)$.

We therefore have the input data for a univariate cubic Hermite interpolant, and the desired tangent ribbon assumes the form

$$\mathbf{x}_v(u, 0) = \mathbf{x}_v(0, 0)H_0^3(u) + \mathbf{x}_{uv}(0, 0)H_1^3(u) + \mathbf{x}_{uv}(1, 0)H_2^3(u) + \mathbf{x}_v(1, 0)H_3^3(u).$$
$$(20.12)$$

The remaining three tangent ribbons are computed analogously.

We have thus found a (new) way to pass a C^1 surface through a C^1
network of curves. All that is required is the ability to estimate the twists
at the data points.

20.6   Problems

1. Verify the caption to Figure 20.3 algebraically.

2. Show that the bilinearly blended Coons patch is not in the convex
   hull of its boundary curves. Is this a good or a bad property?

3. Show that the bilinearly blended Coons patch, when applied to cubic
   boundary curves, yields a bicubic patch.

4. Show that Adini's twist from Section 17.3 is the twist of the bilinearly
   blended Coons patch for the four boundary cubics.

5. As we have seen, two adjacent bilinearly blended Coons patches are
   not C^1 in general. What are the conditions for the boundary curves
   of the two patches such that the Coons patches *are* C^1?

21

Coons Patches: Additional Material

21.1 Compatibility

A situation may arise where one is not free to generate the tangent ribbon information as we did in the previous section. In some cases, the cross-boundary derivatives may be prescribed and must then be adhered to. The bicubically blended Coons patch (20.11) was designed to cope with exactly that situation, so we should be ready to address that problem.

Let us first return to the case of the bilinearly blended Coons patch. It is an obvious requirement that the four prescribed boundary curves meet in the corners; in other words, we must exclude data configurations as shown in Figure 21.1. This condition on the prescribed data is known as a *compatibility condition*. An incompatibility of that form can usually be overcome by adjusting boundary curves so that they meet at the patch corners.

The bicubically blended Coons patch suffers from a more difficult compatibility problem. It results from the appearance of the twist terms in the tensor product term $\mathbf{h}_{cd}$ in (20.10). The problem was not recognized by Coons, and only later did R. Barnhill and J. Gregory discover it; see Gregory [185].

From calculus, we know that we can usually interchange the order of differentiation when taking mixed partials: we can set $\mathbf{x}_{uv} = \mathbf{x}_{vu}$ if $\mathbf{x}(u,v)$ is twice continuously differentiable. Unfortunately, this simplification does

Figure 21.1. Compatibility problems: in the case of a bilinearly blended Coons patch, compatible boundary curves must be prescribed. Data as shown lead to ill-defined interpolants.

not apply to our situation. Let us examine why: at $\mathbf{x}(0,0)$, two given "tangent ribbons" meet. We can obtain the twist at $\mathbf{x}(0,0)$ by differentiating the "ribbon" $\mathbf{x}_v(u,0)$ with respect to u:

$$\mathbf{x}_{uv}(0,0) = \lim_{u \to 0} \frac{\partial}{\partial u} \mathbf{x}_v(u,0),$$

or the other way around:

$$\mathbf{x}_{vu}(0,0) = \lim_{v \to 0} \frac{\partial}{\partial v} \mathbf{x}_u(0,v).$$

If the two twists $\mathbf{x}_{uv}(0,0)$ and $\mathbf{x}_{vu}(0,0)$ are equal, there are no problems: enter this twist term into the matrix in (20.10), and the bicubically blended Coons patch is well-defined.

However, as Figure 21.2 illustrates, these two terms need by no means be equal. Now we have a serious dilemma: entering either one of the two values yields a surface that only partially interpolates to the given data. Entering zero twist vectors only aggravates matters, since they will in general not agree with even one of the two twists above.

There are two ways out of this dilemma. One is to try to adjust the given data so that the incompatibilities disappear. Or, if the data cannot be changed, one can use a method known as *Gregory's square*. This method replaces the constant twist terms in the matrix in (20.10) by *variable twists*.

Figure 21.2. Compatibility problems: we show the example of tangent ribbons that are represented in cubic Bézier form. Note how we obtain two different interior Bézier points, and thus two different corner twists.

The variable twists are computed from the tangent ribbons:

$$
\mathbf{x}_{uv}(0,0) = \frac{u\frac{\partial}{\partial v}\mathbf{x}_u(0,0) + v\frac{\partial}{\partial u}\mathbf{x}_v(0,0)}{u+v},
$$

$$
\mathbf{x}_{uv}(0,1) = \frac{-u\frac{\partial}{\partial v}\mathbf{x}_u(0,1) + (v-1)\frac{\partial}{\partial u}\mathbf{x}_v(0,1)}{-u+v-1},
$$

$$
\mathbf{x}_{uv}(1,0) = \frac{(1-u)\frac{\partial}{\partial v}\mathbf{x}_u(1,0) + v\frac{\partial}{\partial u}\mathbf{x}_v(1,0)}{1-u+v},
$$

$$
\mathbf{x}_{uv}(1,1) = \frac{(u-1)\frac{\partial}{\partial v}\mathbf{x}_u(1,1) + (v-1)\frac{\partial}{\partial u}\mathbf{x}_v(1,1)}{u-1+v-1}.
$$

The resulting surface does not have a continuous twist at the corners. In fact, it is *designed* to be discontinuous: it assumes two different values, depending from where the corner is approached. If we approach $\mathbf{x}(0,0)$, say, along the isoparametric line $u = 0$, we should get the $u-$partial of the given tangent ribbon $\mathbf{x}_v(u,0)$ as the twist $\mathbf{x}_{uv}(0,0)$. If we approach the same corner along $v = 0$, we should get the v-partial of the given ribbon $\mathbf{x}_u(0,v)$ to be $\mathbf{x}_{uv}(0,0)$.

An interesting application of Gregory's square was developed by Chiyokura and Kimura [78]: suppose we are given four boundary curves of a patch in cubic Bézier form, and suppose that the cross boundary derivatives also vary cubically. Let us consider the corner $\mathbf{x}_{00}$ and the two boundary curves that meet there. These curves define the Bézier points $\mathbf{b}_{0j}$ and $\mathbf{b}_{i0}$. The cross boundary derivatives determine $\mathbf{b}_{1j}$ and $\mathbf{b}_{i1}$. Note that $\mathbf{b}_{11}$ is defined twice! This situation is illustrated in Figure 21.2. Chiyokura and Kimura made $\mathbf{b}_{11}$ a function of u and v:

$$\mathbf{b}_{11} = \mathbf{b}_{11}(u,v) = \frac{u\mathbf{b}_{11}(v) + v\mathbf{b}_{11}(u)}{u+v},$$

where $\mathbf{b}_{11}(u)$ denotes the point $\mathbf{b}_{11}$ that would be obtained from the cross boundary derivative $\mathbf{x}_u(0,v)$, etc. Similar expressions hold for the remaining three interior Bézier points, all following the pattern of Gregory's square.

Although a solution to the posed problem, one should note that Gregory's square (or the Chiyokura and Kimura application) is not free of problems. First, even with polynomial input data, it will produce a rational patch. This may not be acceptable in certain environments, since it requires its own kind of data structure.[1] Secondly, there are singularities at the corners. These are removable, but require special attention. In situations where one is not forced to use incompatible cross-boundary derivatives, it is therefore advisable first to estimate corner twists and then to use (20.12) as a cross-boundary derivative generator.

21.2   Control Nets from Coons Patches

Consider the following design situation: four boundary curves of a surface are given, all four in B-spline or Bézier form, i.e., by their control polygons. Let us assume that opposite boundary curves are defined over the same knot sequence and are of the same degrees. The problem: find the control net of a B-spline or Bézier surface that fits between the boundary curves. This situation is illustrated in Figure 21.3.

That control net may be obtained in a surprisingly simple way: interpret the boundary control polygons as piecewise linear curves and compute the bilinearly blended Coons patch that interpolates to them. This Coons patch is piecewise bilinear. Its vertices can be interpreted as vertices of a control net for a B-spline or Bézier surface. As it turns out, that surface is precisely the bilinearly blended Coons patch to the original boundary curves! The proof is straightforward and relies on the fact that both the B-spline and Bézier methods have linear precision (Farin [122]) .

The same principle is also applicable to interpolating spline curves and surfaces. Suppose we are given points on all four boundary curves of a surface (same number of points and same parametrization for opposite curves,

---

[1]It is not the data structure that describes a rational patch from Chapter 15, but a more specialized one that is closer to the standard bicubic Hermite form.

Figure 21.3. Coons patches: the bilinearly blended Coons patch may be applied to boundary control polygons.

of course!). We can construct the cubic spline interpolant to all four point sets. For the sake of concreteness, suppose that the spline curves are represented as piecewise Bézier curves. These four boundary spline curves define a bilinearly blended Coons patch. We may obtain its piecewise bicubic representation in two ways: first, we could compute an array of points, obtained from the given boundary points by applying the bilinearly blended Coons method to them. We could then apply bicubic spline interpolation to them.

That same surface could be obtained more easily by applying the bilinearly blended Coons method directly to the boundary curves (i.e., to their B-spline, Bézier or Hermite representations).

Using the Coons technique in conjunction with other surface forms is one of the most significant applications of the Coons method, implemented in `netcoons` below. It can reduce computation cost considerably and is a

Figure 21.4. Translational surfaces: the Bézier net of a translational tensor product surface. The control polygons in each direction are translates of each other.

quick way of fitting surfaces between boundary curves.[2] If the boundaries happened to be rational, then Coons blending should be applied to the homogeneous representation in four-space.

21.3   Translational Surfaces

There is an alternative way to derive the bilinearly blended Coons patch, based on the two concepts of *translational surfaces* and *convex combinations*.

A translational surface has the simple structure of being generated by two curves: let $\mathbf{c}_1(u)$ and $\mathbf{c}_2(v)$ be two such curves, intersecting at a common point $\mathbf{a} = \mathbf{c}_1(0) = \mathbf{c}_2(0)$. A translational surface $\mathbf{t}(u,v)$ is now defined by

$$\mathbf{t}(u,v) = \mathbf{c}_1(u) + \mathbf{c}_2(v) - \mathbf{a}. \tag{21.1}$$

Why the name "translational?" It is justified by considering an arbitrary isoparametric line of the surface, say, $u = \hat{u}$. We obtain $\mathbf{t}(\hat{u}, v) = \mathbf{c}_2(v) + (-\mathbf{a} + \mathbf{c}_1(\hat{u}))$, that is, all isoparametric lines are *translates* of one of the input curves; see also Figure 21.4.

An interesting property of translational surfaces is that their twist is identically zero everywhere:

$$\frac{\partial^2}{\partial u \partial v}\mathbf{t}(u,v) \equiv \mathbf{0}.$$

This property follows directly from the definition (21.1). Since both input curves may be arbitrarily shaped, the resulting surface may well have high

---

[2]A warning: it does not always produce 'optimal' shapes, see Nachman [262].

curvatures. This dispels the myth that zero twists are identical to flat spots. In fact, twists are not related to the shape of a surface – rather, they are a result of a particular parametrization.

How are translational surfaces related to Coons patches? A translational surface can be viewed as the solution to an interpolation problem: given two intersecting curves, find a surface that contains them as boundary curves. If four boundary curves are given, as in the problem definition for the bilinearly blended Coons patch, we can form four translational surfaces, one for each corner. Let us denote by $\mathbf{t}_{i,j}$ the translational surface that interpolates to the boundary curves meeting at the corner (i, j); $i, j \in \{0, 1\}$.

Now the bilinearly blended Coons patch $\mathbf{x}(u, v)$ can be written as

$$\mathbf{x}(u, v) = \begin{bmatrix} 1 - u & u \end{bmatrix} \begin{bmatrix} \mathbf{t}_{00}(u, v) & \mathbf{t}_{01}(u, v) \\ \mathbf{t}_{10}(u, v) & \mathbf{t}_{11}(u, v) \end{bmatrix} \begin{bmatrix} 1 - v \\ v \end{bmatrix}. \qquad (21.2)$$

The form (21.2) of the bilinearly blended Coons patch is called a *convex combination*. It blends together four surfaces, weighting each with a *weight function*. The weight functions sum to one (a necessity: nonbarycentric combinations are disallowed) and are nonnegative for $u, v \in \{0, 1\}$. Note that the weight functions are zero where the corresponding $\mathbf{t}_{i,j}$ is "wrong."

The weight functions in (21.2) are linear in both u and v, another justification for the term *bilinearly* blended Coons patch.

21.4   Gordon Surfaces

Gordon surfaces are a generalization of Coons patches. They were developed in the late sixties by W. Gordon [178], [180], [177], [179], who was then working for the General Motors Research labs.

It is often not sufficient to model a surface from only four boundary curves. A more complicated (and realistic) situation arises when a *network* of curves is prescribed, as shown in Figure 21.5. We will construct a surface $\mathbf{g}$ that interpolates to all these curves – they will then be isoparametric curves $\mathbf{g}(u_i, v); i = 0, \ldots, m$ and $\mathbf{g}(u, v_j); j = 0, \ldots, n$. We shall therefore refer to these input curves in terms of the final surface $\mathbf{g}$. The idea behind the construction of this *Gordon surface* $\mathbf{g}$ is the same as for the Coons patch: find a surface $\mathbf{g}_1$ that interpolates to one family of isoparametric curves, for instance to the $\mathbf{g}(u_i, v)$. Next, find a surface $\mathbf{g}_2$ that interpolates to the $\mathbf{g}(u, v_j)$. Finally, add both together and subtract a surface $\mathbf{g}_{12}$.

Let us start with the task of finding the surface $\mathbf{g}_1$. If there are only two curves $\mathbf{g}(u_0, v)$ and $\mathbf{g}(u_1, v)$, the surface $\mathbf{g}_1$ reduces to the lofted surface $\mathbf{g}_1(u, v) = L_0^1(u)\mathbf{g}(u_0, v) + L_1^1(u)\mathbf{g}(u_1, v)$, where the L_i^1 are the linear

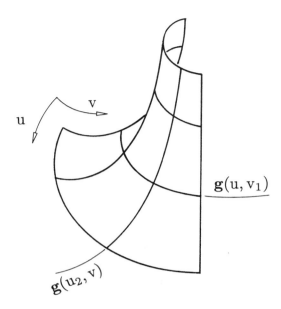

Figure 21.5. Gordon surfaces: a rectilinear network of curves is given and an interpolating surface is sought.

Lagrange polynomials from Section 6.2. If we have more than two input curves, we might want to try higher degree Lagrange polynomials:

$$\mathbf{g}_1(u, v) = \sum_{i=0}^{m} \mathbf{g}(u_i, v) L_i^m(u). \tag{21.3}$$

Simple algebra verifies that we have successfully generalized the concept of a lofted surface.

Let us return to the construction of the Gordon surface, for which $\mathbf{g}_1$ will only be a building block. The second building block, $\mathbf{g}_2$, is obtained by analogy:

$$\mathbf{g}_2(u, v) = \sum_{j=0}^{n} \mathbf{g}(u, v_j) L_j^n(v).$$

The third building block, $\mathbf{g}_{12}$, is simply the interpolating tensor product surface

$$\mathbf{g}_{12}(u, v) = \sum_{i=0}^{m} \sum_{j=0}^{n} \mathbf{g}(u_i, v_j) L_i^m(u) L_j^n(v).$$

The Gordon surface $\mathbf{g}$ now becomes

$$\mathbf{g} = \mathbf{g}_1 + \mathbf{g}_2 - \mathbf{g}_{12}. \tag{21.4}$$

It is left as an exercise for the reader to verify that (21.4) in fact interpolates to all given curves. Note that for the actual computation of $\mathbf{g}$, we do not have to use the Lagrange polynomials. We only have to be able to solve the univariate polynomial interpolation problem, for example, by using the Vandermonde approach.

We have derived Gordon surfaces as based on polynomial interpolation. Much more generality is available. Equation (21.4) is also true if we use interpolation methods other than polynomial interpolation. The essence of (21.4) may be stated as follows: take a univariate interpolation scheme, apply it to all curves $\mathbf{g}(u, v_j)$ and to all curves $\mathbf{g}(u_i, v)$, add the resulting two surfaces and subtract the tensor product interpolant that is defined by the univariate scheme. We may replace polynomial interpolation by spline interpolation, in which case we speak of *spline-blended* Gordon surfaces. The basis functions of the univariate interpolation scheme are called *blending functions*.

21.5   Boolean Sums

Our development of Coons patches was quite straightforward, yet it is slightly flawed from a geometric viewpoint. When we derived the basic equation (20.6), we *added* the two surfaces $\mathbf{r}_c$ and $\mathbf{r}_d$ as an intermediate step. This is illegal – the sum of two surfaces would depend on the choice of a coordinate system, see the discussion in Section 2.1. Although the situation is straightened out by subtracting the bilinear surface $\mathbf{r}_{cd}$, one might ask for a cleaner development. It is provided by the use of *Boolean sums*.

Let us define an operator $\mathcal{P}_1$ that, when applied to a rectangular surface $\mathbf{x}$, returns the ruled surface through $\mathbf{x}(u, 0)$ and $\mathbf{x}(u, 1)$:

$$[\mathcal{P}_1\mathbf{x}](u, v) = (1 - v)\mathbf{x}(u, 0) + v\mathbf{x}(u, 1).$$

Similarly, we define $\mathcal{P}_2$ to return the ruled surface through $\mathbf{x}(0, v)$ and $\mathbf{x}(1, v)$:

$$[\mathcal{P}_2\mathbf{x}](u, v) = (1 - u)\mathbf{x}(0, v) + u\mathbf{x}(1, v).$$

In terms of Section 20.2, $\mathcal{P}_1$ and $\mathcal{P}_2$ yield the surfaces $\mathbf{r}_c$ and $\mathbf{r}_d$.

We would like to formulate the bilinearly blended Coons patch – which we now call $\mathcal{P}\mathbf{x}$ – in terms of $\mathcal{P}_1$ and $\mathcal{P}_2$.

Let us take $\mathcal{P}_1\mathbf{x}$ as a first building block for the Coons patch. Since $\mathcal{P}_1\mathbf{x}$ only interpolates on two boundaries, we will try to add another surface to it, such that the final result will interpolate to all four boundaries. Such a *correction surface* must interpolate to all four boundaries of the error surface $\mathbf{x} - \mathcal{P}_1\mathbf{x}$.[3] It may be obtained by applying $\mathcal{P}_2$ to the error surface. We then obtain

$$\mathcal{P}\mathbf{x} = \mathcal{P}_1\mathbf{x} + \mathcal{P}_2(\mathbf{x} - \mathcal{P}_1\mathbf{x}).$$

This expression for the bilinearly blended Coons patch may be shortened by showing only the involved operators:

$$\mathcal{P} = \mathcal{P}_1 + \mathcal{P}_2(\mathcal{I} - \mathcal{P}_1),$$

where $\mathcal{I}$ is the identity operator. This way of obtaining one operator $\mathcal{P}$ as a combinations of two operators $\mathcal{P}_1, \mathcal{P}_2$ is called a Boolean sum and is often written as

$$\mathcal{P} = \mathcal{P}_1 \oplus \mathcal{P}_2.$$

Of course, one may also multiply out the terms in (21.5). We then obtain

$$\mathcal{P} = \mathcal{P}_1 \oplus \mathcal{P}_2 = \mathcal{P}_1 + \mathcal{P}_2 - \mathcal{P}_1\mathcal{P}_2.$$

We now see that, even with the use of an operator calculus, we still have the same old Coons patch as defined by (20.6): the term $\mathcal{P}_1\mathcal{P}_2$ is simply the bilinear interpolant to the patch corners.

Let us summarize the essence of the Boolean sum approach: An interpolant to the given data is built by applying $\mathcal{P}_1$. A second operator $\mathcal{P}_2$ is then applied to the "failures" of $\mathcal{P}_1$, and the result is added back to the output from $\mathcal{P}_1$. The interpolant $\mathcal{P}_2$ may actually be of a simpler nature than $\mathcal{P}_1$, since it only has to act on zero data where $\mathcal{P}_1$ was "successful." We can illustrate this for the example of univariate cubic Hermite interpolation: we define $\mathcal{P}_1$ to be the (point-valued) linear interpolant between two points $\mathbf{x}_0$ and $\mathbf{x}_1$ and $\mathcal{P}_2$ to be the (vector-valued) cubic Hermite interpolant to a data set $\mathbf{0}, \mathbf{m}_0, \mathbf{m}_1, \mathbf{0}$. Then $\mathcal{P}_1 \oplus \mathcal{P}_2$ is the standard cubic Hermite interpolant.

A note on the notation used in this section: the letter $\mathcal{P}$ that we used to denote our building block interpolants is due to the term *projector*. A projector is an operator, that, if applied to its own output, will not change

---

[3]Note that this error surface is *vector*-valued, since both $\mathbf{x}$ and $\mathcal{P}_1\mathbf{x}$ are *point*-valued.

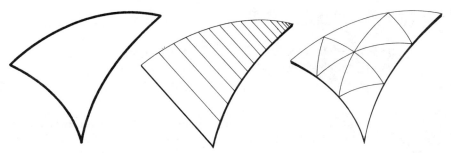

Figure 21.6. BBG interpolation: three boundary curves are given, left. Three ruled surfaces are constructed from them (only one shown, middle). They are combined to yield the final surface, right.

the result.[4] For example, $\mathcal{P}_1\mathbf{x}$ is a ruled surface, and $\mathcal{P}_1\mathcal{P}_1\mathbf{x}$ is the same ruled surface. Operators with the property of being projectors are also called *idempotent*.

It was W. Gordon who realized the underlying algebraic structure of Coons patches. That discovery then led him to the generalization which now bears his name (Section 21.4). Boolean sums may be utilized in the development of many surface interpolation schemes – for an excellent survey, see Barnhill [14].

21.6 Triangular Coons Patches

Just as triangular Bézier patches may be an alternative to the rectangular variety, one may devise a triangular version of Coons patches. Several solutions have been proposed through the years; we will briefly explain the ones by Barnhill, Birkhoff, and Gordon [18] and by Nielson [266].

The C^0 Barnhill, Birkhoff, and Gordon (short: BBG) approach can be explained as follows. Suppose we are given three boundary curves, as shown in Figure 21.6. We seek a surface that interpolates to all three of them, i.e., a *transfinite triangular interpolant*. The construction follows the standard Coons patch development in that it consists of several building blocks which are then combined in a clever way.

Let us denote[5] the three boundary curves by $\mathbf{x}(0,v,w)$, $\mathbf{x}(u,0,w)$, $\mathbf{x}(u,v,0)$. We define three building blocks, each being a ruled surface that

---

[4]The term comes from geometry: if a 3D object is projected into a plane, we may then repeat that projection, yet it will not change the image.

[5]We use the the concept of barycentric coordinates as outlined in Section 18.1.

interpolates to two boundary curves:

$$
\begin{aligned}
\mathcal{P}_1\mathbf{x}(\mathbf{u}) &= (1-r)\mathbf{x}(u,0,w) + r\mathbf{x}(u,v,0); & r &= \tfrac{v}{v+w}, \\
\mathcal{P}_2\mathbf{x}(\mathbf{u}) &= (1-s)\mathbf{x}(u,v,0) + s\mathbf{x}(0,v,w); & s &= \tfrac{w}{w+u}, \\
\mathcal{P}_3\mathbf{x}(\mathbf{u}) &= (1-t)\mathbf{x}(u,0,w) + t\mathbf{x}(0,v,w); & t &= \tfrac{v}{v+u}.
\end{aligned}
\tag{21.5}
$$

There are several combinations of these surfaces that yield an interpolant $\mathcal{P}\mathbf{x}$ to all three boundaries: the Boolean sum of any two – e.g., $\mathcal{P} = \mathcal{P}_1 \oplus \mathcal{P}_3$ – will have that property.

Another possibility is to define $\mathcal{P}$ as a convex combination of the three $\mathcal{P}_i$:

$$
\mathcal{P}\mathbf{x} = u\mathcal{P}_1\mathbf{x} + v\mathcal{P}_2\mathbf{x} + w\mathcal{P}_3\mathbf{x}.
\tag{21.6}
$$

The building blocks that are used in (21.5) are rational in u, v, w, but they are linear in r, s, t. If we were to incorporate cross-boundary derivative data, i.e., to build a C^1 BBG interpolant, we would define $\mathcal{P}_1, \mathcal{P}_2, \mathcal{P}_3$ to be cubic Hermite interpolants in r, s, t:

$$
\begin{aligned}
\mathcal{P}_1\mathbf{x}(\mathbf{u}) &= H_0^3(r)\mathbf{x}(u,0,w) + H_1^3(r)\mathbf{x}_1(u,0,w) \\
&\quad + H_2^3(r)\mathbf{x}_1(u,v,0) + H_3^3(r)\mathbf{x}(u,v,0), \\
\mathcal{P}_2\mathbf{x}(\mathbf{u}) &= H_0^3(s)\mathbf{x}(u,v,0) + H_1^3(s)\mathbf{x}_2(u,v,0) \\
&\quad + H_2^3(s)\mathbf{x}_2(0,v,w) + H_3^3(s)\mathbf{x}(0,v,w), \\
\mathcal{P}_3\mathbf{x}(\mathbf{u}) &= H_0^3(t)\mathbf{x}(u,0,w) + H_1^3(t)\mathbf{x}_3(u,0,w) \\
&\quad + H_2^3(t)\mathbf{x}_3(u,0,w) + H_3^3(t)\mathbf{x}(0,v,w).
\end{aligned}
\tag{21.7}
$$

The terms $\mathbf{x}_i$ are shorthand for directional derivatives of $\mathbf{x}$ taken in a direction parallel to edge i, more precisely:

$$
\begin{aligned}
\mathbf{x}_1(\mathbf{u}) &= (v+w)D_{\mathbf{e2}-\mathbf{e3}}\mathbf{x}(\mathbf{u}), \\
\mathbf{x}_2(\mathbf{u}) &= (u+w)D_{\mathbf{e3}-\mathbf{e1}}\mathbf{x}(\mathbf{u}), \\
\mathbf{x}_3(\mathbf{u}) &= (u+v)D_{\mathbf{e2}-\mathbf{e1}}\mathbf{x}(\mathbf{u}).
\end{aligned}
$$

The factors $(v+w)$ etc. appear because cubic Hermite interpolation is sensitive to interval lengths. A reminder: the terms $\mathbf{e1}, \mathbf{e2}, \mathbf{e3}$ refer to points, *not* to edges!

Again, a Boolean sum of any two of the above operators will provide a solution – provided the cross-boundary derivatives are compatible (which typically they won't be!).

Figure 21.7. Nielson's side-vertex method: three boundary curves are given, left. Three ruled surfaces are constructed from them (only one shown, middle). They are combined to yield the final surface, right.

A different approach is due to G. Nielson [266]. He considers – for a C^0 interpolant – *radial* curves, connecting a patch vertex with a point on the opposite edge, as shown in Figure 21.7. We have

$$
\begin{aligned}
\mathcal{P}_1\mathbf{x}(\mathbf{u}) &= u\mathbf{x}(1,0,0) + (1-u)\mathbf{x}(0,r,1-r); \quad r = \tfrac{v}{v+w} \\
\mathcal{P}_2\mathbf{x}(\mathbf{u}) &= v\mathbf{x}(0,1,0) + (1-v)\mathbf{x}(1-s,0,s); \quad s = \tfrac{u}{u+w} \\
\mathcal{P}_3\mathbf{x}(\mathbf{u}) &= w\mathbf{x}(0,0,1) + (1-w)\mathbf{x}(1-t,t,0); \quad t = \tfrac{u}{u+v}.
\end{aligned}
\tag{21.8}
$$

The final interpolant may then be written as a *triple Boolean sum:*

$$
\begin{aligned}
\mathcal{P} &= \mathcal{P}_1 \oplus \mathcal{P}_2 \oplus \mathcal{P}_3 \\
&= \mathcal{P}_1 + \mathcal{P}_2 + \mathcal{P}_3 \\
&\quad - \mathcal{P}_1\mathcal{P}_2 - \mathcal{P}_1\mathcal{P}_3 - \mathcal{P}_2\mathcal{P}_3 \\
&\quad + \mathcal{P}_1\mathcal{P}_2\mathcal{P}_3.
\end{aligned}
$$

In order to make this scheme C^1, one again replaces the linear interpolants in (21.8) by cubic Hermite interpolants, now with directional derivatives supplied in the radial directions.

For more literature on triangular Coons-type interpolants, consult the following: Barnhill [15], Barnhill and Gregory [22], Gregory and Charrot [186], Marshall and Mitchell [250], Lacombe and Bédard [230], Nielson [264].

21.7 Implementation

The following is a routine that fits a bilinearly blended Coons patch in between four boundary control polygons, as described in Section 21.2. The routine works on one coordinate only, and will have to be called separately for the $x-$, $y-$, and $z-$ components of a control net.

```
void netcoons(net,rows,columns)
/* Uses bilinear Coons blending to complete a control
net of which only the four boundary polygons are used as input.
Works for one coordinate only.
Input:      net:          control net.
            rows, columns: dimensions of net.
Output:     net:          the completed net, with the old boundaries.
*/
        float net[20][20];
        int rows, columns; /*If either of these is >20, adjust*/
                           /*dimensions in previous statement!*/
{
        int i,j;
        float u,v,u1,v1;

        for(i=0; i<=rows;    i++)
        for(j=0; j<=columns; j++)
        {
              u=((float)i)/rows;    u1=1.0-u;
              v=((float)j)/columns; v1=1.0-v;

              net[i][j]=u1*net[0][j] + u*net[rows][j]
                     +v1*net[i][0] + v*net[i][columns]
                   -u1*v1*net[0][0]      - u1*v*net[0][columns]
                   -u *v1*net[rows][0] - u *v*net[rows][columns];
        }
}
```

21.8   Problems

1. What exactly *does* the bilinearly blended Coons patch interpolate to when applied to data as in Figure 21.1?

2. Equation (20.12) generates tangent ribbons from the given boundary curve network. Verify that the resulting surface does not suffer from twist incompatibilities.

3. Translational surfaces have zero twists. Show that the inverse statement is also true: every surface with identically vanishing twists is a translational surface.

4. Find a form analogous to (21.2) for the partially bicubically blended Coons patch and for the bicubically blended Coons patch.

5. Show that bilinearly blended Coons patches have *translational* precision: if the four boundary curves are boundaries of a translational surface, then the bilinearly blended Coons patch reproduces that translational surface.

6. Equation (21.6) shows how one can combine the three surfaces from (21.5) in order to get a complete interpolant. How would one have to blend together the three surfaces from (21.7)?

22

W. Boehm: Differential Geometry II

22.1 Parametric Surfaces and Arc Element

A surface may be given by an *implicit* form $f(x, y, z) = 0$ or, more useful for CAGD, by its parametric form

$$\mathbf{x} = \mathbf{x}(u, v) = \begin{bmatrix} x(u, v) \\ y(u, v) \\ z(u, v) \end{bmatrix} ; \quad \mathbf{u} = \begin{bmatrix} u \\ v \end{bmatrix} \in [\mathbf{a}, \mathbf{b}] \subset I\!R^2, \qquad (22.1)$$

where the cartesian coordinates x, y, z of a surface point are differentiable functions of the parameters u and v and $[\mathbf{a}, \mathbf{b}]$ denotes a rectangle in the $u, v-$plane; see Figure 22.1 (sometimes other domains are used, for example, triangles). In order to avoid potential problems with undefined normal vectors, we will assume that

$$\mathbf{x}_u \wedge \mathbf{x}_v \neq \mathbf{0} \quad \text{for} \quad \mathbf{u} \in [\mathbf{a}, \mathbf{b}],$$

i.e., that both families of isoparametric lines are regular (see Section 11.1) and are nowhere tangent to each other. Such a parametrization is called *regular*.[1]

---

[1] Examples of irregular parametrizations are shown in Figures 16.9, 16.10, and 16.11.

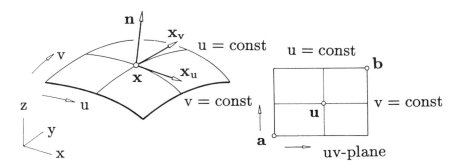

Figure 22.1. A parametric surface.

Any change $\mathbf{r} = \mathbf{r}(\mathbf{u})$ of the parameters will not change the shape of the surface; the new parametrization is regular if $\det[\mathbf{r}_u, \mathbf{r}_v] \neq 0$ for $\mathbf{u} \in [\mathbf{a}, \mathbf{b}]$, i.e., if one can find the inverse $\mathbf{u} = \mathbf{u}(\mathbf{r})$ of $\mathbf{r}$.

A regular curve $\mathbf{u} = \mathbf{u}(t)$ in the $u, v-$plane defines a regular curve $\mathbf{x}(\mathbf{u}(t))$ on the surface. One can easily compute the (squared) arc element (see Section 11.1) of this curve: from $\dot{\mathbf{x}} = \mathbf{x}_u \dot{u} + \mathbf{x}_v \dot{v}$ one immediately obtains

$$\mathrm{d}s^2 = ||\dot{\mathbf{x}}||^2 \mathrm{d}t^2 = (\mathbf{x}_u^2 \dot{u}^2 + 2\mathbf{x}_u \mathbf{x}_v \dot{u}\dot{v} + \mathbf{x}_v^2 \dot{v}^2)\mathrm{d}t^2,$$

which will be written as

$$\mathrm{d}s^2 = E\mathrm{d}u^2 + 2F\mathrm{d}u\mathrm{d}v + G\mathrm{d}v^2, \tag{22.2}$$

where

$$
\begin{aligned}
E &= E(u, v) = \mathbf{x}_u \mathbf{x}_u, \\
F &= F(u, v) = \mathbf{x}_u \mathbf{x}_v, \\
G &= G(u, v) = \mathbf{x}_v \mathbf{x}_v.
\end{aligned}
$$

The squared arc element (22.2) is called the *first fundamental form* in classical differential geometry. It is of great importance for the further development of our material. Note that the arc element $\mathrm{d}s$, being a geometric invariant of the curve through the point $\mathbf{x}$, does not depend on the particular parametrization chosen for the representation (22.1) of the surface.

For the arc length of the surface curve defined by $\mathbf{u} = \mathbf{u}(t)$, one obtains

$$\int_{t_0}^{t} ||\dot{\mathbf{x}}||\mathrm{d}t = \int_{t_0}^{t} \sqrt{E\dot{u}^2 + 2F\dot{u}\dot{v} + G\dot{v}^2}\,\mathrm{d}t.$$

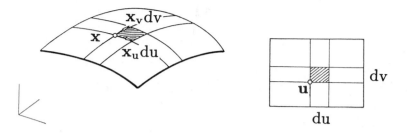

Figure 22.2. Area element.

Remark 1:   The *area element* corresponding to the element $dudv$ of the $u, v-$plane is given by

$$dA = ||\mathbf{x}_u du \wedge \mathbf{x}_v dv|| = ||\mathbf{x}_u \wedge \mathbf{x}_v||dudv;$$

see Figure 22.2. From $||\mathbf{a} \wedge \mathbf{b}||^2 = \mathbf{a}^2\mathbf{b}^2 - (\mathbf{ab})^2$, one obtains

$$D = ||\mathbf{x}_u \wedge \mathbf{x}_v|| = \sqrt{EG - F^2}. \tag{22.3}$$

The quantity D is called *discriminant* of (22.2). Thus the surface area A corresponding to a region U of the $u, v-$plane is given by

$$A = \int\int_U \sqrt{EG - F^2}dudv.$$

Remark 2:   If $F = 0$ at a point of the surface, the two isoparametric lines that meet there are orthogonal to each other. Moreover, if $F \equiv 0$ at every point of the surface, the net of isoparametric lines is orthogonal everywhere.

Remark 3:   Note that for any real[2] du, dv, the first fundamental form ds^2 is strictly positive. However, if $ds^2 = 0$, we have two *imaginary* directions. These are called *isotropic directions* at $\mathbf{x}$.

Remark 4:   Let $\mathbf{u}_1 = \mathbf{u}_1(t_1)$ and $\mathbf{u}_2 = \mathbf{u}_2(t_2)$ define two surface curves, intersecting at $\mathbf{x}$. Both curves are intersecting orthogonally if the *polar form* of $\dot{\mathbf{x}}^2$, given by

$$\dot{\mathbf{x}}_1\dot{\mathbf{x}}_2 = E\dot{u}_1\dot{u}_2 + F(\dot{u}_1\dot{v}_2 + \dot{u}_2\dot{v}_1) + G\dot{v}_1\dot{v}_2,$$

vanishes at $\mathbf{x}$.

---

[2]Note that the vector $[du, dv]$ defines a direction at a point $\mathbf{x}$.

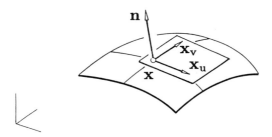

Figure 22.3. The local frame and the tangent plane.

22.2   The Local Frame

The partials $\mathbf{x}_u$ and $\mathbf{x}_v$ at a point $\mathbf{x}$ span the tangent plane to the surface at $\mathbf{x}$. Let $\mathbf{y}$ be any point on this plane. Then

$$\det[\mathbf{y} - \mathbf{x}, \mathbf{x}_u, \mathbf{x}_v] = 0$$

is the implicit equation of the tangent plane. The parametric equation is

$$\mathbf{y}(u, v) = \mathbf{x} + \Delta u \mathbf{x}_u + \Delta v \mathbf{x}_v.$$

The normal $\mathbf{x}_u \wedge \mathbf{x}_v$ of the tangent plane coincides with the normal to the surface at $\mathbf{x}$. The normalized normal

$$\mathbf{n} = \frac{\mathbf{x}_u \wedge \mathbf{x}_v}{||\mathbf{x}_u \wedge \mathbf{x}_v||} = \frac{1}{D}[\mathbf{x}_u \wedge \mathbf{x}_v]$$

together with the unnormalized vectors $\mathbf{x}_u$, $\mathbf{x}_v$ form a local coordinate system, a *frame*, at $\mathbf{x}$. This frame plays the same important role for surfaces as the Frenet frame (see Section 11.2) does for curves. The normal is of unit length and is perpendicular to $\mathbf{x}_u$ and $\mathbf{x}_v$, i.e., $\mathbf{n}^2 = 1$ and $\mathbf{n}\mathbf{x}_u = \mathbf{n}\mathbf{x}_v = 0$. In general the local coordinate system with origin $\mathbf{x}$ and axes $\mathbf{x}_u, \mathbf{x}_v$ forms only an affine system; it is also (unlike the Frenet frame) dependent on the parametrization (22.1).

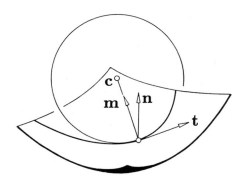

Figure 22.4. Osculating circle

22.3 The Curvature of a Surface Curve

Let $\mathbf{u}(t)$ define a curve on the surface $\mathbf{x}(\mathbf{u})$. From curve theory we know that its curvature $\kappa = \frac{1}{\rho}$ is defined by $\mathbf{t}' = \kappa\mathbf{m}$, the prime "'" denoting differentiation with respect to the arc length of the curve. We will now reformulate this expression in surface terms. Since $\mathbf{t} = \mathbf{x}'$ and $u' = \mathrm{d}u/\mathrm{d}s$, $v' = \mathrm{d}v/\mathrm{d}s$, we have

$$\mathbf{t}' = \mathbf{x}'' = \mathbf{x}_{uu}u'^2 + 2\mathbf{x}_{uv}u'v' + \mathbf{x}_{vv}v'^2 + \mathbf{x}_u u'' + \mathbf{x}_v v''.$$

Let ϕ be the angle between the main normal $\mathbf{m}$ of the curve and the surface normal $\mathbf{n}$ at the point $\mathbf{x}$ under consideration, as illustrated in Figure 22.4. Then

$$\mathbf{t}'\mathbf{n} = \kappa\mathbf{m}\mathbf{n} = \kappa\cos\phi.$$

Inserting $\mathbf{t}'$ from above and keeping in mind that $\mathbf{n}\mathbf{x}_u = \mathbf{n}\mathbf{x}_v = 0$, we have

$$\kappa\cos\phi = \mathbf{n}\mathbf{x}_{uu}u'^2 + 2\mathbf{n}\mathbf{x}_{uv}u'v' + \mathbf{n}\mathbf{x}_{vv}v'^2. \tag{22.4}$$

Furthermore, $\mathbf{n}\mathbf{x}_u = 0$ implies $\mathbf{n}_u\mathbf{x}_u + \mathbf{n}\mathbf{x}_{uu} = 0$ etc. Thus, using the abbreviations

$$
\begin{aligned}
L = L(u,v) \quad &= -\mathbf{x}_u\mathbf{n}_u \quad &&= \mathbf{n}\mathbf{x}_{uu}, \\
M = M(u,v) \quad &= -\tfrac{1}{2}(\mathbf{x}_u\mathbf{n}_v + \mathbf{x}_v\mathbf{n}_u) \quad &&= \mathbf{n}\mathbf{x}_{uv}, \\
N = N(u,v) \quad &= -\mathbf{x}_v\mathbf{n}_v \quad &&= \mathbf{n}\mathbf{x}_{vv},
\end{aligned}
\tag{22.5}
$$

equation (22.4) can be written as

$$\kappa\cos\phi\,\mathrm{d}s^2 = L\,\mathrm{d}u^2 + 2M\,\mathrm{d}u\,\mathrm{d}v + N\,\mathrm{d}v^2. \tag{22.6}$$

This expression is called the *second fundamental form* in classical differential geometry. For any given direction du/dv in the $u, v-$plane and any given angle ϕ, the second fundamental form, together with the first fundamental form (22.2), allows us to compute the curvature κ of a surface curve having that tangent direction.

Remark 5: Note that the arc length in the above development was only used in a theoretical context; for applications, it does not have to be actually computed.

Remark 6: Note that κ depends only on the tangent direction and the angle ϕ. It will change its sign, however, if there is a change in the orientation of $\mathbf{n}$.

22.4 Meusnier's Theorem

The right-hand side of (22.4) does not contain terms involving ϕ. For $\phi = 0$, i.e., $\cos \phi = 1$, we have that $\mathbf{m} = \mathbf{n}$: the osculating plane of the curve is perpendicular to the surface tangent plane at $\mathbf{x}$. The curvature κ_0 of such a curve is called the *normal curvature* of the surface at $\mathbf{x}$ in the direction of $\mathbf{t}$ (defined by du/dv). The normal curvature is given by

$$\kappa_0 = \kappa_0(\mathbf{x}; \mathbf{t}) = \frac{1}{\rho_0} = \frac{2^{\text{nd}}\text{fundamental form}}{1^{\text{st}}\text{fundamental form}}. \tag{22.7}$$

Now (22.6) takes the very short form

$$\rho = \rho_0 \cos \phi. \tag{22.8}$$

This simple formula has an interesting and important interpretation, known as Meusnier's Theorem. It is illustrated in Figure 22.5: the osculating circles of all surface curves through $\mathbf{x}$ having the same tangent $\mathbf{t}$ there form a sphere. This sphere and the surface have a common tangent plane at $\mathbf{x}$; the radius of the sphere is ρ_0.

As a consequence of Meusnier's Theorem, it is sufficient to study curves at $\mathbf{x}$ with $\mathbf{m} = \mathbf{n}$; moreover, these curves may be planar. Such curves, called *normal sections*, can be thought of as the intersection of the surface with a plane through $\mathbf{x}$ and containing $\mathbf{n}$, as illustrated in Figure 22.6.

Remark 7: If the direction of the normal is chosen as in Figure 22.5, we have $0 \leq \rho \leq \rho_0$, and $\rho = 0$ only if $\phi = \pi/2$, i.e., if the osculating plane $\mathbf{O}$ coincides with the tangent plane.

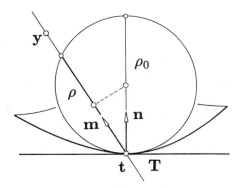

Figure 22.5. Meusnier's sphere viewed in the direction of **t**.

22.5 Lines of Curvature

For Meusnier's Theorem, we considered (osculating) planes that contained a fixed tangent at a point on a surface; we will now look at (osculating) planes containing the normal vector at a fixed point **x**. We will drop the subscript of κ_0 to simplify the notation. Setting $\lambda = dv/du = \tan\alpha$ (see Figure 22.6), we can rewrite (22.7) as

$$\kappa(\mathbf{x}, \mathbf{t}) = \kappa(\lambda) = \frac{L + 2M\lambda + N\lambda^2}{E + 2F\lambda + G\lambda^2}.$$

In the special case where $L : M : N = E : F : G$, the normal curvature κ is independent of λ. Points **x** with that property are called *umbilical points*.

In the general case, where κ changes as λ changes, $\kappa = \kappa(\lambda)$ is a rational quadratic function, as illustrated in Figure 22.7. The extreme values κ_1

Figure 22.6. Normal section of a surface.

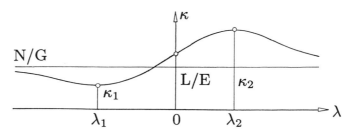

Figure 22.7. The function $\kappa = \kappa(\lambda)$.

and κ_2 of $\kappa(\lambda)$ occur at the roots λ_1 and λ_2 of

$$
\det \begin{bmatrix} \lambda^2 & -\lambda & 1 \\ E & F & G \\ L & M & N \end{bmatrix} = 0. \tag{22.9}
$$

It can be shown that λ_1 and λ_2 are always real. The extreme values κ_1 and κ_2 themselves are the roots of

$$
\det \begin{bmatrix} \kappa E - L & \kappa F - M \\ \kappa F - M & \kappa G - N \end{bmatrix} = 0. \tag{22.10}
$$

The quantities λ_1 and λ_2 define directions in the (u, v)−plane; the corresponding directions in the tangent plane are called *principal directions*. The net of lines that have these directions at all of their points is called the net of *lines of curvature*. If necessary, it may be constructed by integrating (22.9).

Therefore, this net of lines of curvature can be used as a parametrization of the surface; then (22.9) must be satisfied by $du = 0$ and by $dv = 0$. This implies, excluding umbilical points, that

$$
F \equiv 0 \quad \text{and} \quad M \equiv 0.
$$

The first equation, $F \equiv 0$, states that lines of curvature are orthogonal to each other; the second equation states that they are conjugate to each other as defined in Section 22.9.

At an umbilical point, the principal directions are undefined; see also Remark 9.

Remark 8: For a surface of revolution, the net of lines of curvature is defined by the meridians and the parallels; an example is shown in Figure 22.8.

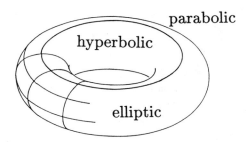

Figure 22.8. Lines of curvature on a torus. Also shown are the regions of elliptic, parabolic, and hyperbolic points.

22.6   Gaussian and Mean Curvature

The extreme values κ_1 and κ_2 of $\kappa = \kappa(\lambda)$ are called *principal curvatures* of the surface at $\mathbf{x}$. A comparison of (22.10) with $\kappa^2 - (\kappa_1 + \kappa_2)\kappa + \kappa_1\kappa_2 = 0$ yields

$$\kappa_1\kappa_2 = \frac{LN - M^2}{EG - F^2},\qquad(22.11)$$

and

$$\kappa_1 + \kappa_2 = \frac{NE - 2MF + LG}{EG - F^2}.\qquad(22.12)$$

The term $K = \kappa_1\kappa_2$ is called *Gaussian curvature*, while $H = \frac{1}{2}(\kappa_1 + \kappa_2)$ is called *mean curvature*. Note that both κ_1 and κ_2 change sign if the normal $\mathbf{n}$ is reversed, but K is not affected by such a reversal.

If κ_1 and κ_2 are of the same sign, i.e., if $K > 0$, the point $\mathbf{x}$ under consideration is called *elliptic*. For example, all points of an ellipsoid are elliptic points. If κ_1 and κ_2 have different signs, i.e., $K < 0$, the point $\mathbf{x}$ under consideration is called *hyperbolic*. For example, all points of a hyperboloid are hyperbolic points. Finally, if either $\kappa_1 = 0$ or $\kappa_2 = 0$, K vanishes, the point $\mathbf{x}$ under consideration is called *parabolic*. For example, all points of a cylinder are parabolic points. In the special case where both K and H vanish, one has a *flat* point.

The Gaussian curvature K depends on the coefficients of the first and second fundamental forms. It is a very important result, due to Gauss, that K can also be expressed only in terms of E, F, and G and their derivatives. This is known as the *Theorema Egregium* and states that K depends only on the *intrinsic geometry* of the surface. This means it does not change if the surface is deformed in a way that does not change length measurement within it.

Remark 9: All points of a sphere are umbilic. The Gaussian and mean curvatures of a sphere are constant.

Remark 10: Any *developable*, i.e., a surface that can be deformed to planar shape without changing length measurements in it, must have $K \equiv 0$. Conversely, every surface with $K \equiv 0$ can be developed into a plane (if necessary, by applying cuts). See also Section 22.10.

22.7   Euler's Theorem

The normal curvatures in different directions $\mathbf{t}$ at a point $\mathbf{x}$ are not independent of each other. For simplicity, let the isoparametric curves of a surface be lines of curvature; then we have $F \equiv M \equiv 0$ (see Section 22.5). As a consequence, we have

$$\kappa_1 = \frac{L}{E} \quad \text{and} \quad \kappa_2 = \frac{N}{G},$$

and $\kappa(\lambda)$ may be written as

$$\kappa(\lambda) = \frac{L + N\lambda^2}{E + G\lambda^2} = \kappa_1 \frac{E}{E + G\lambda^2} + \kappa_2 \frac{G\lambda^2}{E + G\lambda^2}. \tag{22.13}$$

The coefficients of κ_1 and κ_2 have a nice geometric meaning: let Ψ denote the angle between $\mathbf{x}_u$ and the tangent vector $\dot{\mathbf{x}} = \mathbf{x}_u \dot{u} + \mathbf{x}_v \dot{v}$ of the curve under consideration, as illustrated in Figure 22.9. We obtain

$$\cos \Psi = \frac{\dot{\mathbf{x}} \mathbf{x}_u}{\|\dot{\mathbf{x}}\| \, \|\mathbf{x}_u\|} = \frac{\sqrt{E}}{\sqrt{E + G\lambda^2}}$$

and

$$\sin \Psi = \frac{\dot{\mathbf{x}} \mathbf{x}_v}{\|\dot{\mathbf{x}}\| \, \|\mathbf{x}_v\|} = \frac{\sqrt{G}\lambda}{\sqrt{E + G\lambda^2}},$$

where $\lambda = \dot{v}/\dot{u}$ as before. Hence $\kappa(\lambda)$ may be written as

$$\kappa(\lambda) = \kappa_1 \cos^2 \Psi + \kappa_2 \sin^2 \Psi.$$

This important result was found by L. Euler.

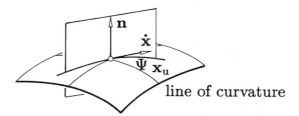

Figure 22.9. Configuration for Euler's Theorem

22.8   Dupin's Indicatrix

Euler's Theorem has the following geometric implication. If we introduce polar coordinates $r = \sqrt{\rho}$ and Ψ for a point $\mathbf{y}$ of the tangent plane at $\mathbf{x}$ by setting $y_1 = \sqrt{\rho}\cos\Psi$, $y_2 = \sqrt{\rho}\sin\Psi$, then setting $\kappa_1 = \frac{1}{\rho_1}$ and $\kappa_2 = \frac{1}{\rho_2}$, Euler's Theorem can be written as

$$\frac{y_1^2}{\rho_1} + \frac{y_2^2}{\rho_2} = 1.$$

This is the equation of a conic Section, the *Dupin's indicatrix*, see Figure 22.10. Its points $\mathbf{y}$ in the direction given by Ψ have distance $\sqrt{\rho}$ from $\mathbf{x}$. Taking into account that a reversal of the direction of $\mathbf{n}$ will effect a change in the sign of ρ, this conic section is an ellipse if $K > 0$, a pair of hyperbolas if $K < 0$ (corresponding to $\sqrt{\rho}$ and $\sqrt{-\rho}$), and a pair of parallel lines if $K = 0$ (but $H \neq 0$).

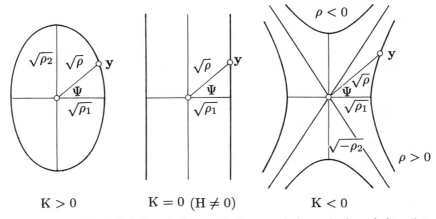

Figure 22.10. Dupin's indicatrix for an elliptic, a parabolic, and a hyperbolic point.

Figure 22.11. Dupin's indicatrix, scale $1 : m$.

Dupin's indicatrix has a nice geometric interpretation: we may approximate our surface at $\mathbf{x}$ by a paraboloid, that is, a Taylor expansion with terms up to second order. Then Remark 7 of Chapter 11 leads to a very simple interpretation of Dupin's indicatrix: the indicatrix, scaled down by a factor of $1 : m$, can be viewed as the intersection of the surface with a plane parallel to the tangent plane at $\mathbf{x}$ in the distance $\epsilon = \frac{1}{2m^2}$. This is illustrated in Figure 22.11.

Remark 11:   This illustrates the appearance of a pair of hyperbolas in Figure 22.10; they appear when intersecting the surface in distances $\epsilon = \pm\frac{1}{2m^2}$. We can thus assign a *sign* to the Dupin Indicatrix, depending on its being "above" or "below" the tangent plane.

22.9   Asymptotic Lines and Conjugate Directions

The asymptotic directions of Dupin's indicatrix have a simple geometric meaning: surface curves passing through $\mathbf{x}$ and having a tangent in an asymptotic direction there have zero curvature at $\mathbf{x}$; in other words, these directions are defined by

$$L\mathrm{d}u^2 + 2M\mathrm{d}u\mathrm{d}v + N\mathrm{d}v^2 = 0. \tag{22.14}$$

They are real and different if $K < 0$, real but coalescing if $K = 0$, and complex if $K > 0$.

The net of lines having these directions in all their points is called the *net of asymptotic lines*. If necessary, it may be calculated by integrating (22.14). In a hyperbolic region of the surface it is real and regular and can be used for a real parametrization.

For this parametrization, one has

$$L \equiv 0 \ \text{ and } \ N \equiv 0,$$

and vice versa.

As above, let $\mathbf{y}$ be a point on Dupin's indicatrix at a point $\mathbf{x}$. Let $\dot{\mathbf{y}}$ denote its tangent direction at $\mathbf{y}$. The direction $\dot{\mathbf{y}}$ is called *conjugate* to the direction $\dot{\mathbf{x}}$ from $\mathbf{x}$ to $\mathbf{y}$. Consider two surface curves $\mathbf{u}_1(t_1)$ and $\mathbf{u}_2(t_2)$ that have tangent directions $\dot{\mathbf{x}}_1$ and $\dot{\mathbf{x}}_2$ at $\mathbf{x}$. Some elementary calculations yield that $\dot{\mathbf{x}}_1$ is conjugate to $\dot{\mathbf{x}}_2$ if

$$L\dot{u}_1\dot{u}_2 + M(\dot{u}_1\dot{v}_2 + \dot{u}_2\dot{v}_1) + N\dot{v}_1\dot{v}_2 = 0.$$

Note that this expression is symmetric in $\dot{\mathbf{u}}_1, \dot{\mathbf{u}}_2$. By definition asymptotic directions are *self-conjugate*.

Remark 12: Isoparametric curves of a surface are conjugate if $M \equiv 0$ and vice versa.

Remark 13: The principal directions, defined by (22.9), are orthogonal and conjugate; they bisect the angles between the asymptotic directions; i.e., they are the axis directions of Dupin's indicatrix (see Figure 22.10).

Remark 14: The tangent planes of two "consecutive" points on a surface curve intersect in a straight line $\mathbf{s}$. Let the curve have direction $\mathbf{t}$ at a point $\mathbf{x}$ on the surface. Then $\mathbf{s}$ and $\mathbf{t}$ are conjugate to each other. In particular, if $\mathbf{t}$ is an asymptotic direction, $\mathbf{s}$ coincides with $\mathbf{t}$. If $\mathbf{t}$ is one of the principal directions at $\mathbf{x}$, then $\mathbf{s}$ is orthogonal to $\mathbf{t}$ and vice versa. These properties characterize lines of curvature and asymptotic lines and may be used to define them geometrically.

22.10 Ruled Surfaces and Developables

If a surface contains a family of straight lines it is called a *ruled surface*. It is convenient to use these straight lines as one family of isoparametric lines. Then the ruled surface may be written as

$$\mathbf{x} = \mathbf{x}(t, v) = \mathbf{p}(t) + v\mathbf{q}(t), \tag{22.15}$$

where $\mathbf{p}$ is a point and $\mathbf{q}$ is a vector, both depending on t. The isoparametric lines $t = const$ are called the *generatrices* of the surface; see Figure 22.12.

The partials of a ruled surface are given by $\mathbf{x}_t = \dot{\mathbf{p}} + v\dot{\mathbf{q}}$ and $\mathbf{x}_v = \mathbf{q}$. The normal $\mathbf{n}$ at $\mathbf{x}$ is given by

$$\mathbf{n} = \frac{(\dot{\mathbf{p}} + v\dot{\mathbf{q}}) \wedge \mathbf{q}}{||(\dot{\mathbf{p}} + v\dot{\mathbf{q}}) \wedge \mathbf{q}||}.$$

A point $\mathbf{y}$ on the tangent plane at $\mathbf{x}$ satisfies

$$\det[\mathbf{y} - \mathbf{p}, \dot{\mathbf{p}}, \mathbf{q}] + v\det[\mathbf{y} - \mathbf{p}, \dot{\mathbf{q}}, \mathbf{q}] = 0;$$

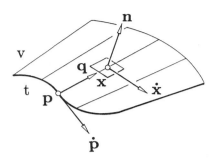

Figure 22.12. Ruled surface.

in other words, the tangent planes along a generatrix form a pencil of planes. However, if $\dot{\mathbf{p}}, \dot{\mathbf{q}}$, and $\mathbf{q}$ are linearly dependent, i.e. if

$$\det[\dot{\mathbf{p}}, \dot{\mathbf{q}}, \mathbf{q}] = 0, \qquad (22.16)$$

the tangent plane does not vary with v.

If (22.16) holds for all t, the tangent planes are fixed along each generatrix; hence all tangent planes of the surface form a one parameter family of planes. Conversely, any one parameter family of planes envelopes a developable surface that may be written as a ruled surface (22.15), satisfying condition (22.16); see also Remark 10.

Remark 15: The generatrices of any ruled surface coalesce with one family of its asymptotic lines. As a consequence of asymptotic lines being real, one has $K \leq 0$.

Remark 16: In particular, the generatrices of a developable surface agree with its coalescing asymptotic lines, also forming one family of its lines of curvature. The second family of lines of curvature is formed by the orthogonal trajectories of the generatrices.

Remark 17: It can be shown that any developable surface is a cone $\mathbf{p} = \mathbf{const}$, a cylinder $\mathbf{q} = \mathbf{const}$, or a surface formed by all tangents of a space curve, that is, $\mathbf{q} = \dot{\mathbf{p}}$; see Figure 22.13.

Remark 18: The normals along a line of curvature of any surface form a developable surface. This property characterizes and defines lines of curvature.

Remark 19: The tangent planes along a curve $\mathbf{x} = \mathbf{x}(\mathbf{u}(t))$ on any surface form a developable surface. It may be developed into a plane; if by this process the curve $\mathbf{x}(\mathbf{u}(t))$ happens to be developed into a straight line, the curve $\mathbf{x}(\mathbf{u}(t))$ is called a *geodesic*. At any point $\mathbf{x}$ of a geodesic, one finds that

$$\det[\dot{\mathbf{x}}, \ddot{\mathbf{x}}, \mathbf{n}] = 0. \qquad (22.17)$$

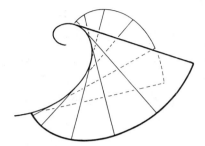

Figure 22.13. General developable surface.

Equation (22.17) is the differential equation of a geodesic; it is of second order. Geodesics may also be characterized as providing the shortest path between two points on the surface.

22.11   Nonparametric Surfaces

Let $z = f(x, y)$ be a function of two variables as shown in Figure 22.14. The surface

$$\mathbf{x} = \mathbf{x}(u, v) = \begin{bmatrix} u \\ v \\ z(u, v) \end{bmatrix}$$

is then called a nonparametric surface. From the above, one immediately finds

$$E = 1 + z_u^2, \quad F = z_u z_v, \quad G = 1 + z_v^2,$$

$$D^2 = EG - F^2 = 1 + z_u^2 + z_v^2,$$

$$\mathbf{n} = \frac{1}{D} \begin{bmatrix} -z_u \\ -z_v \\ 1 \end{bmatrix},$$

$$L = \frac{1}{D} z_{uu}, \quad M = \frac{1}{D} z_{uv}, N = \frac{1}{D} z_{vv},$$

$$K = \frac{1}{D^2} (z_{uu} z_{vv} - z_{uv}^2).$$

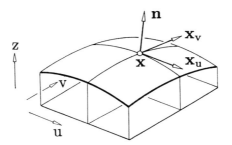

Figure 22.14. Nonparametric surface.

22.12   Composite Surfaces

A surface $\mathbf{x} = \mathbf{x}(u,t)$ with global parameters u and t may be composed
of patches or segments of different surfaces. Let $\mathbf{x}_- = \mathbf{x}_-(t)$ denote the
right boundary curve and $\mathbf{x}_+ = \mathbf{x}_+(t)$ the left boundary curve of two such
patches, connected along $\mathbf{x} = \mathbf{x}(t)$, $t \in [a, b]$, as illustrated in Figure 22.15.
Both patches are tangent plane continuous if $\mathbf{n}_- = \pm\mathbf{n}_+$ at all $\mathbf{x}(t)$. This
may also be written as

$$\alpha\mathbf{x}_{-u} = \beta\mathbf{x}_{+v} + \gamma\dot{\mathbf{x}}, \qquad (22.18)$$

where α, β, γ are functions of t and the product $\alpha\beta$ is nonvanishing.

The two patches are curvature continuous if they are tangent plane continuous and both Dupin's indicatrices agree along the common boundary, in the sense of Remark 11.

If the common boundary is C^1, both indicatrices have a pair of points in common which are opposed to each other in the direction of the boundary tangent. Although a conic section is defined by five points (see Section

Figure 22.15. Composite surface.

Figure 22.16. Common Dupin's indicatrix.

14.5), or by its midpoint and three non-diametrical points, it can be shown that both Dupin's indicatrices coincide if there exists a family of curvature continuous surface curves crossing the common boundary. In particular, this family may be one of asymptotic lines (Pegna and Wolter [274]) or any family of isolines (Boehm [59]) or even any family of unordered directions (Pegna and Wolter [274]). Moreover, if the boundary is C^0 only at a point, there are two directions of curvature continuity there, and so no further conditions have to be met.

Remark 20: A surface is called tangent or curvature continuous if any plane section is tangent or curvature continuous, respectively.

Remark 21: Note that asymptotic directions of both patches may coincide even if they are imaginary.

Remark 22: A consequence of (22.18) is the following:

$$\alpha \mathbf{x}_{-ut} = \beta \mathbf{x}_{+ut} + \gamma \ddot{\mathbf{x}} - \dot{\alpha} \mathbf{x}_{-u} + \dot{\beta} \mathbf{x}_{+v} + \dot{\gamma} \dot{\mathbf{x}}.$$

Remark 23: Note that, although Dupin's indicatrix is a euclidean invariant only, curvature continuity of surfaces is an affinely invariant property.

23

Interrogation and Smoothing

We discussed many methods for curve and surface generation. In this chapter, we shall discuss some ways to inspect the geometric quality of those curves and surfaces and develop a few ideas on how to remove shape imperfections.

23.1 Use of Curvature Plots

A spline curve is typically obtained in one of two ways: as a curve that interpolates to given data points, or as the result of interactive manipulation of a B-spline polygon. In both cases, it is hard to tell from the display on the screen if the shape of the curve is acceptable or not: two curves may look identical on the screen, yet reveal significant shape differences when plotted to full scale on a large flatbed plotter. Such plots are both expensive and time consuming – one needs a tool to analyze curve shape at the CAD terminal.

Such a tool is provided by the *curvature plot* of the curve. For a given curve, we can plot curvature *vs* arc length. The resulting graph is the curvature plot. We have already used curvature plots in Chapter 9. All three curves from Figures 9.2, 9.4, and 9.6 look very similar, yet their curvature plots reveal substantial differences. The same is true for Figures

9.10 and 9.12. What actually constitutes a "substantial" difference depends on the application at hand, of course.

The curvature of a space curve is nonnegative by definition (11.7).[1] Very often, one is interested in the detection of inflection points of the current planar projection, i.e., the points of inflection of the curve as it appears on the screen. If we introduce signed curvature by

$$\kappa(u) = \frac{\ddot{x}(u)\dot{y}(u) - \ddot{y}(u)\dot{x}(u)}{[(\dot{x}(u))^2 + (\dot{y}(u))^2]^{3/2}}, \qquad (23.1)$$

where x, y are the two components of the curve, it is easy to point to changes in the sign of curvature, which indicate inflection points. (Those sign changes can be marked by special symbols on the plot.) Signed curvature is used in all examples in this book.

We now go one step further and use curvature plots for the definition of fair curves: *A curve is fair if its curvature plot is continuous and consists of only a few monotone pieces.*[2] Regions of monotone curvature are separated by points of extreme curvature. The number of curvature extrema of a fair curve should thus be small – curvature extrema should only occur where explicitly desired by the designer, and nowhere else!

This definition of fairness (also suggested by Dill [113], Birkhoff [50], and Su and Liu [67] in similar form) is certainly subjective; however, it has proven to be a practical concept. Once a designer has experienced that "flat spots" on the curve correspond to "almost zero" curvature values and that points of inflection correspond to crossings of the zero curvature line, he or she will use curvature plots as an everyday tool.

23.2   Curve and Surface Smoothing

A typical problem in the design process of many objects is that of *digitizing errors*: data points have been obtained from some digitizing device (a tablet being the simplest), and a fair curve is sought through them. In many cases, however, the digitized data are inaccurate, and this presence of digitizing error manifests itself in a "rough" curvature plot of an interpolating spline curve.[3]

---

[1]See also the Problems section of Chapter 15.

[2]M. Sabin has suggested that "a frequency analysis of the radius of curvature plotted against arc length might give some measure of fairness – the lower the dominant frequency, the fairer the curve." Quoted from Forrest [155].

[3]Typically splines that are obtained from interactive adjustment of control polygons exhibit rough curvature plots as well.

For a given curvature plot of a C^2 cubic spline, we may now search for the largest slope discontinuity of $\kappa(s)$ (s being arc length) and try to "fair" the curve there. Let this largest slope discontinuity occur at $u = u_j$. The slope κ' is given by

$$\frac{d\kappa}{ds} = \frac{\det[\dot{\mathbf{x}}, \dddot{\mathbf{x}}]}{||\dot{\mathbf{x}}||^4} - 3\dot{\mathbf{x}}\ddot{\mathbf{x}}\frac{\det[\dot{\mathbf{x}}, \ddot{\mathbf{x}}]}{||\dot{\mathbf{x}}||^6}, \tag{23.2}$$

where, as usual, dots denote derivatives with respect to the given parameter u (see Pottmann [287]). Note that this formula applies for 2D curves only.

The data point $\mathbf{x}(u_j)$ is potentially in error: so why not move $\mathbf{x}(u_j)$ to a more favorable position? It seems that a more favorable position should be such that the spline curve through the new data no longer exhibits a slope discontinuity.

We now make the following observation: if a spline curve is three (instead of just two) times differentiable at a point $\mathbf{x}(u_j)$, then certainly its curvature is differentiable at u_j; i.e., it does not have a slope discontinuity there (assuming that the tangent vector does not vanish at u_j). Also, the two cubic segments corresponding to the intervals (u_{j-1}, u_j) and (u_j, u_{j+1}) are now part of *one* cubic segment: the knot u_j is only a pseudo-knot, which could be removed from the knot sequence without changing the curve.

We will thus try to *remove* the "offending knot" u_j from the knot sequence, thereby fairing the curve, and then reinsert the knot in order to keep a spline curve with the same number of intervals as the initial one. We discussed knot insertion in Chapter 10. The inverse process, *knot removal*, has no unique solution. Several possibilities are discussed in Farin *et al.* [137], Sapidis [315] and Farin and Sapidis [138]. We present here a simple yet effective solution to the knot removal problem. Let the offending knot u_j be associated with the vertex $\mathbf{d}_j$.[4] We now formulate our knot removal problem: to what position $\hat{\mathbf{d}}_j$ must we move $\mathbf{d}_j$ such that the resulting new curve becomes three times differentiable at u_j? After some calculation (equating the left and the right third derivative of the new spline curve), one verifies that the new vertex $\hat{\mathbf{d}}_j$ is given by

$$\hat{\mathbf{d}}_j = \frac{(u_{j+2} - u_j)\mathbf{l}_j + (u_j - u_{j-2})\mathbf{r}_j}{u_{j+2} - u_{j-2}},$$

where the auxiliary points $\mathbf{l}_j, \mathbf{r}_j$ are given by

$$\mathbf{l}_j = \frac{(u_{j+1} - u_{j-3})\mathbf{d}_{j-1} - (u_{j+1} - u_j)\mathbf{d}_{j-2}}{u_j - u_{j-3}}$$

---

[4]This uses the notation from Chapter 7.

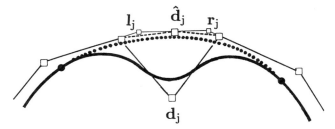

Figure 23.1. Knot removal: if $\mathbf{d}_j$ is moved to $\hat{\mathbf{d}}_j$, the new curve is three times differentiable at u_j.

and

$$\mathbf{r}_j = \frac{(u_{j+3} - u_{j-1})\mathbf{d}_{j+1} - (u_j - u_{j-1})\mathbf{d}_{j+2}}{u_{j+3} - u_j}.$$

The geometry underlying these equations is illustrated in Figure 23.1.

The faired curve now differs from the old curve between $\mathbf{x}(u_{j-2})$ and $\mathbf{x}(u_{j+2})$ – thus this fairing procedure is *local*. Figures 23.2 and 23.3 illustrate an application of this algorithm. Note that the initial and the smoothed curves look identical, and only their curvature plots reveal significant shape differences.

In practice, the improved vertex $\hat{\mathbf{d}}_j$ may be further away from the original vertex $\mathbf{d}_j$ than a prescribed tolerance allows. In that case, one restricts a realistic $\hat{\mathbf{d}}_j$ to be in the direction towards the optimal $\hat{\mathbf{d}}_j$, but within tolerance to the old $\mathbf{d}_j$.

Other methods for curve fairing exist. We mention Kjellander's method [225] that moves a data point to a more favorable location and then interpolates the changed data set with a C^2 cubic spline. This method is global. A method that fairs only data points, not spline curves, is presented by Renz [297]. This method computes second divided differences, smoothes them, and "integrates" back up. Methods that aim at the smoothing of single Bézier curves are discussed by Hoschek [210], [213]. Variations on the described method are given in [138].

23.3 Surface Interrogation

Curvature plots are useful for curves; it is reasonable, therefore, to investigate the analogous concepts for surfaces. Several authors have done this, including Beck et al. [36], Farouki [140], Dill [113], Munchmeyer [261], [260], Forrest [158]; and an interesting early example is on page 197 of

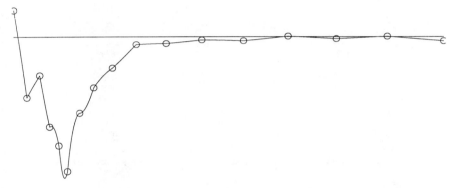

Figure 23.2. Curve smoothing: an initial curve and B-spline polygon with its curvature plot.

Hilbert and Cohn-Vossen [205]. Surfaces have two major kinds of curvature: Gaussian and mean; see Section 22.6. Both kinds can be used for the detection of surface imperfections. Another type of curvature can be useful, too: *absolute curvature* κ_{abs}. It is defined by

$$\kappa_{\text{abs}} = |\kappa_1| + |\kappa_2|,$$

where κ_1 and κ_2 are the maximal and minimal normal curvatures at the point under consideration.

Gaussian curvature does not offer much information about generalized cylinders of the form

$$\mathbf{c}(u, v) = (1 - u)\mathbf{x}(v) + u[\mathbf{x}(v) + \mathbf{v}].$$

Even if the generating curve $\mathbf{x}(v)$ is highly curved, we still have $K \equiv 0$ for these surfaces. A similar statement can be made about the mean curvature

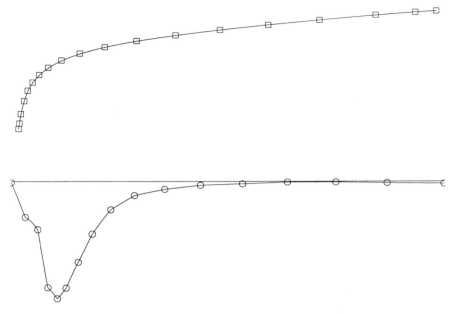

Figure 23.3. Curve smoothing: the smoothed curve and its curvature plot.

H, which is always zero for minimal surfaces, no matter how complicated. Absolute curvature will always recognize curvature in a surface and may be the most reliable of these three curvatures.

All three kinds of curvatures are shown in Plate V. Note how the surface (a wire frame rendering) looks perfectly flat, yet the curvatures detect many concave and convex regions.[5]

Another example is shown in Plate VI: both Gaussian and mean curvature detect regions of uneven curvature where the wire frame rendering (and also absolute curvature) indicate nothing.

Three points of the surface from Plate VI were then perturbed by less than .3 mm (the surface itself having a side length of $\approx$ 800 mm). Again, Gaussian and mean curvatures detect these irregularities easily, while absolute curvature does not.

Plate VII shows the ability of curvature interrogation to detect the effect of a bad choice of twist vectors in surface generation: Gaussian curvature is displayed for the choice of C^2 twists (upper left), Adini's twist (upper right), FMILL twist (lower left), and zero twists (lower right). While the

---

[5]Plates V, VI, VII, VIII and Figures 23.4, 23.5, 23.6 are taken from L. Fayard's Master's thesis [146].

Figure 23.4. Reflection lines: a surface, with a wire frame rendering on the upper left, is shown together with the reflection patterns that are generated by three differently oriented families of "strip lights."

first three methods yield similar plots, the zero twist clearly gives rise to an imperfect surface.

Another method for surface interrogation is the use of *reflection lines*, first described in Klass [227] and later by Poeschl [286]. Reflection lines are a standard surface interrogation tool in the styling shop of a car manufacturer. They are the pattern that is formed on the polished car surface by the mirror images of a number of parallel fluorescent strip lights. If the mirror images are "nice," then the corresponding surface is deemed acceptable. Reflection lights can easily be simulated on a raster graphics device (mark points whose normal points to one of the light sources). With some more effort, they are also computable on a line drawing device (see Klass [227]).

Figures 23.4 and 23.5 show two surfaces together with a family of reflection lines. The first surface is the one from Plate VI. The second one is a perturbed version of this surface, with perturbations about 10 times as large as those leading to the surface in Plate VII.

Reflection lines and curvature "paintings" have different usages: reflection lines are not as fine-tuned as curvatures are; they are prone to miss local shape defects of a surface.[6] On the other hand, curvatures of a surface may look perfect, yet it might not have a "pleasant" overall shape – reflection lines have a better chance of flagging global imperfections. Figure 23.6 gives an example: a bilinearly blended Coons surface, applied to the four

---

[6]This is so because reflection lines may be viewed as a first order interrogation tool (involving only first derivatives), while curvature plots are second order interrogation tools.

Figure 23.5. Reflection lines: the same surface as before, but now with some "dents."

shown boundary curves, yields a surface that is too flat. The reflection lines reveal this shape imperfection; they are not parallel as a "perfect" shape would require.[7]

Once imperfections are detected in a tensor product B-spline surface, one would want methods to remove them without time-consuming interactive adjustment of control polygons. One such method is to apply the curve smoothing method from Section 23.2 above in a tensor product way: smooth all control net rows, then all control net columns. The resulting

Figure 23.6. Global shape imperfections: a bilinearly blended Coons patch, applied to four torus boundary curves, yields a surface that is too flat. This may be inferred from the top right family of reflection lines.

---

[7]Methods to overcome this drawback of the Coons method have been studied at various places; the one that R. Goldman implemented for Ford is described (in a B-spline version) by L. Nachman [262]. Classical methods, based on proportional development, are discussed by Faux and Pratt [145].

surface is usually smoother than the original surface. More involved methods for surface fairing exist; they aim for the enforcement of convexity constraints in tensor product spline surfaces. We mention Andersson *et al.* [7] and Jones [222], and Kaufmann and Klass [224].

23.4 Implementation

The routine **curvatures** may be used to generate curvature values of a rational Bézier curve. It writes the values into a file that might be read by another program that generates a curvature plot.

In order to compute the curvature at the parameter value t, the curve is subdivided using the (rational) de Casteljau algorithm. Of the two subpolygons that are generated, the larger one is selected, and its beginning curvature is computed. Since the subdivision routine **rat_subdiv** orders both subpolygons beginning at the subdivision point, only one curvature routine **curvature_0** is needed.

```
#include <usercore.h>
#include <stdio.h>
#include <math.h>
extern FILE *outfile;

void curvatures(coeffx,coeffy,weight,degree,dense)
/*     writes  signed curvatures of  a rational  Bezier curve into
       a file.
input:
     coeffx, coeffy:  2D Bezier polygon
     weight:          the weights
     degree:          the degree
     dense:           how many curvature values to compute
output:
     written into file outfile
*/
     float coeffx[], coeffy[], weight[];
     int degree, dense;
{
     float bleftx[10],blefty[10],brightx[10],brighty[10];
     float wleft[10], wright[10];
     float dist,t,delt,h;
     int i,j;
     float curvature_0();

     delt=1.0/(float)dense;
```

```
      i=0;
      for(t=0.0; t<0.5; t=t+delt)
      {
            rat_subdiv(degree,coeffx,weight,t,bleftx,brightx,wleft,wright);
             rat_subdiv(degree,coeffy,weight,t,blefty,brighty,wleft,wright);
            h=curvature_0(brightx,brighty,wright,degree);
            fprintf(outfile,"%2.3f  %f\n",t,h);    /* note: the output   */
            i=i+1;                                 /* file is of the form */
                                             /* t_i, kappa_i -- ready for use in*/
      }                                      /* a display program.          */


      for(t=t; t<=1.00001; t=t+delt)
      {
            rat_subdiv(degree,coeffx,weight,t,bleftx,brightx,wleft,wright);
             rat_subdiv(degree,coeffy,weight,t,blefty,brighty,wleft,wright);
            h=curvature_0(bleftx,blefty,wleft,degree);
            h=0.0-h;
            /*
             minus sign since order of polygon traversal is reversed!
            */
            fprintf(outfile,"%2.3f   %f\n",t,h);
            i=i+1;
      }


}
```

The routine curvature_0 is a simple application of equation 11.10:

```
#include <math.h>
float curvature_0(bez_x,bez_y,weight,degree)
/* computes curvature of rational  Bezier curve at t=0 */
      float bez_x[], bez_y[], weight[];
      int degree;
{
      float b0[2],b1[2],b2[2];
      float dist;
      float area();

      b0[0]=bez_x[0]; b1[0]=bez_x[1]; b2[0]=bez_x[2];
      b0[1]=bez_y[0]; b1[1]=bez_y[1]; b2[1]=bez_y[2];

      dist = sqrt( (b1[0]-b0[0])*(b1[0]-b0[0])+
                  (b1[1]-b0[1])*(b1[1]-b0[1])  );

      return (2.0*(degree-1)*weight[0]*weight[2]*area(b0,b1,b2)
```

```
                /(degree*weight[1]*weight[1]*dist*dist*dist) );
}
```

The **area** routine is somewhat trivial:

```
float area(p1,p2,p3)
/* find area of triangle p1,p2,p3 */

    float p1[2], p2[2], p3[2];
{
    return( (p2[0]-p1[0])*(p3[1]-p1[1])-(p2[1]-p1[1])*(p3[0]-p1[0]))/2.0;
}
```

Note, however, that **area** returns a negative value if the the input points are ordered clockwise!

24

Evaluation of Some Methods

In this chapter, we will examine some of the many methods that have been presented. We will try to point out the relative strengths and weaknesses of each, a task that is necessarily influenced by personal experience and opinion.

24.1   Bézier Curves or B-spline Curves?

Taken at face value, this is a meaningless question: Bézier curves are a special case of B-spline curves. Any system that contains B-splines in their full generality, allowing for multiple knots, is capable of representing a Bézier curve or, for that matter, a piecewise Bézier curve.

In fact, several systems use both concepts simultaneously. A curve may be stored as an array holding B-spline control vertices, knots, and knot multiplicities. For evaluation purposes, the curve may then be converted to the piecewise Bézier form.

24.2   Spline Curves or B-spline Curves?

This question is often asked, yet it does not make much sense. B-splines form a basis for all splines, so any spline curve can be written as a B-spline curve.

What is often meant is the following: if we want to design a curve, should we pass an interpolating spline curve through data points, or should we design a curve by interactively manipulating a B-spline polygon? Now the question has become one concerning curve *generation* methods, rather than curve *representation* methods.

A flexible system should have both: interpolation and interactive manipulation. The interpolation process may of course be formulated in terms of B-splines. Since many designers do not favor interactive manipulation of control polygons, one should allow them to generate curves using interpolation. Subsequent curve modification may also take place without display of a control polygon: for instance, the designer might move one (interpolation) point to a new position. The system could then compute the B-spline polygon modification that would produce exactly that effect. So a user might actually work with a B-spline package, but a system that is adapted to his or her needs might hide that fact. See "inverse design" in Section 7.11 for details.

We finally note that every C^2 B-spline curve may be generated as an interpolating spline curve: read off junction points, end tangent vectors, and knot sequence from the B-spline curve. Feed these data into a C^2 cubic spline interpolator, and the original curve will be regenerated.

24.3   The Monomial or the Bézier Form?

We have made the point in this book that the monomial form[1] is *less geometric* than the Bézier form for a polynomial curve. A software developer, however, might not care much about the beauty of geometric ideas – in the workplace, the main priority is performance. Since the fundamental work by Farouki and Rajan [144] and [143], one important performance issue has been resolved: the Bézier form is *numerically more stable* than the monomial form. Farouki and Rajan observed that numerical inaccuracies, unavoidable with the use of finite precision computers, affect curves in the monomial form significantly more than those in Bézier form. More precisely, they show that the condition number of simple roots of a polynomial [2] is smaller in the Bernstein basis than in the monomial basis. If one decides to use the Bézier form for stability reasons, then it is essential that no conversions are made to other representations; these will destroy the accuracy gained by the use of the Bézier form. For example, it is not advisable from a stability viewpoint to store data in the monomial form

---

[1]This form is also called the power basis form.

[2]This number indicates by how much the location of a root is perturbed as a result of a perturbation of the coefficients of the given polynomial.

Figure 24.1. A piecewise monomial surface: the patches miss the points (1,1) due to roundoff.

and to convert to Bézier form to perform certain operations. More details are in Daniel and Daubisse [91].

As a consequence of its numerical instability, the monomial form is not very reliable for the representation of curves or surfaces. For the case of surfaces, Figure 24.1 gives an illustration (in somewhat exaggerated form). Since the monomial form is essentially a Taylor expansion around the local coordinate (0,0) of each patch, it is quite close to the intended surface there. Further away from (0,0) however, roundoff takes its toll. The point (1,1) is *computed* and therefore missed. For an adjacent patch, the actual point is *stored* as a patch corner, thus giving rise to the discontinuities shown in Figure 24.1. The significance of this phenomenon increases dramatically when curves or surfaces of high degrees are used.

One should not forget to mention the main attraction of the monomial form: speed. Horner's method is faster than the de Casteljau algorithm; its is also faster than the routine **hornbez**. There is a tradeoff therefore between stability and speed. (Given modern hardware, things are not quite that clear cut, however: T. DeRose and T. Holman [112] have developed a multiprocessor architecture that hardwires the de Casteljau algorithm into a network of processors and now outperforms Horner's method.)

24.4   The B-spline or the Hermite Form?

Cubic B-spline curves are numerically more stable than curves in the piecewise cubic Hermite form. This comes as no surprise, since some of the Hermite basis functions are negative, giving rise to numerically unstable nonconvex combinations. However, there is an argument in favor of the piecewise Hermite form: it stores interpolation points explicitly. In the B-spline form, they must be computed. Even if this computation is stable, it may produce roundoff.

As another argument in favor of the Hermite form, one might add that end conditions for C^2 spline interpolation are more easily formulated in the Hermite form than in the B-spline form.

A significant argument against the use of the Hermite form points to its lack of invariance under affine parameter transformations. Everyone who has programmed the Hermite form has probably experienced the trauma resulting from miscalculated tangent lengths. A programmer should not be burdened with the subtleties of the interplay between tangent lengths and parameter interval lengths.

An important advantage of the B-spline form is *storage*. For B-spline curves, one needs a control point array of length $n + 2$ plus a knot vector array of length $n + 1$ for a curve with n data points, resulting in an overall storage requirement of $4n + 7$ reals.[3] For the piecewise Hermite form, one needs an data array of length $2n$ (position and tangent at each data point) plus a knot vector of length $n + 1$, resulting in a storage requirement of $7n + 1$ reals. For surfaces (with same degrees in u and v for simplicity), the discrepancy becomes even larger: $3(n + 2)^2 + 2(n + 1)$ *vs* $12n^2 + 2(n + 1)$ reals (for the Hermite form, we have to store position, $u-$ and $v-$tangents, and twist for each data point).

When both forms are used for tensor product interpolation, the Hermite form must solve three sets of linear equations (see Section 17.6) while the B-spline form must solve only two sets (see Section 17.4).

24.5   Triangular or Rectangular Patches?

Most of the early CAD efforts were developed in the car industry, and this is perhaps the main reason for the predominance of rectangular patches in most CAD systems; the first applications of CAD methods to car body design were to the outer panels such as roof, doors, hood, etc. These parts basically have a rectangular geometry, hence it is natural to break them down into smaller rectangles. These smaller rectangles were then represented by rectangular patches.

Once a CAD system had been successfully applied to a design problem, it seemed natural to extend its use to other tasks: the design of the interior car body panels, for instance. Such structures do not possess a notably rectangular structure, and rectangular patches are therefore not a natu-

---

[3]We are not storing knot multiplicities. We would then be able to represent curves that are only C^0, which the cubic Hermite form is not capable of.

ral choice for modeling these complicated geometries. However, rectangle-based schemes already existed, and the obvious approach was to make them work in "unnatural" situations also. They do the job, although with some difficulties, which arise mainly in the case of degenerate rectangular patches.

Triangular patches do not suffer from such degeneracies and are thus better suited to describe complex geometries than are rectangular patches. It seems obvious, therefore, to advise any CAD system developer to add triangular patches to the system.

There is a catch: the very addition of a new patch type to an existing system is a formidable task in itself. This new patch type must be interfaced with every existing function that the system offers: a routine must be written for triangular patch/plane intersection, for the offset surface of a triangular patch, and so on. Adding the nice features of triangular patches to an existing system has its price, both in the development of new code and in its subsequent maintenance.

A different situation arises if a completely new system is to be developed. The extra cost for the inclusion of triangular patches into an emerging system is not nearly as high as that for the addition to an existing system. Such a new system would most likely profit from the additional flexibility offered by triangular patches enough to justify a higher implementation cost. Similar arguments hold for other non-four-sided patch types, as described in Sabin [306], Sabin and Kimura [308], Hosaka and Kimura [209], Gregory [184], and Varady [341].

We should add that a development of rectangular patches has blurred the clear distinction between patch types: This is the trimmed surface as discussed in Section 17.9. It can mimick multisided patches and seems to be a reasonable way to upgrade a rectangular surface system towards more versatility.

25

Quick Reference of Curve and Surface Terms

[1] **ab initio design**   Latin: from the beginning. Used to describe design processes in which the designer inputs his or her ideas directly into the computer, without constraints such as →interpolatory constraints.

Affine invariance   A property of a curve or surface generation scheme: it does not matter if computation of a point on a curve or surface occurs before or after an affine map is applied to the input data.

Affine map   Any map that is composed of translations, rotations, scalings, and shears. Maps parallels to parallels. Leaves ratios of →collinear points unchanged.

Affine combination   Same as a →barycentric combination.

Approximation   Fitting a curve or surface to given data. As opposed to →interpolation, the curve or surface approximation only has to be close to data.

Barycentric combination   A weighted average where the sum of the weights equals one.

Barycentric coordinates   A point in $I\!E^2$ may be written as a unique →barycentric combination of three points. The coefficients in this combination are its barycentric coordinates.

---

[1] Arrows refer to terms that are defined elsewhere in this glossary.

Basis function   Functions form linear spaces, which have bases. The elements of these bases are the basis functions.

Bernstein polynomial   The basis functions for →Bézier curves.

Beta-spline curve   A → G^2 piecewise cubic curve that is defined over a uniform knot sequence.

Bézier curve   A polynomial curve that is expressed in terms of →Bernstein polynomials.

Bézier polygon   The coefficients in the expansion of a →Bézier curve in terms of →Bernstein polynomials are → points. Connected according to their natural numbering, they form the Bézier polygon.

Bilinear patch   A patch that is →ruled in two directions. Or: a hyperbolic paraboloid.

Blossoming   The procedure of applying several →de Casteljau algorithm steps or several de Boor algorithm steps, but each one for a different parameter value.

B-spline   A piecewise polynomial function. It is defined over a →knot partition, has →local support, and is nonnegative. If a →spline curve is expressed in terms of B-splines, it is called a B-spline curve.

B-spline polygon   The coefficients in the expansion of a →B-spline curve in terms of →B-splines are →points. Connected according to their natural numbering, they form the B-spline polygon.

Breakpoint   Same as a →knot.

CAGD   Computer Aided Geometric Design.

Collinear   Being on a straight line.

Compatibility   For some interpolation problems, the input data may not be arbitrary but must satisfy some consistency constraints, called compatibility conditions.

Conic section   The intersection curve between a cone and a plane. Or: the projective image of a parabola. A nondegenerate conic is either an ellipse, a parabola, or a hyperbola.

Control polygon   See →Bézier polygon or →B-spline polygon.

Convex hull   The smallest convex set that contains a given set.

Convex curve   A planar curve that is a subset of the boundary of its convex hull.

Convex set   A set such that the straight line connecting any two points of the set is completely contained within the set.

Coons patch   A →patch that is fitted between four arbitrary boundary curves.

Cross plot   Breaking down the plot of a parametric curve into the plots of each coordinate function.

Curve   The path of a point moving through space. Or: the image of the real line under a continuous map.

Curvature   At a point on a curve, curvature is the inverse of the radius of the →osculating circle. Also: curvature measures by how much a curve deviates from a straight line at a given point.

de Boor algorithm   The algorithm that recursively computes a point on a →B-spline curve.

de Casteljau algorithm   The algorithm that recursively computes a point on a →Bézier curve.

Direct G^2 splines G^2 piecewise cubics that are generated by specifying a control polygon and some Bézier points.

Domain   The preimage of a curve or surface.

End condition   In cubic →spline curve interpolation, one can supply an extra condition at each of the two endpoints. Examples of such end conditions: prescribed tangents or zero curvature.

Frenet frame   At each point of a (nondegenerate) curve, the first, second, and third derivative vectors are linearly independent. Applying Gram-Schmidt orthonormalization to them yields the Frenet frame of the curve at the given point.

Functional curve or surface: A curve of the form $y = f(x)$ or a surface of the form $z = f(x, y)$.

G^2 spline curve   A C^1 piecewise cubic curve that is twice differentiable with respect to arc length.

γ-spline   A $\rightarrow G^2$ spline that is C^1 over a given knot sequence.

Geometric continuity   Smoothness properties of a curve or a surface that are more general than its order of differentiability.

Gordon surface   A generalization of → Coons patches. Interpolates to a rectilinear network of curves.

Hermite interpolation   Generating a curve or surface from data which consist of points and first and/or second derivatives.

Hodograph   The first derivative curve of a parametric curve.

Horner's scheme   An efficient method to evaluate a polynomial in → monomial form by nested multiplication.

Inflection point   A point on a curve where the tangent intersects the curve. Often corresponds to points with zero curvature.

Interior Bézier points   For curves: those Bézier points that are not →junction points. For surfaces: those Bézier points that are not boundary points.

Interpolation   Finding a curve or surface that satisfies some imposed constraints exactly. The most common constraint is the requirement of passing through a set of given points.

Junction point   A →spline curve is composed of →segments. The common point shared by two segments is called the junction point. See also →knot.

Knot   A →spline curve is defined over a partition of an interval of the real line. The points that define the partition are called knots. If evaluated at a knot, the spline curve passes through a →junction point.

Knot insertion   Adding a new knot to the knot sequence of a →B-spline curve without changing the graph of the curve.

Lagrange interpolation   Finding a polynomial curve through a given set of data points.

Linear precision   A property of many curve schemes: if the curve generation scheme is applied to equidistant points on a straight line, that straight line is reproduced.

Local control   A curve or surface scheme has the local control property if a change in the input data only changes the curve or surface in a region near the changed data.

Lofting   creating a →ruled surface between two given curves.

Minmax box   Smallest 2D or 3D box with edges parallel to the coordinate axes that completely contains a given object.

Monomial form   A polynomial is in monomial form if it is expressed in terms of the monomials $1, t, t^2, \ldots$

Node   A term that is used inconsistently in the literature: it sometimes refers to a knot, sometimes to a control vertex.

NURB   Nonuniform rational B-spline curve.

ν-spline   An →interpolating $\rightarrow G^2$ spline curve that is C^1 over a given knot sequence.

Osculating circle   At a given point, the osculating circle approximates the curve "better" than any other circle.

Osculating plane   The plane that contains the →osculating circle of a curve at a given point.

Oslo algorithm   The process of simultaneously inserting several →knots into a →B-spline curve.

Parametrization   Assigning parameter values to →junction points in →spline curves. Also used with a different meaning: the function that describes the speed of a point traversing a curve.

Patch   Complicated →surfaces are usually broken down into smaller units, called patches. For example, a →bicubic spline surface consists of a collection of → bicubic patches.

Point   A location in →space. If one uses coordinate systems to describe space, a point is represented as an $n-$tuple of real numbers.

Precision   A curve or surface generation scheme has n^{th} order precision if it reproduces polynomials of degree n.

Projective map   A map that is composed of →affine maps and central projections. Leaves cross ratios of →collinear points unchanged. Does (in general) not map parallels to parallels.

Quadric   A surface with the implicit representation $f(x, y, z) = 0$, where f is a quadratic polynomial. Or: the projective image of an elliptic paraboloid, a hyperbolic paraboloid, or a parabolic cylinder.

Rational curves and surfaces   Projections of nonrational (integral) curves or surfaces from 4-space into 3-space.

Ruled surface   A surface containing a family of straight lines. Obtained as linear interpolation between two given curves.

Segment   An individual polynomial (or rational polynomial) curve in an assembly of such curves to form a →spline curve. The bivariate analog of a segment is a →patch.

Shape parameter   A degree of freedom (usually one or several real numbers) in a curve or surface representation that can be used to fine tune the shape of that curve or surface.

Solid Modeling   The description of objects that are bounded by surfaces.

Space   The collection of all →points.

Spline curve   A continuous curve that is composed of several polynomial →segments. Spline curves are often represented in terms of →B-spline functions. They may be the result of an →interpolation process or of an →ab initio design process. If the segments are rational polynomials, we have a rational spline curve.

Subdivision   Breaking a curve or surface down into smaller pieces, usually recursively.

Support   The region over which a function is nonzero.

Surface   The locus of all points of a moving and deforming →curve. Or: the image of a region in 2-space under a continuous map. A surface is often broken down into →patches.

Tangent   The straight line that best approximates a smooth curve at a point on it. This straight line is parallel to the →tangent vector.

Tangent vector   The first derivative of a differentiable curve at a point on it. The length of the tangent vector depends on the →parametrization of the curve.

Tensor product   A method to generate rectangular surfaces using curve methods.

Torsion   A measure of how much a curve "curves away" from the →osculating plane at a given point.

Transfinite interpolation   Interpolating to curves, with infinitely, i.e., transfinitely many points on it, as opposed to discrete interpolation, which only interpolates to finitely many points.

Translational surface   A surface that is obtained by sweeping one curve along another one.

Triangular patch   A →patch whose →domain is is a triangle.

Trimmed surface   If the domain of a parametric surface is divided into "valid" and "invalid" regions, the image of the valid regions is called a trimmed surface.

Twist vector   The mixed second partial of a surface at a point. Note: not a geometric property of the surface, but parametrization dependent.

Variation diminution   Intuitively: a curve or surface scheme has this property if its output "wiggles less" than the data it is constructed from.

Vector   A direction. Usually the difference of two →points.

Volume deformation   A surface or a collection of surfaces may be embedded in a cube. That cube may then be deformed using some trivariate Bézier or B-spline method – this is the volume distortion – in order to change the shape of the initial surface(s).

Appendix 1

List of Programs

The following list contains all programs that are contained in the text.

Appendix 2

Notation

Here is the notation used in this book:

$\wedge$	cross product
$\dot{}, \ddot{}$	curve derivatives with respect to the current parameter
$', ''$	curve derivatives with respect to arc length
a, b, α, β	real numbers or real-valued functions
$\mathbf{0}$	short for (0,0,0)
$\mathbf{a}, \mathbf{b}$	points or vectors (possibly in terms of barycentric coordinates)
A, B	matrices
$\mathbf{A}, \mathbf{B}$	matrices whose elements are points ("hypermatrices")
$\mathbf{b}_i^r$	intermediate points in the de Casteljau algorithm
$B_i^n, B_{\mathbf{i}}^n$	Bernstein polynomials of degree n
$\mathbf{e1}, \mathbf{e2}, \mathbf{e3}$	short for (1,0,0), (0,1,0), and (0,0,1)
$I\!\!E^d$	$d-$dimensional euclidean space
$D_{\mathbf{d}}f$	directional derivative of f in the direction $\mathbf{d}$
Δ_i	difference in parameter intervals (i.e., $\Delta_i = u_{i+1} - u_i$)
Δ^r	iterated forward difference
H_i^3	cubic Hermite polynomials
$\mathbf{P}$	control polygon
Φ	an affine map
$\mathcal{P}_i$	operators
$||\mathbf{v}||$	(euclidean) length of the vector $\mathbf{v}$
$\mathbf{x}_u$	u-partial of $\mathbf{x}(u, v)$

Bibliography

[1] S. Abi-Ezzi. *The Graphical Processing of B-splines in a Highly Dynamic Environment*. PhD thesis, RPI, 1989. Rensselaer Design Research Center.

[2] T. Ackland. On osculatory interpolation, where the given values of the function are at unequal intervals. *J. Inst. Actuar.*, 49:369–375, 1915.

[3] J. Ahlberg, E. Nilson, and J. Walsh. *The Theory of Splines and their Applications*. Academic Press, 1967.

[4] H. Akima. A new method of interpolation and smooth curve fitting based on local procedures. *J. ACM*, 17(4):589–602, 1970.

[5] P. Alfeld. A bivariate C^2 Clough-Tocher scheme. *Computer Aided Geometric Design*, 1:257–267, 1984.

[6] P. Alfeld and L. Schumaker. The dimension of bivariate spline spaces of smoothness r and degree $d \geq 4r + 1$. *Constructive Approximation*, 3:189–197, 1987.

[7] R. Andersson, E. Andersson, M. Boman, B. Dahlberg, T. Elmroth, and B. Johansson. The automatic generation of convex surfaces. In R. Martin, editor, *The Mathematics of Surfaces II*, pages 427–446, Oxford University Press, 1987.

[8] A. Ball. Consurf I: introduction of the conic lofting tile. *Computer Aided Design*, 6(4):243–249, 1974.

[9] A. Ball. Consurf II: description of the algorithms. *Computer Aided Design*, 7(4):237–242, 1975.

[10] A. Ball. Consurf III: how the program is used. *Computer Aided Design*, 9(1):9–12, 1977.

[11] A. Ball. The parametric representation of curves and surfaces using rational polynomial functions. In R. Martin, editor, *The Mathematics of Surfaces II*, pages 39–62, Oxford University Press, 1987.

[12] A. Ball. Reparametrization and its application in computer-aided geometric design. *Int J for Num Methods in Eng*, 20:197–216, 1984.

[13] R. Barnhill. Coons' patches. *Computers in Industry*, 3:37–43, 1982.

[14] R. Barnhill. Representations and approximation of surfaces. In J. R. Rice, editor, *Mathematical Software III*, Academic Press, 1977.

[15] R. Barnhill. Smooth interpolation over triangles. In R. Barnhill and R. Riesenfeld, editors, *Computer Aided Geometric Design*, pages 45–70, Academic Press, 1974.

[16] R. Barnhill. Surfaces in computer aided geometric design: a survey with new results. *Computer Aided Geometric Design*, 2:1–17, 1985.

[17] R. Barnhill. A survey of the representation and design of surfaces. *IEEE Computer Graphics and Applications*, 3:9–16, 1983.

[18] R. Barnhill, G. Birkhoff, and W. Gordon. Smooth interpolation in triangles. *J. Approx. Theory*, 8(2):114–128, 1973.

[19] R. Barnhill, J. Brown, and I. Klucewicz. A new twist in CAGD. *Computer Graphics and Image Processing*, 1978.

[20] R. Barnhill and G. Farin. C^1 quintic interpolation over triangles: two explicit representations. *Int. J. Num Methods in Engineering*, 17:1763–1778, 1981.

[21] R. Barnhill, G. Farin, M. Jordan, and B. Piper. Surface / surface intersection. *Computer Aided Geometric Design*, 4(1-2):3–16, 1987.

[22] R. Barnhill and J. Gregory. Blending function interpolation to boundary data on triangles. *Mathematics of Computation*, 29(131):726–735, 1975.

[23] R. Barnhill and R. F. Riesenfeld, editors. *Computer Aided Geometric Design*. Academic Press, 1974.

[24] P. Barry and R. Goldman. De Casteljau-type subdivision is peculiar to Bézier curves. *Computer Aided Design*, 20(3):114–116, 1988.

[25] P. Barry and R. Goldman. A recursive proof of a B-spline identity for degree elevation. *Computer Aided Geometric Design*, 5(2):173–175, 1988.

[26] B. Barsky. *The Beta-spline: a local representation based on shape parameters and fundamental geometric measures*. PhD thesis, Dept. of computer science, University of Utah, 1981.

[27] B. Barsky. *Computer Graphics and Geometric Modeling using Beta-splines*. Springer Verlag, 1988.

[28] B. Barsky. Exponential and polynomial methods for applying tension to an interpolating spline curve. *Computer Vision, Graphics, and Image Processing*, 27:1–18, 1984.

[29] B. Barsky and J. Beatty. *Varying the Betas in Beta-splines*. Technical Report CS-82-49, University of Waterloo, Waterloo, Ontario, Canada N31 3G1, December 1982.

[30] B. Barsky and T. DeRose. The beta2-spline: a special case of the beta-spline curve and surface representation. *IEEE Computer Graphics and Applications*, 5(9):46–58, 1985.

[31] B. Barsky and T. DeRose. *Geometric Continuity of Parametric Curves*. Technical Report UCB/CSB 84/205, University of California, Computer Science Division, University of California, Berkley, California 94720, October 1984.

[32] B. Barsky and D. Greenberg. Determining a set of B-spline control vertices to generate an interpolating surface. *Computer Graphics and Image Processing*, 14:203–209, 1979.

[33] B. Barsky and S. Thomas. TRANSPLINE – a system for representing curves using transformations among four spline formulations. *The Computer J*, 24(3):271–277, 1981.

[34] R. Bartels, J. Beatty, and B. Barsky. *An Introduction to Splines for Use in Computer Graphics and Geometric Modeling*. Morgan Kaufmann, 1987.

[35] R. Bartles and J. Beatty. *Beta-Splines with a Difference*. Technical Report CS-83-40, University of Waterloo, Computer Science Department, University of Waterloo, Waterloo, Ontario, Canada N2L 3G1, May 1984.

[36] J. Beck, R. Farouki, and J. Hinds. Surface analysis methods. *IEEE Computer Graphics and Applications*, 6(12):18–36, 1986.

[37] E. Beeker. Smoothing of shapes designed with free-form surfaces. *Computer Aided Design*, 18(4):224–232, 1986.

[38] G. Behforooz and N.Papamichael. End conditions for interpolatory cubic splines with unequally spaced knots. *J of Comp Appl Math*, 6(1), 1980.

[39] M. Berger. *Geometry I*. Springer-Verlag, 1987.

[40] S. Bernstein. Démonstration du théorème de Weierstrass fondeé sur le calcul des probabilités. *Harkov Soobs. Matem ob-va*, 13:1–2, 1912.

[41] H. Bez. On invariant curve forms. *Computer Aided Geometric Design*, 3(3):193–204, 1986.

[42] P. Bézier. Définition numérique des courbes et surfaces I. *Automatisme*, 11:625–632, 1966.

[43] P. Bézier. Définition numérique des courbes et surfaces II. *Automatisme*, 12:17–21, 1967.

[44] P. Bézier. *Essay de définition numérique des courbes et des surfaces expérimentales*. PhD thesis, University of Paris VI, 1977.

[45] P. Bézier. General distortion of an ensemble of biparametric patches. *Computer Aided Design*, 10(2):116–120, 1978.

[46] P. Bézier. Mathematical and practical possibilities of UNISURF. In R. Barnhill and R. Riesenfeld, editors, *Computer Aided Geometric Design*, Academic Press, 1974.

[47] P. Bézier. *The Mathematical Basis of the UNISURF CAD System*. Butterworths, London, 1986.

[48] P. Bézier. *Numerical Control: Mathematics and Applications*. Wiley, 1972. translated by R. Forrest.

[49] P. Bézier. Procédé de définition numérique des courbes et surfaces non mathématiques. *Automatisme*, XIII(5), 1968.

[50] G. Birkhoff. *Aesthetic Measure*. Harvard University Press, 1933.

[51] W. Boehm. Cubic B-spline curves and surfaces in computer aided geometric design. *Computing*, 19:29–34, 1977.

[52] W. Boehm. Curvature continuous curves and surfaces. *Computer Aided Geometric Design*, 2(2):313–323, 1985.

[53] W. Boehm. Generating the Bézier points of B-splines. *Computer Aided Design*, 13(6), 1981.

[54] W. Boehm. Inserting new knots into B-spline curves. *Computer Aided Design*, 12(4):199–201, 1980.

[55] W. Boehm. On Cubics: A Survey. *Computer Graphics and Image Processing*, 19:201–226, 1982.

[56] W. Boehm. On the definition of geometric continuity. *Computer Aided Design*, 20(7):370–372, 1988. Letter to the editor.

[57] W. Boehm. Parameterdarstellung kubischer und bikubischer Splines. *Computing*, 17:87–92, 1976.

[58] W. Boehm. Rational geometric splines. *Computer Aided Geometric Design*, 4(1-2):67–78, 1987.

[59] W. Boehm. Smooth curves and surfaces. In G. Farin, editor, *Geometric Modeling: Algorithms and New Trends*, pages 221–234, SIAM, Philadelphia, 1987.

[60] W. Boehm. Visual continuity. *Computer Aided Design*, 20(6):307–311, 1988.

[61] W. Boehm, G. Farin, and J. Kahmann. A survey of curve and surface methods in CAGD. *Computer Aided Geometric Design*, 1(1):1–60, 1984.

[62] G. Bol. *Projective Differential Geometry, Vol. 1*. Vandenhoeck and Ruprecht, Goettingen, 1950. In German.

[63] J. Brewer and D. Anderson. Visual interaction with Overhauser curves and surfaces. *Computer Graphics*, 11(2):132–137, 1977.

[64] I. Brueckner. Construction of Bézier points of quadrilaterals from those of triangles. *Computer Aided Design*, 12(1):21–24, 1980.

[65] P. Brunet. Increasing the smoothness of bicubic spline surfaces. *Computer Aided Geometric Design*, 2(1-3):157–164, 1985.

[66] B. Buchberger. Applications of Groebner bases in non-linear computational geometry. In J. Rice, editor, *Mathematical Aspects of Scientific Software*, Springer-Verlag, 1988.

[67] Su Bu-Qing and Liu Ding-Yuan. *Computational Geometry*. Academic Press, 1989.

[68] C. Calladine. Gaussian curvature and shell structures. In J. Gregory, editor, *The Mathematics of Surfaces*, pages 179–196, Clarendon Press, 1986.

[69] M. Casale and J. Bobrow. A set operation algorithm for sculptured solids modeled with trimmed patches. *Computer Aided Geometric Design*, 6(3):235–248, 1989.

[70] E. Catmull and J. Clark. Recursively generated B-spline surfaces on arbitrary topological meshes. *Computer Aided Design*, 10(6):350–355, 1978.

[71] E. Catmull and R. Rom. A class of interpolating splines. In R. Barnhill and R. Riesenfeld, editors, *Computer Aided Geometric Design*, pages 317–326, Academic Press, 1974.

[72] G. Chaikin. An algorithm for high speed curve generation. *Computer Graphics and Image Processing*, 3:346–349, 1974.

[73] G. Chang. Matrix formulation of Bézier technique. *Computer Aided Design*, 14(6), 1982.

[74] G. Chang and P. Davis. The convexity of Bernstein polynomials over triangles. *J Approx Theory*, 40:11–28, 1984.

[75] G. Chang and Y. Feng. An improved condition for the convexity of Bernstein-Bézier surfaces over triangles. *Computer Aided Geometric Design*, 1:279–283, 1985.

[76] S. Chang, M. Shantz, and R. Rochetti. Rendering cubic curves and surfaces with integer adaptive forward differencing. *Computer Graphics*, 23(3):157–166, 1989. SIGGRAPH '89 Proceedings.

[77] P. Charrot and J. Gregory. A pentagonal surface patch for computer aided geometric design. *Computer Aided Geometric Design*, 1(1), 1984.

[78] H. Chiyokura and F. Kimura. Design of solids with free-form surfaces. *Computer Graphics*, 17(3):289–298, 1983.

[79] R. Clough and J. Tocher. Finite element stiffness matrices for analysis of plates in blending. In *Proceedings of Conference on Matrix Methods in Structural Analysis*, 1965.

[80] J. Cobb. Letter to the editor. *Computer Aided Geometric Design*, 6:85, 1989. Concerning Piegl's sphere approximation.

[81] J. Cobb. *A rational bicubic representation of the sphere.* Technical Report, Computer science, U. of Utah, 1988.

[82] E. Cohen. A new local basis for designing with tensioned splines. *ACM Transactions on Graphics*, 6:81–112, 1987.

[83] E. Cohen, T. Lyche, and R. Riesenfeld. Discrete B-splines and subdivision techniques in computer aided geometric design and computer graphics. *Comp. Graphics and Image Process.*, 14(2):87–111, 1980.

[84] S. Coons. *Méthode Matricielle.* Hermes, Paris, 1987. Translation from English by P. Bézier and M. Moronval.

[85] S. Coons. *rational bicubic surface patches.* Technical Report, MIT, 1968. Project MAC.

[86] S. Coons. Surface patches and B-spline curves. In R. Barnhill and R. Riesenfeld, editors, *Computer Aided Geometric Design*, Academic Press, 1974.

[87] S. Coons. *Surfaces for computer aided design.* Technical Report, MIT, 1964. Available as AD 663 504 from the National Technical Information service, Springfield, VA 22161.

[88] S. Coons. *Surfaces for computer aided design of space forms.* Technical Report, MIT, 1967. Project MAC-TR 41.

[89] M. Cox. *The numerical evaluation of B-splines.* DNAC 4, National Physical Laboratory, 1971.

[90] H. Coxeter. *Introduction to Geometry.* Wiley, 1961.

[91] M. Daniel and J. Daubisse. The numerical problem of using Bézier curves and surfaces in the power basis. *Computer Aided Geometric Design*, 6(2):121–128, 1989.

[92] P. Davis. *Interpolation and Approximation.* Dover, New York, 1975. first edition 1963.

[93] P. Davis. Lecture notes on CAGD. 1976. Given at the Univ. of Utah.

[94] C. de Boor. B-form basics. In G. Farin, editor, *Geometric Modeling: Algorithms and New Trends*, pages 131–148, SIAM, Philadelphia, 1987.

[95] C. de Boor. Bicubic spline interpolation. *J. Math. Phys.*, 41:212–218, 1962.

[96] C. de Boor. Cutting corners always works. *Computer Aided Geometric Design*, 4(1-2):125–132, 1987.

[97] C. de Boor. On calculating with B-splines. *J. Approx. Theory*, 6:50–62, 1972.

[98] C. de Boor. *A Practical Guide to Splines.* Springer, 1978.

[99] C. de Boor and R. de Vore. A geometric proof of total positivity for spline interpolation. *Mathematics of Computation*, 45(172):497–504, 1985.

[100] C. de Boor and K. Hollig. B-splines without divided differences. In G. Farin, editor, *Geometric Modeling - Algorithms and New Trends*, pages 21–27, SIAM, Philadelphia, 1987.

[101] C. de Boor, K. Hollig, and M. Sabin. High accuracy geometric Hermite interpolation. *Computer Aided Geometric Design*, 4(4):269–278, 1988.

[102] P. de Casteljau. *Courbes et surfaces à poles*. Technical Report, A. Citroen, Paris, 1963.

[103] P. de Casteljau. *Outillages méthodes calcul*. Technical Report, A. Citroen, Paris, 1959.

[104] P. de Casteljau. *Shape Mathematics and CAD*. Kogan Page, London, 1986.

[105] G. de Rham. Sur une courbe plane. *J. Math. Pures Appl.*, 35:25–42, 1956. Also in Collected Works, 696-713.

[106] G. de Rham. Un peu de mathématique à propos d'une courbe plane. *Elem. Math*, 2:73–76; 89–97, 1947. Also in Collected Works, 678-689.

[107] A. DeRose. *Geometric Continuity: A Parametrization Independent Measure of Continuity for Computer Aided Geometric Design*. PhD thesis, Berkeley, 1985. also tech report UCB/CSD 86/255.

[108] T. DeRose. Composing Bézier simplices. *ACM Transactions on Graphics*, 7(3):198–221, 1988.

[109] T. DeRose. Geometric programming. In R. Goldman, editor, *SIGGRAPH '88 course notes*, 1988.

[110] T. DeRose. Necessary and sufficient conditions for G^1 continuity of adjacent Bézier patches. 1989. submitted for publication.

[111] T. DeRose and B. Barsky. Geometric continuity, shape parameters, and geometric constructions for Catmull-Rom splines. *ACM Transactions on Graphics*, 7(1):1–41, 1988.

[112] T. DeRose and T. Holman. *The triangle: a multiprocessor architecture for fast curve and surface generation*. Technical Report, Computer Science Department, Univ. of Washington, 1987. Tech Report 87-08-07.

[113] J. Dill. An application of color graphics to the display of surface curvature. *Computer Graphics*, 15:153–161, 1981.

[114] M. do Carmo. *Differential Geometry of Curves and Surfaces*. Prentice Hall, Englewood Cliffs, 1976.

[115] T. Dokken. Finding intersections of B-spline represented geometries using recursive subdivision techniques. *Computer Aided Geometric Design*, 2(1-3):1189–196, 1985.

[116] Tor Dokken, Vibeke, and Anne-Marie Ytrehus. Recursive subdivision and iteration in intersections and related problems. In T. Lyche and L. Schumaker, editors, *Mathematical Methods in Computer Aided Geometric Design*, pages 207–214, Academic Press, 1989.

[117] D. Doo and M. Sabin. Behaviour of recursive division surfaces near extraordinary points. *Computer Aided Design*, 10(6):356–360, 1978.

[118] N. Dyn and C. Micchelli. *Piecewise polynomial spaces and geometric continuity of curves.* Technical Report, IBM report RCC11390, Yorktown Heights, 1985.

[119] M. Epstein. On the influence of parametrization in parametric interpolation. *SIAM J. Numer. Anal*, 13:261–268, 1976.

[120] G. Farin. Algorithms for rational Bézier curves. *Computer Aided Design*, 15(2):73–77, 1983.

[121] G. Farin. *Bézier polynomials over triangles and the construction of piecewise C^r polynomials.* Technical Report TR/91, Brunel University, Uxbridge, England, 1980.

[122] G. Farin. Commutativity between tensor product and coons-type operators. *Rocky Mountain J. of Mathematics*, 1989. to appear.

[123] G. Farin. A construction for the visual C^1 continuity of polynomial surface patches. *Computer Graphics and Image Processing*, 20:272–282, 1982.

[124] G. Farin. Curvature continuity and offsets for piecewise conics. *ACM Transactions on Graphics*, 8(2):89–99, 1989.

[125] G. Farin. Designing C^1 surfaces consisting of triangular cubic patches. *Computer Aided Design*, 14(5):253–256, 1982.

[126] G. Farin. *Konstruktion und Eigenschaften von Bézier-Kurven und - Flächen.* Master's thesis, Technical University Braunschweig, FRG, 1977.

[127] G. Farin. Piecewise triangular C^1 surface strips. *Computer Aided Design*, 18(1):45–47, 1986.

[128] G. Farin. Some aspects of car body design at Daimler-Benz. In R. Barnhill and W. Boehm, editors, *Surfaces in Computer Aided Geometric Design*, North-Holland, 1982.

[129] G. Farin. Some remarks on V^2 - splines. *Computer Aided Geometric Design*, 2(2):325–328, 1985.

[130] G. Farin. *Subsplines ueber Dreiecken.* PhD thesis, Technical University Braunschweig, FRG, 1979.

[131] G. Farin. Triangular Bernstein-Bézier patches. *Computer Aided Geometric Design*, 3(2):83–128, 1986.

[132] G. Farin. Visually C^2 cubic splines. *Computer Aided Design*, 14(3):137–139, 1982.

[133] G. Farin and P. Barry. A link between Lagrange and Bézier curve and surface schemes. *Computer Aided Design*, 18:525–528, 1986.

[134] G. Farin and H. Hagen. Local twist estimation. submitted for publication.

[135] G. Farin, D. Hansford, and A. Worsey. Results on the singular cases for interpolating γ-splines. *Computer Aided Geometric Design*, 7, 1990.

[136] G. Farin, B. Piper, and A. Worsey. The octant of a sphere as a non-degenerate triangular Bézier patch. *Computer Aided Geometric Design*, 4(4):329–332, 1988.

[137] G. Farin, G. Rein, N. Sapidis, and A. Worsey. Fairing cubic B-spline curves. *Computer Aided Geometric Design*, 4(1-2):91–104, 1987.

[138] G. Farin and N. Sapidis. Curvature and the fairness of curves and surfaces. *IEEE Computer Graphics and Applications*, 9(2):52–57, 1989.

[139] R. Farouki. The approximation of non-degenerate offset surfaces. *Computer Aided Geometric Design*, 3(1):15–44, 1986.

[140] R. Farouki. Direct surface section evaluation. In G. Farin, editor, *Geometric Modeling: Algorithms and New Trends*, pages 319–334, SIAM, Philadelphia, 1987.

[141] R. Farouki. Exact offset procedures for simple solids. *Computer Aided Geometric Design*, 2(4):257–279, 1985.

[142] R. Farouki and J. Hinds. A hierarchy of geometric forms. *IEEE Computer Graphics and Applications*, 5(5):51–78, 1985.

[143] R. Farouki and V. Rajan. Algorithms for polynomials in Bernstein form. *Computer Aided Geometric Design*, 5(1):1–26, 1988.

[144] R. Farouki and V. Rajan. On the numerical condition of polynomials in Bernstein form. *Computer Aided Geometric Design*, 4(3):191–216, 1987.

[145] I. Faux and M. Pratt. *Computational Geometry for Design and Manufacture*. Ellis Horwood, 1979.

[146] L. Fayard. *The use of curvatures as a surface interrogation tool*. Master's thesis, Arizona State Univ., 1988.

[147] D. Ferguson. Construction of curves and surfaces using numerical optimization techniques. *Computer Aided Design*, 18(1):15–21, 1986.

[148] J. Ferguson. Multivariable curve interpolation. *JACM*, II/2:221–228, 1964.

[149] D. Field. Mathematical problems in solid modeling: a brief survey. In G. Farin, editor, *Geometric Modeling: Algorithms and New Trends*, pages 91–108, SIAM, Philadelphia, 1987.

[150] D. Filip. Adaptive subdivision algorithms for a set of Bézier triangles. *Computer Aided Design*, 18(2):74–78, 1986.

[151] N. Fog. Creative definition and fairing of ship hulls using a B-spline surface. *Computer Aided Design*, 16(4):225–230, 1984.

[152] J. Foley and A. Van Dam. *Fundamentals of Interactive Computer Graphics*. Addison-Wesley, 1982.

[153] T. Foley. Interpolation with interval and point tension controls using cubic weighted ν − splines. *ACM Transactions on Math. Software*, 13(1):68–96, 1987.

[154] T. Foley. Local control of interval tension using weighted splines. *Computer Aided Geometric Design*, 3(4):281–294, 1986.

[155] A. Forrest. *Curves and surfaces for computer-aided design.* PhD thesis, Cambridge, 1968.

[156] A. Forrest. Interactive interpolation and approximation by Bézier polynomials. *Computer J*, 15:71–79, 1972.

[157] A. Forrest. On Coons and other methods for the representation of curved surfaces. *Computer Graphics and Image Processing*, 1:341–359, 1972.

[158] A. Forrest. On the rendering of surfaces. *Computer Graphics*, 13:253–259, 1979.

[159] A. Forrest. The twisted cubic curve: a computer-aided geometric design approach. *Computer Aided Design*, 12(4):165–172, 1980.

[160] L. Frederickson. *Triangular spline interpolation/Generalized triangular splines.* Technical Report, Lakehead University, Canada, 1971. Math reports no. 6 / 70 and 7/71.

[161] F. Fritsch. Energy comparison of Wilson-Fowler splines with other interpolating splines. In G. Farin, editor, *Geometric Modeling: Algorithms and New Trends*, pages 185–202, SIAM, Philadelphia, 1987.

[162] F. Fritsch and R. Carlson. Monotone piecewise cubic interpolation. *SIAM J. Numer. Anal.*, 17(2):238–246, 1980.

[163] D. Gans. *Transformations and Geometries.* Appleton-Century-Crofts, 1969.

[164] G. Geise. Über berührende Kegelschnitte ebener Kurven. *ZAMM*, 42:297–304, 1962.

[165] A. Geisow. *Surface interrogations.* PhD thesis, Univ. of East Anglia, 1983.

[166] A. Glassner, editor. *An Introduction to Ray Tracing.* Academic Press, 1989.

[167] R. Goldman. Illicit expressions in vector algebra. *ACM Transactions on Graphics*, 4(3):223–243, 1985.

[168] R. Goldman. The method of resolvents: a technique for the implicitization, inversion, and intersection of non-planar, parametric, rational cubic curves. *Computer Aided Geometric Design*, 2(4):237–255, 1985.

[169] R. Goldman. Using degenerate Bézier triangles and tetrahedra to subdivide Bézier curves. *Computer Aided Design*, 14(6):307–312, 1982.

[170] R. Goldman and T. DeRose. Recursive subdivision without the convex hull property. *Computer Aided Geometric Design*, 3(4):247–266, 1986.

[171] R. Goldman and C. Micchelli. Algebraic aspects of geometric continuity. In T. Lyche and L. Schumaker, editors, *Mathematical Methods in Computer Aided Geometric Design*, pages 313–332, Academic Press, 1989.

[172] H. Gonska and J. Meier. A bibliography on approximation of functions by Bernstein type operators. In L. Schumaker and K. Chui, editors, *Approximation Theory IV*, Academic Press, 1983.

[173] T. Goodman. Properties of Beta-splines. *J. Approx. Theory*, 44(2):132–153, 1985.

[174] T. Goodman. *Shape preserving interpolation by parametric rational cubic splines*. Technical Report, University of Dundee, 1988. Department of Mathematics and Computer Scinece.

[175] T. Goodman and K. Unsworth. Generation of β-spline curves using a recurrence relation. *NATO ASI series F*, 17:325–353, 1985.

[176] T. Goodman and K. Unsworth. Manipulating shape and producing geometric continuity in beta-spline surfaces. *IEEE Computer Graphics and Applications*, 6(2):50–56, 1986.

[177] W. Gordon. Blending-function methods of bivariate and multivariate interpolation and approximation. *SIAM J Num Analysis*, 8(1):158–177, 1969.

[178] W. Gordon. Distributive lattices and the approximation of multivariate functions. In I. Schoenberg, editor, *Approximation with Special Emphasis on Splines*, University of Wisconsin Press, Madison, 1969.

[179] W. Gordon. *Free-form Surface Interpolation through Curve Networks*. Technical Report GMR-921, General Motors Research Laboratories, 1969.

[180] W. Gordon. Spline-blended surface interpolation through curve networks. *J of Math and Mechanics*, 18(10):931–952, 1969.

[181] W. Gordon and R. Riesenfeld. B-spline curves and surfaces. In R. E. Barnhill and R. F. Riesenfeld, editors, *Computer Aided Geometric Design*, pages 95–126, Academic Press, 1974.

[182] T. Gossing. Bulge, shear and squash: a representation for the general conic arc. *Computer Aided Design*, 13(2):81–84, 1981.

[183] T. Grandine. Computing zeroes of splines functions. *Computer Aided Geometric Design*, 6(2):129–136, 1989.

[184] J. Gregory. N-sided surface patches. In J. Gregory, editor, *The Mathematics of Surfaces*, pages 217–232, Clarendon Press, 1986.

[185] J. Gregory. Smooth interpolation without twist constraints. In R. E. Barnhill and R. F. Riesenfeld, editors, *Computer Aided Geometric Design*, pages 71–88, Academic Press, 1974.

[186] J. Gregory and P. Charrot. A C^1 triangular interpolation patch for computer-aided geometric design. *Computer Graphics and Image Processing*, 13:80–87, 1980.

[187] J. Gregory and J. Hahn. Geometric continuity and convex combination patches. *Computer Aided Geometric Design*, 4(1-2):79–90, 1987.

[188] John A. Gregory. Geometric continuity. In T. Lyche and L. Schumaker, editors, *Mathematical Methods in Computer Aided Geometric Design*, pages 353–372, Academic Press, 1989.

[189] T. Greville. Introduction to spline functions. In T. Greville, editor, *Theory and Applications of Spline Functions*, pages 1–36, Academic Press, 1969.

[190] T. Greville. On the normalization of the B-splines and the location of the nodes for the case of unequally spaced knots. In O. Shisha, editor, *Inequalities*, Academic Press, 1967. Supplement to the paper 'On spline functions' by I. Schoenberg.

[191] E. Grosse. Tensor spline approximation. *Linear Algebra and its Applications*, 34:29–41, 1980.

[192] H. Hagen. Bézier-curves with curvature and torsion continuity. *Rocky Mtn. J. of Math.*, 16(3):629–638, 1986.

[193] H. Hagen. Geometric spline curves. *Computer Aided Geometric Design*, 2(1-3):223–228, 1985.

[194] H. Hagen. Geometric surface patches without twist constraints. *Computer Aided Geometric Design*, 3:179–184, 1986.

[195] H. Hagen and H. Pottmann. Curvature continuous triangular interpolants. In T. Lyche and L. Schumaker, editors, *Mathematical Methods in Computer Aided Geometric Design*, pages 373–384, Academic Press, 1989.

[196] H. Hagen and G. Schulze. Automatic smoothing with geometric surface patches. *Computer Aided Geometric Design*, 4(3):231–236, 1987.

[197] J. Hahn. Geometric continuous patch complexes. *Computer Aided Geometric Design*, 6(1):11–22, 1989.

[198] J. Hands. Reparametrisation of rational surfaces. In R. Martin, editor, *The Mathematics of Surfaces II*, pages 87–100, Oxford University Press, 1987.

[199] S. Hanna, J. Abel, and D. Greenberg. Intersection of parametric surfaces by means of lookup tables. *IEEE Computer Graphics and Applications*, 3(7):39–48, 1983.

[200] P. Hartley and C. Judd. Parametrization and shape of B-spline curves. *Computer Aided Design*, 12(5):235–238, 1980.

[201] P. Hartley and C. Judd. Parametrization of Bézier-type B-spline curves. *Computer Aided Design*, 10(2):130–1345, 1978.

[202] J. Hayes. *New Shapes from Bicubic Splines*. Technical Report, National Physics Laboratory, 1974.

[203] L. Hering. Closed C^2 and C^3 continuous Bézier and B-spline curves with given tangents. *Computer Aided Design*, 15(1):3–6, 1983.

[204] G. Herron. Techniques for visual continuity. In G. Farin, editor, *Geometric Modeling*, pages 163–174, SIAM, Philadelphia, 1987.

[205] D. Hilbert and S. Cohn-Vossen. *Geometry and the Imagination*. Chelsea, New York, 1952.

[206] G. Hoelzle. Knot placement for piecewise polynomial approximation of curves. *Computer Aided Design*, 15(5):295–296, 1983.

[207] C. Hoffmann. *Geometric & Solid Modeling*. Morgan Kaufmann, 1989.

[208] J. Holladay. Smoothest curve approximation. *Math. Tables Aids Computation*, 11:233–243, 1957.

[209] M. Hosaka and F. Kimura. Non-four-sided patch expressions with control points. *Computer Aided Geometric Design*, 1(1), 1984.

[210] J. Hoschek. Detecting regions with undesirable curvature. *Computer Aided Geometric Design*, 18(2):183–192, 1984.

[211] J. Hoschek. Dual Bézier curves and surfaces. In R. Barnhill and W. Boehm, editors, *Surfaces in Computer Aided Geometric Design*, pages 147–156, North-Holland, 1985.

[212] J. Hoschek. Offset curves in the plane. *Computer Aided Design*, 17(2), 1985.

[213] J. Hoschek. Smoothing of curves and surfaces. *Computer Aided Geometric Design*, 2(1-3):97–105, 1985.

[214] J. Hoschek. Spline approximation of offset curves. *Computer Aided Geometric Design*, 5(1):33–40, 1988.

[215] J. Hoschek and D. Lasser. *Grundlagen derGeometrischen Datenverarbeitung*. B.G. Teubner, Stuttgart, 1989.

[216] J. Hoschek and D. Liu. Conditions for G1 continuity of adjacent Bézier patches. 1989. submitted for publication.

[217] J. Hoschek and N. Wissel. Optimal approximate conversion of spline curves and spline approximation of offse curves. *Computer Aided Design*, 20(8):475–483, 1988.

[218] E. Houghton, E. Emnett, R. Factor, and L. Sabharwal. Implementation of a divide-and-conquer-method for the intersection of parametric surfaces. *Computer Aided Geometric Design*, 2(1-3):173–184, 1985.

[219] T. Jensen. Assembling triangular and rectangular patches and multivariate splines. In G. Farin, editor, *Geometric Modeling: Algorithms and New Trends*, pages 203–222, SIAM, Philadelphia, 1987.

[220] A. Jones. *An Algorithm for Convex Parametric Splines*. Technical Report ETA-TR-29, Boeing Computer Services, 1985.

[221] A. Jones. Nonrectangular surface patches with curvature continuity. *Computer Aided Design*, 20(6):3325–335, 1988.

[222] A. Jones. Shape control of curves and surfaces through constrained optimization. In G. Farin, editor, *Geometric Modeling: Algorithms and New Trends*, pages 265–280, SIAM, Philadelphia, 1987.

[223] J. Kahmann. Continuity of curvature between adjacent Bézier patches. In R. Barnhill and W. Boehm, editors, *Surfaces in Computer Aided Geometric Design*, pages 65–76, North-Holland, 1982.

[224] E. Kaufmann and R. Klass. Smoothing surfaces using reflection lines for families of splines. *Computer Aided Design*, 20(6):312–316, 1988.

[225] J. Kjellander. Smoothing of bicubic parametric surfaces. *Computer Aided Design*, 15(5):288–293, 1983.

[226] J. Kjellander. Smoothing of cubic parametric splines. *Computer Aided Design*, 15(3):175–179, 1983.

[227] R. Klass. Correction of local surface irregularities using reflection lines. *Computer Aided Design*, 12(2):73–77, 1980.

[228] R. Klass. An offset spline approximation for plane cubics. *Computer Aided Design*, 15(5):296–299, 1983.

[229] P. Korovkin. *Linear Operators and Approximation Theory*. Hindustan Publishing Co., Delhi, 1960.

[230] C. Lacombe and C. Bédard. Interpolation functin over a general triangular mid-edge finite element. *Comp. Math. Appl.*, 12A(3):362–373, 1986.

[231] P. Lancaster and K. Salkauskas. *Curve and Surface Fitting*. Academic Press, 1986.

[232] J. Lane and R. Riesenfeld. A geometric proof for the variation diminishing property of B-spline approximation. *J of Approx Theory*, 37:1–4, 1983.

[233] J. Lane and R. Riesenfeld. A theoretical development for the computer generation and display of piecewise polynomial surfaces. *IEEE Trans. Pattern Anal. Machine Intell.*, 2(1):35–46, 1980.

[234] D. Lasser. Bernstein-Bézier representation of volumes. *Computer Aided Geometric Design*, 2(1-3):145–150, 1985.

[235] D. Lasser. Intersection of parametric surfaces in the Bernstein-Bézier representation. *Computer Aided Design*, 18(4):186–192, 1986.

[236] B. Lee and D. Fredericks. Intersection of parametric surface patches and a plane. *IEEE Computer Graphics and Applications*, 4(8):48–51, 1984.

[237] E. Lee. Choosing nodes in parametric curve interpolation. *Computer Aided Design*, 21(6), 1989. Presented at the SIAM Applied Geometry meeting, Albany, N.Y., 1987.

[238] E. Lee. The rational Bézier representation for conics. In G. Farin, editor, *Geometric Modeling: Algorithms and New Trends*, pages 3–19, SIAM, Philadelphia, 1987.

[239] J. Levin. Mathematical models for determining the intersection of quadric surfaces. *Computer Graphics and Image Processing*, 11:73–87, 1979.

[240] G. Levner, P. Tassinari, and D. Marini. A simple method for raytracing bicubic surfaces. In R. Earnshaw, editor, *Theoretical Foundations of Computer Graphics and CAD*, pages 805–820, Springer Verlag, 1988.

[241] J. Lewis. 'B-spline' bases for splines under tension, nu-splines, and fractional order splines. 1975. Presented at the SIAM-SIGNUM-meeting, San Francisco, Dec. 3-5.

[242] S. Lien, M. Shantz, and V. Pratt. Adaptive forward differencing for rendering curves and surfaces. *Computer Graphics*, 21, 1987. SIGGRAPH '87 proceedings.

[243] R. Liming. *Mathematics for Computer Graphics*. Aero publishers, 1979.

[244] R. Liming. *Practical Analytical Geometry with Applications to Aircraft*. Macmillan, 1944.

[245] G. Lorentz. *Bernstein Polynomials*. Toronto press, 1953.

[246] T. Lyche and V. Morken. Knot removal for parametric B-spline curves and surfaces. *Computer Aided Geometric Design*, 4(3):217–230, 1987.

[247] J.R. Manning. Continuity conditions for spline curves. *The Computer Journal*, 17:181–186, 1974.

[248] M. Mantyla. *An Introduction to Solid Modeling*. Computer Science Press, Rockville, Md, 1988.

[249] R. Markot and R. Magedson. Solutions of tangential surface and curve intersections. *Computer Aided Design*, 21(7):421–429, 1989.

[250] J. Marshall and A. Mitchell. Blending interpolants in the finite element method. *Int. J. Numer. Meth. Eng.*, 77–83, 1978.

[251] D. McAllister and J. Roulier. Interpolation by convex quadratic splines. *Mathematics of Computation*, 32(144):1154–1162, 1978.

[252] D. McConalogue. Algorithm 66 - an automatic French-curve procedure for use with an incremental plotter. *Computer Journal*, 14:207–209, 1971.

[253] D. McConalogue. A quasi-intrinsic scheme for passing a smooth curve through a discrete set of points. *Computer Journal*, 13:392–396, 1970.

[254] H. McLaughlin. Shape preserving planar interpolation: an algorithm. *IEEE Computer Graphics and Applications*, 3(3):58–67, 1985.

[255] H. Meier and H. Nowacki. Interpolating curves with gradual changes in curvature. *Computer Aided Geometric Design*, 4(4):297–306, 1988.

[256] C. Micchelli and H. Prautzsch. Computing surfaces invariant under subdivision. *Computer Aided Geometric Design*, 4(4):321–328, 1988.

[257] J. Miller. Sculptured surfaces in solid models: issues and alternative approaches. *IEEE Computer Graphics and Applications*, 6(12):37–48, 1986.

[258] F. Moebius. *August Ferdinand Moebius, Gesammelte Werke*. Verlag von S. Hirzel, 1885. also published by Dr. M. Saendig oHG, Wiesbaden, FRG, 1967.

[259] M. Mortenson. *Geometric Modeling*. Wiley, 1985.

[260] F. Munchmeyer. On surface imperfections. In R. Martin, editor, *The Mathematics of Surfaces II*, pages 459–474, Oxford University Press, 1987.

[261] F. Munchmeyer. Shape interrogation: a case study. In G. Farin, editor, *Geometric Modeling: Algorithms and New Trends*, pages 291–302, SIAM, Philadelphia, 1987.

[262] L. Nachman. Blended tensor product B-spline surface. *Computer Aided Design*, 20(6):336–340, 1988.

[263] G. Nielson. Coordinate free scattered data interpolation. In L. Schumaker, editor, *Topics in Multivariate Approximation*, Academic Press, 1987.

[264] G. Nielson. Minimum norm interpolation in triangles. *SIAM J Numer Anal*, 17:46–62, 1980.

[265] G. Nielson. A rectangular nu-spline for interactive surface design. *IEEE Computer Graphics and Applications*, 6(2):35–41, 1986.

[266] G. Nielson. The side-vertex method for interpolation in triangles. *J of Approx Theory*, 25:318–336, 1979.

[267] G. Nielson. Some piecewise polynomial alternatives to splines under tension. In R. E. Barnhill and R. F. Riesenfeld, editors, *Computer Aided Geometric Design*, pages 209–235, Academic Press, 1974.

[268] G. Nielson. A transfinite, visually continuous, triangular interpolant. In G. Farin, editor, *Geometric Modeling: Algorithms and New Trends*, pages 235–246, SIAM, Philadelphia, 1987.

[269] G. Nielson and T. Foley. A survey of applications of an affine invariant norm. In T. Lyche and L. Schumaker, editors, *Mathematical aspects in Computer Aided Geometric Design*, pages 445–468, Academic Press, 1989.

[270] H. Nowacki and D. Reese. Design and fairing of ship surfaces. In R. Barnhill and W. Boehm, editors, *Surfaces in Computer Aided Geometric Design*, pages 121–134, North-Holland, 1982.

[271] A. Overhauser. *Analytic definition of curves and surfaces by parabolic blending*. Technical Report, Ford Motor Company, 1968.

[272] R. Patterson. Projective transformations of the parameter of a rational Bernstein-Bézier curve. *ACM Transactions on Graphics*, 4:276–290, 1986.

[273] T. Pavlidis. Curve fitting with conic splines. *ACM Transactions on Graphics*, 2:1–31, 1983.

[274] J. Pegna and F. Wolter. A simple pratical criterion to guarantee second order smoothness of blend surfaces. 1988. Preprint MIT.

[275] Q. Peng. An algorithm for finding the intersection lines between two B-spline surfaces. *Computer Aided Design*, 191–196, 1984.

[276] M. Penna and R. Patterson. *Projective Geometry and its Applications to Computer Graphics*. Prentice Hall, 1986.

[277] G. Peters. Interactive computer graphics application of the parametric bi-cubic surface to engineering design problems. In R. Barnhill and R. Riesenfeld, editors, *Computer Aided Geometric Design*, Academic Press, 1974.

[278] C. Petersen. Adaptive contouring of three-dimensional surfaces. *Computer Aided Geometric Design*, 1:61–74, 1984.

[279] L. Piegl. A geometric investigation of the rational Bézier scheme in computer aided geometric design. *Computers in Industry*, 7:401–410, 1987.

[280] L. Piegl. Hermite- and Coons-like interpolants using rational Bézier approximation form with infinite control points. *Computer Aided Design*, 20(1):2–10, 1988.

[281] L. Piegl. Interactive data interpolation by rational Bézier curves. *IEEE Computer Graphics and Applications*, 7(4):45–58, 1987.

[282] L. Piegl. On the use of infinite control points in CAGD. *Computer Aided Geometric Design*, 4:155–166, 1987.

[283] L. Piegl. The sphere as a rational Bézier surface. *Computer Aided Geometric Design*, 3(1):45–52, 1986.

[284] L. Piegl and W. Tiller. Curve and surface constructions using rational B-splines. *Computer Aided Design*, 19(9):485–98, 1987.

[285] B. Piper. Visually smooth interpolation with triangular Bézier patches. In G. Farin, editor, *Geometric Modeling: Algorithms and New Trends*, pages 221–234, SIAM, Philadelphia, 1987.

[286] T. Poeschl. Detecting surface irregularities using isophotes. *Computer Aided Geometric Design*, 18(2):163–168, 1984.

[287] H. Pottmann. Curves and tensor product surfaces with third order geometric continuity. In *Proceedings of the Third International Conference on Engineering Graphics and Descriptive Geometry*, pages 107–116, 1988.

[288] H. Pottmann. Projectively invariant classes of geometric continuity for CAGD. *Computer Aided Geometric Design*, 6(4):307–322, 1989.

[289] M. Pratt and A. Geisow. Surface/surface intersection problems. In J. Gregory, editor, *The Mathematics of Surfaces*, Clarendon Press, 1986.

[290] H. Prautzsch. Degree elevation of B-spline curves. *Computer Aided Geometric Design*, 18(12):193–198, 1984.

[291] H. Prautzsch and C. Micchelli. Computing curves invariant under halving. *Computer Aided Geometric Design*, 4(1-2):133–140, 1987.

[292] L. Ramshaw. Béziers and B-splines as multiaffine maps. In R. Earnshaw, editor, *Theoretical Foundations of Computer Graphics and CAD*, pages 757–776, Springer Verlag, 1988.

[293] L. Ramshaw. *Blossoming: A Connect-the-Dots Approach to Splines*. Technical Report, Digital Systems Research Center, Palo Alto, Ca, 1987.

[294] D. Reese, M. Reidger, and R. Lang. *Flaechenhaftes Glaetten und Veraendern von Schiffsoberflaechen*. Technical Report MTK 0243, Technische Universitaet Berlin, 1983.

[295] G. Renner. Inter-patch continuity of surfaces. In R. Martin, editor, *The Mathematics of Surfaces II*, pages 237–254, Oxford University Press, 1987.

[296] A. Renyi. *Wahrscheinlichkeitsrechnung*. VEB Deutscher Verlag der Wissenschaften, 1962.

[297] W. Renz. Interactive smoothing of digitized point data. *Computer Aided Design*, 14(5):267–269, 1982.

[298] A. Requicha. Representations for rigid solids: theory, methods, and systems. *ACM Comp. Surveys*, 12:437–464, 1980.

[299] R. Riesenfeld. *Applications of b-spline approximation to geometric problems of computer-aided design.* PhD thesis, Syracuse Univ., 1973.

[300] R. Riesenfeld. On Chaikin's algorithm. *IEEE Computer Graphics and Applications*, 4:304–310, 1975.

[301] J. Rossignac and A. Requicha. Offsetting operations in solid modelling. *Computer Aided Geometric Design*, 3(2):129–148, 1986.

[302] J. Roulier and E. Passow. Monotone and convex spline interpolation. *SIAM J. Num Analysis*, 14(5), 1977.

[303] C. Runge. Ueber empirische Funktionen und die Interpolation zwischen aequidistanten Ordinaten. *ZAMM*, 46:224–243, 1901.

[304] M. Sabin. A method for displaying the intersection curve of two quadric surfaces. *The Computer Journal*, 19:336–338, 1976.

[305] M. Sabin. Recursive subdivision. In J. Gregory, editor, *The Mathematics of Surfaces*, pages 269–281, Clarendon Press, 1986.

[306] M. Sabin. Some negative results in n-sided patches. *Computer Aided Design*, 18(1):38–44, 1986.

[307] M. Sabin. *The use of piecewise forms for the numerical representation of shape.* PhD thesis, Hungarian Academy of Sciences, Budapest, Hungary, 1976.

[308] M. Sabin and F. Kimura. Letters to the editor. *Computer Aided Geometric Design*, 1(3):289–290, 1984. Concerning n-sided patches.

[309] P. Sablonniere. *Bases de Bernstein et approximants splines.* PhD thesis, Univ. of Lille, 1982.

[310] P. Sablonniere. Bernstein-Bézier methods for the construction of bivariate spline approximants. *Computer Aided Geometric Design*, 2(1-3):29–36, 1985.

[311] P. Sablonniere. Composite finite elements of class C^k. *J of Computational and Appl Math*, 12,13:542–550, 1985.

[312] P. Sablonniere. Interpolation by quadratic splines on triangles and squares. *Computers in Industry*, 3:45–52, 1982.

[313] P. Sablonniere. Spline and Bézier polygons associated with a polynomial spline curve. *Computer Aided Design*, 10(4):257–261, 1978.

[314] K. Salkauskas. C^1 splines for interpolation of rapidly varying data. *Rocky Mtn J of Math*, 14(1):239–250, 1984.

[315] N. Sapidis. *Algorithms for locally fairing B-spline curves.* Master's thesis, Univ. of Utah, 1987.

[316] R. Sarraga. Errata: G^1 interpolation of generally unrestricted cubic Bézier curves. *Computer Aided Geometric Design*, 6(2):167–172, 1989.

[317] R. Sarraga. G^1 interpolation of generally unrestricted cubic Bézier curves. *Computer Aided Geometric Design*, 4(1-2):23–40, 1987.

[318] I. Schoenberg. Contributions to the problem of approximation of equidistant data by analytic functions. *Quart. Appl. Math*, 4:45–99, 1946.

[319] I. Schoenberg. On spline functions. In O. Shisha, editor, *Inequalities*, pages 255–291, Academic Press, 1967.

[320] I. Schoenberg. On variation diminishing approximation methods. In R. E. Langer, editor, *On Numerical Approximation*, pages 249–274, Univ. of Wisconsin Press, 1953.

[321] L. Schumaker. On shape preserving quadratic spline interpolation. *SIAM J Numer Anal*, 20:854–864, 1983.

[322] L. Schumaker. *Spline functions: Basic Theory*. Wiley, 1981.

[323] L. Schumaker and W. Volk. Efficient evaluation of multivariate polynomials. *Computer Aided Geometric Design*, 3(2):149–154, 1986.

[324] A. Schwartz. Subdividing Bézier curves and surfaces. In G. Farin, editor, *Geometric Modeling: Algorithms and New Trends*, pages 55–66, SIAM, Philadelphia, 1987.

[325] T. Sederberg. Improperly parametrized rational curves. *Computer Aided Geometric Design*, 1(3):67–75, 1986.

[326] T. Sederberg. Steiner surface patches. *IEEE Computer Graphics and Applications*, 5(5):23–36, 1985.

[327] T. Sederberg, H. Christiansen, and S. Katz. Improved test for closed loops in surface intersections. *Computer Aided Design*, 21(8):505–508, 1989.

[328] T. Sederberg and R. Meyers. Loop detection in surface patch intersections. *Computer Aided Geometric Design*, 5(2):161–172, 1988.

[329] T. Sederberg and S. Parry. Comparison of three curve intersection algorithms. *Computer Aided Design*, 18(1):58–64, 1986.

[330] T. Sederberg and S. Parry. Free-form deformation of solid geometric models. *Computer graphics*, 20(4):151–160, 1986. SIGGRAPH proceedings.

[331] T. Sederberg, S. White, and A. Zundel. Fat arcs: a bounding region with cubic convergence. *Computer Aided Geometric Design*, 6(3):205–218, 1989.

[332] S. Selesnick. Local invariants and twist vectors in CAGD. *Computer Graphics and Image Processing*, 17:145–160, 1981.

[333] M. Shantz and S. Chang. Rendering trimmed NURBS with adaptive forward differencing. *Computer Graphics*, 22(4):189–198, 1988.

[334] L. Shirman and C. Séquin. Local surface interpolation with Bézier patches. *Computer Aided Geometric Design*, 4(4):279–296, 1988.

[335] E. Staerk. *Mehrfach differenzierbare Bézierkurven und Bézierflächen.* PhD thesis, Technical Univ. Braunschweig, 1976.

[336] D. Stancu. Some Bernstein polynomials in two variables and their applications. *Soviet Mathematics*, 1:1025–1028, 1960.

[337] W. Tiller. Rational B-splines for curve and surface representation. *IEEE Computer Graphics and Applications*, 3(6), 1983.

[338] W. Tiller and E. Hanson. Offsets of two-dimensional profiles. *IEEE Computer Graphics and Applications*, 4:36–46, 1984.

[339] P. Todd and R. McLeod. Numerical estimation of the curvature of surfaces. *Computer Aided Design*, 18(1):33–37, 1986.

[340] J. van Wijk. Bicubic patches for approximating non-rectangular control-point meshes. *Computer Aided Geometric Design*, 3(1):1–13, 1986.

[341] T. Varady. Survey and new results in n-sided patch generation. In R. Martin, editor, *The Mathematics of Surfaces II*, pages 203–236, Oxford University Press, 1987.

[342] T. Varady and M.J. Pratt. Design techniques for the definition of solid objects with free-form geometry. *Computer Aided Geometric Design*, 1(3):207–225, 1984.

[343] D. Vernet. Expression mathématique des formes. *Ingenieurs de l'Automobile*, 10:509–520, 1971.

[344] M. Veron, G. Ris, and J. Musse. Continuity of biparametric surface patches. *Computer Aided Design*, 8(4):267–273, 1976.

[345] K. Vesprille. *Computer aided design application of the rational B-spline approximation form.* PhD thesis, Syracuse University, 1975.

[346] A. Vinacua and P. Brunet. A construction for VC^1 continuity for rational Bezier patches. In T. Lyche and L. Schumaker, editors, *Mathematical Methods in Computer Aided Geometric Design*, pages 601–611, Academic Press, 1989.

[347] H. Walter. *Numerical representation of surfaces using an optimum principle.* PhD thesis, University of Munich, 1971. In German.

[348] C. Wang. Shape classification of the parametric cubic curve and parametric B-spline cubic curve. *Computer Aided Design*, 13(4):199–296, 1981.

[349] M. Watkins and A. Worsey. Degree reduction for Bézier curves. *Computer Aided Design*, 20(7):398–405, 1988.

[350] R. Wielinga. Constrained interpolation using Bézier curves as a new tool in computer aided geometric design. In R. Barnhill and R. Riesenfeld, editors, *Computer Aided Geometric Design*, pages 153–172, Academic Press, 1974.

[351] A. Worsey and G. Farin. An n-dimensional Clough-Tocher element. *Constructive Approximation*, 3:99–110, 1987.

[352] F. Yamaguchi. *Curves and Surfaces in Computer Aided Geometric Design.* Springer, 1988.

[353] A. Zenisek. Interpolation polynomials on the triangle. *Numerische Math*, 15:283–296, 1970.

[354] A. Zenisek. Polynomial approximation on tetrahedrons in the finite element method. *J of Approx Theory*, 7:334–351, 1973.

[355] J. Zhou. *The positivity and convexity of Bézier polynomials over triangles*. PhD thesis, Beijing univ., 1985.

Index